THE
HOLY
BIBLE
KJV
2023

CONTAINING THE

NEW TESTAMENT

The *King James Version 2023 Edition New Testament* is a modernized rendition of the original *King James Version,* written in contemporary English while preserving the timeless meaning of the traditional text.

King James Version 2023 Edition

1611-2023

CONTAINING THE

NEW TESTAMENT

KING JAMES VERSION 2023 EDITION

New Testament

Copyright 2023 by Nick Sayers

All Rights Reserved.

Any excerpts and quotations from King James Version 2023 Edition New Testament may be used in articles, magazines, newsletters, reviews, or bulletins, without the written permission of Nick Sayers. Please let each such use be accompanied by the following credit line:

From the King James Version 2023 Edition, copyright ©2023, Nick Sayers. Used by permission

We invite your suggestions, participation, and support. For more information, please contact:

Nick Sayers

TextusReceptusBibles@gmail.com

Published by Nick Sayers

Australia

www.tr.org.au

CONTENTS

THE NEW TESTAMENT

Book	Page	Book	Page
Matthew	1	1 Timothy	338
Mark	54	2 Timothy	344
Luke	88	Titus	349
John	146	Philemon	352
Acts	189	Hebrews	354
Romans	245	James	371
1 Corinthians	267	1 Peter	377
2 Corinthians	289	2 Peter	383
Galatians	303	1 John	387
Ephesians	311	2 John	393
Philippians	319	3 John	394
Colossians	325	Jude	395
1 Thessalonians	333	Revelation	397
2 Thessalonians	338		

THE GOSPEL ACCORDING TO
MATTHEW

CHAPTER 1

¹ The book of the generation of Jesus Christ, the Son of David, the Son of Abraham.

² Abraham begot Isaac, and Isaac begot Jacob, and Jacob begot Judah and his brethren.

³ And Judah begot Perez and Zerah by Tamar, and Perez begot Hezron, and Hezron begot Ram.

⁴ And Ram begot Amminadab, and Amminadab begot Nahshon, and Nahshon begot Salmon.

⁵ And Salmon begot Boaz by Rahab, and Boaz begot Obed by Ruth, and Obed begot Jesse,

⁶ and Jesse begot David the king, and David the king begot Solomon by her *who had been the wife* of Uriah.

⁷ And Solomon begot Rehoboam, and Rehoboam begot Abijah, and Abijah begot Asa.

⁸ And Asa begot Jehoshaphat, and Jehoshaphat begot Joram, and Joram begot Uzziah.

⁹ And Uzziah begot Jotham, and Jotham begot Ahaz, and Ahaz begot Hezekiah.

¹⁰ And Hezekiah begot Manasseh, and Manasseh begot Amon, and Amon begot Josiah.

¹¹ And Josiah begot Jechoniah and his brethren, about the time they were carried away to Babylon.

¹² And after they were brought to Babylon, Jechoniah begot Shealtiel, and Shealtiel begot Zerubbabel.

¹³ And Zerubbabel begot Abiud, and Abiud begot Eliakim, and Eliakim begot Azor.

¹⁴ And Azor begot Zadoc, and Zadoc begot Achim, and Achim begot Eliud.

¹⁵ And Eliud begot Eleazar, and Eleazar begot Matthan, and Matthan begot Jacob.

¹⁶ And Jacob begot Joseph the husband of Mary, of whom was born Jesus, who is called Christ.

¹⁷ So all the generations from Abraham to David *are* fourteen generations, and from David until the carrying away into Babylon *are* fourteen generations, and from the carrying away into Babylon to Christ *are* fourteen generations.

¹⁸ Now the birth of Jesus Christ happened this way: After His mother Mary was betrothed to Joseph, before they came together, she was found with child from the Holy Spirit.

¹⁹ Then Joseph her husband, being a just *man*, and not willing to make her a public example, was minded to put her away privately.

²⁰ But while he thought on these things, behold, the angel of the Lord appeared to him in a dream, saying, "Joseph, son of David, do not be afraid to take to yourself

Mary your wife, because that which is conceived in her is from the Holy Spirit.

²¹ And she will bear a Son, and you shall call His name JESUS, because He will save His people from their sins."

²² So all this was done that it might be fulfilled which was spoken by the Lord through the prophet, saying:

²³ "Behold, a virgin will be with child, and will bear a Son, and they will call His name Immanuel," which being translated is, "God with us."

²⁴ Then Joseph being raised from sleep, did as the angel of the Lord had commanded him, and took to him his wife,

²⁵ and did not know her until she had brought forth her firstborn Son. And he called His name JESUS.

CHAPTER 2

¹ Now when Jesus was born in Bethlehem of Judea in the days of Herod the king, behold, wise men from the east came to Jerusalem,

² saying, "Where is He who has been born King of the Jews? As we have seen His star in the east and have come to worship Him."

³ When Herod the king had heard *these things*, he was troubled, and all Jerusalem with him.

⁴ And when he had gathered all the chief priests and scribes of the people together, he demanded of them where Christ would be born.

⁵ And they said to him, "In Bethlehem of Judea, because, thus it is written by the prophet:

⁶ 'And you Bethlehem, *in* the land of Judah, are not the least among the rulers of Judah; because out of you will come a Ruler that will rule My people Israel.' "

⁷ Then Herod, when he had privately called the wise men, diligently inquired of them what time the star appeared.

⁸ And he sent them to Bethlehem and said, "Go and search diligently for the young Child, and when you have found *Him*, bring back word to me, that I may come and worship Him also."

⁹ After they heard the king, they departed; and behold, the star which they had seen in the east, went before them, until it came and stood over where the young Child was.

¹⁰ When they saw the star, they rejoiced with exceedingly great joy.

¹¹ And when they had come into the house, they saw the young Child with Mary His mother, and fell down, and worshiped Him. And when they had opened their treasures, they presented gifts to Him: gold, frankincense, and myrrh.

¹² And being warned by God in a dream that they should not return to Herod, they departed into their own country another way.

¹³ Now when they had departed, behold, the angel of the Lord

appeared to Joseph in a dream, saying, "Arise, take the young Child and His mother, flee into Egypt, and wait there until I bring you word; because Herod will seek the young Child to destroy Him."

¹⁴ When he arose, he took the young Child and His mother by night and departed into Egypt,

¹⁵ and was there until the death of Herod, that it might be fulfilled which was spoken by the Lord through the prophet, saying, "Out of Egypt I have called My Son."

¹⁶ Then Herod, when he saw that he was mocked because of the wise men, was exceedingly angry; and he sent forth and killed all the children who were in Bethlehem and in all of its districts, from two years old and under, according to the time which he had diligently inquired of the wise men.

¹⁷ Then was fulfilled that which was spoken through Jeremiah the prophet, saying:

¹⁸ "A voice was heard in Ramah, lamentation, weeping, and great mourning, Rachel weeping *for* her children, and would not be comforted, because they are no more."

¹⁹ But when Herod was dead, behold, an angel of the Lord appeared in a dream to Joseph in Egypt,

²⁰ saying, "Arise, and take the young Child and His mother, and go into the land of Israel, because those who sought the young Child's life are dead."

²¹ Then he arose, and took the young Child and His mother, and came into the land of Israel.

²² But when he heard that Archelaus was reigning in Judea in the position of his father Herod, he was afraid to go there. However, being warned of God in a dream, he turned aside into the region of Galilee.

²³ And he came and dwelt in a city called Nazareth, that it might be fulfilled which was spoken through the prophets, "He will be called a Nazarene."

CHAPTER 3

¹ In those days John the Baptist came preaching in the wilderness of Judea,

² and saying, "Repent, because the kingdom of heaven is at hand!"

³ Because, this is he who was spoken of through the prophet Isaiah, saying: "The voice of one shouting out in the wilderness: 'Prepare the way of the LORD; make His paths straight.' "

⁴ Now John himself was clothed in camel's hair, with a leather belt around his waist; and his food was locusts and wild honey.

⁵ Then Jerusalem, all Judea, and all the region around the Jordan went out to him

⁶ and were baptized by him in the Jordan, confessing their sins.

⁷ But when he saw many of the Pharisees and Sadducees coming to his baptism, he said to them, "O

generation of vipers! Who has warned you to escape from the wrath to come?

⁸ Therefore bear fruits worthy of repentance,

⁹ and do not think to say within yourselves, 'we have Abraham as *our* father.' Because, I say to you that God is able to raise up children to Abraham from these stones.

¹⁰ And even now the axe is laid to the root of the trees. Therefore every tree which does not produce good fruit is cut down and thrown into the fire.

¹¹ I indeed baptize you with water for repentance, but He who is coming after me is mightier than me, whose sandals I am not worthy to carry. He will baptize you with the Holy Spirit and *with* fire.

¹² His winnowing fan *is* in His hand, and He will thoroughly clean His threshing floor, and gather His wheat into the barn; but He will burn up the chaff with unquenchable fire."

¹³ Then Jesus came from Galilee to John at the Jordan to be baptized by him.

¹⁴ But John prevented Him, saying, "I need to be baptized by You, and are You coming to me?"

¹⁵ But Jesus answered and said to him, "Permit *it to be so* now, because it is fitting for us to fulfill all righteousness." Then he allowed Him.

¹⁶ And when He was baptized, Jesus came up immediately from the water; and behold, the heavens were opened to Him, and He saw the Spirit of God descending like a dove, and lighting upon Him.

¹⁷ And behold a voice from heaven, saying, "This is My beloved Son, in whom I am well pleased."

CHAPTER 4

¹ Then Jesus was led up by the Spirit into the wilderness to be tempted by the devil.

² And when He had fasted forty days and forty nights, afterward He was hungry.

³ Now when the tempter came to Him, he said, "If You are the Son of God, command that these stones become bread."

⁴ But He replied and said, "It is written, 'Man will not live by bread alone, but by every word that proceeds from the mouth of God.'"

⁵ Then the devil took Him up into the holy city, and set Him on a pinnacle of the temple,

⁶ and said to Him, "If You are the Son of God, throw Yourself down. Because it is written: 'He will give His angels orders concerning You,' and, 'in *their* hands they will hold You up, lest at any time You strike Your foot against a stone.'"

⁷ Jesus said to him, "It is written again, 'You shall not tempt the LORD your God.'"

⁸ Again, the devil took Him up onto a very high mountain, and showed Him all the kingdoms of the world and their glory.

⁹ And he said to Him, "I will give

You all these things, if You will fall down and worship me."

¹⁰ Then Jesus said to him, "Leave Satan! Because it is written, 'You shall worship the LORD your God, and Him only shall you serve.' "

¹¹ Then the devil left Him, and behold, angels came and ministered to Him.

¹² Now when Jesus had heard that John had been thrown into prison, He departed to Galilee.

¹³ And leaving Nazareth, He came and dwelt in Capernaum, which is by the sea coast, in the regions of Zebulun and Naphtali,

¹⁴ that it might be fulfilled which was spoken through Isaiah the prophet, saying:

¹⁵ "The land of Zebulun and the land of Naphtali, *by* the way of the sea, beyond the Jordan, Galilee of the Gentiles:

¹⁶ The people who sat in darkness have seen a great Light, and upon those who sat in the region and shadow of death Light has dawned."

¹⁷ From that time Jesus began to preach, and to say, "Repent, because the kingdom of heaven is at hand."

¹⁸ And Jesus, walking by the sea of Galilee, saw two brethren, Simon called Peter, and Andrew his brother, casting a net into the sea; because they were fishermen.

¹⁹ And He said to them, "Follow Me, and I will make you fishers of men."

²⁰ And they immediately left *their* nets, and followed Him.

²¹ And going on from there, He saw two more brethren, James the son of Zebedee, and John his brother, in a boat with Zebedee their father, mending their nets, and He called them.

²² And immediately they left the boat and their father, and followed Him.

²³ Then Jesus went about all Galilee, teaching in their synagogues, and preaching the gospel of the kingdom, and healing all types of sickness and every kind of disease among the people.

²⁴ And His fame went throughout all Syria; and they brought to Him every sick person who was afflicted with various diseases and torments, and those who were possessed with demons, those who were insane, and paralytics; and He healed them.

²⁵ And large crowds of people followed Him from Galilee, and *from* Decapolis, Jerusalem, Judea, and beyond the Jordan.

CHAPTER 5

¹ And seeing the crowds, He went up on a mountain, and when He was seated His disciples came to Him.

² Then He opened His mouth and taught them, saying:

³ "Blessed *are* the poor in spirit, because theirs is the kingdom of heaven.

⁴ Blessed *are* those who mourn, because they will be comforted.

⁵ Blessed *are* the meek, because

they will inherit the earth.

⁶ Blessed *are* those who hunger and thirst for righteousness, because they will be filled.

⁷ Blessed *are* the merciful, because they will obtain mercy.

⁸ Blessed *are* the pure in heart, because they will see God.

⁹ Blessed *are* the peacemakers, because they will be called the children of God.

¹⁰ Blessed *are* those who are persecuted for righteousness' sake, because theirs is the kingdom of heaven.

¹¹ "Blessed *are* you, when *men* revile you, persecute *you*, and say all kinds of evil against you falsely, for My sake.

¹² Rejoice, and be exceedingly glad, because great is your reward in heaven, because they also persecuted the prophets who were before you.

¹³ "You are the salt of the earth; but if the salt has lost its flavor, how shall it be salted? It is then good for nothing but to be thrown out and to be trampled underfoot by men.

¹⁴ "You are the light of the world. A city that is set on a hill cannot be hidden.

¹⁵ Nor do men light a lamp and put it under a basket, but on a lampstand, and it gives light to all who are in the house.

¹⁶ Let your light shine like this before men, that they may see your good works and glorify your Father who is in heaven.

¹⁷ "Do not think that I came to destroy the law or the prophets. I did not come to destroy but to fulfill.

¹⁸ Because, truly, I say to you, until heaven and earth pass away, one jot or one tittle will by no means pass from the law, until all is fulfilled.

¹⁹ Whoever therefore breaks one of these least commandments, but teaches men so, he will be called the least in the kingdom of heaven; but whoever does and teaches *them*, they will be called great in the kingdom of heaven.

²⁰ Because, I say to you, that unless your righteousness exceeds *the righteousness* of the scribes and Pharisees, you will by no means enter into the kingdom of heaven.

²¹ "You have heard that it was said by those of old times, 'You shall not murder, and whoever murders will be in danger of the judgment.'

²² But I say to you that whoever is angry with his brother without a cause will be in danger of the judgment. And whoever shall say to his brother, 'Raca!' will be in danger of the council. But whoever says, 'You fool!' will be in danger of hell fire.

²³ Therefore if you bring your gift to the altar, and there remember that your brother has something against you,

²⁴ leave your gift there before the altar, and go your way. First be reconciled to your brother, and then come and offer your gift.

²⁵ Agree with your adversary quickly, while you are on the way with him, lest at any time your adversary deliver you to the judge, and the judge deliver you to the officer, and you be thrown into prison.

²⁶ Truly, I say to you, you will by no means come out of there until you have paid the last penny.

²⁷ "You have heard that it was said by those of old times, 'You shall not commit adultery.'

²⁸ But I say to you that whoever looks on a woman to lust after her has committed adultery with her already in his heart.

²⁹ And if your right eye offends you, pluck it out, and cast *it* from you; because, it is more profitable for you that one of your members should perish, and not *that* your entire body to be thrown into hell.

³⁰ And if your right hand offends you, cut it off and cast *it* from you; because, it is more profitable for you that one of your members should perish, and not *that* your entire body be thrown into hell.

³¹ "It has been said, 'whoever divorces his wife, let him give her a certificate of divorce.'

³² But I say to you, that whoever puts away his wife for any reason except sexual immorality, causes her to commit adultery; and whoever marries a woman who is divorced commits adultery.

³³ "Again, you have heard that it has been said to those of old times, 'You shall not swear falsely, but shall perform your oaths to the Lord.'

³⁴ But I say to you, do not swear at all: neither by heaven, because it is God's throne;

³⁵ nor by the earth, because it is His footstool; nor by Jerusalem, because it is the city of the great King.

³⁶ Neither shall you swear by your head, because you cannot make one hair white or black.

³⁷ But let your communication be, 'yes,' 'yes,' *or* 'no,' 'no.' Because whatever goes beyond these is from evil.

³⁸ "You have heard that it has been said, ' An eye for an eye, and a tooth for a tooth.'

³⁹ But I tell you that you should not resist a wicked *person*. But whoever slaps you on your right cheek, turn the other to him also.

⁴⁰ And if anyone wants to sue you at the law and take away your coat, let him have *your* cloak also.

⁴¹ And whoever compels you to go one mile, go two with him.

⁴² Give to him who asks you, and from him who wants to borrow from you do not turn away.

⁴³ "You have heard that it has been said, 'You shall love your neighbor and hate your enemy.'

⁴⁴ But I say to you, Love your enemies, bless those who curse you, do good to those who hate you, and pray for those who spitefully use you and persecute you,

⁴⁵ that you may be the children of

your Father who is in heaven; because, He makes His sun to rise on the evil and on the good, and sends rain on the just and on the unjust.

⁴⁶ Because, if you love those who love you, what reward do you gain? Do not even the tax collectors do the same?

⁴⁷ And if you only greet your brethren, what do you do more *than others*? Do not even tax collectors do so?

⁴⁸ Therefore be perfect, just as your Father in heaven is perfect.

CHAPTER 6

¹ "Beware that you do not do your charitable deeds in front of men, to be seen by them. Otherwise you have no reward from your Father who is in heaven.

² Therefore, when you do *your* charitable deeds, do not sound a trumpet before you, as the hypocrites do in the synagogues and in the streets, that they may have glory from men. Truly, I say to you, they have their reward.

³ But when you do charitable deeds, do not let your left hand know what your right hand is doing,

⁴ that your charitable deeds may be in secret; and your Father who sees in secret will Himself reward you openly.

⁵ "And when you pray, you shall not be like the hypocrites *are*. Because, they love to pray standing in the synagogues and in the corners of the streets, that they may be seen by men. Truly, I say to you, they have their reward.

⁶ But you, when you pray, go into your room, and when you have shut your door, pray to your Father who is in secret; and your Father who sees in secret will reward you openly.

⁷ But when you pray, do not use vain repetitions, as the heathen *do*. Because, they think that they will be heard because of their many words.

⁸ "Therefore do not be like them. Because, your Father knows the things you have need of before you ask Him.

⁹ In this manner, therefore, pray: Our Father who is in heaven, hallowed be Your name.

¹⁰ Your kingdom come. Your will be done, on earth, as it is in heaven.

¹¹ Give us this day our daily bread.

¹² And forgive us our debts, as we forgive our debtors.

¹³ And do not lead us into temptation, but deliver us from evil. Because, Yours is the kingdom and the power and the glory forever. Amen.

¹⁴ "Because, if you forgive men their trespasses, your heavenly Father will also forgive you.

¹⁵ But if you do not forgive men their trespasses, neither will your Father forgive your trespasses.

¹⁶ "Moreover, when you fast, do not be like the hypocrites, with a sad countenance. Because, they dis-

figure their faces, that they may appear to men to be fasting. Truly, I say to you, they have their reward.

[17] But you, when you fast, anoint your head, and wash your face,

[18] *so* that you do not appear to men to be fasting, but to your Father who is in *that* secret *place*; and your Father who sees in secret, will reward you openly.

[19] "Do not store up for yourselves treasures on earth, where moth and rust corrupts, and where thieves break in and steal;

[20] but store up for yourselves treasures in heaven, where neither moth nor rust corrupts, and where thieves do not break in nor steal.

[21] Because, where your treasure is, there will your heart be also.

[22] "The light of the body is the eye. Therefore if your eye is single, your entire body will be full of light.

[23] But if your eye is corrupt, your entire body will be filled with darkness. Therefore if the light that is in you is darkness, how great *is* that darkness!

[24] "No one can serve two masters; because, either he will hate the one and love the other, or else he will be loyal to the one and despise the other. You cannot serve God and mammon.

[25] "Therefore I say to you, do not be anxious about your life, what you shall eat or what you shall drink; nor about your body, what you shall put on. Is not this life more than food and the body more than clothing?

[26] Look at the birds of the air, because, they neither sow nor reap nor gather into barns; yet your heavenly Father feeds them. Are you not of much more value than them?

[27] Which of you by being anxious can add one cubit to his stature?

[28] "So why do you worry about clothing? Consider the lilies of the field, how they grow: they neither toil nor spin;

[29] and yet I say to you that even Solomon in all his glory was not arrayed like one of these.

[30] Now if God clothes the grass of the field like that, which today exists, and tomorrow is thrown into the oven, *will He* not much more *clothe* you, O you of little faith?

[31] "Therefore do not worry, saying, 'What shall we eat?' or, 'What shall we drink?' or, 'What shall we wear?'

[32] (Because, the Gentiles seek after all these things.) Because your heavenly Father knows that you have need of all these things.

[33] But you, seek first the kingdom of God and His righteousness, and all these things will be added to you.

[34] Therefore do not worry about tomorrow, because tomorrow will be concerned for the issues of itself. Sufficient for the day *is* its own evil.

CHAPTER 7

[1] "Judge not, that you be not

judged.

² Because, with the judgment you judge, you will be judged; and with the measure you use, it will be measured back to you.

³ And why do you look at the speck that is in your brother's eye, but do not consider the plank that *is* in your own eye?

⁴ Or how can you say to your brother, 'Let me remove the speck from your eye'; and behold, a plank is in your own eye?

⁵ You hypocrite! First take out the plank from your own eye, and then you will see clearly to take out the speck from your brother's eye.

⁶ "Do not give that which is holy to the dogs; nor cast your pearls before swine, lest they trample them under their feet, and turn again and attack you.

⁷ "Ask, and it will be given to you; seek, and you will find; knock, and it will be opened to you.

⁸ Because, everyone who asks receives, and he who seeks finds, and to him that knocks it will be opened.

⁹ Or what man is there among you, who if his son asks for bread, will give him a stone?

¹⁰ Or if he asks for a fish, will he give him a serpent?

¹¹ If you then, being evil, know how to give good gifts to your children, how much more will your Father who is in heaven give good things to those who ask Him?

¹² Therefore, everything you would like men to do to you, so likewise you do to them, because this is the Law and the Prophets.

¹³ "Enter in through the narrow gate; because, the gate *is* wide and the way *is* broad that leads to destruction, and there are many who go in through it.

¹⁴ Because, the gate is narrow and the way is narrow that leads to life, and there are few who find it.

¹⁵ "Beware of false prophets, who come to you in sheep's clothing, but inwardly they are ravenous wolves.

¹⁶ You will know them by their fruits. Do men gather grapes from thornbushes, or figs from thistles?

¹⁷ Likewise every good tree bears good fruit, but a bad tree bears bad fruit.

¹⁸ A good tree cannot bear bad fruit, nor *can* a bad tree bear good fruit.

¹⁹ Every tree that does not bear good fruit is cut down and thrown into the fire.

²⁰ Therefore by their fruits you will know them.

²¹ "Not everyone who says to Me, 'Lord, Lord,' shall enter into the kingdom of heaven, but he who does the will of My Father who is in heaven.

²² Many will say to Me in that day, 'Lord, Lord, have we not prophesied in Your name, cast out demons in Your name, and done many wonderful works in Your name?'

²³ And then will I declare to them, 'I never knew you; depart from Me, you who practice iniquity!'

²⁴ "Therefore whoever hears these sayings of Mine, and does them, I will liken him to a wise man, who built his house on a rock:

²⁵ and the rain descended, and the floods came, and the winds blew and beat upon that house; and it did not fall, because it was founded on a rock.

²⁶ "But everyone who hears these sayings of Mine, and does not do them, will be likened to a foolish man who built his house on the sand:

²⁷ and the rain descended, the floods came, and the winds blew and beat upon that house; and it fell. And great was its fall."

²⁸ And so it happened, when Jesus had ended these sayings, that the people were astonished at His doctrine,

²⁹ because, He taught them as *one* having authority, and not as the scribes.

CHAPTER 8

¹ When He had come down from the mountain, large crowds followed Him.

² And behold, a leper came and worshiped Him, saying, "Lord, if you are willing, You can make me clean."

³ And Jesus put out *His* hand, and touched him, saying, "I am willing; be cleansed." And immediately his leprosy was cleansed.

⁴ And Jesus said to him, "See that you tell no one; but go your way, show yourself to the priest, and offer the gift that Moses commanded, as a testimony to them."

⁵ Now when Jesus had entered into Capernaum, a centurion came to Him, pleading with Him,

⁶ saying, "Lord, my servant is lying at home paralyzed, afflicted terribly.

⁷ And Jesus said to him, "I will come and heal him."

⁸ The centurion replied and said, "Lord, I am not worthy that You should come under my roof. But only speak a word, and my servant will be healed.

⁹ Because, I also am a man under authority, having soldiers under me. And I say to this *man*, 'Go,' and he goes; and to another, 'Come,' and he comes; and to my servant, 'Do this,' and he does *it*."

¹⁰ When Jesus heard *it*, He marveled, and said to those who followed, "Truly I say to you, I have not found such great faith, no, not even in Israel!

¹¹ And I say to you, that many will come from the east and west, and will sit down with Abraham, Isaac, and Jacob, in the kingdom of heaven.

¹² But the children of the kingdom will be thrown out into outer darkness. There will be weeping and gnashing of teeth."

¹³ And Jesus said to the centurion, "Go your way; and as you have believed, so let it be done for you." And his servant was healed that

same hour.

¹⁴ Now when Jesus had come into Peter's house, He saw his wife's mother lying down, and sick with a fever.

¹⁵ So He touched her hand, and the fever left her. And she arose, and ministered to them.

¹⁶ When the evening had come, they brought to Him many who were possessed with demons. And He cast out the spirits with *His* word, and healed all who were sick, ¹⁷ that it might be fulfilled which was spoken through Isaiah the prophet, saying, "He Himself took our weaknesses, and bore *our* sicknesses."

¹⁸ Now when Jesus saw large crowds around Him, He gave orders to depart to the other side.

¹⁹ Then a certain scribe came and said to Him, "Teacher, I will follow You wherever You go."

²⁰ And Jesus said to Him, "The foxes have holes and the birds of the air *have* nests, but the Son of Man has nowhere to lay *His* head."

²¹ Then another of His disciples said to Him, "Lord, firstly permit me to go and bury my father."

²² But Jesus said to him, "Follow Me; and let the dead bury their dead."

²³ Now when He got into a boat, His disciples followed Him.

²⁴ And behold, a large tempest arose on the sea, so much so that the boat was covered with the waves. But He was asleep.

²⁵ Then His disciples came to *Him*, and woke Him, saying, "Lord, save us! We are perishing."

²⁶ But He said to them, "Why are you fearful, O you of little faith?" Then He arose, and rebuked the winds and the sea, and there was a great calm.

²⁷ So the men marveled, saying, "What type of man is this, that even the winds and the sea obey Him?"

²⁸ And when He had come to the other side, to the country of the Gergesenes, there met Him two demon possessed *men*, coming out of the tombs, exceedingly fierce, so that no one could pass through that way.

²⁹ And behold they shouted out, saying, "What have we to do with You, Jesus, You Son of God? Have You come here to torment us before the time?

³⁰ Now a long distance away from them there was a herd of many swine feeding.

³¹ So the demons begged Him, saying, "If You cast us out, permit us to go away into the herd of swine."

³² And He said to them, "Go." So when they had come out, they went into the herd of swine. And, behold the entire herd of swine ran violently down a steep place into the sea, and drowned in the waters.

³³ Then those who kept them fled, and they went away into the city and told everything, including what had happened to the demon possessed men.

³⁴ And, behold, the entire city came out to meet Jesus. And when they saw Him, they begged *Him* that He would depart from their region.

CHAPTER 9

¹ So He got into a boat, crossed over, and came into His own city.

² Then behold, they brought to Him a paralytic lying on a bed. And Jesus seeing their faith said to the paralytic, "Son, be of good cheer; your sins are forgiven you."

³ And, immediately some of the scribes said within themselves, "This *Man* blasphemes!"

⁴ But Jesus knowing their thoughts said, "Why do you think evil in your hearts?

⁵ Because which is easiest to say, '*Your* sins are forgiven you,' or to say, 'Rise up and walk?'

⁶ But that you may know that the Son of Man has authority on earth to forgive sins," then He said to the paralytic, "Rise up, take up your bed, and go to your house."

⁷ And he rose up, and departed to his house.

⁸ Now when the crowds saw *it*, they marveled, and glorified God, who had given such authority to men.

⁹ And as Jesus passed on from there, He saw a man named Matthew sitting at the tax office. And He said to him, "Follow Me." So he rose up, and followed Him.

¹⁰ Now it happened, as Jesus sat at the table in the house, behold, many tax collectors and sinners came and sat down with Him and His disciples.

¹¹ And when the Pharisees saw *it*, they said to His disciples, "Why does your Teacher eat with tax collectors and sinners?"

¹² But when Jesus heard *that*, He said to them, "Those who are well have no need of a physician, but those who are sick.

¹³ But go and learn what *this* means: 'I desire mercy and not sacrifice.' Because, I did not come to call the righteous, but sinners to repentance."

¹⁴ Then the disciples of John came to Him, saying, "Why do we and the Pharisees fast often, but your disciples do not fast?"

¹⁵ And Jesus said to them, "Can the children of the bridechamber mourn, as long as the bridegroom is with them? But the days will come, when the bridegroom will be taken away from them, and then they will fast.

¹⁶ No man puts a piece of new cloth on old clothing, because, that which is put in to patch it rips away from the clothing, and the tear is made worse.

¹⁷ Neither do they put new grape juice into old containers, or else the containers break, and the grape juice spills out, and the containers perish. But they put new grape juice into new containers, and both are preserved."

¹⁸ While He spoke these things to them, behold, a certain ruler came,

and worshiped Him, saying, "My daughter has just died, but come and lay Your hand upon her, and she will live."

¹⁹ So Jesus rose up, and followed him, and so *did* His disciples.

²⁰ And, suddenly a woman, who had a discharge of blood for twelve years, came from behind *Him*, and touched the edge of His clothes.

²¹ Because she said within herself, "If only I may touch His clothes, I will be made well."

²² But Jesus turned around, and when He saw her, He said, "Be cheerful daughter; your faith has made you well." And the woman was made well from that hour.

²³ And when Jesus came into the ruler's house, and saw the musicians and the people making a noise,

²⁴ He said to them, "Make room, because the girl is not dead, but is sleeping." And they laughed and mocked at Him.

²⁵ But when the people were put outside, He went in and took her by the hand, and the girl arose.

²⁶ And the fame of this went out into all that land.

²⁷ And when Jesus departed from there, two blind men followed Him, shouting out, and saying, "You, Son of David, have mercy on us!"

²⁸ And when He had come into the house, the blind men came to Him. And Jesus said to them, "Do you believe that I am able to do this?" They said to Him, "Yes, Lord."

²⁹ Then He touched their eyes, saying, "According to your faith let it be to you."

³⁰ And their eyes were opened. And Jesus firmly warned them, saying, "See *that* no one knows it."

³¹ But when they had departed, they spread the fame about Him in all that country.

³² As they went out, behold, they brought to Him a mute man possessed with a demon.

³³ And when the demon was cast out, the mute spoke. And the crowds marveled, saying, "It has never been seen like this in Israel!"

³⁴ But the Pharisees said, "He casts out demons by the ruler of the demons."

³⁵ Then Jesus went about all the cities and villages, teaching in their synagogues, preaching the gospel of the kingdom, and healing every sickness and every disease among the people.

³⁶ But when He saw the crowds, He was moved with compassion for them, because they were exhausted, and scattered everywhere, like sheep having no shepherd.

³⁷ Then He said to His disciples, "Truly the harvest *is* plentiful, but the laborers *are* few.

³⁸ Therefore pray the Lord of the harvest that He will send out laborers into His harvest."

CHAPTER 10

¹ And when He had called His

twelve disciples to *Himself*, He gave them authority *against* unclean spirits, to cast them out, and to heal every kind of sickness and every kind of disease.

² Now the names of the twelve apostles are these: The first, Simon, who is called Peter, and Andrew his brother; James the son of Zebedee, and John his brother;

³ Philip and Bartholomew; Thomas and Matthew the tax collector; James the son of Alphaeus, and Lebbaeus, whose surname was Thaddaeus;

⁴ Simon the Canaanite, and Judas Iscariot, who also betrayed Him.

⁵ These twelve Jesus sent out, and commanded them, saying, "Do not go into the way of the Gentiles, and do not enter any city of the Samaritans.

⁶ But rather go to the lost sheep of the house of Israel.

⁷ And as you go, preach, saying, 'The kingdom of heaven is at hand.'

⁸ Heal the sick, cleanse the lepers, raise the dead, cast out demons. Freely you have received, freely give.

⁹ Provide neither gold nor silver nor copper in your money belts,

¹⁰ nor bag for *your* journey, nor two coats, neither sandals, nor staffs; because a worker is worthy of his food.

¹¹ "Now whatever city or town you go into, inquire who is worthy in it, and abide there until you go from it.

¹² And when you go into a household, greet it.

¹³ And if the household is worthy, let your peace come upon it. But if it is not worthy, let your peace return to you.

¹⁴ And whoever shall not receive you nor hear your words, when you depart from that house or city, shake off the dust from your feet.

¹⁵ Truly, I say to you, it will be more tolerable for the land of Sodom and Gomorrah in the day of judgment than for that city!

¹⁶ "Behold, I send you out as sheep in the midst of wolves. Therefore be wise as serpents, and harmless as doves.

¹⁷ But beware of men, because, they will deliver you up to councils and they will scourge you in their synagogues.

¹⁸ And you will be brought before governors and kings for My sake, as a testimony against them and the Gentiles.

¹⁹ But when they deliver you up, do not worry about how or what you shall speak. Because, it will be given to you in that same hour what you shall speak;

²⁰ because it is not you who is speaking, but the Spirit of your Father who speaks in you.

²¹ "Now brother will deliver up brother to death, and the father the child; and the children will rise up against *their* parents and cause them to be put to death.

²² And you will be hated by all *people* for My name's sake. But he who

endures to the end will be saved.

²³ But when they persecute you in one city, flee to another. Because, truly, I say to you, you will not have gone through the cities of Israel, before the Son of Man comes.

²⁴ "The disciple is not above *his* teacher, nor the servant above his master.

²⁵ It is enough for the disciple to be like his teacher, and the servant as his master. If they have called the master of the house Beelzebub, how much more *will they call* those of his household!

²⁶ Therefore do not fear them. Because, there is nothing covered, that will not be revealed, and hidden, that will not be known.

²⁷ "Whatever I tell you in darkness, *that* speak in light; and what you hear in the ear, *that* preach on the housetops.

²⁸ And do not fear those who kill the body but cannot kill the soul. But rather reverence Him who is able to destroy both soul and body in hell.

²⁹ Are not two sparrows sold for a copper coin? And not one of them falls to the ground without your Father's *knowledge*.

³⁰ But the very hairs of your head are all numbered.

³¹ Do not fear therefore; you are of more value than many sparrows.

³² "Therefore whoever confesses Me before men, him I will also confess before My Father who is in heaven.

³³ But whoever denies Me before men, him I will also deny before My Father who is in heaven.

³⁴ "Do not think that I came to bring peace on earth. I did not come to bring peace, but a sword.

³⁵ Because, I have come to 'divide a man against his father, and a daughter against her mother, and a daughter in law against her mother in law,'

³⁶ and 'a man's enemies *shall be* those of his own household.'

³⁷ He who loves father or mother more than Me is not worthy of Me. And he who loves son or daughter more than Me is not worthy of Me.

³⁸ And he who does not take up his cross, and follow after Me, is not worthy of Me.

³⁹ He who finds his life will lose it, and he who loses his life for My sake will find it.

⁴⁰ "He who receives you receives Me, and he who receives Me receives Him who sent Me.

⁴¹ He who receives a prophet in the name of a prophet will receive a prophet's reward. And he who receives a righteous man in the name of a righteous man will receive a righteous man's reward.

⁴² And whoever gives one of these little ones just a cup of cold *water* to drink in the name of a disciple, truly I say to you, he will by no means lose his reward."

CHAPTER 11

¹ And it came to pass, when Jesus had finished commanding His twelve disciples, that He departed from there to teach and to preach in their cities.

² Now when John had heard in the prison about the works of Christ, he sent two of his disciples,

³ And said to Him, "Are You He who should come, or do we look for another?"

⁴ Jesus answered and said to them, "Go and show John again those things which you hear and see:

⁵ The blind receive their sight and the lame walk; the lepers are cleansed and the deaf hear; the dead are raised up and the poor have the gospel preached to them.

⁶ And blessed is *he*, who is not offended because of Me."

⁷ And as they departed, Jesus began to say to the crowds concerning John: "What did you go out into the wilderness to see? A reed shaken by the wind?

⁸ But what did you go out to see? A man clothed in fine clothing? Behold, those who wear fine *clothing* are in kings' houses.

⁹ But what did you go out to see? A prophet? Yes, I say to you, and more than a prophet.

¹⁰ Because, this is *he*, of whom it is written: 'Behold, I send My messenger before Your face, who will prepare Your way before You.'

¹¹ "Truly I say to you, among those born of women there has not risen one greater than John the Baptist; but he who is least in the kingdom of heaven is greater than him.

¹² And from the days of John the Baptist until now the kingdom of heaven suffers violence, and the violent take it by force.

¹³ Because, all the prophets and the law prophesied until John.

¹⁴ And if you are willing to receive *it*, this is Elijah who was to come beforehand.

¹⁵ He who has ears to hear, let him hear!

¹⁶ But to what shall I liken this generation? It is likened to children sitting in the marketplaces, and calling to their friends,

¹⁷ and saying: 'We played the flute for you, and you did not dance; we have mourned to you, and you did not lament.'

¹⁸ Because, John came neither eating nor drinking, and they say, 'He has a demon.'

¹⁹ The Son of Man came eating and drinking, and they say, 'Behold a gluttonous man, and a wine drinker, a friend of tax collectors and sinners!' But wisdom is justified by her children."

²⁰ Then He began to rebuke the cities in which most of His mighty works had been done, because they did not repent:

²¹ "Woe to you, Chorazin! Woe to you, Bethsaida! Because, if the mighty works, which were done in you, had been done in Tyre and Sidon, they would have repented long ago in sackcloth and ashes.

²² But I say to you, it will be more tolerable for Tyre and Sidon in the day of judgment than for you. ²³ And you, Capernaum, who are exalted to heaven, will be brought down to hell; because, if the mighty works, which were done in you, had been done in Sodom, it would have remained until this day. ²⁴ But I say to you that it will be more tolerable for the land of Sodom in the day of judgment than for you."

²⁵ At that time Jesus responded and said, "I thank you, O Father, Lord of heaven and earth, because You have hidden these things from the wise and prudent, and have revealed them to babes.

²⁶ Even so Father, because in this manner it seemed good in Your sight.

²⁷ All things are delivered to Me by My Father, and no one knows the Son, except for the Father. Neither does anyone know the Father, except for the Son, and to *the one* whom the Son wills to reveal *Him*.

²⁸ Come to Me, all you who labor and have a heavy burden, and I will give you rest.

²⁹ Take My yoke upon you, and learn from Me, because, I am meek and lowly in heart, and you will find rest for your souls.

³⁰ Because, My yoke is easy, and My burden is light."

CHAPTER 12

¹ At that time Jesus went through the grainfields on the Sabbath day. And His disciples were hungry, and began to pluck the heads of grain and to eat.

² But when the Pharisees saw *it*, they said to Him, "Look, Your disciples are doing what is not lawful to do on the Sabbath day!"

³ But He said to them, "Have you not read what David did when he was hungry, and those who were with him:

⁴ how he entered into the house of God, and ate the showbread, which was not lawful for him to eat, nor for those who were with him, but only for the priests?

⁵ Or have you not read in the law, that on the Sabbath days the priests in the temple profane the Sabbath, and are blameless?

⁶ But I say to you that in this place there is *One* greater than the temple.

⁷ And if you had known what *this* means, 'I desire mercy, and not sacrifice,' you would not have condemned the guiltless.

⁸ Because the Son of Man is Lord even of the Sabbath day"

⁹ Now when He had departed from there, He went into their synagogue.

¹⁰ And behold, there was a man who had a withered hand. And they asked Him, saying, "Is it lawful to heal on the Sabbath days?" That they might accuse Him.

¹¹ And He said to them, "What man would there be among you, who has

one sheep, and if it falls into a pit on the Sabbath day, will not lay hold of it and lift *it* out?

¹² How much better then is a man than a sheep? Therefore it is lawful to do good on the Sabbath days."

¹³ Then He said to the man, "Stretch out your hand." And he stretched *it* out, and it was restored as whole as the other.

¹⁴ Then the Pharisees went out and held a council against Him, how they might destroy Him.

¹⁵ But when Jesus knew *it*, He withdrew Himself from there. And large crowds followed Him, and He healed them all.

¹⁶ And commanded them that they should not make Him known,

¹⁷ that it might be fulfilled which was spoken through Isaiah the prophet, saying:

¹⁸ "Behold! My Servant, whom I have chosen, My beloved, in whom My soul is well pleased! I will put My Spirit upon Him, and He will show justice to the Gentiles.

¹⁹ He will not strive, nor shout out, nor will anyone hear His voice in the streets.

²⁰ A bruised reed He will not break, and smoking flax He will not quench, until He sends forth justice to victory;

²¹ And in His name shall the Gentiles trust."

²² Then one was brought to Him who was possessed with a demon, blind and mute; and He healed him, so that the blind and mute both spoke and saw.

²³ And all the people were amazed and said, "Is not this the Son of David?"

²⁴ But when the Pharisees heard *it*, they said, "This one does not cast out demons, except by Beelzebub, the ruler of the demons."

²⁵ But Jesus knew their thoughts, and said to them: "Every kingdom divided against itself is brought to desolation, and every city or house divided against itself will not stand.

²⁶ And if Satan casts out Satan, he is divided against himself. How then will his kingdom stand?

²⁷ And if I cast out demons by Beelzebub, by whom do your children cast *them* out? Therefore they will be your judges.

²⁸ But if I cast out demons by the Spirit of God, then the kingdom of God has come to you.

²⁹ Or else how can one enter a strong man's house, and plunder his goods, unless he first binds the strong man? And then he shall plunder his house.

³⁰ He that is not with Me is against Me; and he that does not gather with Me scatters abroad.

³¹ "Therefore I say to you, every type of sin and blasphemy will be forgiven men, but the blasphemy *against* the *Holy* Spirit will not be forgiven men.

³² And whosoever speaks a word against the Son of Man, it will be forgiven him; but whoever speaks against the Holy Spirit, it will not be

forgiven him, neither in this age, nor in the *age* to come.

³³ "Either make the tree good, and its fruit good, or else make the tree bad, and its fruit bad: because the tree is known by *its* fruit.

³⁴ O generation of vipers, how can you being evil, speak good things? Since out of the abundance of the heart the mouth speaks!

³⁵ A good man out of the good treasure of the heart brings forth good things, and an evil man out of the evil treasure brings forth evil things.

³⁶ But I say to you that every idle word that men will speak, they will give account of it in the day of judgment.

³⁷ Because, by your words you will be justified, and by your words you will be condemned."

³⁸ Then some of the scribes and Pharisees responded, saying, "Teacher, we want to see a sign from You."

³⁹ But He replied and said to them, "An evil and adulterous generation seeks after a sign, and no sign will be given to it except the sign of the prophet Jonah.

⁴⁰ Because, as Jonah was three days and three nights in the whale's belly, so will the Son of Man be three days and three nights in the heart of the earth.

⁴¹ The men of Nineveh will rise in judgment with this generation will and condemn it, because they repented at the preaching of Jonah; and behold, a greater than Jonah *is* here.

⁴² The queen of the south will rise up in the judgment with this generation and will condemn it, because, she came from the ends of the earth to hear the wisdom of Solomon; and behold, a greater than Solomon *is* here.

⁴³ "When an unclean spirit goes out of a man, he goes through dry places, seeking rest, and finds none.

⁴⁴ Then he says, 'I shall return to my house from which I came out.' And when he has come, he finds *it* empty, swept, and put in order.

⁴⁵ Then he goes, and takes with him seven other spirits more wicked than himself, and they enter in and dwell there; and the last *state* of that man is worse than the first. Even so will it be to this wicked generation."

⁴⁶ While He was still talking to the people, behold, *His* mother and His brethren stood outside, wanting to speak with Him.

⁴⁷ Then one said to Him, "Look, Your mother and Your brethren are standing outside, wanting to speak with You."

⁴⁸ But He replied and said to him who told Him, "Who is My mother and who are My brethren?

⁴⁹ And He stretched out His hand toward His disciples, and said, "Behold, My mother and My brethren!

⁵⁰ Because, whoever does the will of My Father who is in heaven, that

one is My brother and sister and mother."

CHAPTER 13

¹ That same day Jesus went out of the house, and sat beside the sea.

² And large crowds were gathered about Him, so that He got into a boat, and sat; and the entire crowd stood on the shore.

³ Then He spoke many things to them in parables, saying: "Behold, a sower went out to sow.

⁴ And as he sowed, some *seeds* fell by the way side; and the birds came and devoured them.

⁵ Some fell on stony places, where they did not have much earth; and they immediately sprang up because they had no depth of earth.

⁶ But when the sun was up they were scorched, and because they had no root they withered away.

⁷ And some fell among thorns, and the thorns sprung up and choked them.

⁸ But others fell into good ground and bore fruit: some a hundredfold, some sixty, some thirty.

⁹ He who has ears to hear, let him hear!"

¹⁰ And the disciples came and said to Him, "Why do You speak to them in parables?"

¹¹ He answered and said to them, "Because, it has been given to you to know the mysteries of the kingdom of heaven, but to them it has not been given.

more will be given, and he will have abundance; but whoever does not have, even what he has will be taken away from him.

¹³ Therefore I speak to them in parables, because, seeing they do not see, and hearing they do not hear, nor do they understand.

¹⁴ And in them the prophecy of Isaiah is fulfilled, which says: 'By hearing you will hear, and will not understand, and seeing you will see, and will not perceive;

¹⁵ because the hearts of this people have grown dull, their ears are dull of hearing, and their eyes they have closed, lest they should see with *their* eyes and hear with *their* ears, and should understand with *their* hearts and would be converted, so that I should heal them.'

¹⁶ But blessed *are* your eyes because they see, and your ears because they hear;

¹⁷ because truly, I say to you, that many prophets and righteous *men* have desired to see those things which you see, and did not see *it*, and *hear* those things which you hear, and did not hear *it*.

¹⁸ "Therefore all of you, hear the parable of the sower:

¹⁹ When anyone hears the word of the kingdom, and does not understand *it*, then the wicked *one* comes and snatches away what was sown in his heart. This is the one which received seed by the wayside.

²⁰ But he who received the seed on stony places, this is the one who hears the word and immediately receives it with joy;

²¹ yet he has no root in himself, but endures only for a while. Because when tribulation or persecution arises because of the word, immediately he stumbles.

²² Now he who received seed among the thorns is he who hears the word, and the worries of this world and the deceitfulness of riches choke the word, and he becomes unfruitful.

²³ But he who received seed on the good ground is he who hears the word and understands *it*, who also bears fruit and produces: some a hundredfold, some sixty, some thirty."

²⁴ He put before them another parable, saying: "The kingdom of heaven is like a man who sowed good seed in his field;

²⁵ but while men slept, his enemy came and sowed tares among the wheat and went his way.

²⁶ So when the grain had sprouted and produced a crop, then the tares also appeared.

²⁷ So the servants of the householder came and said to him, 'Sir, did you not sow good seed in your field? How then does it have tares?'

²⁸ He said to them, 'An enemy has done this.' The servants said to him, 'Do you want us then to go and gather them up?'

²⁹ But he said, 'No, lest while you gather up the tares you also uproot the wheat with them.

³⁰ Let both grow together until the harvest, and at harvest time I will tell the reapers, "First gather together the tares and bind them in bundles to burn them, but gather the wheat into my barn." ' "

³¹ He put before them another parable, saying: "The kingdom of heaven is like a grain of mustard seed, that a man took and sowed in his field,

³² which indeed is the least of all seeds; but when it is grown it is the greatest among the herbs and becomes a tree, so that the birds of the air come and nest in its branches."

³³ He spoke another parable to them: "The kingdom of heaven is like leaven, which a woman took and hid inside three measures of flour until it was all leavened."

³⁴ Jesus spoke all these things to the crowds in parables; and He did not speak to them without a parable,

³⁵ that it might be fulfilled which was spoken through the prophet, saying: "I will open My mouth in parables; I will utter things which have been kept secret since the foundation of the world."

³⁶ Then Jesus sent the crowd away and went into the house. And His disciples came to Him, saying, "Explain to us the parable of the tares of the field."

³⁷ He replied and said to them: "He who sows the good seed is the Son of Man.

³⁸ The field is the world, the good seed are the children of the king-

dom, but the tares are the children of the wicked *one*.

⁃³⁹ The enemy who sowed them is the devil, the harvest is the end of the age, and the reapers are the angels.

⁴⁰ Therefore as the tares are gathered and burned in the fire, so it will be at the end of this age.

⁴¹ The Son of Man will send out His angels, and they will gather out of His kingdom all things that cause offense, and those who practice iniquity,

⁴² and will throw them into a furnace of fire. There will be weeping and gnashing of teeth.

⁴³ Then the righteous will shine forth as the sun in the kingdom of their Father. He who has ears to hear, let him hear!

⁴⁴ "Again, the kingdom of Heaven is like treasure hidden in a field, which when a man finds, he hides; and for joy over it he goes and sells all that he has and buys that field.

⁴⁵ "Again, the kingdom of Heaven is like a merchant man seeking choice pearls,

⁴⁶ who, when he had found one pearl of great price, went and sold all that he had and bought it.

⁴⁷ "Again, the kingdom of heaven is like a dragnet that was cast into the sea and gathered some of every kind,

⁴⁸ which, when it was full, they drew to shore; and sat down and gathered the good into vessels, but threw the bad away.

⁴⁹ So it will be at the end of the age. The angels will come forth, separate the wicked from among the just,

⁵⁰ and will throw them into the furnace of fire. There will be weeping and gnashing of teeth."

⁵¹ Jesus said to them, "Have you understood all these things?" They said to Him, "Yes, Lord."

⁵² Then He said to them, "Therefore every scribe *which* is instructed concerning the kingdom of heaven is like a man *who* is a householder who brings out of his treasure *things* new and old."

⁵³ Now it came to pass, when Jesus had finished these parables, that He departed from there.

⁵⁴ And when He had come to His own country, He taught them in their synagogue, so that they were astonished and said, "Where did this *Man* get this wisdom and *these* mighty works?

⁵⁵ Is this not the carpenter's son? Is not His mother called Mary? And His brothers James, Joses, Simon, and Judas?

⁵⁶ And His sisters, are they not all with us? Where then did this *Man* get all these things?"

⁵⁷ So they were offended at Him. But Jesus said to them, "A prophet is not without honor except in his own country and in his own house."

⁵⁸ So He did not do many mighty works there because of their unbelief.

CHAPTER 14

¹ At that time Herod the tetrarch heard about the fame of Jesus,

² and said to his servants, "This is John the Baptist; he is risen from the dead, and therefore mighty works display themselves in *him*."

³ Because, Herod had laid hold of John and bound him, and put *him* in prison because of Herodias, his brother Philip's wife.

⁴ Because, John said to him, "It is not lawful for you to have her."

⁵ And when he wanted to put him to death, he feared the crowds, because, they considered him to be a prophet.

⁶ But when Herod's birthday was celebrated, the daughter of Herodias danced before them and pleased Herod.

⁷ So he promised with an oath to give her whatever she might ask.

⁸ So she being instructed beforehand by her mother said, "Give me John the Baptist's head here on a platter."

⁹ And the king was grieved: nevertheless because of the oaths and those who sat with him at the table, he commanded it to be given to her.

¹⁰ So he sent, and beheaded John in the prison.

¹¹ And his head was brought on a platter, and given to the girl, and she brought it to her mother.

¹² Then his disciples came, and took away the body, and buried it, and went and told Jesus.

¹³ When Jesus heard *this*, He departed from there by boat into a deserted place by Himself. But when the crowds heard *of it*, they followed Him on foot from the cities.

¹⁴ And Jesus went out and saw a large crowd; and was moved with compassion for them and He healed their sick.

¹⁵ Now when it was evening, His disciples came to Him, saying, "This is a desert place, and the hour is already late. Send the crowds away, that they may go into the villages and buy sustenance for themselves."

¹⁶ But Jesus said to them, "They do not need to leave. You give them something to eat."

¹⁷ And they said to Him, "We have only five loaves, and two fish with us."

¹⁸ He said, "Bring them here to Me."

¹⁹ Then He commanded the crowds to sit down on the grass. And He took the five loaves and the two fish, and looking up to heaven, He blessed and broke, and gave the loaves to His disciples; and the disciples to the crowds.

²⁰ So they all ate and were filled, and they took up twelve baskets full of the fragments that remained.

²¹ Now those who had eaten were about five thousand men, besides women and children.

²² And immediately Jesus made His disciples to get into a boat and go before Him to the other side, while

He sent the crowds away.

²³ And when He had sent the crowds away, He went up on a mountain by Himself to pray. Now when the evening came, He was there alone.

²⁴ But the boat was now in the midst of the sea, tossed by the waves, because the wind was contrary.

²⁵ Now in the fourth watch of the night Jesus went to them, walking on the sea.

²⁶ And when the disciples saw Him walking on the sea, they were troubled, saying, "It is a spirit!" And they shouted out through fear.

²⁷ But immediately Jesus spoke to them, saying, "Be cheerful! It is Me; do not be afraid."

²⁸ And Peter replied to Him and said, "Lord, if it is You, tell me to come to You on the water."

²⁹ And He said, "Come." And when Peter had come down out of the boat, he walked on the water to go to Jesus.

³⁰ But when he saw the wind was strong, he was afraid; and beginning to sink, he shouted out, saying, "Lord, save me!"

³¹ And immediately Jesus stretched out *His* hand, and caught him, and said to him, "O you of little faith, why did you doubt?"

³² And when they got into the boat, the wind ceased.

³³ Then those who were in the boat came and worshiped Him, saying, "Truly You are the Son of God."

³⁴ And when they had crossed over, they came into the land of Gennesaret.

³⁵ And when the men of that place recognized Him, they sent out into all that surrounding region, and brought to Him all who were sick,

³⁶ and begged Him that they might only touch the edge of His clothes. And as many as touched it were made perfectly well.

CHAPTER 15

¹ Then the scribes and Pharisees who were from Jerusalem came to Jesus saying,

² "Why do Your disciples transgress the tradition of the elders? Because they do not wash their hands when they eat bread."

³ But He answered and said to them, "Why do you also transgress the commandment of God by your tradition?

⁴ Because, God commanded, saying, Honor your father and mother; and, He who curses father or mother, let him be put to death.

⁵ But you say, 'Whosoever says to *his* father or his mother, "Whatever profit you may have received from me *has become* a gift,"

⁶ and does not honor his father or his mother, *because he will be exempt.*' Thus you have made the commandment of God of no effect by your tradition.

⁷ *You* hypocrites! Isaiah correctly prophesied about you, saying:

⁸ 'These people draw near to Me with their mouth, and honor Me

with *their* lips, but their heart is far from Me.

⁹ But in vain they worship Me, teaching as doctrines the commandments of men.' "

¹⁰ Then He called the crowds and said to them, "Hear and understand:

¹¹ Not what goes into the mouth defiles a man; but what comes out of the mouth, this defiles a man."

¹² Then His disciples came and said to Him, "Do You know that the Pharisees were offended when they heard this saying?"

¹³ But He answered and said, "Every plant which My heavenly Father has not planted will be uprooted.

¹⁴ Leave them alone. They are blind leaders of the blind. And if the blind leads the blind, both will fall into the ditch."

¹⁵ Then Peter replied and said to Him, "Explain this parable to us."

¹⁶ And Jesus said, "Are you also still without understanding?

¹⁷ Do you still not understand that whatever enters into the mouth goes into the stomach, and is cast out into the drain?

¹⁸ But those things which proceed out of the mouth come from the heart, and they defile a man.

¹⁹ Because, out of the heart comes evil thoughts, murders, adulteries, fornications, thefts, false witness, blasphemies.

²⁰ These are *the things* which defile a man, but to eat with unwashed hands does not defile a man."

²¹ Then Jesus went out from there and departed to the region of Tyre and Sidon.

²² And behold, a woman of Canaan came from that region, and shouted out to Him, saying, "Have mercy on me, O Lord, You Son of David! My daughter is severely tormented with a demon."

²³ But He did not reply one word to her. And His disciples came and asked Him, saying, "Send her away; because, she shouts out to us."

²⁴ But He replied and said, "I am not sent except to the lost sheep of the house of Israel."

²⁵ Then she came and worshiped Him, saying, "Lord, help me!"

²⁶ But He replied and said, "It is not good to take the children's bread, and cast *it* to dogs."

²⁷ And she said, "True, Lord, yet the dogs eat the crumbs which fall from their masters' table."

²⁸ Then Jesus replied and said to her, "O woman, great is your faith! Let it be to you as you desire." And her daughter was healed from that very hour.

²⁹ Then Jesus left there, and came near to the sea of Galilee, and went up on a mountain, and sat down there.

³⁰ And large crowds came to Him, having with them *those who were* lame, blind, mute, maimed, and many others; and they placed them down at Jesus' feet; and He healed them.

³¹ So the crowds marveled when

they saw the mute speaking, the maimed made whole, the lame walking, and the blind seeing; and they glorified the God of Israel.

³² Then Jesus called His disciples *to Himself* and said, "I have compassion on the crowd, because, they have continued with Me for three days now and have nothing to eat. And I do not want to send them away fasting, lest they faint on the way."

³³ And His disciples said to Him, "Where could we get enough bread in the wilderness to fill such a large crowd?"

³⁴ And Jesus said to them, "How many loaves do you have?" And they said, "Seven, and a few small fish."

³⁵ And He commanded the crowd to sit down on the ground.

³⁶ And He took the seven loaves and the fish and gave thanks, then broke *them* and gave to His disciples; and the disciples to the crowd.

³⁷ So they all ate, and were filled, and they took up seven large baskets full of the *fragments* that were left.

³⁸ Now those who ate were four thousand men, besides women and children.

³⁹ And He sent the crowd away, got into a boat, and came into the region of Magdala.

CHAPTER 16

¹ The Pharisees also with the Sadducees came, and testing Him asked that He would show them a sign from heaven.

² He answered and said to them, "When it is evening, you say, '*It will be* fair weather, because the sky is red';

³ and in the morning, '*It will be* foul weather today, because the sky is red and overcast.' O you hypocrites! You can discern the face of the sky, but you cannot *discern* the signs of the times?

⁴ A wicked and adulterous generation seeks after a sign; and there will be no sign given to it except the sign of the prophet Jonah." And He left them, and departed.

⁵ Now when His disciples had come to the other side, they had forgotten to take bread.

⁶ Then Jesus said to them, "Take heed and beware of the leaven of the Pharisees and of the Sadducees."

⁷ And they reasoned among themselves, saying, "*It is* because we have not taken bread."

⁸ *Which* when Jesus perceived it He said to them, "O you of little faith, why do you reason among yourselves because you have brought no bread?

⁹ Do you still not understand, or remember the five loaves of the five thousand and how many baskets you took up?

¹⁰ Nor the seven loaves of the four thousand and how many huge baskets you took up?

¹¹ How is it that you do not understand that I did not speak *this* to you concerning bread, but that you should beware of the leaven of the Pharisees and the Sadducees?"

¹² Then they understood that He did not tell *them* to beware of the leaven of bread, but of the doctrine of the Pharisees and of the Sadducees.

¹³ When Jesus came into the region of Caesarea Philippi, He asked His disciples, saying, "Who do men say that I the Son of Man, am?"

¹⁴ So they said, "Some *say that* You *are* John the Baptist, some, Elijah, and others Jeremiah, or one of the prophets."

¹⁵ He said to them, "But who do you say that I am?"

¹⁶ And Simon Peter answered and said, "You are the Christ, the Son of the living God."

¹⁷ And Jesus replied and said to him, "Blessed are you, Simon Bar-Jonah, because flesh and blood has not revealed *this* to you, but My Father who is in heaven.

¹⁸ And I also say to you that you are Peter, and upon this rock I will build My church; and the gates of hell will not prevail against it.

¹⁹ And I will give you the keys of the kingdom of heaven, and whatever you will bind on earth will be bound in heaven, and whatever you will loose on earth will be loosed in heaven."

²⁰ Then He commanded His disciples that they should not tell anyone that He was Jesus the Christ.

²¹ From that time forward Jesus began to show to His disciples how that He must go to Jerusalem, and suffer many things from the elders and chief priests and scribes, and be killed, and be raised again the third day.

²² Then Peter took Him *aside*, and began to rebuke Him, saying, "Let this be far from You Lord; this will not happen to You!"

²³ But He turned and said to Peter, "Get behind Me Satan! You are an offense to Me, because, you are not thinking things that are of God, but those that are of man."

²⁴ Then said Jesus to His disciples, "If anyone desires to come after Me, let him deny himself, and take up his cross, and follow Me.

²⁵ Because, whoever desires to save his life will lose it, but whoever desires to lose his life for My sake will find it.

²⁶ Because, what does a man profit if he gains the entire world, and loses his own soul? Or what shall a man give in exchange for his soul?

²⁷ Because, the Son of Man will come in the glory of His Father with His angels, and then He will reward everyone according to his works.

²⁸ Truly, I say to you, there are some standing here who will not taste death, until they see the Son of Man coming in His kingdom.

CHAPTER 17

¹ Now after six days Jesus took Peter, James, and John his brother, and led them up on a high mountain by themselves;

² and He was transfigured before them, so His face shone like the sun, and His clothes became as white as the light.

³ And behold, Moses and Elijah appeared to them there, talking with Him.

⁴ Then Peter responded and said to Jesus, "Lord, it is good for us to be here; if you want to, let us make three tabernacles here; one for You, one for Moses, and one for Elijah."

⁵ While he still spoke, behold, a bright cloud overshadowed them; and behold a voice came out of the cloud, saying, "This is My beloved Son, in whom I am well pleased. Hear Him!"

⁶ And when the disciples heard *it*, they fell on their faces and were greatly afraid.

⁷ But Jesus came and touched them and said, "Arise, and do not be afraid."

⁸ And when they had lifted up their eyes, they saw no one, except Jesus only.

⁹ Now as they came down from the mountain, Jesus commanded them, saying, "Tell the vision to no one until the Son of Man is risen again from the dead."

¹⁰ Then His disciples asked Him, saying, "Why then do the scribes say that Elijah must come first?"

¹¹ So Jesus answered and said to them, "Truly Elijah is coming first, and will restore all things.

¹² But I say to you, that Elijah has come already and they did not know him, but did to him whatever they desired. Likewise the Son of Man will suffer by them also."

¹³ Then the disciples understood that He spoke to them about John the Baptist.

¹⁴ And when they came to the crowd, *a certain* man came to Him, kneeling down to Him and saying,

¹⁵ "Lord, have mercy on my son, because, he is crazy, and suffers greatly; because he often falls into the fire and often into the water.

¹⁶ And I brought him to Your disciples, but they could not cure him."

¹⁷ Then Jesus responded and said, "O faithless and perverse generation, how long shall I be with you? How long shall I put up with you? Bring him here to Me."

¹⁸ And Jesus rebuked the demon, and he came out of him; and the child was cured from that very hour.

¹⁹ Then the disciples came to Jesus privately and said, "Why could we not cast him out?"

²⁰ And Jesus said to them, "Because of your unbelief; because, truly, I say to you, if you have faith as a grain of mustard seed, you shall say to this mountain, 'Move from here to there,' and it will move; and nothing will be impossible for you.

²¹ However this kind does not go

out except by prayer and fasting."

²² Now while they were staying in Galilee, Jesus said to them, "The Son of Man will be betrayed into the hands of men,

²³ and they will kill Him, and the third day He will be raised again." And they were exceedingly sorrowful.

²⁴ And when they had come to Capernaum, those who received tax *money* came to Peter, and said, "Does your Teacher not pay tax?"

²⁵ He said, "Yes." And when he had come into the house, Jesus intercepted him, saying, "What do you think, Simon? From whom do the kings of the earth take customs or taxes, from their own children, or from strangers?"

²⁶ Peter said to Him, "From strangers." Jesus said to him, "Then the children are free.

²⁷ Nevertheless, lest we should offend them, go to the sea, and cast in a hook, and take up the first fish that comes up. And when you have opened its mouth, you will find a piece of money; take that, and give it to them for Me and you."

CHAPTER 18

¹ At the same time the disciples came to Jesus, saying, "Who is the greatest in the kingdom of heaven?"

² And Jesus called a little child to Himself, and set him in the midst of them,

³ and said, "Truly, I say to you, unless you are converted, and become as little children, you will not enter into the kingdom of heaven.

⁴ Therefore whoever humbles himself as this little child, they are the greatest in the kingdom of heaven.

⁵ And whoever receives one little child like this in My name receives Me.

⁶ But whoever causes one of these little ones who believe in Me to stumble, it would be better for him if a millstone were hung around his neck, and *that* he were drowned in the depth of the sea.

⁷ Woe to the world because of offenses! Because, offenses must come, but woe to that man by whom the offense comes!

⁸ So if your hand or your foot offends you, cut them off and cast *them* away from you. It is better for you to enter into life lame or maimed, rather than having two hands or two feet, to be thrown into everlasting fire.

⁹ And if your eye offends you, pluck it out and cast *it* away from you. It is better for you to enter into life with one eye, rather than having two eyes, to be thrown into hell fire.

¹⁰ Beware that you do not despise one of these little ones, because, I say to you that in heaven their angels always behold the face of My Father who is in heaven.

¹¹ Because the Son of Man has come to save that which was lost.

¹² "What do you think? If a man has a hundred sheep, and one of them goes astray, does he not leave the ninety nine and go to the mountains to seek the one that has gone astray?

¹³ And if he happens to find it, truly, I say to you, he rejoices more over that *sheep* than over the ninety nine that did not go astray.

¹⁴ Likewise it is not the will of your Father who is in heaven that one of these little ones should perish.

¹⁵ "Also if your brother sins against you, go and tell him his fault between you and him alone. If he hears you, you have gained your brother.

¹⁶ But if he will not hear *you, then* take with you one or two more, that 'by the mouth of two or three witnesses every word may be established.'

¹⁷ And if he refuses to hear them, tell *it* to the church. But if he refuses even to listen to the church, let him be to you as a heathen and a tax collector.

¹⁸ "Truly, I say to you, whatever you will bind on earth will be bound in heaven and whatever you will loose on earth will be loosed in heaven.

¹⁹ "Again I say to you that if two of you agree on earth concerning anything that they ask, it will be done for them by My Father who is in heaven.

²⁰ Because, where two or three are gathered together in My name, I am there in the midst of them."

²¹ Then Peter came to Him and said, "Lord, how often shall my brother sin against me, and I forgive him? Until seven times?"

²² Jesus said to him, "I do not say to you, until seven times, but until seventy times seven.

²³ Therefore the kingdom of heaven is like a certain king who wanted to settle accounts with his servants.

²⁴ And when he had begun to settle accounts, one was brought to him who owed him ten thousand talents.

²⁵ But since he had no means to pay, his master commanded him to be sold, with his wife and children and all that he owned, and that payment be made.

²⁶ So the servant fell down and worshiped him, saying, 'Master, have patience with me, and I will repay everything to you.'

²⁷ Then the Master of that servant was moved with compassion, released him, and forgave him the debt.

²⁸ "But the same servant went out and found one of his fellow servants, who owed him a hundred denarii: and he laid hands on him and took *him* by the throat, saying, 'Pay me what you owe!'

²⁹ So his fellow servant fell down at his feet and begged him, saying, 'Have patience with me, and I will repay everything to you.'

³⁰ And he would not, but went and threw him into prison until he should pay the debt.

³¹ So when his fellow servants saw what had been done, they were very grieved, and came and told their master all that was done.

³² Then his master, after he had summoned him, said to him, 'O you wicked servant! I forgave you all that debt because you begged me.

³³ Should you not also have had compassion on your fellow servant, just as I had pity on you?'

³⁴ And his master was angry, and delivered him to the torturers until he should pay all that was due to him.

³⁵ "So likewise will My heavenly Father also do to you if each of you, from his heart, does not forgive his brother their trespasses."

CHAPTER 19

¹ Now it came to pass, when Jesus had finished these sayings, *that* He departed from Galilee and came to the region of Judea beyond the Jordan.

² And large crowds followed Him, and He healed them there.

³ The Pharisees also came to Him, testing Him, and saying to Him, "Is it lawful for a man to put away his wife for just any reason?"

⁴ And He answered and said to them, "Have you not read that He who made *them* in the beginning 'made them male and female,'

⁵ And said, 'For this reason a man shall leave his father and mother and be joined to his wife, and the two will be one flesh?'

⁶ Therefore they are no longer two but one flesh. Therefore what God has joined together, let not man separate."

⁷ They said to Him, "Why then did Moses command to give a certificate of divorce, and to separate from her?"

⁸ He said to them, "Moses, because of the hardness of your hearts, permitted you to put away your wives, but from the beginning it was not so.

⁹ And I say to you, whoever puts away his wife, except *it be* for sexual immorality, and marries another, commits adultery; and whoever marries her who is put away commits adultery."

¹⁰ His disciples said to Him, "If this is the situation of the man with *his* wife, it is not good to marry."

¹¹ But He said to them, "Not all *men* can accept this saying, except *those* to whom it is given:

¹² Because, there are some eunuchs who were born so from *their* mother's womb, and there are some eunuchs who were made eunuchs by men, and there are eunuchs who have made themselves eunuchs for the sake of the kingdom of heaven. He who is able to accept *it*, let him accept *it*."

¹³ Then little children were brought to Him so that He might lay *His* hands on them and pray, but the disciples rebuked them.

¹⁴ But Jesus said, "Permit little children to come to Me and do not

forbid them; because, of such is the kingdom of heaven."

¹⁵ And He laid *His* hands on them and departed from there.

¹⁶ And, behold, one came and said to Him, "Good Teacher, what good thing should I do that I may have eternal life?"

¹⁷ And He said to him, "Why do you call Me good? No one *is* good except One, *that is*, God. But if you want to enter into life, keep the commandments."

¹⁸ He said to Him, "Which ones?" Jesus said, " 'You shall not murder,' 'You shall not commit adultery,' 'You shall not steal,' 'You shall not bear false witness,'

¹⁹ 'Honor your father and *your* mother,' and, 'You shall love your neighbor as yourself.' "

²⁰ The young man said to Him, "I have kept all these things from my youth. What do I still lack?"

²¹ Jesus said to Him, "If you want to be perfect, *go* and sell what you have and give to the poor, and you will have treasure in heaven; and come *and* follow Me."

²² But when the young man heard that saying, he went away sorrowful, because he had many possessions.

²³ Then Jesus said to His disciples, "Truly, I say to you, that it is hard for a rich man to enter into the kingdom of heaven.

²⁴ And again I say to you, it is easier for a camel to go through the eye of a needle than for a rich man to enter into the kingdom of God."

²⁵ When His disciples heard *it*, they were greatly amazed, saying, "Who then can be saved?"

²⁶ But Jesus looked at *them* and said to them, "With men this is impossible, but with God all things are possible."

²⁷ Then Peter replied and said to Him, "Look, we have left everything, and followed You. Therefore what shall we have?"

²⁸ And Jesus said to them, "Truly, I say to you, that in the regeneration when the Son of Man sits on the throne of His glory, you who have followed Me will also sit upon twelve thrones, judging the twelve tribes of Israel.

²⁹ And everyone who has left houses or brothers or sisters or father or mother or wife or children or lands, for My name's sake, will receive a hundredfold, and will inherit everlasting life.

³⁰ But many *who are* first will be last, and the last *will be* first."

CHAPTER 20

¹ "Because, the kingdom of heaven is likened to a man *who* is a householder who went out early in the morning to hire laborers for his vineyard.

² Now when he had agreed with the laborers for a denarius a day, he sent them into his vineyard.

³ And he went out about the third hour, and saw others standing idle in the marketplace,

⁴ and said to them, 'You also go into the vineyard, and whatever is right I will give you.' So they went their way.

⁵ Again he went out about the sixth and ninth hour, and did likewise.

⁶ And about the eleventh hour he went out and found others standing idle and said to them, 'Why have you been standing here idle all day?'

⁷ They said to him, 'Because no one has hired us.' He said to them, 'You also go into the vineyard, and whatever is right *that* you will receive.'

⁸ So when evening had come, the master of the vineyard said to his steward, 'Call the laborers and give them *their* wages, beginning from the last to the first.'

⁹ And when those came who were *hired* about the eleventh hour, everyone received a denarius each.

¹⁰ But when the first came, they supposed that they would receive more; and they likewise received a denarius each.

¹¹ And when they had received *it*, they murmured against the good householder,

¹² saying, 'These last have worked *only* one hour, and you have made them equal to us who have endured the burden and heat of the day.'

¹³ But he responded to one of them and said, 'Friend, I am doing you no wrong. Did you not agree with me for a denarius?

¹⁴ Take *what* is yours, and go your way. I desire to give to the last, the same as you.

¹⁵ Is it not lawful for me to do what I want with my own things? Is your eye corrupt because I am good?'

¹⁶ So the last will be first, and the first last. Because many are called, but few are chosen"

¹⁷ Now Jesus, going up to Jerusalem, took the twelve disciples aside on the road, and said to them,

¹⁸ "Behold, we are going up to Jerusalem, and the Son of Man will be betrayed to the chief priests and to the scribes; and they will condemn Him to death,

¹⁹ and will deliver Him to the Gentiles to mock and to scourge and to crucify *Him*. And the third day He will rise again."

²⁰ Then the mother of Zebedee's children came to Him with her sons, worshiping *Him*, and asking something from Him.

²¹ And He said to her, "What do you desire?" She said to Him, "Permit that these two sons of mine may sit, one on Your right hand and the other on the left, in Your kingdom."

²² But Jesus answered and said, "You do not know what you ask. Are you able to drink of the cup that I will drink of, and to be baptized with the baptism that I am baptized with?" They said to Him, "We are able."

²³ So He said to them, "You will indeed drink My cup, and be baptized with the baptism that I am baptized with; but to sit on My right hand

and on My left is not Mine to give, but it *will be given to those* for whom it is prepared by My Father."

²⁴ And when the ten heard *it*, they were moved with indignation with the two brethren.

²⁵ But Jesus called them to *Himself*, and said, "You know that the rulers of the Gentiles dominate over them, and those who are great exercise authority over them.

²⁶ But it will not be so among you; but whoever wants to be great among you, let him be your servant.

²⁷ And whoever wants to be first among you, let him be your servant,

²⁸ just as the Son of Man did not come to be served, but to serve, and to give His life a ransom for many."

²⁹ Now as they departed from Jericho, a large crowd followed Him.

³⁰ And, behold, two blind men sitting by the road, when they heard that Jesus was passing by, shouted out, saying, "Have mercy on us, O Lord, *You* Son of David!"

³¹ And the crowd rebuked them, that they should keep silent; but they shouted all the more, saying, "Have mercy on us, O Lord, *You* Son of David!"

³² Then Jesus stood still and called them, and said, "What do you want Me to do for you?"

³³ They said to Him, "Lord, that our eyes may be opened."

³⁴ So Jesus had compassion *on them*, and touched their eyes. And immediately their eyes received sight, and they followed Him.

CHAPTER 21

¹ Now when they drew near to Jerusalem, and came to Bethphage, at the mount of Olives, then Jesus sent out two disciples,

² saying to them, "Go into the village opposite you, and immediately you will find a donkey tied, and a colt with her. Loose them, and bring them to Me.

³ And if anyone says anything to you, you shall say, 'The Lord has need of them,' and he will immediately send them."

⁴ All this was done that it might be fulfilled which was spoken through the prophet, saying:

⁵ "Tell the daughter of Zion, 'Behold, your King is coming to you, humble, and sitting on a donkey, a colt, the foal of a donkey.'"

⁶ Then the disciples went, and did as Jesus commanded them,

⁷ and brought the donkey and the colt, put their clothes on them, and they set Him on them.

⁸ And a very large crowd spread their clothes on the road; others cut down branches from the trees and spread them on the road.

⁹ And the crowds who went before and those who followed shouted out, saying: "Hosanna to the Son of David! Blessed is He who comes in the name of the LORD! Hosanna in the highest!"

¹⁰ And when He came into Jerusalem, the entire city was moved saying, "Who is this?"

¹¹ Then the crowd said, "This is

Jesus the prophet from Nazareth of Galilee."

¹² And Jesus went into the temple of God, and threw out all those who bought and sold in the temple, and turned over the tables of the moneychangers, and the seats of those who sold doves,

¹³ and said to them, "It is written, 'My house shall be called the house of prayer,' but you have made it a 'den of thieves.'"

¹⁴ Then the blind and the lame came to Him in the temple, and He healed them.

¹⁵ But when the chief priests and scribes saw the wonderful things that He did, and the children shouting out in the temple, and saying, "Hosanna to the Son of David!" they were very annoyed.

¹⁶ and said to Him, "Do You hear what they are saying?" And Jesus said to them, "Yes. Have you never read, 'Out of the mouth of babes and nursing infants You have perfected praise'?"

¹⁷ Then He left them, and went out of the city to Bethany; and He stayed there.

¹⁸ Now in the morning as He returned to the city, He was hungry.

¹⁹ And when He saw a fig tree beside the road, He came to it, and found nothing on it but only leaves, and said to it, "Let no fruit grow on you ever again." And immediately the fig tree withered away.

²⁰ So when the disciples saw it, they marveled, saying, "How did the fig tree wither away so suddenly!"

²¹ Jesus answered and said to them, "Truly, I say to you, if you have faith and do not doubt, you will not only do what was done to the fig tree, but also if you will say to this mountain, 'Be removed, and be cast into the sea' it will be done.

²² And anything, whatever things you ask in prayer, believing, you will receive."

²³ Now when He came to the temple, the chief priests and the elders of the people confronted Him as He was teaching, and said, "By what authority are You doing these things? And who gave You this authority?"

²⁴ But Jesus answered and said to them, "I will also ask you one thing, which if you tell me, I likewise will tell you by what authority I do these things.

²⁵ The baptism of John, where was it from? From heaven, or from men?" And they reasoned among themselves, saying, "If we shall say, 'From heaven,' He will say to us, 'Why then did you not believe him?'

²⁶ But if we shall say, 'From men,' we fear the crowds, because everyone counts John as a prophet."

²⁷ So they answered Jesus, and said, "We do not know." And He said to them, "Neither will I tell you by what authority I do these things.

²⁸ "But what do you think? A certain man had two sons, and he came to the first and said, 'Son, go,

work today in my vineyard.'

²⁹ He replied and said, 'I will not,' but afterward he repented, and went.

³⁰ Then he came to the second and said likewise. And he replied and said, 'I will go, sir,' but he did not go.

³¹ Which of those two did the will of his father?" They said to Him, "The first." Jesus said to them, "Truly, I say to you, that tax collectors and prostitutes enter the kingdom of God before you.

³² Because, John came to you in the way of righteousness, and you did not believe him; but tax collectors and prostitutes believed him; and you, when you saw it, did not afterward repent that you might believe him.

³³ "Hear another parable: There was a certain householder who planted a vineyard and made a hedge around it, dug a grape juice press in it and built a tower. And leased it out to farmers, and went into a country far away.

³⁴ Now when the time of harvest drew near, he sent his servants to the farmers, that they might receive its fruit.

³⁵ But the farmers took his servants, beat one, killed one, and stoned another.

³⁶ Again, he sent other servants more than the first, and they did the same to them.

³⁷ Then last of all he sent his son to them, saying, 'They will respect my son.'

³⁸ But when the farmers saw the son, they said among themselves, 'This is the heir. Come, let us kill him, and let us seize on his inheritance.'

³⁹ So they took him, and threw him out of the vineyard, and killed him.

⁴⁰ Therefore when the owner of the vineyard comes, what shall he do to those farmers?

⁴¹ They said to Him, "He will viciously destroy those wicked men, and will lease out his vineyard to other farmers who will present to him the fruits in their seasons."

⁴² Jesus said to them, "Have you never read in the Scriptures: 'The stone which the builders rejected has become the chief cornerstone. This is the LORD'S doing, and it is marvelous in our eyes'?

⁴³ "Therefore I say to you, the kingdom of God will be taken from you and given to a nation bearing the fruits of it.

⁴⁴ And whoever falls on this stone will be broken; but on whomever it falls, it will grind him to powder."

⁴⁵ Now when the chief priests and Pharisees had heard His parables, they perceived that He spoke about them.

⁴⁶ But when they sought to lay hands on Him, they feared the crowds, because, they counted Him as a prophet.

CHAPTER 22

¹ And Jesus responded and spoke to them again by parables and said:

² "The kingdom of heaven is like a certain king who arranged a marriage for his son,

³ and sent out his servants to call those who were invited to the wedding; and they would not come.

⁴ Again, he sent out other servants, saying, 'Tell those who are invited, "Behold, I have prepared my dinner; my oxen and *my* fatted cattle *are* slaughtered, and all things *are* ready. Come to the marriage." '

⁵ But they made light of *it*, and went their ways, one to his farm, another to his business.

⁶ And the rest took his servants, and treated *them* spitefully, and killed them.

⁷ But when the king heard *about* it, he was very angry. And he sent out his armies, and destroyed those murderers, and burned up their city.

⁸ Then he said to his servants, 'The wedding is ready, but those who were invited were not worthy.

⁹ Therefore go into the highways, and as many as you can find, invite to the marriage.'

¹⁰ So those servants went out into the highways, and gathered together as many as they could find, both bad and good. And the wedding was filled with guests.

¹¹ "But when the king came in to see the guests, he saw a man there who did not have a wedding garment on.

¹² And he said to him, 'Friend, how did you come in here without a wedding garment?' And he was speechless.

¹³ Then the king said to the servants, 'Bind him hand and foot, and take him away, and throw *him* into outer darkness; there will be weeping and gnashing of teeth.'

¹⁴ "Because, many are called, but few are chosen."

¹⁵ Then the Pharisees went, and plotted how they might entangle Him in *His* speech.

¹⁶ And they sent out to Him their disciples with the Herodians, saying, "Teacher, we know that You are true, and teach the way of God in truth; nor do You gratify anyone, because You do not regard the person of men.

¹⁷ Tell us, therefore, what do You think? Is it lawful to pay taxes to Caesar, or not?"

¹⁸ But Jesus perceived their wickedness, and said, "Why do you test Me, you hypocrites?

¹⁹ Show Me the tax money." So they gave a denarius to Him.

²⁰ And He said to them, "Whose image and inscription *is* this?"

²¹ They said to Him, "Caesar's." Then He said to them, "Therefore render to Caesar the things that are Caesar's, and to God the things that are God's."

²² When they had heard *these words*, they marveled, and left Him and went their way.

²³ The same day the Sadducees who say that there is no resurrection, came to Him and asked Him,

²⁴ saying: "Teacher, Moses said, that if a man dies, having no children, his brother shall marry his wife, and raise up offspring for his brother.
²⁵ Now there were with us seven brothers. So the first died after he had married a wife, and having no offspring, left his wife to his brother.
²⁶ Likewise the second also, and the third, until the seventh.
²⁷ Then last of all the woman died also.
²⁸ Therefore in the resurrection, whose wife of the seven shall she be, because they all had her?"
²⁹ Jesus answered and said to them, "You are mistaken, not knowing the Scriptures, nor the power of God.
³⁰ Because, in the resurrection they neither marry nor are given in marriage, but are as the angels of God in heaven.
³¹ But concerning the resurrection of the dead, have you not read what was spoken to you by God, saying,
³² 'I am the God of Abraham, the God of Isaac, and the God of Jacob'? God is not the God of the dead, but of the living."
³³ And when the crowd heard *this*, they were astonished at His doctrine.
³⁴ But when the Pharisees heard that He had silenced the Sadducees, they were gathered together.
³⁵ Then one of them, *who was* a lawyer, asked *Him a question*, testing Him, and saying,
³⁶ "Teacher, which *is* the greatest commandment in the law?"
³⁷ Jesus said to him, "'You shall love the LORD your God with all your heart, with all your soul, and with all your mind.'
³⁸ This is the first and great commandment.
³⁹ And the second *is* like it, 'You shall love your neighbor as yourself.'
⁴⁰ On these two commandments hang all the Law and the Prophets."
⁴¹ while the Pharisees were gathered together, Jesus asked them,
⁴² saying, "What do you think of Christ? Whose Son is He?" They said to Him, "*The Son* of David."
⁴³ He said to them, "How then does David in the Spirit call Him 'Lord,' saying:
⁴⁴ "The LORD said to my Lord, 'sit at My right hand, until I make Your enemies Your footstool? '"
⁴⁵ If David then calls Him 'Lord,' how is He his Son?"
⁴⁶ And no one was able to answer Him a word, nor did anyone ask Him any more *questions* from that day on.

CHAPTER 23

¹ Then Jesus spoke to the crowd and to His disciples,
² saying: "The scribes and the Pharisees sit in Moses' seat.
³ Everything then, whatever they tell you to observe, *that* observe and

do, but do not do according to their works; because they preach, and do not *practice*.

⁴ Because, they bind heavy burdens, hard to carry, and lay *them* on men's shoulders; but they *themselves* will not move them with one of their fingers.

⁵ But they do their works to be seen by men. They make their phylacteries broad and enlarge the edges of their garments.

⁶ They love the best places at feasts, the first seats in the synagogues,

⁷ greetings in the markets, and to be called by men, 'Rabbi, Rabbi.'

⁸ But you, do not be called 'Rabbi'; because, One is your Teacher, *that is*, Christ, and you are all brethren.

⁹ And do not call anyone on earth your father; because One is your Father, who is in heaven.

¹⁰ Nor be called teachers; because One is your Teacher, *that is*, Christ.

¹¹ But he who is greatest among you shall be your servant.

¹² And whoever exalts himself will be humbled, and he who humbles himself will be exalted.

¹³ "But woe to you, scribes and Pharisees, hypocrites! Because, you shut up the kingdom of heaven against men; because you neither go in *yourselves*, nor do you permit those who are entering to go in.

¹⁴ Woe to you, scribes and Pharisees, hypocrites! Because, you devour widows' houses, and for a show make long prayers. Therefore you will receive the greater damnation.

¹⁵ Woe to you, scribes and Pharisees, hypocrites! Because, you travel land and sea to make one proselyte, and when he is converted, you make him twice as much the child of hell as yourselves.

¹⁶ "Woe to you, *you* blind guides, who say, 'Whoever swears by the temple, it is nothing; but whoever swears by the gold of the temple, he is obligated!'

¹⁷ *You* fools and blind! Because which is greater, the gold or the temple that sanctifies the gold?

¹⁸ And, 'Whoever swears by the altar, it is nothing; but whoever swears by the gift that is on it, he is obligated.'

¹⁹ *You* fools and blind! Because which *is* greater, the gift or the altar that sanctifies the gift?

²⁰ Therefore whoever swears by the altar, swears by it and by all things on it.

²¹ And whoever swears by the temple, swears by it, and by Him who dwells in it.

²² And he who swears by heaven, swears by the throne of God and by Him who sits upon it.

²³ Woe to you, scribes and Pharisees, hypocrites! Because, you pay tithe of mint and anise and cummin, and have omitted the weightier *matters* of the law: justice, mercy, and faith. You should have done these, without leaving the others undone.

²⁴ You blind guides, who strain at a

gnat, and swallow a camel!

²⁵ "Woe to you, scribes and Pharisees, hypocrites! Because, you clean the outside of the cup and dish, but inside they are full of extortion and excess.

²⁶ *You* blind Pharisee, first cleanse that *which is* inside of the cup and dish, that the outside of them may be clean also.

²⁷ "Woe to you, scribes and Pharisees, hypocrites! Because, you are like whitewashed tombs which indeed appear beautiful outwardly, but inside are full of dead *men's* bones and all uncleanness.

²⁸ Even so you also outwardly appear righteous to men, but inside you are full of hypocrisy and iniquity.

²⁹ "Woe to you, scribes and Pharisees, hypocrites! Because, you build the tombs of the prophets and decorate the tombs of the righteous,

³⁰ and say, 'If we had been in the days of our fathers, we would not have been partakers with them in the blood of the prophets.'

³¹ "Therefore you are witnesses against yourselves that you are the children of those who killed the prophets.

³² Fill up then the measure of your fathers.

³³ *You* serpents, *you* generation of vipers, how can you escape the damnation of hell?

³⁴ Therefore, behold, I send to you prophets, wise men, and scribes: and *some* of them you will kill and crucify, and *some* of them you will scourge in your synagogues, and persecute *them* from city to city,

³⁵ that upon you may come all the righteous blood shed on the earth, from the blood of righteous Abel to the blood of Zechariah son of Berechiah, whom you murdered between the temple and the altar.

³⁶ Truly, I say to you, all these things will come upon this generation.

³⁷ "O Jerusalem, Jerusalem, *you* who kills the prophets, and stone those who are sent to you! How often I wanted to gather your children together, just as a hen gathers her chicks under *her* wings, but you were not willing!

³⁸ Behold! Your house is left to you desolate;

³⁹ because, I say to you, You will see Me no more until you shall say, 'Blessed *is* He who comes in the name of the LORD.' "

CHAPTER 24

¹ Then Jesus went out and departed from the temple, and His disciples came to *Him* to show Him the buildings of the temple.

² And Jesus said to them: "Do you not see all these things? Truly, I say to you, there will not be left here one stone upon another that will not be thrown down."

³ Now as He sat on the Mount of Olives, the disciples came to Him privately, saying, "Tell us, when

shall these things happen? And what *shall be* the sign of Your coming, and of the end of the age?"

⁴ And Jesus answered and said to them, "Beware that no one deceives you.

⁵ Because, many will come in My name, saying, 'I am Christ,' and will deceive many.

⁶ And you will hear of wars and rumors of wars. See that you are not troubled; because, all *these things* must come to pass, but the end is not yet.

⁷ Because, nation will rise against nation, and kingdom against kingdom. And there will be famines, pestilences, and earthquakes in various places.

⁸ All these *are* the beginning of sorrows.

⁹ Then they will deliver you up to be afflicted, and will kill you, and you will be hated by all nations for My name's sake.

¹⁰ And then many will be offended, will betray one another, and will hate one another.

¹¹ Then many false prophets will rise up and will deceive many.

¹² And because iniquity will abound, the love of many will go cold.

¹³ But he who endures to the end, they will be saved.

¹⁴ And this gospel of the kingdom will be preached in all the world as a witness to all nations, and then the end will come.

¹⁵ "Therefore when you see the 'abomination of desolation,' spoken of by Daniel the prophet, standing in the holy place," (whoever reads, let him understand),

¹⁶ "then let those who are in Judea flee to the mountains.

¹⁷ Let him who is on the housetop not go down to take anything out of his house,

¹⁸ nor let him who is in the field return back to take his clothes.

¹⁹ But woe to those who are pregnant and to those who are nursing babes in those days!

²⁰ And pray that your flight may not be in the winter nor on the Sabbath day.

²¹ Because, then there will be great tribulation, such as has not been since the beginning of the world until this time, no, nor ever will be.

²² And unless those days were shortened, no flesh would be saved; but for the sake of the elect those days will be shortened.

²³ "Then if anyone says to you, 'Look, here *is* Christ,' or 'There!' Do not believe *it*.

²⁴ Because, false christs and false prophets will arise and will show great signs and wonders; so much so that, if it were possible, they would deceive even the elect.

²⁵ Behold, I have told you in advance.

²⁶ "Therefore if they say to you, 'Look, He is in the desert!' do not go out; or 'Look, He is in the secret chambers!' Do not believe it.

²⁷ Because, as the lightning comes

out of the east and flashes to the west, so also will the coming of the Son of Man be.

²⁸ Because, wherever the corpse is, there the eagles will be gathered together.

²⁹ Immediately after the tribulation of those days the sun will be darkened, and the moon will not give her light; the stars will fall from heaven, and the powers of the heavens will be shaken.

³⁰ And then the sign of the Son of Man will appear in heaven, and then all the tribes of the earth will mourn, and they will see the Son of Man coming in the clouds of heaven with power and great glory.

³¹ And He will send His angels with a large sound of a trumpet, and they will gather together His elect from the four winds, from one end of heaven to the other.

³² "Now learn this parable from the fig tree: When its branch is still tender and grows out leaves, you know that summer *is* near.

³³ So you likewise, when you see all these things, know that it is near, *even* at the doors!

³⁴ Truly, I say to you, this generation will not pass away, until all these things are fulfilled.

³⁵ Heaven and earth will pass away, but My words will not pass away.

³⁶ But of that day and hour no *one* knows, no, not the angels of heaven, but My Father only.

³⁷ But as the days of Noah *were*, so also will the coming of the Son of Man be.

³⁸ Because, as in the days that were before the flood they were eating and drinking, marrying and giving in marriage, until the day that Noah entered into the ark,

³⁹ and did not know until the flood came and took them all away, so also will the coming of the Son of Man be.

⁴⁰ Then two will be in the field: the one will be taken and the other left.

⁴¹ Two *women will* be grinding at the mill: one will be taken and the other left.

⁴² Therefore watch, because, you do not know what hour your Lord is coming.

⁴³ But know this, that if the master of the house had known what hour the thief would come, he would have watched and not allowed his house to be broken into.

⁴⁴ Therefore you likewise be ready, because the Son of Man is coming at an hour you do not expect.

⁴⁵ "Who then is a faithful and wise servant, whom his master made ruler over his household, to provide them with food in the appropriate season?

⁴⁶ Blessed *is* that servant, whom his master, when he comes, will find doing that.

⁴⁷ Truly, I say to you, that he will make him ruler over all his goods.

⁴⁸ But if that evil servant says in his heart, 'My master is delaying his coming,'

⁴⁹ and begins to beat *his* fellow ser-

vants, and to eat and drink with the drunkards,

⁵⁰ the master of that servant will come on a day when he is not looking for *him* and at an hour that he is not aware of,

⁵¹ and will cut him in two, and appoint him his portion with the hypocrites. There will be weeping and gnashing of teeth.

CHAPTER 25

¹ "Then the kingdom of heaven will be likened to ten virgins who took their lamps and went out to meet the bridegroom.

² Now five of them were wise, and five *were* foolish.

³ Those who *were* foolish took their lamps and took no oil with them,

⁴ but the wise took oil in their vessels with their lamps.

⁵ while the bridegroom was delayed, they all slumbered and slept.

⁶ "And at midnight a shout was made, 'Behold, the bridegroom is coming; go out to meet him!'

⁷ Then all those virgins arose, and trimmed their lamps.

⁸ And the foolish said to the wise, 'Give us some of your oil, because, our lamps have gone out.'

⁹ But the wise replied, saying, 'No, lest there shall not be enough for us and you; but rather go to those who sell, and buy for yourselves.'

¹⁰ And while they went to buy, the bridegroom came, and those who were ready went in with him to the wedding; and the door was shut.

¹¹ "Afterward the other virgins came also, saying, 'Lord, Lord, open to us!'

¹² But he replied and said, 'Truly, I say to you, I do not know you.'

¹³ "Watch therefore, because, you know neither the day nor the hour in which the Son of Man is coming.

¹⁴ "Because, *the kingdom of heaven is* like a man travelling into a far country, *who* called his own servants and distributed his goods to them.

¹⁵ And to one he gave five talents, to another two, and to another one, to each according to his own ability; and immediately he went on a journey.

¹⁶ Then he who had received the five talents went and traded with them, and made *those into* another five talents.

¹⁷ And likewise he who *had received* two, he gained two more also.

¹⁸ But he who had received one went and dug in the earth, and hid his lord's money.

¹⁹ After a long time the lord of those servants came and settled accounts with them.

²⁰ "And so he who had received five talents came and brought another five talents, saying, 'Lord, you distributed to me five talents; look, I have gained five more talents besides them.

²¹ His lord said to him, 'Well done, *you* good and faithful servant; you have been faithful over a few things, I will make you ruler over

many things. Enter into the joy of your lord.'

²² He also who had received two talents came and said, 'Lord, you distributed to me two talents; look, I have gained two more talents besides them.'

²³ His lord said to him, 'Well done, good and faithful servant; you have been faithful over a few things, I will make you ruler over many things. Enter into the joy of your lord.'

²⁴ "Then he who had received the one talent came and said, 'Lord, I knew you to be a hard man, reaping where you have not sown, and gathering where you have not scattered seed.

²⁵ And I was afraid, and went and hid your talent in the ground. Look, *there* you have *what is* yours.'

²⁶ "His lord replied and said to him, '*You* wicked and lazy servant, you knew that I reap where I have not sown, and gather where I have not scattered seed.

²⁷ Therefore you should have deposited my money with the bankers, and *then* at my coming I would have received back my own with interest.

²⁸ Therefore take the talent from him, and give *it* to him who has ten talents.

²⁹ 'Because, to everyone who has, more will be given, and he will have abundance; but from him who does not have, even what he has will be taken away.

³⁰ And throw the unprofitable servant into outer darkness. There will be weeping and gnashing of teeth.'

³¹ "When the Son of Man comes in His glory, and all the holy angels with Him, then He will sit upon the throne of His glory.

³² And all the nations will be gathered before Him, and He will separate them one from another, like a shepherd divides *his* sheep from the goats.

³³ And He will set the sheep on His right hand, but the goats on the left.

³⁴ Then the King will say to those on His right hand, 'Come, you blessed of My Father, inherit the kingdom prepared for you from the foundation of the world:

³⁵ because, I was hungry and you gave Me food; I was thirsty and you gave Me a drink; I was a stranger and you took Me in;

³⁶ naked, and you clothed Me; I was sick, and you visited Me; I was in prison, and you came to Me.'

³⁷ "Then the righteous will reply to Him, saying, 'Lord, when did we see You hungry and feed *You*, or thirsty and gave *You* a drink?'

³⁸ When did we see You a foreigner and take *You* in, or naked and clothe *You*?

³⁹ Or when did we see You sick, or in prison, and come to You?'

⁴⁰ And the King will answer and say to them, 'Truly, I say to you, inasmuch as you did it to one of the least of these My brethren, you did

it to Me.'

⁴¹ "Then He will also say to those on the left hand, 'Depart from Me, you cursed, into everlasting fire, prepared for the devil and his angels:

⁴² because, I was hungry and you did not give Me food; I was thirsty and you did not give Me a drink;

⁴³ I was a foreigner and you did not take Me in, naked, and you did not clothe Me, sick, and in prison, and you did not visit Me.'

⁴⁴ "Then they also will reply to Him, saying, 'Lord, when did we see You hungry or thirsty or a foreigner or naked or sick or in prison and did not minister to You?'

⁴⁵ Then He will answer them, saying, 'Truly, I say to you, inasmuch as you did not do *it* to one of the least of these, you did not do *it* to Me.'

⁴⁶ And these will depart into everlasting punishment, but the righteous into life eternal."

CHAPTER 26

¹ Now it came to pass, when Jesus had finished all these sayings, He said to His disciples,

² "You know that after two days is *the Feast* of the Passover, and the Son of Man will be betrayed to be crucified."

³ Then the chief priests, the scribes, and the elders of the people assembled together to the palace of the high priest, who was called Caiaphas,

⁴ and plotted how they might seize Jesus by deception and kill *Him*.

⁵ But they said, "Not on the feast *day*, lest there be an uproar among the people."

⁶ Now when Jesus was in Bethany, in the house of Simon the leper,

⁷ a woman came to Him having an alabaster flask of very precious ointment, and poured it on His head as He was sitting at the table.

⁸ But when His disciples saw *it*, they were indignant, saying, "For what purpose *is* this waste?

⁹ As this ointment might have been sold for much and given to the poor."

¹⁰ When Jesus knew *this*, He said to them, "Why do you trouble the woman? Since she has performed a good work towards Me."

¹¹ Because, you have the poor with you always, but Me you do not have always.

¹² Because, in pouring this ointment on My body, she did *it* for My burial.

¹³ Truly, I say to you, wherever this gospel is preached in the entire world, *there* also will this, what this woman has done, be told as a memorial to her."

¹⁴ Then one of the twelve called Judas Iscariot, went to the chief priests

¹⁵ and said *to them*, "What will you give me, and I will deliver Him to you?" And they covenanted with him for thirty pieces of silver.

¹⁶ So from that time he sought opportunity to betray Him.

¹⁷ Now on the first *day* of the *Feast*

of Unleavened Bread the disciples came to Jesus, saying to Him, "Where do You want us to prepare for You to eat the Passover?"

¹⁸ And He said, "Go into the city to a certain man, and say to him, 'The Teacher says, "My time is at hand; I will keep the Passover at your house with My disciples."'"

¹⁹ So the disciples did as Jesus had directed them; and they made preparations for the Passover.

²⁰ Now when the evening had come, He sat down with the twelve.

²¹ And as they were eating, He said, "Truly I say to you, that one of you will betray me."

²² And they were exceedingly sorrowful, and each of them began to say to Him, "Lord, am I the one?"

²³ And He answered and said, "He who dips *his* hand with Me in the dish, he will betray Me.

²⁴ The Son of Man goes *just* as it is written of Him, but woe to that man by whom the Son of Man is betrayed! It would have been good for that man if he had not been born."

²⁵ Then Judas, who betrayed Him, replied and said, "Rabbi, am I the one?" He said to him, "You have said it."

²⁶ And as they were eating, Jesus took bread, blessed *it*, and broke *it*, and gave *it* to the disciples and said, "Take, eat; this is My body."

²⁷ Then He took the cup, and gave thanks, and gave *it* to them, saying, "Drink from it all of you.

²⁸ Because, this is My blood of the new testament, which is shed for many for the remission of sins.

²⁹ But I say to you, I will not drink of this fruit of the vine from now on until that day when I drink it new with you in My Father's kingdom."

³⁰ And when they had sung a song, they went out to the Mount of Olives.

³¹ Then Jesus said to them, "All of you will be made to stumble because of Me this night, because, it is written: 'I will strike the Shepherd, and the sheep of the flock will be scattered.'

³² But after I am raised up again, I will go before you to Galilee."

³³ Peter replied and said to Him, "Even if all *men* are made to stumble because of You, *yet* I will never be made to stumble."

³⁴ Jesus said to him, "Truly, I say to you, that this night, before the rooster crows, you will deny Me three times."

³⁵ Peter said to Him, "Even if I have to die with You, yet I will not deny You!" And all the disciples said likewise.

³⁶ Then Jesus came with them to a place called Gethsemane, and said to the disciples, "Sit here, while I go and pray over there."

³⁷ And He took Peter and the two sons of Zebedee with Him, and began to be sorrowful and deeply troubled.

³⁸ Then He said to them, "My soul is exceedingly sorrowful, even to

death. Stay here and watch with Me."

³⁹ And He went a little further, fell on His face, and prayed, saying, "O My Father, if it is possible, let this cup pass from Me; nevertheless not as I will, but as You *will*."

⁴⁰ Then He came to the disciples and found them sleeping, and said to Peter, "What! Could you not watch with Me one hour?

⁴¹ Watch and pray, that you do not enter into temptation. The spirit indeed is willing, but the flesh *is* weak."

⁴² He went away again the second time and prayed, saying, "O My Father, if this cup cannot pass away from Me unless I drink it, Your will be done."

⁴³ And He came and found them asleep again, because their eyes were heavy.

⁴⁴ So He left them, went away again, and prayed the third time, saying the same words.

⁴⁵ Then He came to His disciples, and said to them, "Sleep on now and take *your* rest. Behold, the hour is at hand, and the Son of Man is being betrayed into the hands of sinners.

⁴⁶ Rise, let us be going. See, My betrayer is at hand."

⁴⁷ And while He was still speaking, behold, Judas, one of the twelve, and with him a large crowd with swords and clubs, came from the chief priests and elders of the people.

⁴⁸ Now His betrayer had given them a sign, saying, "Whomever I kiss, He is the One; seize Him."

⁴⁹ And immediately he went up to Jesus, and said, "Greetings Rabbi!" and kissed Him.

⁵⁰ But Jesus said to him, "Friend, why have you come?" Then they came and laid hands on Jesus and took Him.

⁵¹ And suddenly, one of those who were with Jesus stretched out his hand and drew his sword, and struck a servant of the high priest and cut off his ear.

⁵² Then Jesus said to him, "Put your sword in its place, because all those who take the sword will die by the sword.

⁵³ Or do you think that I cannot now pray to My Father, and He will provide Me with more than twelve legions of angels?

⁵⁴ But how then shall the Scriptures be fulfilled, that it must happen this way?"

⁵⁵ In that same hour Jesus said to the crowds, "Have you come out as against a thief with swords and clubs to take Me? I sat with you daily, teaching in the temple, and you did not seize Me.

⁵⁶ But all this was done that the Scriptures of the prophets might be fulfilled." Then all the disciples forsook Him, and fled.

⁵⁷ And those who had laid hold of Jesus led *Him* away to Caiaphas the high priest, where the scribes and the elders were assembled.

⁵⁸ But Peter followed Him at a distance to the high priest's courtyard and went in and sat with the servants to see the end.

⁵⁹ Now the chief priests, elders, and all the council, sought false testimony against Jesus, to put Him to death,

⁶⁰ but found none. Yes, although many false witnesses came forward, *yet* they found none. But at last two false witnesses came forward

⁶¹ and said, "This *Man* said, 'I am able to destroy the temple of God and to build it in three days.' "

⁶² And the high priest arose and said to Him, "Do You answer nothing? What *is it that* these witness against You?"

⁶³ But Jesus kept silent. And the high priest responded and said to Him, "I adjure You by the living God, that You tell us if You are the Christ, the Son of God!"

⁶⁴ Jesus said to Him, "You have said it, nevertheless I say to you all, after this you will see the Son of Man sitting at the right hand of Power, and coming in the clouds of heaven."

⁶⁵ Then the high priest tore his clothes, saying, "He has spoken blasphemy! What further need do we have of witnesses? Look, now you have heard His blasphemy!

⁶⁶ what do you think?" They answered and said, "He is worthy of death."

⁶⁷ Then they spat in His face and beat Him; and others struck *Him* with the palms of their hands,

⁶⁸ saying, "Prophesy to us, You Christ! Who is the one who struck You?"

⁶⁹ Now Peter sat outside in the courtyard. And a servant girl came to him, saying, "You were also with Jesus of Galilee."

⁷⁰ But he denied it before *them* all, saying, "I do not know what you are saying."

⁷¹ And when he had gone out to the gateway, another *girl* saw him, and said to those who were there, "This *man* was also with Jesus of Nazareth."

⁷² But again he denied with an oath, "I do not know the Man."

⁷³ And after a while those who stood by came up to *him* and said to Peter, "Surely you also are *one* of them, because your speech exposes you."

⁷⁴ Then he began to curse and to swear, *saying*, "I do not know the Man!" And immediately the rooster crowed.

⁷⁵ And Peter remembered the word of Jesus, which said to Him "Before the rooster crows, you will deny Me three times." So he went out and wept bitterly.

CHAPTER 27

¹ When the morning came, all the chief priests and elders of the people took counsel against Jesus to put Him to death.

² And when they had bound Him,

they led *Him* away and delivered Him to Pontius Pilate the governor.

³ Then Judas, who had betrayed Him, observing that He was condemned, was remorseful and returned the thirty pieces of silver to the chief priests and the elders,

⁴ saying, "I have sinned by betraying the innocent blood." And they said, "What *is that* to us? You see *to it*."

⁵ Then he threw down the pieces of silver in the temple and departed, and went and hung himself.

⁶ And the chief priests took the silver pieces and said, "It is not lawful to put them into the treasury, because it is the payment for blood."

⁷ And they took counsel and bought with them the potter's field, to bury strangers in.

⁸ Therefore that field has been called, the Field of Blood, to this day.

⁹ Then was fulfilled what was spoken through Jeremiah the prophet, saying, "And they took the thirty pieces of silver, the value of Him that was priced, whom they of the children of Israel priced,

¹⁰ and gave them for the potter's field, as the LORD appointed me."

¹¹ Now Jesus stood before the governor. And the governor asked Him, saying, "Are You the King of the Jews?" And Jesus said to him, "*It is* as you say."

¹² And while He was being accused by the chief priests and elders, He did not reply.

¹³ Then Pilate said to Him, "Do You not hear how many things they testify against You?"

¹⁴ But He answered him not one word, so that the governor marveled greatly.

¹⁵ Now at *that* feast the governor was accustomed to release to the people a prisoner, whoever they desired.

¹⁶ And at that time they had an infamous prisoner called Barabbas.

¹⁷ Therefore, when they had gathered together, Pilate said to them, "Whom do you want me to release to you? Barabbas, or Jesus who is called Christ?"

¹⁸ Because, he knew that they had handed Him over because of envy.

¹⁹ while he was sitting on the judgment seat, his wife sent to him, saying, "Have nothing to do with that just Man, because, I have suffered many things today in a dream because of Him."

²⁰ But the chief priests and elders persuaded the crowd that they should ask for Barabbas and destroy Jesus.

²¹ The governor responded and said to them, "Which of the two do you want me to release to you?" They said, "Barabbas!"

²² Pilate said to them, "What shall I do with Jesus who is called Christ?" *They* all said to him, "Let Him be crucified!"

²³ And the governor said, "Why, what evil has He done?" But they

shouted out all the more, saying, "Let Him be crucified!"

²⁴ When Pilate saw that he could not prevail at all, but rather *that* an uproar occurred, he took water, and washed *his* hands before the crowd, saying, "I am innocent of the blood of this just Person. You see *to it*."

²⁵ Then all the people replied and said, "His blood *be* upon us, and upon our children."

²⁶ Then he released Barabbas to them; and when he had scourged Jesus, he delivered *Him* to be crucified.

²⁷ Then the soldiers of the governor took Jesus into the common hall and gathered the entire garrison *of soldiers* around Him.

²⁸ And they stripped Him and put a scarlet robe on Him.

²⁹ And when they had platted a crown of thorns, they put *it* on His head, and a reed in His right hand. And they bowed the knee before Him and mocked Him, saying, "Hail, King of the Jews!"

³⁰ Then they spat on Him, and took the reed and struck Him on the head.

³¹ And after they had mocked Him, they took the robe off Him, put His own clothes on Him, and led Him away to crucify *Him*.

³² Now as they came out, they found a man of Cyrene, Simon by name. They compelled him to carry His cross.

³³ And when they came to a place called Golgotha, that is to say, Place of a Skull,

³⁴ they gave Him vinegar to drink mixed with gall. But when He had tasted *of it*, He would not drink.

³⁵ Then they crucified Him, and divided His clothes, casting lots, that it might be fulfilled which was spoken through the prophet: "They divided My garments among them, and for My clothing they cast lots."

³⁶ And sitting down, they watched over Him there.

³⁷ And they put over His head the charge written against Him: THIS IS JESUS THE KING OF THE JEWS.

³⁸ Then two thieves were crucified with Him, one on the right, and another on the left.

³⁹ And those who passed by reviled Him, shaking their heads

⁴⁰ and saying, "You who destroy the temple, and build *it* in three days, save Yourself! If You are the Son of God, come down from the cross."

⁴¹ Likewise the chief priests also, mocking *Him* with the scribes and elders, said,

⁴² "He saved others; He cannot save Himself! If He is the King of Israel, let Him now come down from the cross, and we will believe Him.

⁴³ He trusted in God; let Him deliver Him now, if He will have Him; since He said, 'I am the Son of God.' "

⁴⁴ The thieves also, who were crucified with Him, threw the same thing in His face.

⁴⁵ Now from the sixth hour until the ninth hour there was darkness

over all the land.

⁴⁶ And about the ninth hour Jesus shouted out with a loud voice, saying, "Eli, Eli, lama sabachthani?" that is to say, "My God, My God, why have You forsaken Me?"

⁴⁷ Some of those who stood there when they heard that, said, "This Man is calling for Elijah."

⁴⁸ And immediately one of them ran and took a sponge, filled *it* with vinegar, they put *it* on a reed, and offered it to Him to drink.

⁴⁹ The rest said, "Leave Him alone; let us see whether Elijah will come to save Him."

⁵⁰ Jesus shouted out again with a loud voice and gave up His spirit.

⁵¹ Then, behold, the veil of the temple was torn in two from top to the bottom; and the earth quaked, and the rocks split open,

⁵² and the graves were opened; and many bodies of the saints who were asleep were raised up,

⁵³ and came out of the graves after His resurrection, and went into the holy city, and appeared to many.

⁵⁴ So when the centurion and those with Him, who were watching over Jesus, saw the earthquake and the things that occurred, they feared greatly, saying, "Truly this was the Son of God."

⁵⁵ And many women who followed Jesus from Galilee ministering to Him, were there watching from afar,

⁵⁶ among whom were Mary Magdalene, and Mary the mother of James and Joses, and the mother of Zebedee's children.

⁵⁷ Now when the evening had come, there came a rich man from Arimathaea, named Joseph, who himself was also Jesus' disciple.

⁵⁸ He went to Pilate and asked for the body of Jesus. Then Pilate commanded the body to be given.

⁵⁹ And when Joseph had taken the body, he wrapped it in a clean linen cloth,

⁶⁰ and laid it in his own new tomb which he had cut out in the rock; and he rolled a large stone against the door of the tomb, and departed.

⁶¹ And Mary Magdalene was there, and the other Mary, sitting opposite the tomb.

⁶² On the next day, which followed the Day of the Preparation, the chief priests and Pharisees gathered together to Pilate,

⁶³ saying, "Sir, we remember, while He was still alive, how that deceiver said, 'After three days I will rise again.'

⁶⁴ Therefore command that the tomb be made secure until the third day, lest His disciples come by night and steal Him away, and say to the people, 'He is risen from the dead.' So the last deception will be worse than the first."

⁶⁵ Pilate said to them, "You have a guard; go your way, make *it* as secure as you can."

⁶⁶ So they went and made the tomb secure, sealing the stone and setting the guard.

CHAPTER 28

¹ At the end of the Sabbath, as the first *day* of the week began to dawn, Mary Magdalene and the other Mary came to see the tomb.

² And behold, there was a large earthquake; because, the angel of the Lord descended from heaven and came and rolled back the stone from the door, and sat on it.

³ His countenance was like lightning, and his clothing as white as snow.

⁴ And the guards shook for fear of him, and became like dead *men*.

⁵ But the angel responded and said to the women, "Do not be afraid, because I know that you seek Jesus who was crucified.

⁶ He is not here; because He is risen, as He said. Come, see the place where the Lord lay.

⁷ And go quickly and tell His disciples that He is risen from the dead, and behold, He is going before you into Galilee; there you will see Him. Behold, I have told you."

⁸ So they went out quickly from the tomb with fear and great joy, and ran to tell His disciples.

⁹ And as they went to tell His disciples, behold, Jesus met them, saying, "Greetings." And they came and held Him by the feet and worshiped Him.

¹⁰ Then Jesus said to them, "Do not be afraid. Go and tell My brethren to go to Galilee, and there they will see Me."

¹¹ Now while they were going, behold, some of the guard came into the city, and reported to the chief priests all the things that had happened.

¹² When they had assembled with the elders and took counsel, they gave a large amount of money to the soldiers,

¹³ saying, "Tell them, 'His disciples came at night and stole Him *away* while we slept.'

¹⁴ And if this comes to the governor's ears, we will persuade him and protect you."

¹⁵ So they took the money and did as they were instructed; and this saying is commonly reported among the Jews until this day.

¹⁶ Then the eleven disciples went away into Galilee, to a mountain where Jesus had appointed for them.

¹⁷ And when they saw Him, they worshiped Him; but some doubted.

¹⁸ And Jesus came and spoke to them, saying, "All authority has been given to Me in heaven and on earth.

¹⁹ "Go therefore and teach all nations, baptizing them in the name of the Father and of the Son and of the Holy Spirit,

²⁰ teaching them to observe all things that I have commanded you; and behold, I am with you always, *even* to the end of the age." Amen.

THE GOSPEL ACCORDING TO
MARK

CHAPTER 1

¹ The beginning of the gospel of Jesus Christ, the Son of God.

² As it is written in the prophets: "Behold, I send My messenger before Your face, who will prepare Your way before You."

³ "The voice of one shouting out in the wilderness: 'Prepare the way of the LORD; make His paths straight.'"

⁴ John baptized in the wilderness and preached the baptism of repentance for the remission of sins.

⁵ And all the land of Judea, and those from Jerusalem, went out to him and were all baptized by him in the Jordan River, confessing their sins.

⁶ Now John was clothed with camel's hair and a leather belt around his waist, and he ate locusts and wild honey.

⁷ And he preached, saying, "After me there is coming One mightier than myself, whose sandal strap I am not worthy to stoop down and loose.

⁸ I indeed have baptized you with water, but He will baptize you with the Holy Spirit."

⁹ And it came to pass in those days that Jesus came from Nazareth of Galilee and was baptized by John in the Jordan.

¹⁰ And immediately, coming up from the water, He saw the heavens opened, and the Spirit descending upon Him like a dove.

¹¹ And there came a voice from heaven, *saying*, "You are My beloved Son, in whom I am well pleased."

¹² And immediately the Spirit drove Him into the wilderness.

¹³ And He was there in the wilderness forty days, tempted by Satan, and was with the wild beasts; and the angels ministered to Him.

¹⁴ Now after John was put in prison, Jesus came to Galilee, preaching the gospel of the kingdom of God,

¹⁵ and saying, "The time is fulfilled, and the kingdom of God is at hand. Repent, and believe the gospel."

¹⁶ Now as He walked by the sea of Galilee, He saw Simon and Andrew his brother casting a net into the sea; because they were fishermen.

¹⁷ And Jesus said to them, "Follow after Me, and I will make you become fishers of men."

¹⁸ And immediately they left their nets and followed Him.

¹⁹ And when He had gone a little further from there, He saw James the *son* of Zebedee, and John his brother, who also were in the boat mending their nets.

²⁰ And immediately He called them, and they left their father Zebedee in the boat with the hired servants,

and went after Him.

²¹ Then they went into Capernaum, and immediately on the Sabbath day He entered into the synagogue and taught.

²² And they were astonished at His doctrine, because, He taught them as one that had authority, and not as the scribes.

²³ Now there was a man in their synagogue with an unclean spirit. And he shouted out,

²⁴ saying, "Leave us alone! What have we to do with You, Jesus of Nazareth? Have You come to destroy us? I know You, who You are, the Holy One of God!"

²⁵ But Jesus rebuked him, saying, "Be quiet, and come out of him!"

²⁶ And when the unclean spirit had convulsed him and shouted out with a loud voice, he came out of him.

²⁷ Then they were all amazed, so that they questioned among themselves, saying, "What is this? What new doctrine is this? Because, with authority He commands even the unclean spirits, and they obey Him."

²⁸ And immediately His fame spread out throughout all the region around Galilee.

²⁹ Now as soon as they had come out of the synagogue, they entered into the house of Simon and Andrew, with James and John.

³⁰ But Simon's wife's mother lay sick with a fever, and they quickly told Him about her.

³¹ So He came and took her by the hand and lifted her up, and immediately the fever left her. And she ministered to them.

³² And at evening, when the sun had set, they brought to Him all who were sick and those who were demon possessed.

³³ And the entire city was gathered together at the door.

³⁴ And He healed many who were sick with various diseases, and cast out many demons; and He did not permit the demons to speak, because they knew Him.

³⁵ Now in the morning, having risen a long while before daylight, He went out and departed to an isolated place, and prayed there.

³⁶ And Simon and those who were with Him searched for Him.

³⁷ And when they had found Him, they said to Him, "Everyone is looking for You."

³⁸ And He said to them, "Let us go into the next towns, that I may preach there as well, because for this purpose I have come forth."

³⁹ And He preached in their synagogues throughout all Galilee, and cast out demons.

⁴⁰ Now a leper came to Him, begging Him, kneeling down to Him and saying to Him, "If You are willing, You can make me clean."

⁴¹ Then Jesus, moved with compassion, stretched out *His* hand, and touched him, and said to him, "I am willing; be cleansed."

⁴² And as soon as He had spoken,

immediately the leprosy left him, and he was cleansed.

⁴³ And He strictly warned him and immediately sent him away,

⁴⁴ and said to him, "See that you say nothing to anyone; but go your way, show yourself to the priest, and offer for your cleansing those things which Moses commanded, as a testimony to them."

⁴⁵ However, he went out and began to proclaim it freely, and to spread the matter abroad, so that Jesus could no longer openly enter into the city, but was outside in deserted places; and they came to Him from every direction.

CHAPTER 2

¹ And after *a few* days He entered into Capernaum again, and it was told that He was in the house.

² And immediately many were gathered together, so that there was no room to receive *them*, not even near the door. And He preached the word to them.

³ Then they came to Him, bringing a paralytic who was carried by four men.

⁴ And when they could not come near to Him because of the crowd, they uncovered the roof where He was. So when they had broken through, they let down the bed upon which the paralytic was lying.

⁵ When Jesus saw their faith, He said to the paralytic, "Son, your sins are forgiven you."

⁶ However some of the scribes were sitting there and reasoning in their hearts,

⁷ "Why does this *Man* speak blasphemies like this? Who can forgive sins but God alone?"

⁸ But immediately, when Jesus perceived in His spirit that they reasoned like this within themselves, He said to them, "Why do you reason these things in your hearts?

⁹ Which is easier, to say to the paralytic, '*Your* sins are forgiven you,' or to say, 'Arise, take up your bed and walk'?

¹⁰ But that you may know that the Son of Man has authority on earth to forgive sins," He said to the paralytic,

¹¹ "I say to you, arise, take up your bed, and go to your house."

¹² And immediately he arose, took up the bed, and went out in front of them all, so that they were all amazed, and glorified God, saying, "We never saw anything like this!"

¹³ Then He went out again by the sea; and all the crowds came to Him, and He taught them.

¹⁴ And as He passed by, He saw Levi the *son* of Alphaeus sitting at the tax office, and said to him, "Follow Me." And he arose and followed Him.

¹⁵ Now it happened, as Jesus was dining in Levi's house, that many tax collectors and sinners also sat together with Jesus and His disciples; because there were many, and they followed Him.

¹⁶ And when the scribes and Pharisees saw Him eating with tax collectors and sinners, they said to His disciples, "How come He eats and drinks with tax collectors and sinners?"

¹⁷ When Jesus heard *it*, He said to them, "Those who are well have no need of a physician, but those who are sick. I did not come to call the righteous, but sinners, to repentance."

¹⁸ And the disciples of John and of the Pharisees used to fast. Then they came and said to Him, "Why do the disciples of John and of the Pharisees fast, but Your disciples do not fast?"

¹⁹ And Jesus said to them, "Can the children of the bridechamber fast while the bridegroom is with them? As long as they have the bridegroom with them they cannot fast.

²⁰ But the days will come, when the bridegroom will be taken away from them, and then they will fast in those days.

²¹ And no one sews a piece of new cloth on old clothing; or else the new piece that took its place rips away from the old, and the tear is made worse.

²² And no one puts new grape juice into old containers; or else the new grape juice bursts the containers, the grape juice is spilled, and the containers are ruined. But new grape juice must be put into new containers."

²³ Now it happened that He went through the grainfields on the Sabbath day; and as they went His disciples began to pluck the heads of grain.

²⁴ And the Pharisees said to Him, "Look, why do they do what is not lawful on the Sabbath day?"

²⁵ But He said to them, "Have you never read what David did when he had need and was hungry, he and those who were with him:

²⁶ how he went into the house of God in the days of Abiathar the high priest, and ate the showbread, which is not lawful to eat except for the priests, and also gave some to those who were with him?"

²⁷ And He said to them, "The Sabbath was made for man, and not man for the Sabbath.

²⁸ Therefore the Son of Man is also Lord of the Sabbath."

CHAPTER 3

¹ And He entered into the synagogue again, and a man was there who had a withered hand.

² So they watched Him, whether He would heal him on the Sabbath day, so that they might accuse Him.

³ And He said to the man who had the withered hand, "Stand in the midst."

⁴ Then He said to them, "Is it lawful on the Sabbath days to do good or to do evil, to save life, or to kill?" But they kept silent.

⁵ And when He had looked around at them with anger, being grieved because of the hardness of their

hearts, He said to the man, "Stretch out your hand." And he stretched it out, and his hand was restored as whole as the other.

⁶ Then the Pharisees went out and immediately took counsel with the Herodians against Him, how they might destroy Him.

⁷ But Jesus withdrew Himself with His disciples to the sea. And a large crowd from Galilee and from Judea followed Him,

⁸ also from Jerusalem and Idumea and *from* beyond the Jordan; and those from Tyre and Sidon, when they heard about the many things He was doing, a large crowd came to Him.

⁹ So He told His disciples that a small boat should be kept ready for Him because of the crowd, lest they should swarm Him,

¹⁰ because, He had healed many, so that as many as had afflictions swarmed about Him to touch Him.

¹¹ And unclean spirits, whenever they saw Him, fell down before Him and shouted out, saying, "You are the Son of God."

¹² But He warned them strictly that they should not make Him known.

¹³ And He went up on a mountain and called to *Him* those whom He wanted. And they came to Him.

¹⁴ Then He ordained twelve, that they might be with Him and that He might send them out to preach,

¹⁵ and to have power to heal sicknesses and to cast out demons:

¹⁶ And Simon He surnamed Peter;

¹⁷ James the *son* of Zebedee, and John the brother of James, to whom He surnamed Boanerges, which is, "The Sons of Thunder";

¹⁸ and Andrew, and Philip, and Bartholomew, and Matthew, and Thomas, and James the son of Alphaeus, and Thaddaeus, and Simon the Cananite;

¹⁹ and Judas Iscariot, who also betrayed Him. And they went into a house.

²⁰ And the crowd came together again, so that they could not so much as eat bread.

²¹ But when His friends heard *about this*, they went out to lay hold of Him, because they said, "He is out of His mind."

²² And the scribes who came down from Jerusalem said, "He has Beelzebub," and "By the ruler of the demons He casts out demons."

²³ So He called them to *Himself* and said to them in parables: "How can Satan cast out Satan?

²⁴ And if a kingdom is divided against itself, that kingdom cannot stand.

²⁵ And if a house is divided against itself, that house cannot stand.

²⁶ And if Satan has risen up against himself, and is divided, he cannot stand, but has an end.

²⁷ No one can enter into a strong man's house and plunder his goods, unless he first binds the strong man. And then he shall plunder his house.

²⁸ "Truly, I say to you, all sins will be forgiven the sons of men, and

whatever blasphemies they may speak;
²⁹ but he who blasphemes against the Holy Spirit never has forgiveness, but is in danger of eternal damnation,"
³⁰ because they said, "He has an unclean spirit."
³¹ Then His brethren and His mother came, and standing outside they sent to Him, calling Him.
³² And the crowd sat around Him; and they said to Him, "Look, Your mother and Your brethren are outside seeking You."
³³ But He replied to them, saying, "Who is My mother, or My brethren?"
³⁴ And He looked around at those who sat about Him, and said, "Behold My mother and My brethren!
³⁵ Because, whoever does the will of God is My brother and My sister and mother."

CHAPTER 4

¹ And again He began to teach by the sea side. And a large crowd was gathered to Him, so that He got into a boat and sat *in it* on the sea. Then the entire crowd was by the sea on the land.
² Then He taught them many things by parables, and said to them in His doctrine:
³ "Listen! Behold, a sower went out to sow.
⁴ And it happened, as he sowed, some fell by the wayside, and the birds of the air came and devoured it.
⁵ And some fell on stony ground, where it did not have much earth; and immediately it sprang up because it had no depth of earth.
⁶ But when the sun was up it was scorched, and because it had no root it withered away.
⁷ And some fell among thorns; and the thorns grew up and choked it, and it yielded no fruit.
⁸ But the other fell on good ground, and yielded fruit that sprang up, increased, and produced: some thirtyfold, some sixty, and some a hundred."
⁹ And He said to them, "He who has ears to hear, let him hear."
¹⁰ But when He was alone, those around Him with the twelve asked Him about the parable.
¹¹ And He said to them, "To you it has been given to know the mystery of the kingdom of God; but to those who are outside, all *these* things come in parables,
¹² so that 'Seeing they may see and not perceive, and hearing they may hear and not understand; lest they should be converted at any time, and *their* sins be forgiven them.' "
¹³ And He said to them, "Do you not understand this parable? So how then shall you understand all parables?
¹⁴ The sower sows the word.
¹⁵ And these are those by the wayside where the word is sown. But when they have heard, Satan

comes immediately and takes away the word that was sown in their hearts.

¹⁶ And likewise these are those which are sown on stony ground who, when they have heard the word, immediately receive it with gladness;

¹⁷ but they have no root in themselves, and so endure only for a time. Afterward, when affliction or persecution arises for the word's sake, immediately they stumble.

¹⁸ Now these are the ones sown among thorns; those who hear the word,

¹⁹ but the cares of this world, the deceitfulness of riches, and the desires for other things entering in choke the word, and it becomes unfruitful.

²⁰ But these are they which are sown on good ground, those who hear the word, receive *it*, and bear fruit: some thirtyfold, some sixty, and some a hundred."

²¹ And He said to them, "Is a lamp brought to be put under a basket or under a bed? Is it not to be set on a lampstand?

²² Because, there is nothing hidden which will not be revealed, nor has anything been kept secret but that it should come to light.

²³ If anyone has ears to hear, let him hear."

²⁴ Then He said to them, "Take heed what you hear. With the same measure you use, it will be measured to you; and to you who hear, more will be given.

²⁵ Because, whoever has, to him more will be given; but whoever does not have, even what he has will be taken away from him."

²⁶ And He said, "The kingdom of God is like as if a man should scatter seed on the ground,

²⁷ and should sleep by night and rise by day, and the seed should sprout and grow, he himself does not know how.

²⁸ Because, the earth yields crops from itself: first the blade, then the head, after that the full grain in the head.

²⁹ So when the grain ripens, immediately he puts in the sickle, because the harvest has come."

³⁰ Then He said, "To what shall we liken the kingdom of God? Or with what comparison shall we compare it?

³¹ *It is* like a grain of mustard seed which, when it is sown on the ground, is smaller than all the seeds that are in the earth;

³² but when it is sown, it grows up and becomes greater than all herbs, and shoots out large branches, so that the birds of the air may nest under its shade."

³³ And with many such parables He spoke the word to them as they were able to hear *it*.

³⁴ But He did not speak to them without a parable. And when they were alone, He expounded all things to His disciples.

³⁵ And the same day, when evening

had come, He said to them, "Let us cross over to the other side."

³⁶ Now when they had sent the crowd away, they took Him in the boat just as He was. And there were also with Him other little boats.

³⁷ And a large windstorm arose, and the waves beat into the boat, so that it was already full.

³⁸ But He was in the back of the boat, asleep on a pillow. And they awoke Him and said to Him, "Teacher, do You not care that we are perishing?"

³⁹ Then He arose and rebuked the wind, and said to the sea, "Peace, be still!" And the wind ceased and there was a great calm.

⁴⁰ But He said to them, "Why are you so fearful? How is it that you have no faith?"

⁴¹ And they feared exceedingly, and said to one another, "What type of man is this, that even the wind and the sea obey Him!"

CHAPTER 5

¹ Then they came over to the other side of the sea, into the countryside of the Gadarenes.

² And when He had come out of the boat, immediately there met Him out of the tombs a man with an unclean spirit,

³ who had *his* dwelling among the tombs; and no one could bind him, not even with chains,

⁴ because he had often been bound with shackles and chains. And the chains had been pulled apart by him, and the shackles broken in pieces; neither could anyone tame him.

⁵ And night and day he was always in the mountains and in the tombs, yelling out and cutting himself with stones.

⁶ When he saw Jesus from afar, he ran and worshiped Him.

⁷ And he shouted out with a loud voice and said, "What have I to do with You, Jesus, *You* Son of the Most High God? I beg You by God that You do not torment me."

⁸ Because He said to him, "Come out of the man, *you* unclean spirit!"

⁹ Then He asked him, "What is your name?" And he answered, saying, "My name is Legion; because, we are many."

¹⁰ And he begged Him earnestly that He would not send them out of the region.

¹¹ Now a large herd of swine was feeding there near the mountains.

¹² And all the demons begged Him, saying, "Send us into the swine, that we may enter into them."

¹³ And immediately Jesus gave them permission. Then the unclean spirits went out and entered into the swine (there were about two thousand); and the herd ran violently down the steep place into the sea, and drowned in the sea.

¹⁴ And those who fed the swine fled, and told *it* in the city, and in the countryside. And they went out to see what it was that had happened.

¹⁵ Then they came to Jesus, and saw

the one who had been demon possessed and had the legion, sitting and clothed and in his right mind. And they were afraid.

¹⁶ And those who saw *it* told them how it happened to him who had been demon possessed, and *also* concerning the swine.

¹⁷ Then they began to plead with Him to depart from their region.

¹⁸ And when He got into the boat, he who had been demon possessed begged Him that he might be with Him.

¹⁹ However, Jesus did not permit him, but said to him, "Go home to your friends, and tell them what great things the Lord has done for you, and how He has had compassion on you."

²⁰ And he departed and began to proclaim in Decapolis all the great things that Jesus had for him; and everyone marveled.

²¹ Now when Jesus had crossed over again by boat to the other side, many people gathered to Him; and He was near the sea.

²² And behold, one of the rulers of the synagogue came, Jairus by name. And when he saw Him, he fell at His feet

²³ and begged Him earnestly, saying, "My little daughter lies at the point of death. *I beg you*, come and lay Your hands on her, that she may be healed, and she will live."

²⁴ So *Jesus* went with him, and a large crowd followed Him and swarmed Him.

²⁵ Now a certain woman had a flow of blood for twelve years,

²⁶ and had suffered many things from many physicians. She had spent all that she had and was no better, but rather grew worse.

²⁷ When she heard about Jesus, she came behind Him in the crowd and touched His clothes.

²⁸ Because, she said, "If only I may touch His clothes, I will be made well."

²⁹ And immediately the fountain of her blood was dried up, and she felt in her body that she was healed of the affliction.

³⁰ And Jesus, immediately knowing in Himself that virtue had gone out of Him, turned around in the crowd and said, "Who touched My clothes?"

³¹ But His disciples said to Him, "You see the crowd swarming You, and You say, 'Who touched Me?' "

³² And He looked around to see her who had done this thing.

³³ But the woman, fearing and trembling, knowing what had happened to her, came and fell down before Him and told Him the whole truth.

³⁴ And He said to her, "Daughter, your faith has made you well. Go in peace, and be healed of your affliction."

³⁵ While He was still speaking, there came *some* from the ruler of the synagogue's *house* who said, "Your daughter is dead. Why trouble the Teacher any further?"

³⁶ As soon as Jesus heard the word that was spoken, He said to the ruler of the synagogue, "Do not be afraid; only believe."

³⁷ And He permitted no one to follow Him except Peter, James, and John the brother of James.

³⁸ Then He came to the house of the ruler of the synagogue, and saw the tumult and those who wept and wailed loudly.

³⁹ And when He came in, He said to them, "Why make this commotion and weep? The girl is not dead, but sleeping."

⁴⁰ And they ridiculed Him. But when He had put them all outside, He took the father and the mother of the child, and those who were with Him, and entered where the girl was lying.

⁴¹ Then He took the girl by the hand, and said to her, "Talitha, cumi," which is translated, "Little girl, I say to you, arise."

⁴² And immediately the girl arose and walked, because, she was twelve years of age. And they were overcome with great astonishment.

⁴³ But He commanded them strictly that no one should know it, and commanded that something should be given her to eat.

CHAPTER 6

¹ Then He went out from there and came into His own region, and His disciples followed Him.

² And when the Sabbath day had come, He began to teach in the synagogue. And many hearing *Him* were astonished, saying, "Where did this *Man* get these things? And what wisdom *is* this which is given to Him, that even such mighty works are performed by His hands?

³ Is this not the carpenter, the Son of Mary, and the brother of James, Joses, Judas, and Simon? And are not His sisters here with us?" So they were offended at Him.

⁴ But Jesus said to them, "A prophet is not without honor except in his own region, among his own relatives, and in his own house."

⁵ Now He could do no mighty work there, except that He laid His hands on a few sick people and healed *them*.

⁶ And He marveled because of their unbelief. Then He went around about the villages teaching.

⁷ And He called the twelve to *Himself*, and began to send them out two by two, and gave them power over unclean spirits.

⁸ And commanded them that they should take nothing for *their* journey except only a staff, no bag, no bread, no money in *their* money belts;

⁹ but to wear sandals, and not put on two coats.

¹⁰ He also said to them, "In whatever place you enter into a house, stay there until you depart from that place.

¹¹ And whoever will not receive you nor hear you, when you depart from there, shake off the dust

under your feet for a testimony against them. Truly, I say to you, it will be more tolerable for Sodom and Gomorrah in the day of judgment than for that city!"

¹² So they went out, and preached that people should repent.

¹³ And they cast out many demons, and anointed with oil many who were sick, and healed *them*.

¹⁴ Now King Herod heard of *Him*, because His name had become well known. And he said "That John the Baptist was risen from the dead, and therefore these mighty works are at work in him."

¹⁵ Others said, "It is Elijah." And others said, "It is a prophet, or like one of the prophets."

¹⁶ But when Herod heard *of it*, he said, "This is John, whom I beheaded; he has risen from the dead."

¹⁷ Because, Herod himself had sent out and laid hold of John, and bound him in prison for the sake of Herodias, his brother Philip's wife; because he had married her.

¹⁸ Because John had said to Herod, "It is not lawful for you to have your brother's wife."

¹⁹ Therefore Herodias had this disagreement with him, and wanted to kill him, but she could not;

²⁰ because Herod feared John, knowing that he was a just and holy man, and protected him. And when he heard him, he did many things, and heard him gladly.

²¹ Then when a convenient day came that Herod on his birthday gave a feast for his nobles, high officers, and chief *men* of Galilee.

²² And when Herodias' daughter herself came in and danced, and pleased Herod and those who sat with him, the king said to the girl, "Ask me whatever you want, and I will give *it to* you."

²³ He also swore to her, "Whatever you will ask me, I will give it to you, up to half of my kingdom."

²⁴ So she went out, and said to her mother, "What should I ask?" And she said, "The head of John the Baptist!"

²⁵ And swiftly she came in immediately to the king and asked, saying, "I want you to give me the head of John the Baptist on a platter at once."

²⁶ And the king was exceedingly sorry; *yet* because of his oaths and because of those who sat with him, he did not want to refuse her.

²⁷ So immediately the king sent an executioner and commanded his head to be brought. And he went and beheaded him in the prison,

²⁸ brought his head on a platter, and gave it to the girl; and the girl gave it to her mother.

²⁹ And when his disciples heard *of it*, they came and took away his corpse and laid it in a tomb.

³⁰ Then the apostles gathered together to Jesus and told Him everything, both what they had done and what they had taught.

³¹ And He said to them, "Come aside

by yourselves to a deserted place and rest a while." Because, there were many coming and going, and they did not even have time to eat.
³² So they departed by boat to a deserted place privately.
³³ But the crowd saw them departing. And many knew Him and ran there on foot from all the cities, overtook them, and came together to Him.
³⁴ And Jesus, when He came out, saw a large crowd and was moved with compassion for them, because they were like sheep not having a shepherd. So He began to teach them many things.
³⁵ And when the day was now almost over, His disciples came to Him and said, "This is a deserted place, and the time has now passed away.
³⁶ Send them away, that they may go into the surrounding region and into the villages and buy themselves bread; because, they have nothing to eat."
³⁷ He replied and said to them, "You give them something to eat." And they said to Him, "Shall we go and buy two hundred denarii worth of bread and give them something to eat?"
³⁸ He said to them, "How many loaves do you have? Go and see." And when they knew they said, "Five, and two fish."
³⁹ Then He commanded them to make everyone sit down in groups on the green grass.
⁴⁰ So they sat down in ranks, in hundreds and in fifties.
⁴¹ And when He had taken the five loaves and the two fish, He looked up to heaven, and blessed, and broke the loaves, and gave *them* to His disciples to set before them; and the two fish He divided among them all.
⁴² So they all ate and were filled.
⁴³ And they took up twelve baskets full of fragments and of the fish.
⁴⁴ Now those who had eaten the loaves were about five thousand men.
⁴⁵ And immediately He made His disciples get into the boat and go ahead of Him to the other side, to Bethsaida, while He sent the people away.
⁴⁶ And when He had sent them away, He departed to a mountain to pray.
⁴⁷ Now when evening came, the boat was in the midst of the sea; and He was alone on the land.
⁴⁸ Then He saw them straining during rowing, because the wind was against them. Now about the fourth watch of the night He came to them, walking on the sea, and would have passed them by.
⁴⁹ And when they saw Him walking on the sea, they supposed it was a spirit, and shouted out;
⁵⁰ because they all saw Him and were troubled. But immediately He talked with them and said to them, "Be of good cheer! It is Me; do not be afraid."

⁵¹ Then He went up into the boat to them, and the wind ceased. And they were greatly amazed in themselves beyond measure, and marveled.
⁵² Because, they did not consider *the miracle* of the loaves, because their heart was hardened.
⁵³ And when they had crossed over, they came to the land of Gennesaret and drew to the shore.
⁵⁴ And when they came out of the boat, immediately the people recognized Him,
⁵⁵ ran through that entire surrounding region, and began to carry about on beds those who were sick to wherever they heard He was.
⁵⁶ And wherever He entered, into villages, cities, or the countryside, they laid the sick in the streets, and begged Him that they might just touch the edge of His clothes. And as many as touched Him were made well.

CHAPTER 7

¹ Then the Pharisees and some of the scribes came together to Him, having come from Jerusalem.
² Now when they saw some of His disciples eat bread with defiled, that is, with unwashed hands, they found fault.
³ Because, the Pharisees and all the Jews do not eat unless they wash *their* hands often, holding the tradition of the elders.
⁴ And *when they come* from the marketplace, they do not eat unless they wash. And there are many other things which they have received to embrace, like the washing of cups, pots, copper vessels, and couches.
⁵ Then the Pharisees and scribes asked Him, "Why do Your disciples not walk according to the tradition of the elders, but eat bread with unwashed hands?"
⁶ He answered and said to them, "Rightly has Isaiah prophesied of you hypocrites as it is written: 'This people honor Me with *their* lips, but their heart is far from Me.
⁷ Therefore in vain do they worship Me, teaching *as* doctrines the commandments of men.'
⁸ Because laying aside the commandment of God, you embrace the tradition of men, *like* the washing of pots and cups, and many other such things you do."
⁹ And He said to them, "All too well you reject the commandment of God, that you may keep your own tradition.
¹⁰ Because, Moses said, 'Honor your father and your mother'; and, 'He who curses father or mother, let him be put to death.'
¹¹ But you claim, 'If a man says to his father or mother, "Whatever profit you might have received from me is Corban" ' (that is to say, a gift), *then he will be exempt*,
¹² then you no longer permit him to do anything for his father or his mother,

¹³ making the word of God of no effect through your tradition which you have handed down. And many such things you do."

¹⁴ And when He had called all the people to *Himself*, He said to them, "Hear Me, everyone *of you*, and understand:

¹⁵ There is nothing that enters a man from outside which can defile him; but the things which come out of him, those are the things that defile a man.

¹⁶ If anyone has ears to hear, let him hear!"

¹⁷ And when He had entered a house away from the people, His disciples asked Him concerning the parable.

¹⁸ So He said to them, "Are you likewise without understanding also? Do you not perceive that whatever enters a man from outside cannot defile him,

¹⁹ because, it does not enter his heart but the stomach, and goes out into the drain, thus purging all foods?"

²⁰ And He said, "That which comes out of a man, that defiles a man.

²¹ Because, from within, out of the heart of men, proceed evil thoughts, adulteries, fornications, murders,

²² thefts, covetousness, wickedness, deceit, perversion, an evil eye, blasphemy, pride, foolishness.

²³ All these evil things come from within and defile the man."

²⁴ And from there He arose and went to the region of Tyre and Sidon. And He entered into a house and wanted no one to know it, but He could not be hidden.

²⁵ Because, *a certain* woman whose young daughter had an unclean spirit heard about Him, and came and fell at His feet.

²⁶ The woman was a Greek, a Syrophoenician by birth, and she begged Him that He would cast the demon out of her daughter.

²⁷ But Jesus said to her, "Let the children be filled first, because it is not appropriate to take the children's bread and throw *it* to the dogs."

²⁸ And she replied and said to "Yes, Lord, yet even the dogs under the table eat from the children's crumbs."

²⁹ Then He said to her, "Because of this saying go your way; the demon has gone out of your daughter."

³⁰ And when she had come to her house, she found the demon gone out, and her daughter lying upon the bed.

³¹ And again, departing from the region of Tyre and Sidon, He came through the midst of the region of Decapolis to the Sea of Galilee.

³² Then they brought to Him one who was deaf and had an impediment in his speech, and they begged Him to put His hand on him.

³³ And He took him aside from the crowd, and put His fingers in his ears, and He spat and touched his tongue.

³⁴ Then, looking up to heaven, He sighed, and said to him, "Ephphatha," that is, "Be opened."

³⁵ And immediately his ears were opened, and the impediment of his tongue was loosed, and he spoke plainly.

³⁶ Then He commanded them that they should tell no one; but the more He commanded them, the more widely they proclaimed *it*.

³⁷ And they were astonished beyond measure, saying, "He has done all things well. He makes both the deaf to hear and the mute to speak."

CHAPTER 8

¹ In those days, the crowds being very large and having nothing to eat, Jesus called His disciples *to Himself* and said to them,

² "I have compassion on the multitude, because they have now continued with Me three days and have nothing to eat.

³ And if I send them away fasting to their own houses, they will faint on the way; because, some of them have come from afar."

⁴ Then His disciples replied to Him, "How can one satisfy these *people* with bread here in the wilderness?"

⁵ He asked them, "How many loaves do you have?" And they said, "Seven."

⁶ So He commanded the people to sit down on the ground. And He took the seven loaves and gave thanks, and broke, and gave them to His disciples to set before *them*; and they set *them* before the people.

⁷ And they also had a few small fish; and having blessed them, He commanded to set them also before *them*.

⁸ So they ate and were filled, and they took up seven large baskets of leftover *food* fragments.

⁹ Now those who had eaten were about four thousand, and He sent them away.

¹⁰ Then immediately He got into a boat with His disciples, and came to the region of Dalmanutha.

¹¹ And the Pharisees came out and began to dispute with Him, seeking from Him a sign from heaven, testing Him.

¹² But He sighed deeply in His spirit, and said, "Why does this generation seek a sign? Truly, I say to you, no sign will be given to this generation."

¹³ And He left them, and getting into the boat again, departed to the other side.

¹⁴ Now *the disciples* had forgotten to take bread, and they did not have more than one loaf with them in the boat.

¹⁵ And He charged them, saying, "Take heed, beware of the leaven of the Pharisees and the leaven of Herod."

¹⁶ And they reasoned among themselves, saying, "*It is* because we have no bread."

¹⁷ But when Jesus, knew *about it*, He said to them, "Why do you reason

because you have no bread? Do you not yet perceive nor understand? Is your heart still hardened?

¹⁸ Having eyes, do you not see? And having ears, do you not hear? And do you not remember?

¹⁹ And when I broke the five loaves for the five thousand, how many baskets full of fragments did you take up?" They said to Him, "Twelve."

²⁰ "Also, when the seven for the four thousand, how many large baskets full of fragments did you take up?" And they said, "Seven."

²¹ So He said to them, "How is it that you do not understand?"

²² Then He came to Bethsaida; and they brought a blind man to Him, and begged Him to touch him.

²³ So He took the blind man by the hand and led him out of the town. And when He had spat on his eyes and put His hands on him, He asked him if he saw anything.

²⁴ And he looked up and said, "I see men like trees, walking."

²⁵ Then He put *His* hands on his eyes again and made him look up. And he was restored and saw everyone clearly.

²⁶ Then He sent him away to his house, saying, "Neither go into the town, nor tell it to anyone in the town."

²⁷ Now Jesus and His disciples went out to the towns of Caesarea Philippi; and on the road He asked His disciples, saying to them, "Who do men say that I am?"

²⁸ So they answered, "John the Baptist; but some *say*, Elijah; and others, one of the prophets."

²⁹ He said to them, "But who do you say that I am?" Peter answered and said to Him, "You are the Christ."

³⁰ Then He strictly warned them that they should tell no one about Him.

³¹ And He began to teach them that the Son of Man must suffer many things, and be rejected by the elders and *by* chief priests and scribes, and be killed, and after three days rise again.

³² And He spoke this saying openly. Then Peter took Him aside and began to rebuke Him.

³³ But when He had turned around and looked at His disciples, He rebuked Peter, saying, "Get behind Me, Satan! Because, you are not mindful of the things that are of God, but the things that are of men."

³⁴ And when He had called the people to *Himself*, with His disciples also, He said to them, "Whoever desires to come after Me, let him deny himself, and take up his cross, and follow Me.

³⁵ Because, whoever desires to save his life will lose it, but whoever loses his life for My sake and the gospel's they will save it.

³⁶ Because, what shall it profit a man if he gains the entire world, and loses his own soul?

³⁷ Or what shall a man give in exchange for his soul?

³⁸ Because, whoever shall be ashamed of Me and My words in this adulterous and sinful generation, of him the Son of Man will also be ashamed when He comes in the glory of His Father with the holy angels."

CHAPTER 9

¹ And He said to them, "Truly, I say to you that there are some standing here who will not taste death until they see the kingdom of God coming with power."

² Now after six days Jesus took Peter, James, and John, *with Him* and led them up on a high mountain privately by themselves; and He was transfigured before them.

³ And His clothes became shining, exceedingly white, like snow, such as no launderer on earth can whiten them.

⁴ And Elijah appeared to them with Moses, and they were talking with Jesus.

⁵ Then Peter responded and said to Jesus, "Teacher, it is good for us to be here; and let us make three tabernacles: one for You, one for Moses, and one for Elijah,"

⁶ because, he did not know what to say, because, they were greatly afraid.

⁷ And a cloud came and overshadowed them; and a voice came out of the cloud, saying, "This is My beloved Son. Hear Him!"

⁸ Then suddenly, when they had looked around, they saw no one anymore, but only Jesus with themselves.

⁹ Now as they came down from the mountain, He commanded them that they should tell no one the things they had seen, until the Son of Man had risen from the dead.

¹⁰ So they kept this saying to themselves, questioning one another what the rising from the dead meant.

¹¹ And they asked Him, saying, "Why do the scribes say that Elijah must come first?"

¹² Then He answered and told them, "Indeed, Elijah comes first and restores all things; and just like it is written concerning the Son of Man, that He must suffer many things and be treated with contempt.

¹³ But I say to you that Elijah indeed came, and they did to him whatever they wished, as it is written of him."

¹⁴ And when He came to *His* disciples, He saw a large crowd around them, and scribes disputing with them.

¹⁵ And immediately, when they saw Him, all the people were greatly amazed, and running to *Him*, greeted Him.

¹⁶ And He asked the scribes, "What are you disputing with them?"

¹⁷ Then one of the crowd answered and said, "Teacher, I brought my son to You, who has a mute spirit.

¹⁸ And wherever it seizes him, it throws him down; he foams at the mouth, gnashes his teeth, and withers away. So I spoke to Your

disciples, that they should cast it out, but they could not."

¹⁹ He answered him and said, "O faithless generation, how long shall I be with you? How long shall I bear with you? Bring him to Me."

²⁰ Then they brought him to Him. And when he saw Him, immediately the spirit convulsed him, and he fell on the ground and rolled around, foaming at the mouth.

²¹ So He asked his father, "How long has this been happening to him?" And he said, "From childhood.

²² And often it has thrown him both into the fire and into the water to destroy him. But if You can do anything, have compassion on us and help us."

²³ Jesus said to him, "If you can believe, all things *are* possible to him who believes."

²⁴ Immediately the father of the child cried out and said with tears, "Lord, I believe; help my unbelief!"

²⁵ When Jesus saw that the people came running together, He rebuked the unclean spirit, saying to it: "*You* mute and deaf spirit, I command you, come out of him and enter into him no more!"

²⁶ Then *the spirit* shouted out, convulsed him greatly, and came out of him. And he became as one dead, so that many said, "He is dead."

²⁷ But Jesus took him by the hand and lifted him up, and he arose.

²⁸ And when He had come into the house, His disciples asked Him privately, "Why could we not cast it out?"

²⁹ So He said to them, "This kind can come out by nothing but through prayer and fasting."

³⁰ Then they departed from there and passed through Galilee, and He did not want anyone to know *it*.

³¹ Because, He taught His disciples and said to them, "The Son of Man is being delivered into the hands of men, and they will kill Him. And after He is killed, He will rise the third day."

³² But they did not understand this saying, and were afraid to ask Him.

³³ Then He came to Capernaum. And when He was in the house He asked them, "What was it you disputed among yourselves on the road?"

³⁴ But they kept silent, because, on the road they had disputed among themselves who *would* be the greatest.

³⁵ And He sat down, called the twelve, and said to them, "If anyone desires to be first, *he* shall be last of all and servant of all."

³⁶ Then He took a child and set him in the midst of them. And when He had taken him in His arms, He said to them,

³⁷ "Whoever recieves one such child in My name receives Me; and whoever receives Me, receives not Me but Him who sent Me."

³⁸ Now John replied to Him, saying, "Teacher, we saw someone who does not follow us casting out

demons in Your name, and we forbade him because he does not follow us."

³⁹ But Jesus said, "Do not forbid because, there is no one who shall do a miracle in My name who can suddenly speak evil of Me.

⁴⁰ Because he who is not against us is on our side.

⁴¹ Because, whoever gives you a cup of water to drink in My name, because you belong to Christ, truly, I say to you, he will not lose his reward.

⁴² "But whoever causes one of *these* little ones who believe in Me to stumble, it would be better for him if a millstone were hung around his neck, and he were thrown into the sea.

⁴³ And if your hand causes you to offend, cut it off. It is better for you to enter into life maimed, rather than having two hands, to go to hell, into the fire that will never be quenched,

⁴⁴ where 'Their worm does not die and the fire is not quenched.'

⁴⁵ And if your foot causes you to offend, cut it off. It is better for you to enter life lame, rather than having two feet, to be thrown into hell, into the fire that will never be quenched,

⁴⁶ where 'Their worm does not die, and the fire is not quenched.'

⁴⁷ And if your eye causes you to offend, pluck it out. It is better for you to enter the kingdom of God with one eye, rather than having two eyes, to be thrown into hell fire,

⁴⁸ where 'Their worm does not die and the fire is not quenched.'

⁴⁹ "Because, everyone will be seasoned with fire, and every sacrifice will be seasoned with salt.

⁵⁰ Salt *is* good, but if the salt loses its flavor, with what will you season it? Have salt in yourselves, and have peace with one another."

CHAPTER 10

¹ Then He arose from there and came to the region of Judea by the other side of the Jordan. And the people gathered to Him again, and as He was accustomed, He taught them again.

² Then the Pharisees came to Him, and asked Him, "Is it lawful for a man to put away his wife?" testing Him.

³ And He answered and said to them, "What did Moses command you?"

⁴ They said, "Moses permitted a man to write a certificate of divorce, and to dismiss *her*."

⁵ And Jesus replied and said to them, "Because of the hardness of your heart he wrote you this precept.

⁶ But from the beginning of the creation, God 'made them male and female.'

⁷ 'For this reason a man shall leave his father and mother and be joined to his wife,

⁸ and the two will become one

flesh'; so then they are no longer two, but one flesh.

⁹ Therefore what God has joined together, let not man separate."

¹⁰ Then in the house, His disciples asked Him again about the same *matter*.

¹¹ So He said to them, "Whoever puts away his wife and marries another commits adultery against her.

¹² And if a woman puts away her husband and marries another, she commits adultery."

¹³ Then they brought little children to Him, that He might touch them; but *his* disciples rebuked those who brought *them*.

¹⁴ But when Jesus saw *it*, He was greatly displeased and said to them, "Permit the little children to come to Me, and do not forbid them; because, of such is the kingdom of God.

¹⁵ Truly, I say to you, whoever does not receive the kingdom of God as a little child will not enter into it."

¹⁶ And He took them up in His arms, laid *His* hands on them, and blessed them.

¹⁷ Now as He was going out on the road, one came running, knelt before Him, and asked Him, "Good Teacher, what shall I do that I may inherit eternal life?"

¹⁸ So Jesus said to him, "Why do you call Me good? No one *is* good but One, *that is*, God.

¹⁹ You know the commandments: 'Do not commit adultery,' 'Do not murder,' 'Do not steal,' 'Do not bear false witness,' 'Do not defraud,' 'Honor your father and your mother.'"

²⁰ And he replied and said to Him, "Teacher, all these things I have observed from my youth."

²¹ Then Jesus, looking at him, loved him, and said to him, "One thing you lack: Go your way, sell whatever you have and give to the poor, and you will have treasure in heaven; and come, take up the cross, and follow Me."

²² But he was sad at that saying, and went away sorrowful, because he had many possessions.

²³ Then Jesus looked around and said to His disciples, "How hard it is for those who have riches to enter the kingdom of God!"

²⁴And the disciples were astonished at His words. But Jesus responded again and said to them, "Children, how hard it is for those who trust in riches to enter the kingdom of God!

²⁵ It is easier for a camel to go through the eye of a needle than for a rich man to enter into the kingdom of God."

²⁶ And they were greatly astonished, saying among themselves, "Who then can be saved?"

²⁷ But Jesus looking at them said, "With men *it is* impossible, but not with God; because, with God all things are possible."

²⁸ Then Peter began to say to Him, "See, we have left all and have

followed You."

²⁹ So Jesus replied and said, "Truly, I say to you, there is no one who has left house or brothers or sisters or father or mother or wife or children or lands, for My sake and the gospel's,

³⁰ who will not receive a hundredfold now in this time, houses and brothers and sisters and mothers and children and lands, with persecutions, and in the age to come, eternal life.

³¹ But many *who are* first will be last, and the last first."

³² Now they were on the road, going up to Jerusalem, and Jesus was going before them; and they were amazed. And as they followed they were afraid. Then He took aside the twelve again and began to tell them the things that would happen to Him:

³³ Saying, "Behold, we are going up to Jerusalem, and the Son of Man will be delivered to the chief priests and to the scribes; and they will condemn Him to death and deliver Him to the Gentiles;

³⁴ and they will mock Him, and will scourge Him, and will spit on Him, and will kill Him. And the third day He will rise again."

³⁵ Then James and John, the sons of Zebedee, came to Him, saying, "Teacher, we want You to do for us whatever we desire."

³⁶ And He said to them, "What do you want Me to do for you?"

³⁷ They said to Him, "Grant us that we may sit, one on Your right hand and the other on Your left, in Your glory."

³⁸ But Jesus said to them, "You do not know what you ask. Are you able to drink the cup that I drink of, and be baptized with the baptism that I am baptized with?"

³⁹ They said to Him, "We are able." So Jesus said to them, "You will indeed drink the cup that I drink, and with the baptism I am baptized with you will be baptized;

⁴⁰ but to sit on My right hand and on My left hand is not Mine to give, but *it will be given* to those for whom it is prepared."

⁴¹ And when the ten heard it, they began to be greatly displeased with James and John.

⁴² But Jesus called them *to Himself* and said to them, "You know that those who are considered rulers over the Gentiles lord it over them, and their great ones exercise authority over them.

⁴³ Yet it shall not be so among you; but whoever desires to become great among you will be your servant.

⁴⁴ And whoever of you desires to be chief shall be servant of all.

⁴⁵ Because, even the Son of Man did not come to be ministered to, but to minister, and to give His life a ransom for many."

⁴⁶ Now they came to Jericho. As He went out of Jericho with His disciples and a large crowd, blind Bartimaeus, the son of Timaeus, sat

by the roadside begging.

⁴⁷ And when he heard that it was Jesus of Nazareth, he began to shout out and say, "Jesus, *You* Son of David, have mercy on me!"

⁴⁸ Then many warned him that he should be quiet; but he shouted out all the more, "*You* Son of David, have mercy on me!"

⁴⁹ So Jesus stood still and commanded him to be called. Then they called the blind man, saying to him, "Be of good cheer. Rise, He is calling you."

⁵⁰ And throwing aside his coat, he rose and came to Jesus.

⁵¹ So Jesus replied and said to him, "What do you want Me to do for you?" The blind man said to Him, "Lord, that I may receive my sight."

⁵² Then Jesus said to him, "Go your way; your faith has made you well." And immediately he received his sight and followed Jesus on the road.

CHAPTER 11

¹ Now when they came near to Jerusalem, to Bethphage and Bethany, at the Mount of Olives, He sent out two of His disciples;

² and He said to them, "Go your way into the village opposite you; and as soon as you have entered into it you will find a colt tied, on which no one has sat. Loose him and bring *him*.

³ And if anyone says to you, 'Why are you doing this?' say that, 'The Lord has need of him,' and immediately he will send him here."

⁴ So they went their way, and found the colt tied by the door outside in a place where two roads meet, and they loosed him.

⁵ But some of those who stood there said to them, "What are you doing, loosing the colt?"

⁶ And they spoke to them just as Jesus had commanded. So they let them go.

⁷ Then they brought the colt to Jesus and threw their clothes on him, and He sat upon him.

⁸ And many spread their clothes on the road, and others cut down branches from the trees and spread them on the road.

⁹ Then those who went before and those who followed shouted out, saying: "Hosanna! 'Blessed *is* He who comes in the name of the LORD!'

¹⁰ Blessed *be* the kingdom of our father David that comes in the name of the Lord! Hosanna in the highest!"

¹¹ And Jesus entered into Jerusalem and into the temple. So when He had looked around at all things, as the hour was already late, He went out to Bethany with the twelve.

¹² Now the next day, when they had come out from Bethany, He was hungry.

¹³ And seeing from afar a fig tree having leaves, He went to see if perhaps He would find something on it. And when He came to it, He found nothing but leaves, because

it was not yet the season for figs.

¹⁴ And Jesus responded and said to it, "Let no one eat fruit from you ever again." And His disciples heard *it*.

¹⁵ Then they came to Jerusalem. And Jesus went into the temple and began to throw out those who bought and sold in the temple, and overturned the tables of the money changers and the seats of those who sold doves.

¹⁶ And He would not permit anyone to carry *any* vessel through the temple.

¹⁷ Then He taught, saying to them, "Is it not written, 'My house shall be called a house of prayer for all nations'? But you have made it a 'den of thieves.' "

¹⁸ And the scribes and chief priests heard *it* and sought how they might destroy Him; because they feared Him, as all the people were astonished at His doctrine.

¹⁹ And when evening had come, He went out of the city.

²⁰ Now in the morning, as they passed by, they saw the fig tree dried up from the roots.

²¹ And Peter, remembering, said to Him, "Teacher, look! The fig tree which You cursed has withered away."

²² So Jesus replied and said to them, "Have faith in God.

²³ Because, truly, I say to you, whoever shall say to this mountain, 'Be removed and be cast into the sea,' and does not doubt in his heart, but believes that those things he says will come to pass, he will have whatever he says.

²⁴ Therefore I say to you, whatever things you desire when you pray, believe that you receive *them*, and you will have *them*.

²⁵ "And whenever you stand praying, if you have anything against anyone, forgive, that your Father in heaven may also forgive you your trespasses.

²⁶ But if you do not forgive, neither will your Father in heaven forgive your trespasses."

²⁷ Then they came again to Jerusalem. And as He was walking in the temple, the chief priests, the scribes, and the elders came to Him.

²⁸ And they said to Him, "By what authority are You doing these things? And who gave You this authority to do these things?"

²⁹ But Jesus answered and said to them, "I also will ask you one question; then answer Me, and I will tell you by what authority I do these things:

³⁰ The baptism of John, was *it* from heaven or from men? Answer Me."

³¹ And they reasoned among themselves, saying, "If we shall say, 'From heaven,' He will say, 'Why then did you not believe him?'

³² But if we say, 'From men,' " they feared the people, because, everyone counted John to have been a prophet indeed.

³³ So they answered and said to Jesus, "We cannot tell." And Jesus

replied and said to them, "Neither will I tell you by what authority I do these things."

CHAPTER 12

¹ Then He began to speak to them in parables: "A *certain* man planted a vineyard and set a hedge around *it*, dug *a place* for the grape juice vat and built a tower. And he leased it to vinedressers and went into a far region.

² Now when the season came he sent a servant to the vinedressers, that he might receive some of the fruit of the vineyard from the vinedressers.

³ And they took *him* and beat him and sent *him* away empty handed.

⁴ So, again he sent them another servant, and they threw stones at him, wounded *him* in the head, and sent *him* away shamefully treated.

⁵ And again he sent another, and him they killed; and many others, beating some and killing some.

⁶ Therefore still having one son, his dearly beloved, he also sent him to them last, saying, 'They shall reverence my son.'

⁷ But those vinedressers said among themselves, 'This is the heir. Come, let us kill him, and the inheritance will be ours.'

⁸ So they took him and killed *him* and threw *him* out of the vineyard.

⁹ "Therefore what shall the owner of the vineyard do? He will come and destroy the vinedressers, and give the vineyard to others.

¹⁰ Have you not even read this Scripture: 'The stone which the builders rejected has become the chief cornerstone.

¹¹ This was the LORD'S doing, and it is marvelous in our eyes'?"

¹² And they sought to lay hands on Him, but feared the people, because, they knew that He had spoken the parable against them. So they left Him and went their way.

¹³ Then they sent to Him some of the Pharisees and the Herodians, to catch Him in *His* words.

¹⁴ When they had come, they said to Him, "Teacher, we know that You are true, and esteem no one; because, You do not regard the person of men, but teach the way of God in truth. Is it lawful to pay taxes to Caesar, or not?

¹⁵ Should we give, or should we not give?" But He, knowing their hypocrisy, said to them, "Why do you test Me? Bring Me a denarius that I may see *it*."

¹⁶ So they brought *it*. And He said to them, "Whose image and inscription *is* this?" They said to Him, "Caesar's."

¹⁷ And Jesus replied and said to them, "Render to Caesar the things that are Caesar's, and to God the things that are God's." And they marveled at Him.

¹⁸ Then some Sadducees, who say there is no resurrection, came to Him; and they asked Him, saying:

¹⁹ "Teacher, Moses wrote to us that

if a man's brother dies, and leaves *his* wife behind, and leaves no children, that his brother should take his wife and raise up offspring for his brother.

[20] Now there were seven brothers. The first took a wife; and dying, he left no offspring.

[21] And the second took her, and he died; nor did he leave any offspring. And the third likewise.

[22] So the seven had her and left no offspring. Last of all the woman died also.

[23] Therefore, in the resurrection, when they rise, whose wife shall she be? Because all seven had her as wife."

[24] Jesus answered and said to them, "Are you not in error because of this, because, you do not know the Scriptures nor the power of God?

[25] Because, when they rise from the dead, they neither marry nor are given in marriage, but are like the angels who are in heaven.

[26] But concerning the dead, that they rise, have you not read in the book of Moses, how in the bush God spoke to him, saying, '*I am* the God of Abraham, the God of Isaac, and the God of Jacob'?

[27] He is not the God of the dead, but the God of the living. You are greatly in error because of this."

[28] Then one of the scribes came, and having heard them reasoning together, and perceiving that He had answered them well, asked Him, "Which is the first commandment of all?"

[29] And Jesus answered him, "The first of all the commandments is: 'Hear, O Israel, the LORD our God is one LORD.

[30] And you shall love the LORD your God with all your heart, with all your soul, with all your mind, and with all your strength.' This *is* the first commandment.

[31] And the second *is* similar, being this: 'You shall love your neighbor as yourself.' There is no other commandment greater than these."

[32] So the scribe said to Him, "Well *said*, Teacher. You have spoken the truth, because there is one God, and there is no other but He.

[33] And to love Him with all the heart, with all the understanding, with all the soul, and with all the strength, and to love *one's* neighbor as oneself, is more than *all of* the entire burnt offerings and sacrifices."

[34] Now when Jesus saw that he responded wisely, He said to him, "You are not far from the kingdom of God." But after that no one dared ask Him *any questions*.

[35] Then Jesus responded and said, while He taught in the temple, "How is it that the scribes say that Christ is the Son of David?

[36] Because David himself said by the Holy Spirit: 'The LORD said to my Lord, "Sit at My right hand, until I make Your enemies Your footstool." '

[37] Therefore David himself calls

Him 'Lord'; how is He *then* his Son?" And the common people heard Him gladly.

³⁸ Then He said to them in His doctrine, "Beware of the scribes, who desire to go *around* in long robes, *love* greetings in the marketplaces,

³⁹ the best seats in the synagogues, and the best places at feasts,

⁴⁰ who devour widows' houses, and for an exhibition make long prayers. These will receive greater damnation."

⁴¹ Now Jesus sat opposite the treasury and saw how the people put money into the treasury. And many who were rich put in much.

⁴² Then one poor widow came and threw in two mites, which make a quadrans.

⁴³ So He called His disciples to *Himself* and said to them, "Truly, I say to you that this poor widow has put in more than all those who have given into the treasury;

⁴⁴ because, *they* all put in out of their abundance, but she out of her poverty put in all that she had, *even* her entire livelihood."

CHAPTER 13

¹ Then as He went out of the temple, one of His disciples said to Him, "Teacher, see what manner of stones and what buildings *are here*!"

² And Jesus replied and said to him, "Do you see these great buildings? Not one stone will be left upon another, that will not be thrown down."

³ Now as He sat on the Mount of Olives opposite the temple, Peter, James, John, and Andrew asked Him privately,

⁴ "Tell us, when shall these things be? And what *shall* be the sign when all these things shall be fulfilled?"

⁵ And Jesus, answering them, began to say: "Take heed that no *one* deceives you.

⁶ Because, many will come in My name, saying, 'I am *Christ*,' and will deceive many.

⁷ But when you hear of wars and rumors of wars, do not be troubled; because, such things must happen, but the end *will* not *be* yet.

⁸ Because nation will rise against nation, and kingdom against kingdom. And there will be earthquakes in various places, and there will be famines and troubles. These *are* the beginnings of sorrows.

⁹ "But watch out for yourselves, because, they will deliver you up to councils, and you will be beaten in the synagogues. You will be brought before rulers and kings for My sake, for a testimony to them.

¹⁰ And the gospel must first be preached to all the nations.

¹¹ But when they arrest *you* and deliver you up, do not worry beforehand, or premeditate what you will speak. But whatever is given you in that hour, speak that; because it is not you who speaks, but the Holy Spirit.

¹² Now brother will betray brother

to death, and a father his son; and children will rise up against *their* parents and will cause them to be put to death.

¹³ And you will be hated by all *people* for My name's sake. But he who endures to the end, the same will be saved.

¹⁴ "But when you see the 'abomination of desolation,' spoken of by Daniel the prophet, standing where it ought not" (let the reader understand), "then let those who are in Judea flee to the mountains.

¹⁵ Let him who is on the housetop not go down into the house, nor enter *into it* to take anything out of his house.

¹⁶ And let him who is in the field not turn back again to get his clothes.

¹⁷ But woe to those who are pregnant and to those who are nursing babes in those days!

¹⁸ And pray that your flight may not be in the winter.

¹⁹ Because, *in* those days there will be affliction, such as has not been since the beginning of the creation which God created until this time, nor ever will be.

²⁰ And unless the Lord had shortened those days, no flesh would be saved; but for the elect's sake, whom He has chosen, He shortened the days.

²¹ "Then if anyone says to you, 'Look, here is Christ!' or, 'Look, *He* is there!' do not believe *them*.

²² Because, false christs and false prophets will rise and show signs and wonders to seduce, if *it were* possible, even the elect.

²³ But take heed; behold, I have told you all things beforehand.

²⁴ "But in those days, after that tribulation, the sun will be darkened, and the moon will not give her light;

²⁵ the stars of heaven will fall, and the powers in the heavens will be shaken.

²⁶ Then they will see the Son of Man coming in the clouds with great power and glory.

²⁷ And then He will send His angels, and gather together His elect from the four winds, from the farthest part of the earth to the farthest part of heaven.

²⁸ "Now learn this parable from the fig tree: When its branch has already become tender, and puts forth leaves, you know that summer is near.

²⁹ So you also, when you see these things come to pass, know that it is near, *even* at the doors!

³⁰ Truly, I say to you, this generation will not pass away until all these things are done.

³¹ Heaven and earth will pass away, but My words will not pass away.

³² "But of that day and *that* hour no one knows, no, not the angels which are in heaven, nor the Son, but the Father.

³³ Take heed, watch and pray; because, you do not know when the time is.

³⁴ *Because, the Son of Man is* like a

man going to a far region, who left his house and gave authority to his servants, and to every person his work, and commanded the doorkeeper to watch.

35 Watch therefore, because, you do not know when the master of the house is coming, in the evening, at midnight, at the crowing of the rooster, or in the morning,

36 lest, coming suddenly, he find you sleeping.

37 And what I say to you, I say to all: Watch!"

CHAPTER 14

1 After two days it was the *Feast of* the Passover and of Unleavened Bread. And the chief priests and the scribes sought how they might take Him by deception and put *Him* to death.

2 But they said, "Not on the feast *day*, lest there be an uproar of the people."

3 And being in Bethany at the house of Simon the leper, as He sat at the table, a woman came having an alabaster flask of very costly oil of spikenard. Then she broke the flask and poured *it* on His head.

4 But there were some who were indignant among themselves, and said, "Why was this fragrant oil wasted?

5 Because, it might have been sold for more than three hundred denarii and had been given to the poor." And they murmured against her.

6 But Jesus said, "Leave her alone. Why do you trouble her? She has done a good work for Me.

7 Because, you have the poor with you always, and whenever you desire you can do them good; but Me you do not have always.

8 She has done what she could. She has come beforehand to anoint My body for burial.

9 Truly, I say to you, wherever this gospel is preached in the entire world, what this woman has done will also be told as a memorial to her."

10 Then Judas Iscariot, one of the twelve, went to the chief priests to betray Him to them.

11 And when they heard *it*, they were glad, and promised to give him money. So he sought how he might conveniently betray Him.

12 Now *on* the first day of Unleavened Bread, when they killed the Passover, His disciples said to Him, "Where do You want us to go and prepare, that You may eat the Passover?"

13 And He sent out two of His disciples and said to them, "Go into the city, and a man will meet you carrying a pitcher of water; follow him.

14 Wherever he goes in, say to the master of the house, 'The Teacher says, "Where is the guest room in which I may eat the Passover with My disciples?"'

15 Then he will show you a large upper room, furnished *and* prepar-

ed; there make preparations for us."

¹⁶ So His disciples went out, and came into the city, and found it just as He had said to them; and they prepared the Passover.

¹⁷ In the evening He came with the twelve.

¹⁸ Now as they sat and ate, Jesus said, "Truly, I say to you, one of you who eats with Me will betray Me."

¹⁹ And they began to be sorrowful, and to say to Him one by one, "*Is* it I?" And another *said,* "*Is* it I?"

²⁰ He answered and said to them, "*It is* one of the twelve, who dips with Me in the dish.

²¹ The Son of Man indeed goes just as it is written of Him, but woe to that man by whom the Son of Man is betrayed! It would have been good for that man if he had never been born."

²² And as they were eating, Jesus took bread, blessed and broke *it,* and gave it to them and said, "Take, eat; this is My body."

²³ Then He took the cup, and when He had given thanks He gave *it* to them, and they all drank of it.

²⁴ And He said to them, "This is My blood of the new covenant, which is shed for many.

²⁵ Truly, I say to you, I will no longer drink of the fruit of the vine until that day when I drink it new in the kingdom of God."

²⁶ And when they had sung a song, they went out to the Mount of Olives.

²⁷ Then Jesus said to them, "All of you will be made to stumble because of Me this night, because, it is written: 'I will strike the Shepherd, and the sheep will be scattered.'

²⁸ "But after I have been raised, I will go before you to Galilee."

²⁹ But Peter said to Him, "Even if all are made to stumble, yet I *will* not *be.*"

³⁰ Jesus said to him, "Truly, I say to you that today, *even* this night, before the rooster crows twice, you will deny Me three times."

³¹ But he spoke more vehemently, "If I have to die with You, I will not deny You in any way!" And they all said likewise.

³² Then they came to a place which was named Gethsemane; and He said to His disciples, "You sit here while I pray."

³³ And He took Peter, James, and John with Him, and began to be troubled and very distressed.

³⁴ Then He said to them, "My soul is exceedingly sorrowful, *even* to death. Stay here and watch."

³⁵ He went a little farther, and fell on the ground, and prayed that if it were possible, the hour might pass from Him.

³⁶ And He said, "Abba, Father, all things *are* possible for You. Take this cup away from Me; nevertheless, not what I will, but what You *will.*"

³⁷ Then He came and found them sleeping, and said to Peter, "Simon,

are you sleeping? Could you not watch one hour?

³⁸ Watch and pray all of you, lest you enter into temptation. Truly the spirit *is* willing, but the flesh *is* weak."

³⁹ Again He went away and prayed, and spoke the same words.

⁴⁰ And when He returned, He found them asleep again, because their eyes were heavy; and they did not know what to answer Him.

⁴¹ Then He came the third time and said to them, "Sleep now and take *your* rest, it is enough! The hour has come; behold, the Son of Man is being betrayed into the hands of sinners.

⁴² Rise, let us be going. See, he who betrays Me is at hand."

⁴³ And immediately, while He was still speaking, Judas, one of the twelve, with a large crowd with swords and clubs, came from the chief priests and the scribes and the elders.

⁴⁴ Now His betrayer had given them a indication, saying, "Whomever I kiss, He is the One; seize Him and lead *Him* away safely."

⁴⁵ And as soon as he had come, immediately he went up to Him and said to Him, "Teacher, Teacher!" and kissed Him.

⁴⁶ Then they laid their hands on Him and took Him.

⁴⁷ And one of those who stood by drew a sword and struck a servant of the high priest, and cut off his ear.

⁴⁸ Then Jesus responded and said to them, "Have you come out, as against a thief, with swords and clubs to take Me?

⁴⁹ I was daily with you in the temple teaching, and you did not seize Me. But the Scriptures must be fulfilled."

⁵⁰ Then they all forsook Him and fled.

⁵¹ Now a certain young man followed Him, having a linen cloth thrown around *his* naked *body*. And the young men laid hold of him,

⁵² and he left the linen cloth and fled from them naked.

⁵³ And they led Jesus away to the high priest; and with him were assembled all the chief priests, the elders, and the scribes.

⁵⁴ But Peter followed Him at a distance, right into the courtyard of the high priest. And he sat with the servants and warmed himself at the fire.

⁵⁵ Now the chief priests and all the council sought testimony against Jesus to put Him to death, but found none.

⁵⁶ Because, many bore false witness against Him, but their testimonies did not agree.

⁵⁷ Then some rose up and bore false witness against Him, saying,

⁵⁸ "We heard Him say, 'I will destroy this temple that is made with hands, and within three days I will build another made without hands.' "

⁵⁹ But not even then did their tes-

timony agree together.

⁶⁰ And the high priest stood up in the midst and asked Jesus, saying, "Do You answer nothing? What *is it* that these people testify against You?"

⁶¹ But He kept silent and answered nothing. Again the high priest asked Him, saying to Him, "Are You the Christ, the Son of the Blessed?"

⁶² Jesus said, "I am. And you will see the Son of Man sitting at the right hand of the Power, and coming with the clouds of heaven."

⁶³ Then the high priest tore his clothes and said, "What further need do we have of witnesses?

⁶⁴ You have heard the blasphemy! what do you think?" And they all condemned Him to be deserving of death.

⁶⁵ Then some began to spit on Him, and to cover His face, and to beat Him, and to say to Him, "Prophesy!" And the officers struck Him with the palms of their hands.

⁶⁶ Now as Peter was below in the courtyard, one of the servant girls of the high priest came.

⁶⁷ And when she saw Peter warming himself, she looked at him and said, "You also were with Jesus of Nazareth."

⁶⁸ But he denied it, saying, "I neither know nor understand what you are saying." And he went out on the porch, and the rooster crowed.

⁶⁹ And a servant girl saw him again, and began to say to those who stood by, "This is *one* of them."

⁷⁰ But he denied it again. And a little later those who stood by said to Peter again, "Surely you are *one* of them; because, you are a Galilean, and your speech reveals *it*."

⁷¹ Then he began to curse and swear, *saying*, "I do not know this Man of whom you speak!"

⁷² A second time the rooster crowed. Then Peter called to mind the word that Jesus had said to him, "Before the rooster crows twice, you will deny Me three times." And when he thought about it, he wept.

CHAPTER 15

¹ Then immediately, in the morning, the chief priests held a consultation with the elders and scribes and the entire council; and they bound Jesus, led *Him* away, and delivered *Him* to Pilate.

² Then Pilate asked Him, "Are You the King of the Jews?" And He answered and said to him, "*It is as* you say."

³ And the chief priests accused Him of many things, but He answered nothing.

⁴ Then Pilate asked Him again, saying, "Do You answer nothing? See how many things they witness against You!"

⁵ But Jesus still answered nothing, so that Pilate marveled.

⁶ Now at *that* feast he would release one prisoner to them, whomever they requested.

⁷ And there was *one* named Barab-

bas, *who lay* chained with his fellow rebels; they had committed murder in the rebellion.

⁸ Then the crowd, shouting out loudly, began to ask *him to do* just as he had always done for them.

⁹ But Pilate answered them, saying, "Do you want me to release to you the King of the Jews?"

¹⁰ Because he knew that the chief priests had handed Him over because of envy.

¹¹ But the chief priests stirred up the people, so that he should rather release Barabbas to them.

¹² Then Pilate answered and said to them again, "What then do you want me to do *to Him* whom you call the King of the Jews?"

¹³ So they shouted out again, "Crucify Him!"

¹⁴ Then Pilate said to them, "Why, what evil has He done?" But they shouted out all the more earnestly, "Crucify Him!"

¹⁵ And *so* Pilate, wanting to gratify the people, released Barabbas to them; and he delivered Jesus, after he had scourged *Him*, to be crucified.

¹⁶ Then the soldiers led Him away into the hall called Praetorium, and they called together the entire garrison.

¹⁷ And they clothed Him with purple; and they platted a crown of thorns, put it on His *head*,

¹⁸ and began to salute Him, "Hail, King of the Jews!"

¹⁹ Then they struck Him on the head with a reed and spat on Him; and bowing *their* knees, they worshiped Him.

²⁰ And when they had mocked Him, they took the purple off Him, put His own clothes on Him, and led Him out to crucify Him.

²¹ Then they compelled a certain man, Simon a Cyrenian, the father of Alexander and Rufus, as he was coming out of the countryside and passing by, to carry His cross.

²² And they brought Him to the place Golgotha, which is translated, The Place of a Skull.

²³ Then they gave Him wine mingled with myrrh to drink, but He did not take *it*.

²⁴ And when they crucified Him, they divided His clothes, casting lots for them to determine what every man should take.

²⁵ Now it was the third hour, and they crucified Him.

²⁶ And the inscription of His accusation was written above: THE KING OF THE JEWS.

²⁷ And with Him they also crucified two thieves, one on His right hand and the other on His left.

²⁸ So the Scripture was fulfilled which says, "And He was numbered with the transgressors."

²⁹ And those who passed by ridiculed Him, shaking their heads and saying, "Aha! You who destroys the temple and builds *it* in three days,

³⁰ save Yourself, and come down from the cross!"

³¹ Likewise the chief priests also, mocking among themselves with the scribes, said, "He saved others; He cannot save Himself.
³² Let Christ, the King of Israel, descend now from the cross, that we may see and believe." Even those who were crucified with Him reviled Him.
³³ Now when the sixth hour had come, there was darkness over the entire land until the ninth hour.
³⁴ And at the ninth hour Jesus shouted out with a loud voice, saying, "Eloi, Eloi, lama sabachthani?" which is translated, "My God, My God, why have You forsaken Me?"
³⁵ And when they heard *that*, some of those who stood by said, "Behold, He is calling for Elijah!"
³⁶ Then someone ran and filled a sponge full of vinegar, put *it* on a reed, and offered it to Him to drink, saying, "Let Him alone; let us see if Elijah will come to take Him down."
³⁷ And Jesus shouted out with a loud voice, and gave up the spirit.
³⁸ Then the veil of the temple was torn in two from top to bottom.
³⁹ So when the centurion, who stood opposite Him, saw that He shouted out like this and gave up the spirit, he said, "Truly this Man was the Son of God!"
⁴⁰ There were also women looking on from afar, among whom were Mary Magdalene, Mary the mother of James the Less and of Joses, and Salome,
⁴¹ who also followed Him and ministered to Him when He was in Galilee, and many other women who came up with Him to Jerusalem.
⁴² Now when evening had come, because it was the Preparation, that is, the day before the Sabbath,
⁴³ Joseph of Arimathea, an honorable council member, who also waited for the kingdom of God, came, and went in boldly to Pilate and sought the body of Jesus.
⁴⁴ Pilate marveled that He was already dead; and summoning the centurion *to him*, he asked him if He had been dead for some time.
⁴⁵ So when he knew *it* from the centurion, he gave the body to Joseph.
⁴⁶ Then he bought fine linen, took Him down, and wrapped Him in the linen. And he laid Him in a tomb which had been cut out of the rock, and rolled a stone against the door of the tomb.
⁴⁷ And Mary Magdalene and Mary *the mother* of Joses observed where He was laid.

CHAPTER 16

¹ Now when the Sabbath was past, Mary Magdalene, Mary the *mother* of James, and Salome bought sweet spices, that they might come and anoint Him.
² And very early in the morning, on The first *day* of the week, they came to the tomb at the rising of the sun.
³ And they said among themselves,

"Who shall roll away the stone from the door of the tomb for us?"

⁴ But when they looked, they saw that the stone had been rolled away, because, it was very large.

⁵ And entering the tomb, they saw a young man clothed in a long white robe sitting on the right side; and they were afraid.

⁶ But he said to them, "Do not be afraid. You seek Jesus of Nazareth, who was crucified. He is risen! He is not here. Behold the place where they laid Him.

⁷ But go your way, tell His disciples, and Peter, that He is going before you into Galilee; there you will see Him, as He said to you."

⁸ So they went out quickly and fled from the tomb, because they trembled and were astonished. And they said nothing to anyone, because they were afraid.

⁹ Now when *Jesus* was risen early on the first *day* of the week, He appeared first to Mary Magdalene, out of whom He had cast seven demons.

¹⁰ *And* she went and told those who had been with Him, as they mourned and wept.

¹¹ And when they heard that He was alive and had been seen by her, they did not believe.

¹² After that, He appeared in another form to two of them as they walked and went into the countryside.

¹³ And they went and told *it* to the rest, but they did not believe them either.

¹⁴ Later He appeared to the eleven as they sat at the table; and He rebuked their unbelief and hardness of heart, because they did not believe those who had seen Him after He had risen.

¹⁵ And He said to them, "Go into all the world and preach the gospel to every creature.

¹⁶ He who believes and is baptized will be saved; but he who does not believe will be damned.

¹⁷ And these signs will follow those who believe: In My name they will cast out demons; they will speak with new tongues;

¹⁸ they will take up serpents; and if they drink any deadly thing, it will not hurt them; they will lay hands on the sick, and they will recover."

¹⁹ So then, after the Lord had spoken to them, He was received up into heaven, and sat down at the right hand of God.

²⁰ And they went out and preached everywhere, the Lord working with *them* and confirming the word through the signs following them. Amen.

THE GOSPEL ACCORDING TO
LUKE

CHAPTER 1

¹ In as much as many have taken in hand to arrange in order a declaration of those things which are most surely believed among us, ² just as those who from the beginning were eyewitnesses and ministers of the word delivered them to us, ³ it seemed good to me also, having had perfect understanding of all things from the very first, to write to you in order, most excellent Theophilus, ⁴ that you may know the certainty of those things in which you were instructed.

⁵ There was in the days of Herod, the king of Judea, a certain priest named Zacharias, of the division of Abijah, and his wife *was* of the daughters of Aaron, and her name *was* Elizabeth.

⁶ And they were both righteous before God, walking in all the commandments and ordinances of the Lord blameless.

⁷ But they had no child, because Elizabeth was barren, and they were both *now* well advanced in years.

⁸ So it came to pass, that while he was serving in the priest's office before God in the order of his division, ⁹ according to the custom of the priesthood, his lot fell to burn incense when he went into the temple of the Lord.

¹⁰ And the entire crowd of the people were praying outside at the time of incense.

¹¹ Then an angel of the Lord appeared to him, standing on the right side of the altar of incense.

¹² And when Zacharias saw *him*, he was troubled, and fear fell upon him.

¹³ But the angel said to him, "Do not fear, Zacharias, because your prayer is heard; and your wife Elizabeth will bear you a son, and you will call his name John.

¹⁴ And you will have joy and happiness and many will rejoice at his birth.

¹⁵ Because, he will be great in the sight of the Lord and will drink neither grape juice nor strong drink. And he will be filled with the Holy Spirit, even from his mother's womb.

¹⁶ And he will turn many of the children of Israel to the Lord their God.

¹⁷ He will also go before Him in the spirit and power of Elijah, 'to turn the hearts of the fathers to the children,' and the disobedient to the wisdom of the just, to make ready a people prepared for the Lord."

¹⁸ And Zacharias said to the angel, "How shall I know this? Because, I

am an old man, and my wife well advanced in years."

¹⁹ And the angel answered and said to him, "I am Gabriel, who stands in the presence of God, and was sent to speak to you and to show you these glad tidings.

²⁰ But behold, you will be mute and not able to speak until the day that these things will take place, because you did not believe my words which will be fulfilled in their own time."

²¹ And the people waited for Zacharias and marveled that he lingered so long in the temple.

²² But when he came out, he could not speak to them; and they perceived that he had seen a vision in the temple, because he beckoned to them and remained speechless.

²³ So it was, as soon as the days of his service were completed, he departed to his own house.

²⁴ Now after those days his wife Elizabeth conceived; and hid herself five months, saying,

²⁵ "Thus the Lord has dealt with me, in the days when He looked upon *me*, to take away my dishonor among men."

²⁶ Now in the sixth month the angel Gabriel was sent from God to a city of Galilee, named Nazareth,

²⁷ to a virgin betrothed to a man whose name was Joseph, of the house of David. And the virgin's name *was* Mary.

²⁸ And the angel went in to her *presence* and said, "Rejoice, *you who are* highly favored, the Lord *is* with you; blessed *are* you among women!"

²⁹ But when she saw *him*, she was troubled at his saying and considered what manner of greeting this was.

³⁰ Then the angel said to her, "Do not fear, Mary, because, you have found favor with God.

³¹ And behold, you will conceive in your womb and bring forth a Son, and will call His name JESUS.

³² He will be great, and will be called the Son of the Highest; and the Lord God will give to Him the throne of His father David.

³³ And He will reign over the house of Jacob forever, and of His kingdom there will be no end."

³⁴ Then Mary said to the angel, "How can this be, since I do not know a man?"

³⁵ And the angel answered and said to her, "The Holy Spirit will come upon you and the power of the Highest will overshadow you; therefore, also, that Holy One who will be born of you will be called the Son of God.

³⁶ Now behold, Elizabeth your relative has also conceived a son in her old age; and this is the sixth month for her, who was called barren.

³⁷ Because with God nothing will be impossible."

³⁸ Then Mary said, "Behold the maidservant of the Lord! Let it be to me according to your word." And

the angel departed from her.

³⁹ Mary arose in those days and hurried into the hill region, into a city of Judah,

⁴⁰ and entered into the house of Zacharias and greeted Elizabeth.

⁴¹ And it happened, when Elizabeth heard the greeting of Mary, the babe leaped in her womb; and Elizabeth was filled with the Holy Spirit.

⁴² And she spoke out with a loud voice and said, "Blessed *are* you among women, and blessed *is* the fruit of your womb!

⁴³ But why is this *granted* to me, that the mother of my Lord should come to me?

⁴⁴ Because, indeed, as soon as the voice of your greeting sounded in my ears, the babe leaped in my womb for joy.

⁴⁵ And blessed *is* she who believed, because there will be a fulfillment of those things which were told her from the Lord."

⁴⁶ Then Mary said: "My soul magnifies the Lord,

⁴⁷ and my spirit has rejoiced in God my Savior.

⁴⁸ Because, He has regarded the lowly state of His maidservant; because behold, from now on all generations will call me blessed.

⁴⁹ Because, He who is mighty has done great things for me, and holy *is* His name.

⁵⁰ And His mercy *is* on those who reverence Him from generation to generation.

⁵¹ He has shown strength with His arm; He has scattered *the* proud in the imagination of their hearts.

⁵² He has put down the mighty from *their* thrones, and exalted the lowly.

⁵³ He has filled the hungry with good things, and He has sent the rich away empty.

⁵⁴ He has helped His servant Israel, in remembrance of *His* mercy,

⁵⁵ as He spoke to our fathers, to Abraham and to His seed forever."

⁵⁶ Then Mary stayed with her about three months, and returned to her own house.

⁵⁷ Now Elizabeth's full time came for her to be delivered, and she brought forth a son.

⁵⁸ And her neighbors and her relatives heard how the Lord had shown great mercy on her, and they rejoiced with her.

⁵⁹ And so it was, on the eighth day, they came to circumcise the child; and they called him Zacharias, after the name of his father.

⁶⁰ But his mother replied and said, "Not *this*; but he will be called John."

⁶¹ But they said to her, "There is no one from your family that is called by this name."

⁶² So they made signs to his father, what he would have him called.

⁶³ And he asked for a writing tablet, and wrote, saying, "His name is John." So they all marveled.

⁶⁴ And immediately His mouth was opened and his tongue *loosed*, and he spoke and praised God.

⁶⁵ Then reverence came on all who

lived around about them; and all these sayings were discussed throughout all the hill region of Judea.

⁶⁶ And all those who heard *them* kept them in their hearts, saying, "What kind of child shall this be?" And the hand of the Lord was with him.

⁶⁷ Now his father Zacharias was filled with the Holy Spirit, and prophesied, saying,

⁶⁸ "Blessed *is* the Lord God of Israel, because, He has visited and redeemed His people,

⁶⁹ and has raised up a horn of. salvation for us in the house of his servant David,

⁷⁰ as He spoke by the mouth of His holy prophets, who have been since the world began,

⁷¹ that we should be saved from our enemies and from the hand of all who hate us,

⁷² to perform the mercy *promised* to our fathers and to remember His holy covenant,

⁷³ the oath which He swore to our father Abraham:

⁷⁴ That He would grant to us, that we, being delivered out of the hand of our enemies, might serve Him without fear,

⁷⁵ in holiness and righteousness before Him all the days of our life.

⁷⁶ "And you, child, will be called the prophet of the Highest; because, you will go before the face of the Lord to prepare His ways,

⁷⁷ to give knowledge of salvation to His people by the remission of their sins,

⁷⁸ through the tender mercy of our God, with which the Dayspring from on high has visited us;

⁷⁹ to give light to those who sit in darkness and *in* the shadow of death, to guide our feet into the way of peace."

⁸⁰ So the child grew and became strong in spirit, and was in the deserts until the day of his appearance to Israel.

CHAPTER 2

¹ And it came to pass in those days that a decree went out from Caesar Augustus that all the world should be registered.

² *And* this registration first occurred when Quirinius was governor of Syria.

³ And everyone went to be registered, every one into his own city.

⁴ And Joseph also went up from Galilee, out of the city of Nazareth, into Judea, to the city of David, which is called Bethlehem, because he was of the house and lineage of David,

⁵ to be registered with Mary, his betrothed wife, who was large due to pregnancy.

⁶ And so it was, that while they were there, the days were completed for her to be delivered.

⁷ And she brought forth her firstborn Son, and wrapped Him in swaddling clothes and laid Him in a

manger, because there was no room for them in the inn.

⁸ Now there were in the same countryside shepherds staying out in the field, keeping watch over their flock by night.

⁹ And behold, the angel of the Lord came over them, and the glory of the Lord shone around them and they were very afraid.

¹⁰ Then the angel said to them, "Do not fear, because behold, I bring you good news of great joy, which will be to all people.

¹¹ Because, there is born to you this day in the city of David a Savior, who is Christ the Lord.

¹² And this *will* be a sign to you: You will find the Babe wrapped in swaddling clothes, lying in a manger."

¹³ And suddenly there was with the angel a multitude of the heavenly army praising God and saying:

¹⁴ "Glory to God in the highest, and on earth peace, good will toward men!"

¹⁵ So it was, when the angels had gone away from them into heaven, that the shepherds said to each other, "Let us now travel to Bethlehem and see this thing that has come to pass, which the Lord has made known to us."

¹⁶ And they came quickly and found Mary and Joseph, and the Babe lying in a manger.

¹⁷ Now when they had seen *Him*, they made widely known the saying which was told them concerning this Child.

¹⁸ And all those who heard *it* marveled at those things which were told them by the shepherds.

¹⁹ But Mary kept all these things and pondered *them* in her heart.

²⁰ Then the shepherds returned, glorifying and praising God for all the things that they had heard and seen, as it was told to them.

²¹ And when eight days were completed for the circumcision of the Child, His name was called JESUS, the name given by the angel before He was conceived in the womb.

²² When the days of her purification according to the law of Moses were completed, they brought Him to Jerusalem to present *Him* to the Lord

²³ (as it is written in the law of the Lord, "Every male who opens the womb shall be called holy to the LORD"),

²⁴ and to offer a sacrifice according to that which is said in the law of the Lord, "A pair of turtledoves or two young pigeons."

²⁵ And behold, there was a man in Jerusalem, whose name *was* Simeon, and this man *was* just and devout, waiting for the Consolation of Israel, and the Holy Spirit was upon him.

²⁶ And it had been revealed to him by the Holy Spirit that he should not see death before he had seen the Lord's Christ.

²⁷ So he came by the Spirit into the temple. And when the parents

brought in the Child Jesus, to do for Him after the custom of the law,

²⁸ then he took Him up in his arms and blessed God and said:

²⁹ "Lord, now let Your servant depart in peace, according to Your word;

³⁰ Because, my eyes have seen Your salvation

³¹ which You have prepared before the face of all people,

³² A light to bring revelation to the Gentiles, and the glory of Your people Israel."

³³ And Joseph and His mother marveled at those things which were spoken about Him.

³⁴ Then Simeon blessed them, and said to Mary His mother, "Behold, this *Child* is destined for the fall and rising of many in Israel, and for a sign which will be spoken against

³⁵ (yes, a sword will pierce through your own soul also), that the thoughts of many hearts may be revealed."

³⁶ Now there was one, Anna, a prophetess, the daughter of Phanuel, of the tribe of Asher. She was very old and had lived with a husband seven years from her virginity;

³⁷ and she was a widow of about eighty four years, who did not depart from the temple, but served *God* with fastings and prayers night and day.

³⁸ And coming in that instant she also gave thanks likewise to the Lord, and spoke of Him to all those who looked for redemption in Jerusalem.

³⁹ So when they had performed all things according to the law of the Lord, they returned to Galilee, to their own city Nazareth.

⁴⁰ And the Child grew and became strong in spirit, filled with wisdom; and the grace of God was upon Him.

⁴¹ Now His parents went to Jerusalem every year at the Feast of the Passover.

⁴² And when He was twelve years old, they went up to Jerusalem according to the custom of the feast.

⁴³ when they had fulfilled the days, as they returned, the Child Jesus stayed behind in Jerusalem. And Joseph and His mother did not know *about it*;

⁴⁴ but supposing Him to have been in the company, they went a day's journey, and they sought Him among *their* relatives and acquaintances.

⁴⁵ So when they did not find Him, they returned to Jerusalem, seeking Him.

⁴⁶ Now it happened that after three days they found Him in the temple, sitting in the midst of the teachers, both listening to them and asking them questions.

⁴⁷ All who heard Him were astonished at His understanding and answers.

⁴⁸ So when they saw Him, they were amazed; and His mother said to Him, "Son, why have you done this

to us? Look, Your father and I have sought You desperately."

⁴⁹ He said to them, "Why did you seek Me? Did you not know that I must be about My Father's business?"

⁵⁰ But they did not understand the statement which He spoke to them.

⁵¹ Then He went down with them and came to Nazareth, and was subject to them, but His mother kept all these sayings in her heart.

⁵² And Jesus increased in wisdom and stature, and in favor with God and men.

CHAPTER 3

¹ Now in the fifteenth year of the reign of Tiberius Caesar, Pontius Pilate being governor of Judea, Herod being tetrarch of Galilee, his brother Philip tetrarch of Ituraea and of the region of Trachonitis, and Lysanias the tetrarch of Abilene,

² Annas and Caiaphas being the high priests, the word of God came to John the son of Zacharias in the wilderness.

³ And he went into all the region around Jordan, preaching a baptism of repentance for the remission of sins,

⁴ as it is written in the book of the words of Isaiah the prophet, saying: "The voice of one shouting out in the wilderness: 'Prepare the way of the LORD; make His paths straight.

⁵ Every valley will be filled and every mountain and hill will be brought low; and the crooked place will be made straight and the rough ways *will be* made smooth;

⁶ And all flesh will see the salvation of God.' "

⁷ Then he said to the crowds that came out to be baptized by him, "O generation of vipers, who warned you to flee from the wrath to come?

⁸ Therefore bear fruits worthy of repentance, and do not begin to say within yourselves, 'We have Abraham as *our* father.' Because I say to you that God is able to raise up children to Abraham from these stones.

⁹ And even now the axe is laid to the root of the trees. Therefore every tree which does not bear good fruit is cut down and thrown into the fire."

¹⁰ So the people asked him, saying, "What shall we do then?"

¹¹ He answered and said to them, "He who has two coats, let him give to him who has none; and he who has food, let him do likewise."

¹² Then tax collectors also came to be baptized, and said to him, "Teacher, what shall we do?"

¹³ And he said to them, "Collect no more than that which is appointed to you."

¹⁴ Likewise the soldiers demanded of him, saying, "And what shall we do?" So he said to them, "Do not be violent to anyone, nor accuse *anyone* falsely, and be content with your wages."

¹⁵ Now as the people were in ex-

pectation, and everyone reasoned in their hearts about John, whether he was the Christ or not,

¹⁶ John responded, saying to *them* all, "I indeed baptize you with water; but One mightier than I is coming, whose sandal strap I am not worthy to loose. He will baptize you with the Holy Spirit and with fire.

¹⁷ His winnowing fan is in His hand and He will thoroughly clean out His threshing floor, and gather His wheat into His storehouse; but the chaff He will burn with unquenchable fire."

¹⁸ And with many other things in His exhortation he preached to the people.

¹⁹ But Herod the tetrarch, being rebuked by him concerning Herodias, his brother Philip's wife, and for all the evils which Herod had done, ²⁰ also added this, above all, that he shut up John in prison.

²¹ Now when all the people were baptized, it came to pass that Jesus was baptized also; and *while* praying, the heaven was opened.

²² And the Holy Spirit descended in bodily form like a dove upon Him, and a voice came from heaven which said, "You are My beloved Son; in You I am well pleased."

²³ So Jesus Himself began to be about thirty years of age, being (as was supposed) the son of Joseph, who was *the son* of Heli,

²⁴ who was *the son* of Matthat, who was *the son* of Levi, who was *the son* of Melchi, who was *the son* of Janna, who was *the son* of Joseph,

²⁵ who was *the son* of Mattathiah, who was *the son* of Amos, who was *the son* of Nahum, who was *the son* of Esli, who was *the son* of Naggai,

²⁶ who was the son of Maath, who was *the son* of Mattathiah, who was *the son* of Semei, who was *the son* of Joseph, who was *the son* of Judah,

²⁷ who was *the son* of Joannas, who was *the son* of Rhesa, who was *the son* of Zerubbabel, who was *the son* of Shealtiel, who was *the son* of Neri,

²⁸ who was *the son* of Melchi, who was *the son* of Addi, who was *the son* of Cosam, who was *the son* of Elmodam, who was *the son* of Er,

²⁹ who was *the son* of Jose, who was *the son* of Eliezer, who was *the son* of Jorim, who was *the son* of Matthat, who was *the son* of Levi,

³⁰ who was *the son* of Simeon, who was *the son* of Judah, who was *the son* of Joseph, who was *the son* of Jonan, who was *the son* of Eliakim,

³¹ who was *the son* of Melea, who was *the son* of Menan, who was *the son* of Mattathah, who was *the son* of Nathan, *the son* of David,

³² who was *the son* of Jesse, who was *the son* of Obed, who was *the son* of Boaz, who was *the son* of Salmon, who was *the son* of Nahshon,

³³ who was *the son* of Amminadab, who was *the son* of Ram, who was *the son* of Hezron, who was *the son* of Perez, who was *the son* of Judah,

³⁴ who was *the son* of Jacob, who was *the son* of Isaac, who was *the son* of

Abraham, who was *the son* of Terah, who was *the son* of Nahor,

³⁵ who was *the son* of Serug, who was *the son* of Reu, who was *the son* of Peleg, who was *the son* of Eber, who was *the son* of Shelah,

³⁶ who was *the son* of Cainan, who was *the son* of Arphaxad, who was *the son* of Shem, who was *the son* of Noah, who was *the son* of Lamech,

³⁷ who was *the son* of Methuselah, who was *the son* of Enoch, who was *the son* of Jared, who was *the son* of Mahalalel, who was *the son* of Cainan,

³⁸ who was *the son* of Enosh, who was *the son* of Seth, who was *the son* of Adam, who was *the son* of God.

CHAPTER 4

¹ Then Jesus, being filled with the Holy Spirit, returned from the Jordan and was led by the Spirit into the wilderness,

² being tempted forty days by the devil. And in those days He ate nothing, and when they had ended, afterward He was hungry.

³ And the devil said to Him, "If You are the Son of God, command this stone to become bread."

⁴ But Jesus replied to him, saying, "It is written that, 'Man will not live by bread alone, but by every word of God.'"

⁵ Then the devil, taking Him up on a high mountain, showed Him all the kingdoms of the world in a moment of time.

⁶ And the devil said to Him, "I will give You all this authority, and their glory; because, this has been delivered to me and I give it to whomever I wish.

⁷ Therefore, if You will worship me, all will be Yours."

⁸ And Jesus answered and said to him, "Get behind Me, Satan! Because, it is written, 'You shall worship the LORD your God, and Him only shall you serve.'"

⁹ Then he brought Him to Jerusalem, set Him on a pinnacle of the temple, and said to Him, "If You are the Son of God, throw Yourself down from here.

¹⁰ Because, it is written: 'He will give His angels orders concerning you, to protect You,'

¹¹ and, 'In *their* hands they will hold You up, lest at any time You dash Your foot against a stone.'"

¹² And Jesus responding said to him, "It has been said, 'You shall not tempt the LORD your God.'"

¹³ Now when the devil had ended every temptation, he departed from Him for a season.

¹⁴ Then Jesus returned in the power of the Spirit into Galilee, and there His fame went out through all the surrounding region.

¹⁵ And He taught in their synagogues, being glorified by all.

¹⁶ So He came to Nazareth, where He had been brought up. And as His custom was, He went into the synagogue on the Sabbath day, and stood up to read.

¹⁷ And He was handed the book of

the prophet Isaiah. And when He had opened the book, He found the place where it was written:

¹⁸ "The Spirit of the LORD *is* upon Me, because He has anointed Me to preach the gospel to the poor; He has sent Me to heal the brokenhearted, to preach deliverance to the captives and recovery of sight to the blind, to set at liberty those who are oppressed;

¹⁹ to proclaim the acceptable year of the LORD."

²⁰ Then He closed the book, and He gave *it* back to the attendant and sat down. And the eyes of everyone who was in the synagogue were fixed upon Him.

²¹ And He began to say to them, "Today this Scripture is fulfilled in your ears."

²² So all bore witness to Him, and marveled at the gracious words which proceeded out of His mouth. And they said, "Is this not Joseph's son?"

²³ Then He said to them, "You will surely say this proverb to Me, 'Physician, heal yourself! Whatever we have heard done in Capernaum, do also here in Your region.' "

²⁴ And He said, "Truly, I say to you, no prophet is accepted in his own region.

²⁵ But I tell you truly, many widows were in Israel in the days of Elijah, when the heaven was shut up three years and six months, and there was a huge famine throughout all the land;

²⁶ but Elijah was sent to none of them, except to Zarephath, *in the region* of Sidon, to a woman *who was* a widow.

²⁷ And many lepers were in Israel in the time of Elisha the prophet, and none of them was cleansed except Naaman the Syrian."

²⁸ So all those in the synagogue, when they heard these things, were filled with wrath,

²⁹ and rose up and thrust Him out of the city; and they led Him to the brow of the hill on which their city was built, that they might throw Him down over the cliff.

³⁰ But passing through the midst of them He went His way,

³¹ and went down to Capernaum, a city of Galilee, and taught them on the Sabbath days.

³² And they were astonished at His doctrine, because His word was with authority.

³³ Now in the synagogue there was a man who had a spirit of an unclean demon. And he shouted out with a loud voice,

³⁴ saying, "Leave *us* alone! What have we to do with You, *You* Jesus of Nazareth? Did you come to destroy us? I know who You are, the Holy One of God!"

³⁵ But Jesus rebuked him, saying, "Be quiet and come out of him!" And when the demon had thrown him in the midst, it came out of him and did not hurt him.

³⁶ Then they were all amazed and spoke among themselves, saying,

"What a word this is! Because, with authority and power He commands the unclean spirits and they come out."

[37] And His fame went out into every place in the surrounding region.

[38] Now He arose from the synagogue and entered into Simon's house. But Simon's wife's mother was sick with a high fever and they made request of Him concerning her.

[39] So He stood over her and rebuked the fever, and it left her. And immediately she arose and served them.

[40] Now when the sun was setting, all those who had any that were sick with various diseases brought them to Him; and He laid His hands on every one of them and healed them.

[41] And demons also came out of many, shouting out and saying, "You are Christ, the Son of God!" And He, rebuking *them*, did not permit them to speak, because they knew that He was Christ.

[42] Now when it was day, He departed and went into a deserted place. And the people sought Him and came to Him and tried to keep Him from leaving them;

[43] but He said to them, "I must preach the kingdom of God to other cities also, because for this purpose I have been sent."

[44] And He preached in the synagogues of Galilee.

CHAPTER 5

[1] And it happened, as the people pressed about Him to hear the word of God, that He stood by the Lake of Gennesaret,

[2] and saw two boats standing by the lake; but the fishermen had gone from them and were washing *their* nets.

[3] Then He got into one of the boats, which was Simon's, and asked him to put out a little from the land. And He sat down and taught the people from the boat.

[4] Now when He had stopped speaking, He said to Simon, "Launch out into the deep and let down your nets for a catch."

[5] But Simon replied and said to Him, "Master, we have toiled all night and have taken nothing; nevertheless at Your word I will let down the net."

[6] And when they had done this, they caught a great number of fish, and their net was breaking.

[7] So they motioned to *their* partners, who were in the other boat, that they should come and help them. And they came and filled both the boats, so that they began to sink.

[8] When Simon Peter saw *it*, he fell down at Jesus' knees, saying, "Depart from me, because I am a sinful man, O Lord!"

[9] Because, he and all who were with him were astonished at the catch of fish which they had taken;

[10] and so also *were* James and John,

the sons of Zebedee, who were partners with Simon. And Jesus said to Simon, "Do not be afraid. From now on you will catch men."
[11] So when they had brought their boats to land, they forsook everything and followed Him.
[12] And it happened when He was in a certain city, that behold, a man who was full of leprosy seeing Jesus, fell on *his* face and implored Him, saying, "Lord, if You are willing, You can make me clean."
[13] Then He put out *His* hand and touched him, saying, "I am willing; be cleansed." And immediately the leprosy left him.
[14] And He commanded him to tell no one, "But go and show yourself to the priest, and make an offering for your cleansing, as a testimony to them, just as Moses commanded."
[15] However, the fame went around concerning Him all the more; and large crowds came together to hear, and to be healed by Him of their infirmities.
[16] And He withdrew Himself into the wilderness and prayed.
[17] Now it happened on a certain day, as He was teaching, that there were Pharisees and teachers of the law sitting by, who had come out of every town of Galilee, Judea, and Jerusalem. And the power of the Lord was *present* to heal them.
[18] Then behold, men brought on a bed a man who was paralyzed, whom they sought a way to bring in and lay *him* before Him.
[19] And when they could not find how they might bring him in, because of the crowd, they went up on the housetop and let him down with *his* bed through the tiling into the midst before Jesus.
[20] And when He saw their faith, He said to him, "Man, your sins are forgiven you."
[21] And the scribes and the Pharisees began to reason, saying, "Who is this who speaks blasphemies? Who can forgive sins but God alone?"
[22] But when Jesus perceived their thoughts, He responded and said to them, "Why are you reasoning in your hearts?
[23] Which is easier, to say, 'Your sins are forgiven you,' or to say, 'Rise up and walk'?
[24] But that you may know that the Son of Man has authority on earth to forgive sins," He said to the man who was paralyzed, "I say to you, arise, take up your bed, and go to your house."
[25] And immediately he rose up before them, took up what he had been lying on, and departed to his own house, glorifying God.
[26] And they were all amazed, and they glorified God and were filled with reverence, saying, "We have seen strange things today!"
[27] And after these things He went out and saw a tax collector named Levi, sitting at the tax office. And He said to him, "Follow Me."
[28] So he left everything, rose up,

and followed Him.

²⁹ Then Levi made Him a large feast in his own house. And there were a large number of tax collectors and others who sat down with them.

³⁰ And their scribes and the Pharisees complained against His disciples, saying, "Why do You eat and drink with tax collectors and sinners?"

³¹ And Jesus answering said to them, "Those who are well have no need of a physician, but those who are sick.

³² I have not come to call the righteous, but sinners, to repentance."

³³ Then they said to Him, "Why do the disciples of John fast often and make prayers, and likewise *the disciples* of the Pharisees, but Yours eat and drink?"

³⁴ And He said to them, "Can you make the friends of the bridechamber fast while the bridegroom is with them?

³⁵ But the days will come when the bridegroom will be taken away from them; then they will fast in those days."

³⁶ Then He also spoke a parable to them: "No one puts a piece from a new garment on an old one; otherwise the new makes a tear, and also the piece that was *taken* out of the new does not settle with the old.

³⁷ And no one puts new grape juice into old containers; or else the new grape juice will burst the containers and be spilled, and the containers will be ruined.

³⁸ But new grape juice must be put into new containers, and both are preserved.

³⁹ And also, no one having drunk old *grape juice*, immediately desires new; because he says, 'The old is better.' "

CHAPTER 6

¹ Now it happened on the second Sabbath after the first that He went through the grainfields. And His disciples plucked the heads of grain and ate them, rubbing *them* in their hands.

² And some of the Pharisees said to them, "Why are you doing what is not lawful to do on the Sabbath days?"

³ But Jesus answering them said, "Have you not yet read this that David did, when he was hungry, he and those who were with him:

⁴ how he went into the house of God, took and ate the showbread, and also gave some to those with him, which is not lawful to eat but is only for the priests?"

⁵ And He said to them, "The Son of Man is also Lord of the Sabbath."

⁶ Now it happened also on another Sabbath, that He entered into the synagogue and taught. And a man was there whose right hand was withered.

⁷ So the scribes and Pharisees watched Him, whether He would heal on the Sabbath day, that they

might find an accusation against Him.

⁸ But He knew their thoughts, and said to the man who had the withered hand, "Rise up and stand here in the midst." And he arose and stood there.

⁹ Then Jesus said to them, "I will ask you one thing: Is it lawful on the Sabbath days to do good or to do evil, to save life or to destroy *it*?"

¹⁰ And when He had looked around at them all, He said to the man, "Stretch out your hand." And he did so, and his hand was restored as whole as the other.

¹¹ But they were filled with madness, and discussed with one another what they might do to Jesus.

¹² Now it came to pass in those days that He went out to the mountain to pray, and continued all night in prayer to God

¹³ And when it was day, He called His disciples *to Himself*; and from them He chose twelve whom He also named apostles:

¹⁴ Simon, whom He also named Peter and Andrew his brother; James and John; Philip and Bartholomew;

¹⁵ Matthew and Thomas; James the *son* of Alphaeus, and Simon called the Zealot;

¹⁶ Judas *the brother* of James, and Judas Iscariot who also became the traitor.

¹⁷ And He came down with them and stood on a level place with the gathering of His disciples and a large crowd of people from all Judea and Jerusalem, and from the seacoast of Tyre and Sidon, who came to hear Him and be healed of their diseases,

¹⁸ as well as those who were tormented with unclean spirits. And they were healed.

¹⁹ And the entire crowd sought to touch Him, because power went out from Him and healed *them* all.

²⁰ Then He lifted up His eyes toward His disciples, and said: "Blessed *are you* poor, because yours is the kingdom of God.

²¹ Blessed *are you* who hunger now, because you will be filled. Blessed *are you* who weep now, because you will laugh.

²² Blessed are you when men hate you, and when they will separate you *from their company*, and revile *you*, and cast out your name as evil, for the Son of Man's sake.

²³ Rejoice in that day and leap for joy! Because indeed, your reward *is* great in heaven, because in the same manner their fathers did to the prophets.

²⁴ "But woe to you who are rich, because you have received your consolation.

²⁵ Woe to you who are full, because you will hunger. Woe to you who laugh now, because you will mourn and weep.

²⁶ Woe to you when all men speak well of you, because so did their fathers to the false prophets.

27 "But I say to you who hear: Love your enemies, do good to those who hate you,

28 bless those who curse you, and pray for those who spitefully use you.

29 And to him who strikes you on the *one* cheek, offer the other also. And from him who takes away your cloak, do not forbid to *take your* coat as well.

30 Give to everyone who asks of you. And from him who takes away your goods do not ask *them* back.

31 And just as you desire that people should do to you, you also do to them likewise.

32 "Because, if you love those who love you, what credit is that to you? Because even sinners love those who love them.

33 And if you do good to those who do good to you, what credit is that to you? Because even sinners do the same.

34 And if you lend *to those* from whom you hope to receive back, what credit is that to you? Because even sinners lend to sinners to receive as much back.

35 But love your enemies, do good, and lend, hoping for nothing in return; and your reward will be great, and you will be the children of the Most High. Because He is kind to the unthankful and evil.

36 Therefore be merciful, just as your Father also is merciful.

37 "Judge not, and you will not be judged. Condemn not, and you will not be condemned. Forgive, and you will be forgiven.

38 Give, and it will be given to you: good measure, pressed down, shaken together, and running over will men give into your bosom. Because, with the same measure that you use, it will be measured back to you."

39 And He spoke a parable to them: "Can the blind lead the blind? Will they not both fall into the ditch?

40 A disciple is not above his teacher, but everyone who is perfect will be like his teacher.

41 And why do you look at the speck in your brother's eye, but do not perceive the plank in your own eye?

42 Or how can you say to your brother, 'Brother, let me remove the speck that is in your eye,' when you yourself do not see the plank that is in your own eye? You hypocrite! First remove the plank from your own eye, and then you will see clearly to remove the speck that is in your brother's eye.

43 "Because, a good tree does not bear bad fruit, nor does a bad tree bear good fruit.

44 Because, every tree is known by its own fruit. Because, men do not gather figs from thorns, nor do they gather grapes from a bramble bush.

45 A good man out of the good treasure of his heart brings forth that which is good; and an evil man out of the evil treasure of his heart brings forth that which is evil.

Because out of the abundance of the heart his mouth speaks.

⁴⁶ "But why do you call Me 'Lord, Lord,' and not do the things that I say?

⁴⁷ Whoever comes to Me, and hears My sayings and does them, I will show you whom he is like:

⁴⁸ He is like a man who built a house, who dug deep and laid the foundation on the rock. And when the flood arose, the stream beat vehemently against that house, and could not shake it, because it was founded on a rock.

⁴⁹ But he who heard and did nothing is like a man who built a house on the earth without a foundation, against which the stream beat vehemently; and immediately it fell. And the ruin of that house was great."

CHAPTER 7

¹ Now when He concluded all His sayings in the hearing of the people, He entered into Capernaum.

² And a certain centurion's servant, who was dear to him, was sick and ready to die.

³ So when he heard about Jesus, he sent elders of the Jews to Him, pleading with Him that He would come and heal his servant.

⁴ And when they came to Jesus, they begged Him earnestly, saying that the one whom He should do this to was deserving,

⁵ "because, he loves our nation, and has built us a synagogue."

⁶ Then Jesus went with them. And when He was already not far from the house, the centurion sent friends to Him, saying to Him, "Lord, do not trouble Yourself, because, I am not worthy that You should enter under my roof.

⁷ Therefore I did not even think myself worthy to come to You. But say the word, and my servant will be healed.

⁸ Because, I also am a man placed under authority, having soldiers under me. And I say to one, 'Go,' and he goes; and to another, 'Come,' and he comes; and to my servant, 'Do this,' and he does *it*."

⁹ When Jesus heard these things, He marveled at him, and turned around and said to the people that followed Him, "I say to you, I have not found such great faith, not even in Israel!"

¹⁰ And those who were sent, returning to the house, found the servant well who had been sick.

¹¹ Now it happened, the day after, that He went into a city called Nain; and many of His disciples went with Him, and many people.

¹² And when He came near the gate of the city, behold, a dead man was being carried out, the only son of his mother; and she was a widow. And many people from the city were with her.

¹³ And when the Lord saw her, He had compassion on her and said to her, "Do not weep."

¹⁴ Then He came and touched the coffin, and those who carried *him* stood still. And He said, "Young man, I say to you, arise."

¹⁵ So he who was dead sat up and began to speak. And He presented him to his mother.

¹⁶ Then reverence came upon everyone, and they glorified God, saying that: "A great prophet has risen up among us"; and, "God has visited His people."

¹⁷ And this report about Him went forth throughout all Judea and all the surrounding region.

¹⁸ Then the disciples of John reported to him about all these things.

¹⁹ And John, calling two of his disciples *to him*, sent *them* to Jesus, saying, "Are You He who should come, or do we look for another?"

²⁰ When the men had come to Him, they said, "John the Baptist has sent us to You, saying, 'Are You He who should come, or do we look for another?' "

²¹ And that very hour He cured many of their infirmities, diseases, and evil spirits; and to many that were blind He gave sight.

²² So Jesus answering said to them, "Go your way and tell John the things you have seen and heard: that the blind see, the lame walk, the lepers are cleansed, the deaf hear, the dead are raised, the poor have the gospel preached to them.

²³ And blessed is *he* who is not offended because of Me."

²⁴ And when the messengers of John had departed, He began to speak to the people concerning John: "What did you go out into the wilderness to see? A reed shaken by the wind?

²⁵ But what did you go out to see? A man clothed in fine clothing? Indeed those who are wear fine clothes and live in luxury are in kings' courts.

²⁶ But what did you go out to see? A prophet? Yes, I say to you, and much more than a prophet.

²⁷ This is *he* of whom it is written: 'Behold, I send My messenger before Your face, who will prepare Your way before You.'

²⁸ Because, I say to you, among those born of women there is not a greater prophet than John the Baptist; but he who is least in the kingdom of God is greater than him."

²⁹ And all the people who heard *Him*, even the tax collectors justified God, having been baptized with the baptism of John.

³⁰ But the Pharisees and lawyers rejected the counsel of God regarding themselves, not having been baptized by him.

³¹ And the Lord said, "To what then shall I compare the men of this generation, and to what are they like?

³² They are like children sitting in the marketplace and calling to one another, saying: 'We played the flute for you, and you did not dance;

we mourned to you, and you did not weep.'

³³ Because, John the Baptist came neither eating bread nor drinking grape juice, and you say, 'He has a demon.'

³⁴ The Son of Man has come eating and drinking, and you say, 'Look, a glutton and a wine drinker, a friend of tax collectors and sinners!'

³⁵ But wisdom is justified by all her children."

³⁶ Then one of the Pharisees asked Him to eat with him. And He went to the Pharisee's house, and sat down to eat.

³⁷ And behold, a woman in the city who was a sinner, when she knew that *Jesus* sat at the table in the Pharisee's house, brought an alabaster flask of fragrant oil,

³⁸ and stood at His feet behind *Him* weeping; and began to wash His feet with tears, and wiped them with the hair of her head; and kissed His feet and anointed *them* with the fragrant oil.

³⁹ Now when the Pharisee who had invited Him saw *this*, he spoke within himself, saying, "This Man, if He were a prophet, would have known who and what manner of woman *this is* who is touching Him, because she is a sinner."

⁴⁰ And Jesus responded and said to him, "Simon, I have something to say to you." So he said, "Teacher, say it."

⁴¹ "There was a certain creditor who had two debtors. One owed five hundred denarii, and the other fifty.

⁴² And when they had nothing with which to repay, he freely forgave them both. Tell Me, therefore, which of them shall love him most?"

⁴³ Simon answered and said, "I suppose the one whom he forgave more." And He said to him, "You have rightly judged."

⁴⁴ Then He turned to the woman and said to Simon, "Do you see this woman? I entered into your house; you gave Me no water for My feet, but she has washed My feet with her tears and wiped *them* with the hairs of her head.

⁴⁵ You gave Me no kiss, but this woman has not ceased to kiss My feet since the time I came in.

⁴⁶ You did not anoint My head with oil, but this woman has anointed My feet with fragrant oil.

⁴⁷ Therefore I say to you, her sins, which are many, are forgiven, because she loved much. But to whom little is forgiven, *the same* loves little."

⁴⁸ Then He said to her, "Your sins are forgiven."

⁴⁹ And those who sat at the table with Him began to say to themselves, "Who is this who also forgives sins?"

⁵⁰ Then He said to the woman, "Your faith has saved you. Go in peace."

CHAPTER 8

¹ Now it came to pass afterward, that He went through every city and village, preaching and showing the glad tidings of the kingdom of God. And the twelve *were* with Him, ² and certain women who had been healed of evil spirits and infirmities; Mary called Magdalene, out of whom had come seven demons,

³ and Joanna the wife of Chuza, Herod's steward, and Susanna, and many others who provided for Him from their substance.

⁴ And when many people had gathered together, and they had come to Him from every city, He spoke by a parable:

⁵ "A sower went out to sow his seed. And as he sowed, some fell by the wayside; and it was trampled down, and the birds of the air devoured it.

⁶ And some fell on a rock; and as soon as it sprang up, it withered away because it lacked moisture.

⁷ And some fell among thorns, and the thorns sprang up with it and choked it.

⁸ But others fell on good ground, sprang up, and yielded a crop a hundredfold." And when He had said these things He shouted out, "He who has ears to hear, let him hear!"

⁹ Then His disciples asked Him, saying, "What does this parable mean?"

¹⁰ And He said, "To you it has been given to know the mysteries of the kingdom of God, but to the others in parables, that 'Seeing they may not see, and hearing they may not understand.'

¹¹ "Now the parable is this: The seed is the word of God.

¹² Those by the wayside are the ones who hear; then the devil comes and takes away the word out of their hearts, lest they should believe and be saved.

¹³ The ones on the rock *are those* who, when they hear, receive the word with joy; but these have no root, who believe for a while and in time of temptation fall away.

¹⁴ Now the ones that fell among thorns are those who, when they have heard, go out and are choked with cares, riches, and pleasures of *this* life, and bring no fruit to maturity.

¹⁵ But those on the good ground are those who, having heard the word with an honest and good heart, keep *it* and bear fruit with patience.

¹⁶ "No one, when he has lit a lamp, covers it with a vessel or puts *it* under a bed, but sets *it* on a lampstand, that those who enter in may see the light.

¹⁷ Because, nothing is secret that will not be revealed, nor *anything* hidden that will not be known and come to light.

¹⁸ Therefore take heed how you hear. Because, whoever has, to him more will be given; and whoever does not have, even what he seems to have will be taken from him."

¹⁹ Then *His* mother and brethren came to Him, and could not ap-

proach Him because of the crowd. ²⁰ And it was told Him *by some*, who said, "Your mother and Your brethren are standing outside, desiring to see You."

²¹ But He replied and said to them, "My mother and My brethren are these who hear the word of God and do it."

²² Now it happened, on a certain day, that He got into a boat with His disciples. And He said to them, "Let us cross over to the other side of the lake." And they launched out.

²³ But as they sailed He fell asleep. And a windstorm came down on the lake, and they were filling *with water*, and were in jeopardy.

²⁴ And they came to Him and awoke Him, saying, "Master, Master, we are perishing!" Then He arose and rebuked the wind and the raging of the water. And they ceased, and there was a calm.

²⁵ And He said to them, "Where is your faith?" But they being afraid marveled, saying to one another, "What kind of man is this? Because, He commands even the winds and water, and they obey Him!"

²⁶ Then they arrived at the region of the Gadarenes, which is opposite Galilee.

²⁷ And when He went out on the land, there met Him a certain man from the city who had demons for a long time and wore no clothes, nor did he live in a house but in the tombs.

²⁸ When he saw Jesus, he yelled out, fell down before Him, and with a loud voice said, "What have I to do with You, Jesus, *You* Son of the Most High God? I beg You, do not torment me!"

²⁹ Because, He had commanded the unclean spirit to come out of the man. Because, it had often seized him, and he was kept under guard, bound with chains and shackles; and he broke the bonds and was driven by the demon into the wilderness.

³⁰ Jesus asked him, saying, "What is your name?" And he said, "Legion," because many demons had entered him.

³¹ And they begged Him that He would not command them to go out into the abyss.

³² Now a herd of many swine was feeding there on the mountain. So they begged Him that He would permit them to enter them. And He permitted them.

³³ Then the demons went out of the man and entered the swine, and the herd ran violently down a steep place into the lake and drowned.

³⁴ When those who fed *them* saw what had happened, they fled, and went and told *it* in the city and in the countryside.

³⁵ Then they went out to see what had happened, and came to Jesus, and found the man from whom the demons had departed, sitting at the feet of Jesus, clothed and in his right mind. And they were afraid.

³⁶ They also who had seen *it* told

them by what means he who had been demon possessed was healed.

³⁷ Then the entire population of the surrounding region of the Gadarenes begged Him to depart from them, because they were seized with great fear. And He got into the boat and returned back again.

³⁸ Now the man from whom the demons had departed begged Him that he might be with Him. But Jesus sent him away, saying,

³⁹ "Return to your own house, and show what great things God has done for you." And he went his way and proclaimed throughout the entire city what great things Jesus had done for him.

⁴⁰ And it came to pass, when Jesus returned, that the people welcomed Him *gladly*, because they were all waiting for Him.

⁴¹ And behold, there came a man named Jairus, and he was a ruler of the synagogue. And he fell down at Jesus' feet and begged Him that He would come to his house,

⁴² because, he had an only daughter about twelve years of age, and she was dying. But as He went, the people swarmed Him.

⁴³ Now a woman, having a flow of blood for twelve years, who had spent all her livelihood on physicians and could not be healed by any,

⁴⁴ came behind *Him* and touched the edge of His clothes. And immediately her flow of blood stopped.

⁴⁵ And Jesus said, "Who touched Me?" When all denied it, Peter and those with him said, "Master, the crowds swarm and press *You*, and You say, 'Who touched Me?'"

⁴⁶ But Jesus said, "Somebody touched Me, because I perceive power has gone out from Me."

⁴⁷ Now when the woman saw that she was not hidden, she came trembling; and falling down before Him, she declared to Him before all the people the reason she had touched Him and how she was healed immediately.

⁴⁸ And He said to her, "Daughter, be of good cheer; your faith has made you well. Go in peace."

⁴⁹ while He was still speaking, someone came from the ruler of the synagogue's *house*, saying to him, "Your daughter is dead. Do not trouble the Teacher."

⁵⁰ But when Jesus heard *it*, He responded to him, saying, "Do not be afraid; only believe, and she will be made well."

⁵¹ And when He came into the house, He permitted no one to go in except Peter, James, and John, and the father and mother of the girl.

⁵² Now all wept and mourned for her; but He said, "Do not weep; she is not dead, but sleeping."

⁵³ And they ridiculed Him, knowing that she was dead.

⁵⁴ But He put them all outside, took her by the hand and called, saying, "Little girl, arise."

⁵⁵ Then her spirit returned, and she arose immediately. And He com-

manded that she be given food to eat.

⁵⁶ And her parents were astonished, but He commanded them that they should tell no one what had happened.

CHAPTER 9

¹ Then He called His twelve disciples together and gave them power and authority over all demons, and to cure diseases.

² And He sent them to preach the kingdom of God and to heal the sick.

³ And He said to them, "Take nothing for *your* journey, neither staffs nor bag nor bread nor money; and do not have two coats each.

⁴ "Whatever house you enter into, stay there, and from there depart.

⁵ And whoever will not receive you, when you go out of that city, shake off the very dust from your feet as a testimony against them."

⁶ So they departed and went through the towns, preaching the gospel and healing everywhere.

⁷ Now Herod the tetrarch heard of all that was done by Him; and he was perplexed, because it was said by some that John had risen from the dead,

⁸ and by some that Elijah had appeared, and by others that one of the old prophets had risen again.

⁹ And Herod said, "John I have beheaded, but who is this of whom I hear such things?" So he desired to see Him.

¹⁰ And the apostles, when they had returned, told Him all that they had done. Then He took them and went aside privately into a deserted place belonging to the city called Bethsaida.

¹¹ But when the people knew *it*, they followed Him; and He received them and spoke to them about the kingdom of God, and healed those who had need of healing.

¹² And when the day began to wear away, then the twelve came and said to Him, "Send the crowd away, that they may go into the surrounding towns and the countryside, and lodge and get provisions; because we are in a deserted place here."

¹³ But He said to them, "You give them something to eat." And they said, "We have no more than five loaves and two fish, unless we should go and buy food for all these people."

¹⁴ Because, there were about five thousand men. Then He said to His disciples, "Make them sit down in groups of fifty."

¹⁵ And they did so, and made them all sit down.

¹⁶ Then He took the five loaves and the two fish, and looking up to heaven, He blessed and broke them, and gave them to the disciples to set before the crowds.

¹⁷ So they ate and were all filled, and twelve baskets of the leftover fragments were taken up by them.

¹⁸ And it happened, as He was alone

praying, that His disciples were with Him, and He asked them, saying, "Who do the people say that I am?"

[19] They answered and said, "John the Baptist, but some *say* Elijah; and others *say* that one of the old prophets has risen again."

[20] He said to them, "But who do you say that I am?" Peter answered and said, "The Christ of God."

[21] And He strictly warned and commanded *them* to tell this thing to no one,

[22] saying, "The Son of Man must suffer many things, and be rejected by the elders and chief priests and scribes, and be killed, and be raised the third day."

[23] Then He said to *them* all, "If anyone desires to come after Me, let him deny himself, and take up his cross daily, and follow Me.

[24] Because, whoever desires to save his life will lose it, but whoever loses his life for My sake will save it.

[25] Because, what profit is it to a man if he gains the entire world, and is himself thrown away or lost?

[26] Because, whoever is ashamed of Me and of My words, of him the Son of Man will be ashamed when He comes in His own glory, and *in His* Father's, and of the holy angels.

[27] But I tell you truly, there are some standing here who will not taste death until they see the kingdom of God."

[28] Now it came to pass, about eight days after these sayings, that He took Peter, John, and James and went up on the mountain to pray.

[29] As He prayed, the appearance of His face was altered, and His robe *became* white *and* glistening.

[30] And behold, two men talked with Him, who were Moses and Elijah,

[31] who appeared in glory and spoke of His decease which He was about to accomplish at Jerusalem.

[32] But Peter and those with him were heavy with sleep; and when they were awake, they saw His glory and the two men who stood with Him.

[33] Then it happened, as they were parting from Him, that Peter said to Jesus, "Master, it is good for us to be here; and let us make three tabernacles: one for You, one for Moses, and one for Elijah," not knowing what he said.

[34] while he was saying this, a cloud came and overshadowed them; and they were fearful as they entered the cloud.

[35] And a voice came out of the cloud, saying, "This is My beloved Son. Hear Him!"

[36] When the voice had ceased, Jesus was found alone. But they kept quiet, and told no one in those days any of the things that they had seen.

[37] Now it happened on the next day, when they had come down from the mountain, that a large crowd met Him.

[38] Suddenly a man from the crowd shouted out, saying, "Teacher, I

implore You, look on my son, as he is my only child.

³⁹ And behold, a spirit seizes him, and he suddenly yells out; it convulses him so that he froths again; and it departs from him with great difficulty, mauling him.

⁴⁰ So I implored Your disciples to cast it out, but they could not."

⁴¹ Then Jesus responded and said, "O faithless and perverse generation, how long shall I be with you and bear with you? Bring your son here."

⁴² And as he was still coming, the demon threw him down and convulsed *him*. Then Jesus rebuked the unclean spirit, healed the child, and gave him back to his father.

⁴³ And they were all amazed at the mighty power of God. But while everyone marveled at all the things which Jesus did, He said to His disciples,

⁴⁴ "Let these words sink down into your ears, because the Son of Man is about to be delivered into the hands of men."

⁴⁵ But they did not understand this saying, and it was hidden from them so that they did not perceive it; and they were afraid to ask Him about this saying.

⁴⁶ Then a dispute arose among them as to which of them would be greatest.

⁴⁷ And Jesus, perceiving the thought of their heart, took a little child and set him by Him,

⁴⁸ and said to them, "Whoever receives this little child in My name receives Me; and whoever receives Me receives Him who sent Me. Because he who is least among you all, they will be great."

⁴⁹ Now John responded and said, "Master, we saw someone casting out demons in Your name, and we forbade him because he does not follow with us."

⁵⁰ But Jesus said to him, "Do not forbid *him*, because he who is not against us is for us."

⁵¹ Now it came to pass, when the time had come for Him to be received up, that He steadfastly set His face to go to Jerusalem,

⁵² and sent messengers before His face. And as they went, they entered into a village of the Samaritans, to prepare for Him.

⁵³ But they did not receive Him, because His face was set for the journey to Jerusalem.

⁵⁴ And when His disciples James and John saw *this*, they said, "Lord, do You want us to command fire to come down from heaven and consume them, just as Elijah did?"

⁵⁵ But He turned and rebuked them, and said, "You do not know what manner of spirit you are of.

⁵⁶ Because, the Son of Man did not come to destroy men's lives but to save them." And they went to another village.

⁵⁷ Now it happened as they journeyed on the road, that someone said to Him, "Lord, I will follow You wherever You go."

⁵⁸ And Jesus said to him, "Foxes have holes and birds of the air *have* nests, but the Son of Man has nowhere to lay His head."

⁵⁹ Then He said to another, "Follow Me." But he said, "Lord, let me first go and bury my father."

⁶⁰ Jesus said to him, "Let the dead bury their own dead, but you go and preach the kingdom of God."

⁶¹ And another also said, "Lord, I will follow You, but let me first go and say farewell to those who are at my house."

⁶² But Jesus said to him, "No one, having put his hand to the plow, and looking back, is fit for the kingdom of God."

CHAPTER 10

¹ After these things the Lord appointed seventy others also, and sent them two by two before His face into every city and place where He Himself was about to go.

² Then He said to them, "The harvest is truly plentiful, but the laborers *are* few; therefore pray the Lord of the harvest that He would send out laborers into His harvest.

³ Go your way; behold, I send you out as lambs among wolves.

⁴ Carry neither money bag, knapsack, nor sandals; and greet no one along the road.

⁵ But whatever house you enter into, first say, 'Peace *be* to this house.'

⁶ And if a son of peace is there, your peace will rest upon it; if not, it will return to you again.

⁷ And remain in the same house, eating and drinking such things as they give, because the laborer is worthy of his wages. Do not go from house to house.

⁸ And whatever city you enter into, and they receive you, eat such things as are set before you.

⁹ And heal the sick there, and say to them, 'The kingdom of God has come near to you.'

¹⁰ But whatever city you enter into, and they do not receive you, go your way out into the streets of it and say,

¹¹ 'The very dust of your city which clings to us we wipe off against you. Nevertheless be sure of this, that the kingdom of God has come near to you.'

¹² But I say to you that it will be more tolerable in that Day for Sodom than for that city.

¹³ "Woe to you, Chorazin! Woe to you, Bethsaida! Because, if the mighty works which were done in you had been done in Tyre and Sidon, they would have repented long ago, sitting in sackcloth and ashes.

¹⁴ But it will be more tolerable for Tyre and Sidon at the judgment than for you.

¹⁵ And you, Capernaum, who are exalted to heaven, will be thrown down to hell.

¹⁶ He who hears you hears Me, he who rejects you rejects Me, and he who rejects Me rejects Him who

sent Me."

¹⁷ Then the seventy returned again with joy, saying, "Lord, even the demons are subject to us in Your name."

¹⁸ And He said to them, "I saw Satan fall like lightning from heaven.

¹⁹ Behold, I give you the authority to tread on serpents and scorpions, and over all the power of the enemy, and nothing will by any means hurt you.

²⁰ Nevertheless do not rejoice in this, that the spirits are subject to you, but rather rejoice because your names are written in heaven."

²¹ In that hour Jesus rejoiced in spirit and said, "I thank You, O Father, Lord of heaven and earth, that You have hidden these things from the wise and prudent and revealed them to babes. Even so, Father, because so it seemed good in Your sight.

²² All things have been delivered to Me by My Father, and no one knows who the Son is except the Father, and who the Father is except the Son, and *the one* to whom the Son wills to reveal *Him*."

²³ Then He turned to His disciples and said privately, "Blessed *are* the eyes which see the things that you see;

²⁴ because I tell you that many prophets and kings have desired to see these things which you see, and have not seen *them*, and to hear these things which you hear, and have not heard *them*."

²⁵ And behold, a certain lawyer stood up and tested Him, saying, "Teacher, what shall I do to inherit eternal life?"

²⁶ He said to him, "What is written in the law? What is your reading of it?"

²⁷ So he answered and said, " 'You shall love the LORD your God with all your heart, with all your soul, with all your strength, and with all your mind,' and 'your neighbor as yourself.' "

²⁸ And He said to him, "You have answered rightly; do this and you will live."

²⁹ But he, wanting to justify himself, said to Jesus, "And who is my neighbor?"

³⁰ Then Jesus answering said: "A certain *man* went down from Jerusalem to Jericho, and fell among thieves, who stripped him of his clothing, wounded *him*, and departed, leaving *him* half dead.

³¹ Now by chance a certain priest came down that road. And when he saw him, he passed by on the other side.

³² And likewise a Levite, when he arrived at the place, came and looked at him, and passed by on the other side.

³³ But a certain Samaritan, as he journeyed, came where he was. And when he saw him, he had compassion on *him*.

³⁴ So he went to *him* and bandaged his wounds, pouring on oil and wine; and he set him on his own

animal, brought him to an inn, and took care of him.

³⁵ On the next day, when he departed, he took out two denarii, gave *them* to the innkeeper, and said to him, 'Take care of him; and whatever more you spend, when I come again, I will repay you.'

³⁶ So which of these three do you think was neighbor to him who fell among the thieves?"

³⁷ And he said, "He who showed mercy on him." Then Jesus said to him, "You go and do likewise."

³⁸ Now it happened as they went that He entered into a certain village; and a certain woman named Martha welcomed Him into her house.

³⁹ And she had a sister called Mary, who also sat at Jesus' feet and heard His word.

⁴⁰ But Martha was distracted with much serving, and she came to Him and said, "Lord, do You not care that my sister has left me to serve alone? Therefore tell her to help me."

⁴¹ And Jesus answered and said to her, "Martha, Martha, you are worried and troubled about many things.

⁴² But one thing is needed, and Mary has chosen that good part, which will not be taken away from her."

CHAPTER 11

¹ Now it came to pass, as He was praying in a certain place, when He ceased, that one of His disciples said to Him, "Lord, teach us to pray, as John also taught his disciples."

² So He said to them, "When you pray, say: Our Father who is in heaven, Hallowed be Your name. Your kingdom come. Your will be done as in heaven, so *also* on earth.

³ Give us day by day our daily bread.

⁴ And forgive us our sins, because we also forgive everyone who is indebted to us. And do not lead us into temptation, but deliver us from evil."

⁵ And He said to them, "Which of you will have a friend, and will go to him at midnight and say to him, 'Friend, lend me three loaves;

⁶ because, a friend of mine has come to me on his journey, and I have nothing to set before him';

⁷ and he will reply from within and say, 'Do not trouble me; the door is now shut, and my children are with me in bed; I cannot rise and give to you'?

⁸ I say to you, though he will not rise and give to him because he is his friend, yet because of his persistence he will rise and give him as many as he needs.

⁹ "So I say to you, ask, and it will be given to you; seek, and you will find; knock, and it will be opened to you.

¹⁰ Because, everyone who asks receives, and he who seeks finds, and to him who knocks it will be opened.

¹¹ If a son shall ask for bread from

anyone of you that is a father, will he give him a stone? Or if *he asks* for a fish, will he give him a serpent instead of a fish?

¹² Or if he asks for an egg, will he offer him a scorpion?

¹³ If you then, being evil, know how to give good gifts to your children, how much more will *your* heavenly Father give the Holy Spirit to those who ask Him!"

¹⁴ And He was casting out a demon, and it was mute. So it was, when the demon had gone out, that the mute spoke; and the people marveled.

¹⁵ But some of them said, "He casts out demons by Beelzebub, the ruler of the demons."

¹⁶ Others, testing *Him*, sought from Him a sign from heaven.

¹⁷ But He, knowing their thoughts, said to them: "Every kingdom divided against itself is brought to desolation, and a house *divided* against a house falls.

¹⁸ If Satan also is divided against himself, how will his kingdom stand? Because you say I cast out demons by Beelzebub.

¹⁹ And if I cast out demons by Beelzebub, by whom do your sons cast *them* out? Therefore they will be your judges.

²⁰ But if I cast out demons with the finger of God, surely the kingdom of God has come upon you.

²¹ when a strong man, fully armed, guards his own palace, his goods are in peace.

²² But when a stronger than he comes upon him and overcomes him, he takes from him all his armor in which he trusted, and divides his spoils.

²³ He who is not with Me is against Me, and he who does not gather with Me scatters.

²⁴ "When an unclean spirit goes out of a man, he walks through dry places, seeking rest; and finding none, he says, 'I will return to my house from which I came.'

²⁵ And when he comes, he finds *it* swept and put in order.

²⁶ Then he goes and takes *with him* seven other spirits more wicked than himself, and they enter in and dwell there; and the last *state* of that man is worse than the first."

²⁷ And it happened, as He spoke these things, that a certain woman from the crowd raised her voice and said to Him, "Blessed *is* the womb that bore You, and the breasts which You have sucked!"

²⁸ But He said, "Rather, blessed *are* those who hear the word of God and keep it!"

²⁹ And while the people were tightly gathered together, He began to say, "This is an evil generation. It seeks a sign, and no sign will be given to it except the sign of Jonah the prophet.

³⁰ Because, as Jonah became a sign to the Ninevites, so also the Son of Man will be to this generation.

³¹ The queen of the South will rise up in the judgment with the men of this generation and condemn them,

because she came from the ends of the earth to hear the wisdom of Solomon; and behold, a greater than Solomon is here.

³² The men of Nineveh will rise up in the judgment with this generation and will condemn it, because, they repented at the preaching of Jonah; and indeed a greater than Jonah is here.

³³ "No one, when he has lit a lamp, puts *it* in a secret place or under a basket, but on a lampstand, that those who come in may see the light.

³⁴ The lamp of the body is the eye. Therefore, when your eye is single, your entire body also is full of light. But when *your eye* is corrupted, your body also *is* full of darkness.

³⁵ Therefore take heed that the light which is in you is not darkness.

³⁶ If then your entire body *is* full of light, having no part dark, the entire body will be full of light, as when the bright shining of a lamp gives you light."

³⁷ And as He spoke, a certain Pharisee asked Him to dine with him. So He went in and sat down to eat.

³⁸ And when the Pharisee saw *it*, he marveled that He had not first washed before dinner.

³⁹ Then the Lord said to him, "Now you Pharisees make the outside of the cup and dish clean, but your inward part is full of greed and wickedness.

⁴⁰ *You* fools! Did not He who made the outside make the inside also?

⁴¹ But rather give charitable deeds of such things as you have; then indeed all things are clean to you.

⁴² "But woe to you Pharisees! Because you tithe mint and rue and all manner of herbs, and pass over justice and the love of God. These you ought to have done, without leaving the others undone.

⁴³ Woe to you Pharisees! Because, you love the best seats in the synagogues and greetings in the marketplaces.

⁴⁴ Woe to you, scribes and Pharisees, hypocrites! Because, you are like graves which are not seen, and the men who walk over *them* are not aware of *them*."

⁴⁵ Then one of the lawyers responded and said to Him, "Teacher, by saying these things You reproach us also."

⁴⁶ And He said, "Woe to you also, *you* lawyers! Because, you load men with burdens hard to bear, and you yourselves do not touch the burdens with one of your fingers.

⁴⁷ Woe to you! Because, you build the tombs of the prophets, and your fathers killed them.

⁴⁸ In fact, you bear witness that you approve the deeds of your fathers; because, they indeed killed them, and you build their tombs.

⁴⁹ Therefore the wisdom of God also said, 'I will send them prophets and apostles, and *some* of them they will kill and persecute,'

⁵⁰ that the blood of all the prophets which was shed from the foundation of the world may be required of this generation,

⁵¹ from the blood of Abel to the blood of Zechariah who perished between the altar and the temple. Truly, I say to you, it will be required of this generation.

⁵² "Woe to you lawyers! Because, you have taken away the key of knowledge. You did not enter in yourselves, and those who were entering in you hindered."

⁵³ And as He said these things to them, the scribes and the Pharisees began to contest *Him* vehemently, and to provoke Him to speak about many things,

⁵⁴ lying in wait for Him, and seeking to catch Him in something out of His mouth, that they might accuse Him.

CHAPTER 12

¹ In the meantime, when an innumerable multitude of people had gathered together, so that they trampled one another, He began to say to His disciples first of all, "Beware of the leaven of the Pharisees, which is hypocrisy.

² Because, there is nothing covered that will not be revealed, nor hidden that will not be known.

³ Therefore whatever you have spoken in the dark will be heard in the light, and what you have spoken in the ear in inner rooms will be proclaimed upon the house-tops.

⁴ "And I say to you, My friends, do not be afraid of those who kill the body, and after that have no more that they can do.

⁵ But I will forewarn you whom you should reverence: Reverence Him who, after He has killed, has authority to cast into hell; yes, I say to you, reverence Him!

⁶ "Are not five sparrows sold for two copper coins? And not one of them is forgotten before God.

⁷ But even the very hairs of your head are all numbered. Do not fear therefore; you are of more value than many sparrows.

⁸ "Also I say to you, whoever confesses Me before men, him the Son of Man also will confess before the angels of God.

⁹ But he who denies Me before men will be denied before the angels of God.

¹⁰ "And anyone who speaks a word against the Son of Man, it will be forgiven him; but to him who blasphemes against the Holy Spirit, it will not be forgiven.

¹¹ "Now when they bring you to the synagogues and *to* magistrates and authorities, do not worry about how or what you should answer, or what you should say.

¹² Because, the Holy Spirit will teach you in that very hour what you ought to say."

¹³ Then one from the company said to Him, "Teacher, tell my brother to divide the inheritance with me."

¹⁴ But He said to him, "Man, who

made Me a judge or an arbitrator over you?"

¹⁵ And He said to them, "Take heed and beware of covetousness, because, one's life does not consist in the abundance of the things he possesses."

¹⁶ Then He spoke a parable to them, saying: "The ground of a certain rich man yielded plentifully.

¹⁷ And he thought within himself, saying, 'What shall I do, since I have no room to store my crops?'

¹⁸ So he said, 'I will do this: I will pull down my barns and build greater, and there I will store all my crops and my goods.

¹⁹ And I will say to my soul, "Soul, you have many goods laid up for many years; take your ease; eat, drink, *and* be merry." '

²⁰ But God said to him, '*You* fool! This night your soul will be required of you; then whose shall those things be which you have provided?'

²¹ "So *is* he who lays up treasure for himself, and is not rich toward God."

²² Then He said to His disciples, "Therefore I say to you, do not worry about your life, what you shall eat; nor about the body, what you shall put on.

²³ Life is more than food, and the body *is more* than clothing.

²⁴ Consider the ravens, because, they neither sow nor reap, which have neither storehouse nor barn; and God feeds them. Of how much more value are you than the birds?

²⁵ And which of you by worrying can add one cubit to his stature?

²⁶ If you then are not able to do the things that are least, why are you anxious for the rest?

²⁷ Consider the lilies, how they grow: they neither toil nor spin; and yet I say to you, even Solomon in all his glory was not arrayed like one of these.

²⁸ If then God so clothes the grass, which today is in the field and tomorrow is thrown into the oven, how much more *will He clothe* you, O you of little faith?

²⁹ "And do not seek what you should eat or what you should drink, nor have an anxious mind.

³⁰ Because, all these things the nations of the world seek after, and your Father knows that you need these things.

³¹ But instead, seek the kingdom of God, and all these things will be added to you.

³² "Do not fear, little flock, because it is your Father's good pleasure to give you the kingdom.

³³ Sell what you have and give charitable gifts; provide yourselves money bags which do not grow old, a treasure in the heavens that does not fail, where no thief approaches nor moth destroys.

³⁴ Because where your treasure is, there your heart will be also.

³⁵ "Let your waist be girded and *your* lamps burning;

³⁶ and you yourselves be like men

who wait for their master, when he will return from the wedding, that when he comes and knocks they may open to him immediately.

³⁷ Blessed *are* those servants whom the master, when he comes, will find watching. Truly, I say to you that he will gird himself and have them sit down to eat, and will come out and serve them.

³⁸ And if he should come in the second watch, or come in the third watch, and find *them so*, blessed are those servants.

³⁹ But know this, that if the master of the house had known what hour the thief would come, he would have watched and not allowed his house to be broken into.

⁴⁰ Therefore you also be ready, because the Son of Man is coming at an hour you do not expect."

⁴¹ Then Peter said to Him, "Lord, do You speak this parable only to us, or also to everyone?"

⁴² And the Lord said, "Who then is that faithful and wise steward, whom *his* master will make ruler over his household, to give *them their* portion of food in due season?

⁴³ Blessed *is* that servant whom his master will find so doing when he comes.

⁴⁴ Truly, I say to you that he will make him ruler over all that he has.

⁴⁵ But then, if that servant says in his heart, 'My master is delaying his coming,' and begins to beat the male and female servants, and to eat and drink and be drunk,

⁴⁶ the master of that servant will come on a day when he is not looking for *him*, and at an hour when he is not aware, and will cut him in two and will appoint him his portion with the unbelievers.

⁴⁷ And that servant who knew his master's will, and did not prepare *himself* or do according to his will, will be beaten with many *stripes*.

⁴⁸ But he who did not know, yet committed things deserving of stripes, will be beaten with *a* few *stripes*. Because, to whoever much is given, from him much will be required; and to whom much has been committed by men, of him they will ask the more.

⁴⁹ "I came to send fire on the earth, and what do I desire if it were already lit?

⁵⁰ But I have a baptism to be baptized with, and how distressed I am until it is accomplished!

⁵¹ Do you suppose that I came to give peace on earth? I tell you, not at all, but rather division.

⁵² Because, from now on five in one house will be divided: three against two, and two against three.

⁵³ Father will be divided against son and son against father, mother against daughter and daughter against mother, mother in law against her daughter in law and daughter in law against her mother in law."

⁵⁴ Then He also said to the people, "Whenever you see a cloud rising out of the west, immediately you

say, 'A shower is coming'; and so it is.

⁵⁵ And when *you see* the south wind blow, you say, 'There will be hot weather'; and it happens.

⁵⁶ *You* hypocrites! You can discern the face of the sky and of the earth, but how is it you do not discern this time?

⁵⁷ "Yes, and why, even of yourselves, do you not judge what is right?

⁵⁸ When you go with your adversary to the magistrate, make every effort along the way to be delivered from him, lest he drag you to the judge, the judge deliver you to the officer, and the officer throw you into prison.

⁵⁹ I tell you, you will not depart from there until you have paid the very last mite."

CHAPTER 13

¹ There were present at that season some who told Him about the Galileans whose blood Pilate had mingled with their sacrifices.

² And Jesus replied and said to them, "Do you suppose that these Galileans were worse sinners than all other Galileans, because they suffered such things?

³ I tell you, no; but unless you repent you will all likewise perish.

⁴ Or those eighteen on whom the tower in Siloam fell and killed them, do you think that they were worse sinners than all other men who dwelt in Jerusalem?

⁵ I tell you, no; but unless you repent you will all likewise perish."

⁶ He also spoke this parable: "A certain *man* had a fig tree planted in his vineyard, and he came seeking fruit on it and found none.

⁷ Then he said to the keeper of his vineyard, 'Look, for three years I have come seeking fruit on this fig tree and find none. Cut it down; why does it use up the ground?'

⁸ But he answered and said to him, 'Sir, let it alone this year also, until I dig around it and fertilize *it*.

⁹ And if it bears fruit, *well*. But if not, *then* after that you can cut it down.' "

¹⁰ Now He was teaching in one of the synagogues on the Sabbath.

¹¹ And behold, there was a woman who had a spirit of infirmity eighteen years, and was bent over and could in no way lift *herself* up.

¹² But when Jesus saw her, He called *her to Him* and said to her, "Woman, you are loosed from your infirmity."

¹³ And He laid *His* hands on her, and immediately she was made straight, and glorified God.

¹⁴ But the ruler of the synagogue responded with indignation, because Jesus had healed on the Sabbath day; and he said to the people, "There are six days on which men ought to work; therefore come and be healed on them, and not on the Sabbath day."

¹⁵ The Lord then replied to him and said, "*You* hypocrite! Does not each

one of you on the Sabbath loose his ox or his donkey from the stall, and lead *it* away to water *it*?

¹⁶ So ought not this woman, being a daughter of Abraham, whom Satan has bound, behold, for eighteen years, be loosed from this bond on the Sabbath day?"

¹⁷ And when He said these things, all His adversaries were put to shame; and all the people rejoiced for all the glorious things that were done by Him.

¹⁸ Then He said, "What is the kingdom of God like? And to what shall I compare it?

¹⁹ It is like a grain of mustard seed, which a man took and threw in his garden; and it grew and became a large tree, and the birds of the air nested in its branches."

²⁰ And again He said, "To what shall I liken the kingdom of God?

²¹ It is like leaven, which a woman took and hid three measures of meal inside until it was all leavened."

²² And He went through the cities and villages, teaching, and journeying toward Jerusalem.

²³ Then one said to Him, "Lord, are there few who are saved?" And He said to them,

²⁴ "Strive to enter through the narrow gate, because many, I say to you, will seek to enter in and will not be able.

²⁵ When once the Master of the house has risen up and shut the door, and you begin to stand outside and knock at the door, saying, 'Lord, Lord, open for us,' and He will reply and say to you, 'I do not know you, where you are from,'

²⁶ then you will begin to say, 'We ate and drank in Your presence, and You have taught in our streets.'

²⁷ But He will say, 'I tell you I do not know you, where you are from. Depart from Me, all *you* workers of iniquity.'

²⁸ There will be weeping and gnashing of teeth, when you see Abraham and Isaac and Jacob and all the prophets in the kingdom of God, and you *yourselves* thrust out.

²⁹ And they will come from the east and *from* the west, from the north and *from* the south, and will sit down in the kingdom of God.

³⁰ And behold there are last who will be first, and there are first who will be last."

³¹ On the same day some Pharisees came, saying to Him, "Get out and depart from here, because Herod will kill You."

³² And He said to them, "You go and tell that fox, 'Behold, I cast out demons and perform cures today and tomorrow, and the third *day* I will be perfected.'

³³ Nevertheless I must walk today, tomorrow, and the *day* following; because, it cannot be that a prophet should perish outside of Jerusalem.

³⁴ "O Jerusalem, Jerusalem, the one who kills the prophets and stones those who are sent to you! How often I wanted to gather your child-

ren together, as a hen *gathers* her brood under *her* wings, but you were not willing!

³⁵ Behold! Your house is left to you desolate; and truly, I say to you, you will not see Me until *the time* comes when you will say, 'Blessed *is* He who comes in the name of the LORD!' "

CHAPTER 14

¹ Now it happened, as He went into the house of one of the rulers of the Pharisees to eat bread on the Sabbath day, that they watched Him.

² And behold, there was a certain man before Him who had dropsy.

³ And Jesus, responding, spoke to the lawyers and Pharisees, saying, "Is it lawful to heal on the Sabbath day?"

⁴ But they kept silent. And He took *him* and healed him, and let him go.

⁵ Then He responded to them, saying, "Which of you, having a donkey or an ox that has fallen into a pit, will not immediately pull him out on the Sabbath day?"

⁶ And they could not answer Him regarding these things.

⁷ So He told a parable to those who were invited, when He noted how they chose the best places, saying to them:

⁸ "When you are invited by anyone to a wedding feast, do not sit down in the best place, lest one more honorable than you be invited by him;

⁹ and he who invited you and him come and say to you, 'Give place to this man,' and then you begin with shame to take the lowest place.

¹⁰ But when you are invited, go and sit down in the lowest place, so that when he who invited you comes he may say to you, 'Friend, go up higher.' Then you will have glory in the presence of those who sit at the table with you.

¹¹ Because, whoever exalts himself will be humbled, and he who humbles himself will be exalted."

¹² Then He also said to him who invited Him, "When you give a dinner or a supper, do not ask your friends, your brethren, your relatives, nor *your* rich neighbors, lest they also invite you back, and you be repaid.

¹³ But when you give a feast, invite the poor, the maimed, the lame, the blind.

¹⁴ And you will be blessed, because they cannot repay you; because, you will be repaid at the resurrection of the just."

¹⁵ Now when one of those who sat at the table with Him heard these things, he said to Him, "Blessed *is* he who will eat bread in the kingdom of God!"

¹⁶ Then He said to him, "A certain man made a large supper and invited many,

¹⁷ and sent his servant at supper time to say to those who were invited, 'Come, because all things are now ready.'

¹⁸ But they all with one *accord*

began to make excuses. The first said to him, 'I have bought a piece of ground, and I must go and see it. I ask you to have me excused.'

[19] And another said, 'I have bought five yoke of oxen, and I am going to test them. I ask you to have me excused.'

[20] Still another said, 'I have married a wife, and therefore I cannot come.'

[21] So that servant came and reported these things to his master. Then the master of the house, being angry, said to his servant, 'Go out quickly into the streets and lanes of the city, and bring in here the poor and the maimed and the lame and the blind.'

[22] And the servant said, 'Master, it is done as you have commanded, and still there is room.'

[23] Then the master said to the servant, 'Go out into the highways and hedges, and compel *them* to come in, that my house may be filled.

[24] Because, I say to you that none of those men who were invited will taste my supper.'"

[25] Now large crowds went with Him. And He turned and said to them,

[26] "If anyone comes to Me and does not hate his father and mother, wife and children, brothers and sisters, yes, and his own life also, he cannot be My disciple.

[27] And whoever does not bear his cross and come after Me cannot be My disciple.

[28] Because, which of you, intending to build a tower, does not sit down first and count the cost, whether he has *enough* to finish it?

[29] Lest, after he has laid the foundation, and is not able to finish *it*, all who see *it* begin to mock him,

[30] saying, 'This man began to build and was not able to finish.'

[31] Or what king, going to make war against another king, does not sit down first and consider whether he is able with ten thousand to meet him who comes against him with twenty thousand?

[32] Or else, while the other is still a long way off, he sends a delegation and desires conditions of peace.

[33] So likewise, whoever it is of you who does not forsake all that he has cannot be My disciple.

[34] "Salt *is* good; but if the salt has lost its flavor, how will it be seasoned?

[35] It is neither fit for the land nor for the dunghill, *but* men throw it out. He who has ears to hear, let him hear!"

CHAPTER 15

[1] Then all the tax collectors and the sinners drew near to Him to hear Him.

[2] And the Pharisees and scribes murmured, saying, "This Man receives sinners and eats with them."

[3] So He spoke this parable to them, saying:

[4] "What man of you, having a hun-

dred sheep, if he loses one of them, does not leave the ninety nine in the wilderness, and go after the one which is lost until he finds it?

⁵ And when he has found *it*, he lays *it* on his shoulders, rejoicing.

⁶ And when he comes home, he calls together *his* friends and neighbors, saying to them, 'Rejoice with me, because I have found my sheep which was lost!'

⁷ I say to you that likewise there will be more joy in heaven over one sinner who repents than over ninety nine just persons who need no repentance.

⁸ "Or what woman, having ten silver coins, if she loses one coin, does not light a lamp, sweep the house, and search diligently until she finds *it*?

⁹ And when she has found *it*, she calls *her* friends and *her* neighbors together, saying, 'Rejoice with me, because I have found the piece which I lost!'

¹⁰ Likewise, I say to you, there is joy in the presence of the angels of God over one sinner who repents."

¹¹ Then He said: "A certain man had two sons.

¹² And the younger of them said to *his* father, 'Father, give me the portion of goods that falls to *me*.' So he divided to them *his* livelihood.

¹³ And not many days after, the younger son gathered all together, journeyed to a distant region, and there wasted his possessions with riotous living.

¹⁴ But when he had spent everything, there arose a severe famine in that land, and he began to be in need.

¹⁵ Then he went and joined himself to a citizen of that region, and he sent him into his fields to feed swine.

¹⁶ And he would gladly have filled his stomach with the pods that the swine ate, and no one gave *anything* to him.

¹⁷ "But when he came to himself, he said, 'How many of my father's hired servants have enough bread and to spare, and I perish with hunger!

¹⁸ I will arise and go to my father, and will say to him, "Father, I have sinned against heaven and before you,

¹⁹ and I am no longer worthy to be called your son. Make me like one of your hired servants."'

²⁰ "And he arose and came to his father. But when he was still a long way off, his father saw him and had compassion, and ran and fell on his neck and kissed him.

²¹ And the son said to him, 'Father, I have sinned against heaven and in your sight, and am no longer worthy to be called your son.'

²² "But the father said to his servants, 'Bring out the best robe and put *it* on him, and put a ring on his hand and sandals on *his* feet.

²³ And bring the fatted calf here and kill *it*, and let us eat and be merry;

²⁴ because this my son was dead and

is alive again; he was lost and is found.' And they began to be merry.

²⁵ "Now his older son was in the field. And as he came and drew near to the house, he heard music and dancing.

²⁶ So he called one of the servants and asked what these things meant.

²⁷ And he said to him, 'Your brother has come, and because he has received him safe and sound, your father has killed the fatted calf.'

²⁸ "But he was angry and would not go in. Therefore his father came out and pleaded with him.

²⁹ So he replied and said to *his* father, 'Behold, these many years I have been serving you; I never transgressed your commandment at any time; and yet you never gave me a young goat, that I might be merry with my friends.

³⁰ But as soon as this son of yours came, who has devoured your livelihood with harlots, you killed the fatted calf for him.'

³¹ "And he said to him, 'Son, you are always with me, and all that I have is yours.

³² It was right that we should make merry and be glad, because that your brother was dead and is alive again, and was lost and is found.' "

CHAPTER 16

¹ He also said to His disciples: "There was a certain rich man who had a steward, and an accusation was brought to him that this man was wasting his goods.

² So he called him and said to him, 'What is this I hear about you? Give an account of your stewardship, because you can no longer be steward.'

³ "Then the steward said within himself, 'What shall I do? Because, my master is taking the stewardship away from me. I cannot dig; I am ashamed to beg.

⁴ I have resolved what to do, that when I am put out of the stewardship, they may receive me into their houses.'

⁵ "So he called every one of his master's debtors *to him*self, and said to the first, 'How much do you owe my master?'

⁶ And he said, 'A hundred measures of oil.' So he said to him, 'Take your bill, and sit down quickly and write fifty.'

⁷ Then he said to another, 'And how much do you owe?' So he said, 'A hundred measures of wheat.' And he said to him, 'Take your bill, and write eighty.'

⁸ So the master commended the unjust steward because he had dealt shrewdly. Because, the sons of this world are more shrewd in their generation than the children of light.

⁹ "And I say to you, make friends for yourselves by unrighteous mammon, that when you fail, they may receive you into an everlasting home.

¹⁰ He who is faithful in what is least is faithful also in much; and he who

is unjust in what is least is unjust also in much.

¹¹ Therefore if you have not been faithful in the unrighteous mammon, who will commit to your trust the true *riches*?

¹² And if you have not been faithful in what is another man's, who will give you what is your own?

¹³ "No servant can serve two masters; because, either he will hate the one and love the other, or else he will be loyal to the one and despise the other. You cannot serve God and mammon."

¹⁴ Now the Pharisees, who were covetous, also heard all these things, and they derided Him.

¹⁵ And He said to them, "You are those who justify yourselves before men, but God knows your hearts. Because, what is highly esteemed among men is an abomination in the sight of God.

¹⁶ "The law and the prophets *were* until John. Since that time the kingdom of God has been preached, and everyone is pressing into it.

¹⁷ And it is easier for heaven and earth to pass away than for one tittle of the law to fail.

¹⁸ "Whoever puts away his wife and marries another commits adultery; and whoever marries her who is put away from *her* husband commits adultery.

¹⁹ "There was a certain rich man who was clothed in purple and fine linen and lived lavishly every day.

²⁰ But there was a certain beggar named Lazarus, full of sores, who was laid at his gate,

²¹ and desiring to be fed with the crumbs which fell from the rich man's table. Moreover the dogs came and licked his sores.

²² So it happened that the beggar died, and was carried by the angels to Abraham's bosom. The rich man also died and was buried.

²³ And being in torments in Hell, he lifted up his eyes and saw Abraham afar off, and Lazarus in his bosom.

²⁴ "Then he cried out and said, 'Father Abraham, have mercy on me, and send Lazarus that he may dip the tip of his finger in water and cool my tongue; because I am tormented in this flame.'

²⁵ But Abraham said, 'Son, remember that in your lifetime you received your good things, and likewise Lazarus evil things; but now he is comforted and you are tormented.

²⁶ And besides all this, between us and you there is a great gulf fixed, so that those who want to pass from here to you cannot, nor can those who *want to come* from there pass to us.'

²⁷ "Then he said, 'I beg you therefore, father, that you would send him to my father's house,

²⁸ because, I have five brethren, that he may testify to them, lest they also come to this place of torment.'

²⁹ Abraham said to him, 'They have Moses and the prophets; let them

hear them.'

³⁰ And he said, 'No, father Abraham; but if one went to them from the dead, they will repent.'

³¹ But he said to him, 'If they do not hear Moses and the prophets, neither will they be persuaded though one rise from the dead.' "

CHAPTER 17

¹ Then He said to the disciples, "It is impossible that no offenses should come, but woe to *him* through whom they do come!

² It would be better for him if a millstone were hung around his neck, and he were thrown into the sea, than that he should offend one of these little ones.

³ Take heed to yourselves. If your brother sins against you, rebuke him; and if he repents, forgive him.

⁴ And if he sins against you seven times in a day, and seven times in a day returns to you, saying, 'I repent,' you shall forgive him."

⁵ And the apostles said to the Lord, "Increase our faith."

⁶ But the Lord said, "If you have faith as a mustard seed, you can say to this mulberry tree, 'Be pulled up by the roots and be planted in the sea,' and it would obey you.

⁷ And which of you, having a servant plowing or feeding cattle, shall say to him at the end when he has come in from the field, 'Come at once and sit down to eat'?

⁸ But will he not rather say to him, 'Prepare something for my supper, and gird yourself and serve me until I have eaten and drunk, and afterward you will eat and drink'?

⁹ Does he thank that servant because he did the things that were commanded him? I think not.

¹⁰ So likewise you, when you have done all those things which you are commanded, say, 'We are unprofitable servants. We have done what was our duty to do.' "

¹¹ Now it happened as He went to Jerusalem that He passed through the midst of Samaria and Galilee.

¹² Then as He entered into a certain village, there met Him ten men who were lepers, who stood afar off.

¹³ And they lifted up *their* voices and said, "Jesus, Master, have mercy on us!"

¹⁴ So when He saw *them*, He said to them, "Go, show yourselves to the priests." And so it was that as they went, they were cleansed.

¹⁵ And one of them, when he saw that he was healed, returned, and with a loud voice glorified God,

¹⁶ and fell down on *his* face at His feet, giving Him thanks. And he was a Samaritan.

¹⁷ So Jesus responding said, "Were there not ten cleansed? But where *are* the nine?

¹⁸ There are not any found who returned to give glory to God except this foreigner!"

¹⁹ And He said to him, "Arise, go your way. Your faith has made you well."

²⁰ Now when He was demanded by

the Pharisees when the kingdom of God would come, He answered them and said, "The kingdom of God does not come with observation;

²¹ nor will they say, 'Look here!' or 'Look there!' Because indeed, the kingdom of God is within you."

²² Then He said to the disciples, "The days will come when you will desire to see one of the days of the Son of Man, and you will not see *it*.

²³ And they will say to you, 'See here!' or 'See there!' Do not go after *them* or follow *them*.

²⁴ Because, as the lightning that flashes out of one *part* under heaven shines to the other *part* under heaven, so also the Son of Man will be in His day.

²⁵ But first He must suffer many things and be rejected by this generation.

²⁶ And as it was in the days of Noah, so it will be also in the days of the Son of Man:

²⁷ They ate, they drank, they married wives, they were given in marriage, until the day that Noah entered the ark, and the flood came and destroyed them all.

²⁸ Likewise also, as it was in the days of Lot: They ate, they drank, they bought, they sold, they planted, they built;

²⁹ but on the day that Lot went out of Sodom it rained fire and brimstone from heaven and destroyed *them* all.

³⁰ Even so will it be in the day when the Son of Man is revealed.

³¹ "In that day, he who is on the housetop, and his goods *are* in the house, let him not come down to take them away. And he who is in the field, let him not turn back.

³² Remember Lot's wife.

³³ Whoever seeks to save his life will lose it, and whoever loses his life will preserve it.

³⁴ I tell you, in that night there will be two *men* in one bed: the one will be taken and the other will be left.

³⁵ Two *women* will be grinding together: the one will be taken and the other left.

³⁶ Two *men* will be in the field: the one will be taken and the other left."

³⁷ And they replied and said to Him, "Where, Lord?" So He said to them, "Wherever the body is, there the eagles will be gathered together."

CHAPTER 18

¹ Then He spoke a parable to them, *concluding* that men always ought to pray and not lose heart,

² saying: "There was in a certain city a judge who did not reverence God nor regard man.

³ Now there was a widow in that city; and she came to him, saying, 'Avenge me from my adversary.'

⁴ And he would not for a while; but afterward he said within himself, 'Though I do not reverence God nor regard man,

⁵ yet because this widow troubles me I will avenge her, lest by her

continual coming she weary me.' "

⁶ Then the Lord said, "Hear what the unjust judge said.

⁷ And will God not avenge His own elect who cry out day and night to Him, though He bears long with them?

⁸ I tell you that He will avenge them speedily. Nevertheless, when the Son of Man comes, shall He find faith on the earth?"

⁹ Also He spoke this parable to some who trusted in themselves that they were righteous, and despised others:

¹⁰ "Two men went up to the temple to pray, one a Pharisee and the other a tax collector.

¹¹ The Pharisee stood and prayed to himself like this, 'God, I thank You that I am not like other men *are*, extortioners, unjust, adulterers, or even as this tax collector.

¹² I fast twice a week; I give tithes of all that I possess.'

¹³ And the tax collector, standing afar off, would not so much as raise *his* eyes to heaven, but beat his breast, saying, 'God, be merciful to me a sinner!'

¹⁴ I tell you, this man went down to his house justified *rather* than the other; because, everyone who exalts himself will be humbled, and he who humbles himself will be exalted."

¹⁵ Then they also brought infants to Him that He might touch them; but when *His* disciples saw *it*, they rebuked them.

¹⁶ But Jesus called them to *Him* and said, "Permit little children to come to Me, and do not forbid them; because, of such is the kingdom of God.

¹⁷ Truly, I say to you, whoever does not receive the kingdom of God as a little child will by no means enter it."

¹⁸ Now a certain ruler asked Him, "Good Teacher, what shall I do to inherit eternal life?"

¹⁹ So Jesus said to him, "Why do you call Me good? No one *is* good but One, *that is*, God.

²⁰ You know the commandments: 'Do not commit adultery,' 'Do not murder,' 'Do not steal,' 'Do not bear false witness,' 'Honor your father and your mother.' "

²¹ And he said, "All these things I have kept from my youth up."

²² So when Jesus heard these things, He said to him, "You still lack one thing. Sell all that you have and distribute to the poor, and you will have treasure in heaven; and come, follow Me."

²³ But when he heard this, he became very sorrowful, because he was very rich.

²⁴ And when Jesus saw that he became very sorrowful, He said, "How hard it is for those who have riches to enter the kingdom of God!

²⁵ Because, it is easier for a camel to go through the eye of a needle than for a rich man to enter into the kingdom of God."

²⁶ And those who heard *it* said,

"Who then can be saved?"

²⁷ But He said, "The things which are impossible with men are possible with God."

²⁸ Then Peter said, "See, we have saying, left all and followed You."

²⁹ So He said to them, "Truly, I say to you, there is no one who has left house or parents or brethren or wife or children, for the sake of the kingdom of God,

³⁰ who will not receive many times more in this present time, and in the age to come life everlasting."

³¹ Then He took the twelve to *Himself* and said to them, "Behold, we are going up to Jerusalem, and all things that are written by the prophets concerning the Son of Man will be accomplished.

³² Because, He will be delivered to the Gentiles and will be mocked and insulted and spat upon.

³³ Then they will scourge *Him* and put Him to death. And the third day He will rise again."

³⁴ But they understood none of these things; this saying was hidden from them, and they did not know the things which were spoken.

³⁵ Then it happened, as He was coming near Jericho, that a certain blind man sat by the road begging.

³⁶ And hearing the crowd passing by, he asked what it meant.

³⁷ So they told him that Jesus of Nazareth was passing by.

³⁸ And he shouted out, saying, "Jesus, *You* Son of David, have mercy on me!"

³⁹ Then those who went before warned him that he should be quiet; but he shouted out all the more, "*You* Son of David, have mercy on me!"

⁴⁰ So Jesus stood *still* and commanded him to be brought to Him. And when he had come near, He asked him,

⁴¹ saying, "What do you want Me to do for you?" He said, "Lord, that I may receive my sight."

⁴² Then Jesus said to him, "Receive your sight; your faith has saved you."

⁴³ And immediately he received his sight, and followed Him, glorifying God. And all the people, when they saw *it*, gave praise to God.

CHAPTER 19

¹ Then *Jesus* entered and passed through Jericho.

² Now behold, *there was* a man named Zacchaeus who was a chief tax collector, and he was rich.

³ And he sought to see who Jesus was, but could not because of the crowd, because he was of short stature.

⁴ So he ran ahead and climbed up into a sycamore tree to see Him, because He was going to pass that *way*.

⁵ And when Jesus came to the place, He looked up and saw him, and said to him, "Zacchaeus, make haste and come down, because today I must stay at your house."

⁶ So he made haste and came down, and received Him joyfully.

⁷ But when they saw *it*, they all murmured, saying, "He has gone to be a guest with a man who is a sinner."

⁸ Then Zacchaeus stood and said to the Lord, "Look, Lord, I give half of my goods to the poor; and if I have taken anything from anyone by false accusation, I restore fourfold to *them*."

⁹ And Jesus said to him, "Today salvation has come to this house, because he also is the son of Abraham;

¹⁰ because the Son of Man has come to seek and to save that which was lost."

¹¹ Now as they heard these things, He spoke another parable, because He was near Jerusalem and because they thought the kingdom of God would appear immediately.

¹² Therefore He said: "A certain nobleman went into a distant region to receive for himself a kingdom and to return.

¹³ So he called his ten servants, delivered to them ten minas, and said to them, 'Do business until I come.'

¹⁴ But his citizens hated him, and sent a message after him, saying, 'We will not have this *man* to reign over us.'

¹⁵ "And so it was that when he returned, having received the kingdom, he then commanded these servants, to whom he had given the money, to be called to him, that he might know how much every man had gained by trading.

¹⁶ Then came the first, saying, 'Master, your mina has earned ten minas.'

¹⁷ And he said to him, 'Well done, good servant; because you were faithful in a very little, have authority over ten cities.'

¹⁸ And the second came, saying, 'Master, your mina has earned five minas.'

¹⁹ Likewise he said to him, 'You also be over five cities.'

²⁰ "Then another came, saying, 'Master, look, *here* is your mina, which I have kept put away in a handkerchief.

²¹ Because, I feared you, since you are a harsh man. You collect what you did not lay down, and reap what you did not sow.'

²² And he said to him, 'Out of your own mouth I will judge you, *you* wicked servant. You knew that I was a harsh man, collecting what I did not lay down and reaping what I did not sow.

²³ Why then did you not put my money in the bank, that at my coming I might have collected my own with interest?'

²⁴ "And he said to those who stood by, 'Take the mina from him, and give *it* to him who has ten minas.'

²⁵ (they said to him, 'Master, he has ten minas.')

²⁶ 'Because, I say to you, that to

everyone who has will be given; and from him who does not have, even what he has will be taken away from him.

²⁷ But bring here those enemies of mine, who did not want me to reign over them, and slay them before me.' "

²⁸ When He had said this, He went on ahead, going up to Jerusalem.

²⁹ And it came to pass, when He drew near to Bethphage and Bethany, at the mountain called The Mount of Olives, that He sent two of His disciples,

³⁰ saying, "Go into the village opposite *you*, in which as you enter you will find a colt tied, on which no one has ever sat. Loose it and bring *it here*.

³¹ And if anyone asks you, 'Why are you loosing *it*?' you shall say this to him, 'Because the Lord has need of it.' "

³² So those who were sent went their way and found *it* just as He had said to them.

³³ And as they were loosing the colt, the owners of it said to them, "Why are you loosing the colt?"

³⁴ So they said, "The Lord has need of him."

³⁵ Then they brought him to Jesus. And they threw their clothes on the colt, and they set Jesus on him.

³⁶ And as He went, they spread their clothes on the road.

³⁷ Then, as He was drawing near, that is, already at the descent of the Mount of Olives, the entire multitude of the disciples began to rejoice and praise God with a loud voice for all the mighty works that they had seen,

³⁸ saying: " 'Blessed *is* the King who comes in the name of the LORD!' Peace in heaven and glory in the highest!"

³⁹ And from the crowd some of the Pharisees said to Him, "Teacher, rebuke Your disciples."

⁴⁰ But He replied and said to them, "I tell you that if these should keep silent, the stones would immediately shout out."

⁴¹ Now as He drew near, He saw the city and wept over it,

⁴² saying, "If you had known, even you, especially in this your day, the things *that are* for your peace! But now they are hidden from your eyes.

⁴³ Because, the days will come upon you when your enemies will build an embankment around you, surround you and close you in on every side,

⁴⁴ and level you, and your children within you, to the ground; and they will not leave in you one stone upon another, because you did not know the time of your visitation."

⁴⁵ Then He went into the temple and began to drive out those who sold and those who bought in it,

⁴⁶ saying to them, "It is written, 'My house is a house of prayer,' but you have made it a 'den of thieves.' "

⁴⁷ And He was teaching daily in the temple. But the chief priests, the

scribes, and the leaders of the people sought to destroy Him, ⁴⁸ and were unable to do anything; because all the people were very attentive to hear Him.

CHAPTER 20

¹ Now it happened on one of those days, as He taught the people in the temple and preached the gospel, *that* the chief priests and the scribes, together with the elders, confronted *Him*

² and spoke to Him, saying, "Tell us, by what authority are You doing these things? Or who is he who gave You this authority?"

³ But He answered and said to them, "I also will ask you one thing, then answer Me:

⁴ The baptism of John, was it from heaven or from men?"

⁵ And they reasoned among themselves, saying, "If we say, 'From heaven,' He will say, 'Why then did you not believe him?'

⁶ But if we say, 'From men,' all the people will stone us, because they are persuaded that John was a prophet."

⁷ So they answered that they did not know where *it was* from.

⁸ And Jesus said to them, "Neither will I tell you by what authority I do these things."

⁹ Then He began to tell the people this parable: "A certain man planted a vineyard, leased it to vinedressers, and went into a distant region for a long time.

¹⁰ Now at harvest time he sent a servant to the vinedressers, that they might give him some of the fruit of the vineyard. But the vinedressers beat him and sent *him* away empty handed.

¹¹ And again he sent another servant; and they beat him also, treated *him* shamefully, and sent *him* away empty handed.

¹² And again he sent a third; and they wounded him also and cast *him* out.

¹³ "Then the owner of the vineyard said, 'What shall I do? I will send my beloved son. It may be they will respect *him* when they see him.'

¹⁴ But when the vinedressers saw him, they reasoned among themselves, saying, 'This is the heir. Come, let us kill him, that the inheritance may be ours.'

¹⁵ So they cast him out of the vineyard and killed *him*. Therefore what shall the owner of the vineyard do to them?

¹⁶ He will come and destroy those vinedressers and give the vineyard to others." And when they heard *it* they said, "God forbid!"

¹⁷ Then He looked at them and said, "What then is this that is written: 'The stone which the builders rejected has become the chief cornerstone'?

¹⁸ Whoever falls on that stone will be broken; but on whomever it falls, it will grind him to powder."

¹⁹ And the chief priests and the scribes that very hour sought to lay

hands on Him, but they feared the people, because they perceived He had spoken this parable against them.

²⁰ So they watched *Him*, and sent spies who pretended to be righteous men, that they might seize on His words, in order to deliver Him to the power and the authority of the governor.

²¹ Then they asked Him, saying, "Teacher, we know that You say and teach rightly, and You do not show *any* personal favoritism, but teach the way of God in truth:

²² Is it lawful for us to pay taxes to Caesar or not?"

²³ But He perceived their craftiness, and said to them, "Why do you test Me?

²⁴ Show Me a denarius. Whose image and inscription does it have?" They answered and said, "Caesar's."

²⁵ And He said to them, "Render therefore to Caesar the things that are Caesar's, and to God the things that are God's."

²⁶ But they could not catch Him in His words in the presence of the people. And they marveled at His answer and kept silent.

²⁷ Then some of the Sadducees, who deny that there is a resurrection, came to *Him* and asked Him,

²⁸ saying: "Teacher, Moses wrote to us *that* if a man's brother dies, having a wife, and he dies without children, that his brother should take his wife and raise up offspring for his brother.

²⁹ There were seven brothers. And the first took a wife, and died without children.

³⁰ And the second took her as wife, and he died childless.

³¹ Then the third took her, and in like manner the seven also; and they left no children, and died.

³² Last of all the woman died also.

³³ Therefore, in the resurrection, whose wife of them is she? Because all seven had her as wife."

³⁴ And answering Jesus said to them, "The children of this age marry and are given in marriage.

³⁵ But those who will be counted worthy to attain that age, and the resurrection from the dead, neither marry nor are given in marriage;

³⁶ nor can they die anymore, because, they are equal to the angels and are children of God, being children of the resurrection.

³⁷ But even Moses revealed at the bush that the dead are raised, when he called the Lord 'the God of Abraham, the God of Isaac, and the God of Jacob.'

³⁸ Because, He is not the God of the dead but of the living, because all live to Him."

³⁹ Then some of the scribes replied and said, "Teacher, You have spoken well."

⁴⁰ But after that they dared not ask Him *any more questions*.

⁴¹ And He said to them, "How can they say that the Christ is David's Son?

⁴² Now David himself said in the Book of Psalms: 'The LORD said to my Lord, "Sit at My right hand,

⁴³ until I make Your enemies Your footstool." '

⁴⁴ Therefore David calls Him 'Lord'; how is He then his Son?"

⁴⁵ Then, in the hearing of all the people, He said to His disciples,

⁴⁶ "Beware of the scribes, who desire to go around in long robes, love greetings in the marketplaces, the best seats in the synagogues, and the best places at feasts,

⁴⁷ who devour widows' houses, and for a show make long prayers. These will receive greater damnation."

CHAPTER 21

¹ And He looked up and saw the rich ones putting their gifts into the treasury,

² and He also saw a certain poor widow putting in two mites in there.

³ So He said, "Truly I say to you that this poor widow has put in more than they all have;

⁴ because, all these out of their abundance have put in offerings for God, but she out of her poverty has put in all the livelihood that she had."

⁵ Then, as some spoke of the temple, how it was adorned with beautiful stones and donations, He said,

⁶ "*As for* these things which you see, the days will come in which not one stone will be left upon another that will not be thrown down."

⁷ So they asked Him, saying, "Teacher, but when shall these things be? And what sign *shall there be* when these things are about to take place?"

⁸ And He said: "Take heed that you be not be deceived. Because, many will come in My name, saying, 'I am *Christ*,' and, 'The time has drawn near.' Therefore do not go after them.

⁹ But when you hear of wars and commotions, do not be terrified; because, these things must happen first, but the end *is* not yet."

¹⁰ Then He said to them, "Nation will rise against nation, and kingdom against kingdom.

¹¹ And there will be large earthquakes in various places, and famines and pestilences; and there will be fearful sights and great signs from heaven.

¹² But before all these things, they will lay their hands on you and persecute *you*, delivering *you* up to the synagogues and into prisons; being brought before kings and rulers for My name's sake.

¹³ But it will turn out for you as a testimony.

¹⁴ Therefore settle *it* in your hearts not to meditate beforehand on what you will answer;

¹⁵ because, I will give you a mouth and wisdom which all your adversaries will not be able to contradict or resist.

¹⁶ But you will be betrayed also by parents and brethren, relatives and friends; and *some* of you they will cause to be put to death.

¹⁷ And you will be hated by all *people* for My name's sake.

¹⁸ But not a hair of your head will perish.

¹⁹ By your endurance you possess your souls.

²⁰ "But when you see Jerusalem surrounded by armies, then know that its desolation is near.

²¹ Then let those who are in Judea flee to the mountains, let those who are in the midst of it depart out, and let not those who are in the countryside enter into it.

²² Because these are the days of vengeance, that all things which are written may be fulfilled.

²³ But woe to those who are pregnant and to those who are nursing babes in those days! Because there will be great distress in the land and wrath upon this people.

²⁴ And they will fall by the edge of the sword, and be led away captive into all nations. And Jerusalem will be trampled by Gentiles until the times of the Gentiles are fulfilled.

²⁵ "And there will be signs in the sun, in the moon, and in the stars; and on the earth distress of nations, with perplexity, the sea and the waves roaring;

²⁶ men's hearts failing them from fear and the expectation of those things which are coming on the earth, because the powers of heaven will be shaken.

²⁷ And then they will see the Son of Man coming in a cloud with power and great glory.

²⁸ Now when these things begin to happen, look up and lift up your heads, because your redemption draws near."

²⁹ Then He spoke to them a parable: "Look at the fig tree, and all the trees.

³⁰ When they are already budding, you see and know for yourselves that summer is now near.

³¹ So you also, when you see these things happening, know that the kingdom of God is near.

³² Truly, I say to you, this generation will not pass away until all things take place.

³³ Heaven and earth will pass away, but My words will not pass away.

³⁴ "But take heed to yourselves, lest at any time your hearts be weighed down with over indulgence, drunkenness, and cares of this life, and *so* that Day come upon you unexpectedly.

³⁵ Because, it will come as a snare on all those who dwell on the face of the entire earth.

³⁶ Watch therefore, and pray always that you may be counted worthy to escape all these things that will happen, and to stand before the Son of Man."

³⁷ And in the daytime He was teaching in the temple, but at night He went out and stayed on the

mount that is called *The Mount* of Olives.

³⁸ Then early in the morning all the people came to Him in the temple to hear Him.

CHAPTER 22

¹ Now the Feast of Unleavened Bread drew near, which is called The Passover.

² And the chief priests and the scribes sought how they might kill Him, because they feared the people.

³ Then Satan entered into Judas, surnamed Iscariot, who was numbered among the twelve.

⁴ So he went his way, and communed with the chief priests and captains how he might betray Him to them.

⁵ And they were glad, and covenanted to give him money.

⁶ So he promised and sought opportunity to betray Him to them in the absence of the crowd.

⁷ Then came the Day of unleavened Bread, when the Passover must be killed.

⁸ And He sent Peter and John, saying, "Go and prepare the Passover for us, that we may eat."

⁹ So they said to Him, "Where do You want us to prepare?"

¹⁰ And He said to them, "Behold, when you have entered into the city, a man will meet you carrying a pitcher of water; follow him into the house where he enters.

¹¹ Then you will say to the master of the house, 'The Teacher says to you, "Where is the guest room where I may eat the Passover with My disciples?" '

¹² Then he will show you a large, furnished upper room; there make ready."

¹³ So they went and found it just as He had said to them, and they prepared the Passover.

¹⁴ When the hour had come, He sat down, and the twelve apostles with Him.

¹⁵ Then He said to them, "With *fervent* desire I have desired to eat this Passover with you before I suffer;

¹⁶ because, I say to you, I will no longer eat of it until it is fulfilled in the kingdom of God."

¹⁷ Then He took the cup, and gave thanks, and said, "Take this and divide *it* among yourselves;

¹⁸ because, I say to you, I will not drink of the fruit of the vine until the kingdom of God comes."

¹⁹ And He took bread, gave thanks and broke *it*, and gave it to them, saying, "This is My body which is given for you; do this in remembrance of Me."

²⁰ Likewise also the cup after supper, saying, "This cup *is* the new testament in My blood, which is shed for you.

²¹ But behold, the hand of him who betrays Me *is* with Me on the table.

²² And truly the Son of Man goes as it has been determined, but woe to that man by whom He is betrayed!"

²³ Then they began to question among themselves, which of them it was who would do this thing.

²⁴ Now there was also a dispute among them, as to which of them should be considered the greatest.

²⁵ And He said to them, "The kings of the Gentiles exercise lordship over them, and those who exercise authority over them are called 'benefactors.'

²⁶ But you *shall* not *be* like this; but rather, he who is greatest among you, let him be as the younger, and he who rules as he who serves.

²⁷ Because, who *is* greater, he who sits at the table, or he who serves? *Is* it not he who sits at the table? Yet I am among you as He who serves.

²⁸ "You are those who have continued with Me in My trials.

²⁹ And I appoint to you a kingdom, just as My Father has appointed to Me,

³⁰ that you may eat and drink at My table in My kingdom, and sit upon thrones judging the twelve tribes of Israel."

³¹ And the Lord said, "Simon, Simon! Indeed, Satan has desired *to have* you all, that he may sift *you all* like wheat.

³² But I have prayed for you, that your faith should not fail; and when you are converted, strengthen your brethren."

³³ But he said to Him, "Lord, I am ready to go with You, both to prison and to death."

³⁴ Then He said, "I tell you, Peter, the rooster will not crow this day before you will deny three times that you know Me."

³⁵ And He said to them, "When I sent you without money bag, knapsack, and sandals, did you lack anything?" And they said, "Nothing."

³⁶ Then He said to them, "But now, he who has a money bag, let him take *it*, and likewise *his* knapsack; and he who has no sword, let him sell his coat and buy one.

³⁷ Because, I say to you that this which is written must still be accomplished in Me: 'And He was numbered with the transgressors.' Because the things concerning Me have an end."

³⁸ So they said, "Lord, look, here *are* two swords." And He said to them, "It is enough."

³⁹ And He came out, and went to the Mount of Olives, as He was accustomed, and His disciples also followed Him.

⁴⁰ When He came to the place, He said to them, "Pray that you do not enter into temptation."

⁴¹ And He was withdrawn from them about a stone's throw, and He knelt down and prayed,

⁴² saying, "Father, if You are willing, take this cup away from Me; nevertheless not My will, but Yours, be done."

⁴³ Then an angel appeared to Him from heaven, strengthening Him.

⁴⁴ And being in agony, He prayed more earnestly. Then His sweat be-

came like great drops of blood falling down to the ground.

⁴⁵ When He rose up from prayer, and had come to His disciples, He found them sleeping from sorrow.

⁴⁶ Then He said to them, "Why do you sleep? Rise and pray, lest you enter into temptation."

⁴⁷ And while He was still speaking, behold, a crowd; and he who was called Judas, one of the twelve, went before them and drew near to Jesus to kiss Him.

⁴⁸ But Jesus said to him, "Judas, are you betraying the Son of Man with a kiss?"

⁴⁹ When those around Him saw what was going to happen, they said to Him, "Lord, shall we strike with the sword?"

⁵⁰ And one of them struck the servant of the high priest and cut off his right ear.

⁵¹ But Jesus answered and said, "Proceed thus far, all of you." And He touched his ear and healed him.

⁵² Then Jesus said to the chief priests, captains of the temple, and the elders who had come to Him, "Have you come out, as against a robber, with swords and clubs?

⁵³ When I was with you daily in the temple, you did not stretch your hand out against Me. But this is your hour, and the power of darkness."

⁵⁴ Then they took Him, they led *Him* and brought Him into the high priest's house. But Peter followed at a distance.

⁵⁵ Now when they had kindled a fire in the midst of the courtyard and sat down together, Peter sat among them.

⁵⁶ And a certain servant girl, seeing him as he sat by the fire, looked intently at him and said, "This man was also with Him."

⁵⁷ But he denied Him, saying, "Woman, I do not know Him."

⁵⁸ And after a little while another saw him and said, "You also are of them." But Peter said, "Man, I am not!"

⁵⁹ Then after about an hour had passed, after another confidently affirmed, saying, "Surely this *man* was also with Him, because he is a Galilean."

⁶⁰ Then Peter said, "Man, I do not know what you are saying!" And immediately, while he was still speaking, the rooster crowed.

⁶¹ And the Lord turned and looked at Peter. Then Peter remembered the word of the Lord, how He had said to him, "Before the rooster crows, you will deny Me three times."

⁶² So Peter went out and wept bitterly.

⁶³ Now the men who held Jesus mocked Him and beat Him.

⁶⁴ And having blindfolded Him, they struck Him on the face and asked Him, saying, "Prophesy! Who is it who struck You?"

⁶⁵ And many other things they blasphemously spoke against Him.

⁶⁶ As soon as it was day, the elders

of the people, both chief priests and scribes, came together and led Him into their council, saying,

⁶⁷ "Are You the Christ, tell us." But He said to them, "If I tell you, you will not believe.

⁶⁸ And if I also ask *you*, you will not answer Me or let *Me* go.

⁶⁹ After this the Son of Man will sit on the right hand of the power of God."

⁷⁰ Then they all said, "Are You then the Son of God?" So He said to them, "You say that I am."

⁷¹ And they said, "What further witness do we need? Because we have heard it ourselves from His own mouth."

CHAPTER 23

¹ Then the entire multitude of them arose and led Him to Pilate.

² And they began to accuse Him, saying, "We found this *man* perverting the nation, and forbidding to pay taxes to Caesar, saying that He Himself is Christ, a King."

³ Then Pilate asked Him, saying, "Are You the King of the Jews?" And He answered him and said, "You say it ."

⁴ So Pilate said to the chief priests and *to* the people, "I find no fault in this Man."

⁵ But they were the more fierce, saying, "He stirs up the people, teaching throughout all Jewry, beginning from Galilee to this place."

⁶ When Pilate heard of Galilee, he asked if the Man were a Galilean.

⁷ And as soon as he knew that He belonged to Herod's jurisdiction, he sent Him to Herod, who was himself also in Jerusalem at that time.

⁸ Now when Herod saw Jesus, he was exceedingly glad; because, he had desired for a long *time* to see Him, because he had heard many things about Him, and he had hoped to have seen some miracle done by Him.

⁹ Then he questioned Him with many words, but He answered him nothing.

¹⁰ And the chief priests and scribes stood and vehemently accused Him.

¹¹ Then Herod, with his men of war, treated Him with contempt and mocked *Him*, arrayed Him in a gorgeous robe, and sent Him back to Pilate.

¹² That very day Pilate and Herod became friends with each other, because previously they had been at enmity between themselves.

¹³ Then Pilate, when he had called together the chief priests, the rulers, and the people,

¹⁴ said to them, "You have brought this Man to me, as one who perverts the people. And indeed, having examined *Him* in your presence, I have found no fault in this Man concerning those things of which you accuse Him;

¹⁵ no, neither did Herod, because, I sent you to him; and indeed nothing deserving of death has been done to Him.

¹⁶ I will therefore chastise Him and release *Him*"
¹⁷ (because it was necessary for him to release one to them at the feast).
¹⁸ But they all shouted out at once, saying, "Away with this *Man*, and release to us Barabbas,"
¹⁹ who had been thrown into prison for a certain rebellion made in the city, and for murder.
²⁰ Pilate, therefore, willing to release Jesus, spoke to them again.
²¹ But they shouted out, saying, "Crucify *Him*, crucify Him!"
²² Then he said to them the third time, "Why, what evil has He done? I have found no reason for death in Him. I will therefore chastise Him and let *Him* go."
²³ But they were insistent, demanding with loud voices that He be crucified. And the voices of these men and of the chief priests prevailed.
²⁴ So Pilate gave sentence that it should be as they demanded.
²⁵ And he released to them the one they preferred, who for rebellion and murder had been thrown into prison; but he delivered Jesus to their will.
²⁶ Now as they led Him away, they laid hold of a certain man, Simon a Cyrenian, who was coming from the countryside, and on him they laid the cross that he might carry *it* after Jesus.
²⁷ And a large company of the people followed Him, and women who also mourned and lamented Him.
²⁸ But Jesus, turning to them, said, "Daughters of Jerusalem, do not weep for Me, but weep for yourselves and for your children.
²⁹ Because, indeed the days are coming in which they will say, 'Blessed *are* the barren, the wombs that never bore, and breasts which never nursed!'
³⁰ Then they will begin 'to say to the mountains, "Fall on us!" and to the hills, "Cover us!" '
³¹ Because, if they do these things in the green wood, what will be done in the dry?"
³² There were also two others, criminals, led with Him to be put to death.
³³ And when they had come to the place that is called Calvary, there they crucified Him, and the criminals, one on the right hand and the other on the left.
³⁴ Then Jesus said, "Father, forgive them, because they do not know what they do." And they divided His clothes and cast lots.
³⁵ And the people stood looking on. But the rulers, also with them, ridiculed *Him*, saying, "He saved others; let Him save Himself if He is the Christ, the chosen of God."
³⁶ The soldiers also mocked Him, coming to Him and offering Him vinegar,
³⁷ and saying, "If You are the King of the Jews, save Yourself."
³⁸ And an inscription also was written over Him in letters of

Greek, Latin, and Hebrew: THIS IS THE KING OF THE JEWS.

⁹³⁹ Then one of the criminals who were hanged blasphemed Him, saying, "If You are the Christ, save Yourself and us."

⁴⁰ But the other, responding, rebuked him, saying, "Do you not reverence God, seeing you are under the same condemnation?

⁴¹ And we indeed justly, because we receive the due reward of our deeds; but this Man has done nothing wrong."

⁴² Then he said to Jesus, "Lord, remember me when You come into Your kingdom."

⁴³ And Jesus said to him, "Truly, I say to you, today you will be with Me in Paradise."

⁴⁴ Now it was about the sixth hour, and there was darkness over all the earth until the ninth hour.

⁴⁵ Then the sun was darkened, and the veil of the temple was torn in the middle.

⁴⁶ And when Jesus had shouted out with a loud voice, He said, "Father, 'into Your hands I commit My spirit.' " Having said this, He gave up the spirit.

⁴⁷ So when the centurion saw what had happened, he glorified God, saying, "Certainly this was a righteous Man!"

⁴⁸ And all the people who came together to that sight, seeing what had been done, beat their chests and returned.

⁴⁹ But all His acquaintances, and the women who followed Him from Galilee, stood at a distance, watching these things.

⁵⁰ Now behold, *there was* a man named Joseph, a council member, *and he was* a good and just man. ⁵¹ He had not consented to their decision and deed. He was from Arimathea, a city of the Jews, who himself was also waiting for the kingdom of God.

⁵² This *man* went to Pilate and asked for the body of Jesus.

⁵³ Then he took it down, wrapped it in linen, and laid it in a tomb that was hewn out of the rock, where no one had ever lain before.

⁵⁴ That day was the Preparation, and the Sabbath drew near.

⁵⁵ And the women also who had come with Him from Galilee followed after, and they observed the tomb and how His body was laid.

⁵⁶ Then they returned and prepared spices and fragrant oils. And they rested on the Sabbath according to the commandment.

CHAPTER 24

¹ Now on the first *day* of the week, very early in the morning, they, and certain *others* with them, came to the tomb bringing the spices which they had prepared.

² But they found the stone rolled away from the tomb.

³ Then they went in and did not find the body of the Lord Jesus.

⁴ And it happened, as they were greatly perplexed about this, that

behold, two men stood by them in shining clothing.

⁵ Then, as they were afraid and bowed *their* faces to the earth, they said to them, "Why do you seek the living among the dead?

⁶ He is not here, but is risen! Remember how He spoke to you when He was still in Galilee,

⁷ saying, 'The Son of Man must be delivered into the hands of sinful men, and be crucified, and the third day rise again.' "

⁸ And they remembered His words.

⁹ Then *they* returned from the tomb and told all these things to the eleven and to all the rest.

¹⁰ It was Mary Magdalene, Joanna, Mary *the mother* of James, and the other *women that were* with them, who told these things to the apostles.

¹¹ And their words seemed to them like idle tales, and they did not believe them.

¹² But Peter arose and ran to the tomb; and stooping down, he saw the linen cloths lying by themselves; and departed, marveling to himself at what had happened.

¹³ Now behold, two of them were traveling that same day to a village called Emmaus, which was *about* sixty stadiums from Jerusalem.

¹⁴ And they talked together of all these things which had happened.

¹⁵ And it came to pass, while they conversed and reasoned *together,* that Jesus Himself drew near and went with them.

¹⁶ But their eyes were restrained, so that they did not know Him.

¹⁷ And He said to them, "What kind of conversation *is* this that you have with one another as you walk and are sad?"

¹⁸ Then the one whose name was Cleopas answered and said to Him, "Are You only a stranger in Jerusalem, and have You not known the things that happened there in these days?"

¹⁹ And He said to them, "What things?" So they said to Him, "Concerning Jesus of Nazareth, who was a Prophet mighty in deed and word before God and all the people,

²⁰ and how the chief priests and our rulers delivered Him to be condemned to death, and have crucified Him.

²¹ But we were hoping that it was He who was going to redeem Israel. And besides all this, today is the third day since these things were done.

²² Yes, and certain women also of our company, who arrived at the tomb early, astonished us.

²³ And when they did not find His body, they came saying that they had also seen a vision of angels who said He was alive.

²⁴ And certain of those who were with us went to the tomb and found *it* just as the women had said; but Him they did not see."

²⁵ Then He said to them, "O foolish ones, and slow of heart to believe all that the prophets have spoken!

²⁶ Ought not Christ to have suffered these things and to enter into His glory?"
²⁷ And beginning at Moses and all the Prophets, He expounded to them in all the Scriptures the things concerning Himself.
²⁸ Then they drew near to the village where they were going, and He indicated that He would have gone farther.
²⁹ But they constrained Him, saying, "Stay with us, because it is close to evening, and the day is far spent." And He went in to stay with them.
³⁰ Now it came to pass, as He sat at the table with them, that He took bread, blessed and broke *it*, and gave it to them.
³¹ Then their eyes were opened and they knew Him; and He vanished from their sight.
³² And they said to one another, "Did not our heart burn within us while He talked with us on the road, and while He opened the Scriptures to us?"
³³ So they rose up that very hour and returned to Jerusalem, and found the eleven and those who were with them gathered together,
³⁴ saying, "The Lord is risen indeed, and has appeared to Simon!"
³⁵ And they told about the things *that had happened* on the road, and how He was known to them in the breaking of bread.
³⁶ Now as they said these things, Jesus Himself stood in the midst of them, and said to them, "Peace to you."
³⁷ But they were terrified and frightened, and supposed they had seen a spirit.
³⁸ And He said to them, "Why are you troubled? And why do doubts arise in your hearts?
³⁹ Behold My hands and My feet, that it is Me Myself. Handle Me and see, because a spirit does not have flesh and bones as you see I have."
⁴⁰ When He had said this, He showed them *His* hands and *His* feet.
⁴¹ But while they still did not believe for joy, and marveled, He said to them, "Have you any food here?"
⁴² So they gave Him a piece of a broiled fish and some honeycomb.
⁴³ And He took *it* and ate in their presence.
⁴⁴ Then He said to them, "These *are* the words which I spoke to you while I was still with you, that all things must be fulfilled which were written in the Law of Moses and *in* the Prophets and *in* the Psalms concerning Me."
⁴⁵ And He opened their understanding, that they might understand the Scriptures.
⁴⁶ Then He said to them, "Thus it is written, and thus it was necessary for Christ to suffer and to rise from the dead the third day,
⁴⁷ and that repentance and remission of sins should be preached in His name to all nations, beginning at Jerusalem.

⁴⁸ And you are witnesses of these things.

⁴⁹ And behold, I send the Promise of My Father upon you; but wait in the city of Jerusalem until you are endued with power from on high."

⁵⁰ And He led them out as far as Bethany, and He lifted up His hands and blessed them.

⁵¹ Now it came to pass, while He blessed them, that He was parted from them and carried up into heaven.

⁵² And they worshiped Him, and returned to Jerusalem with great joy,

⁵³ and were continually in the temple praising and blessing God. Amen.

THE GOSPEL ACCORDING TO
JOHN

CHAPTER 1

¹ In the beginning was the Word, and the Word was with God, and the Word was God.

² He was in the beginning with God.

³ All things were made by Him, and without Him nothing was made that was made.

⁴ In Him was life, and the life was the light of men.

⁵ And the light shines in darkness, and the darkness did not comprehend it.

⁶ There was a man sent from God, whose name *was* John.

⁷ This man came for a witness, to bear witness of the Light, that all *men* through him might believe.

⁸ He was not that Light, but *was sent* to bear witness of that Light.

⁹ *That* was the true Light which gives light to every man who comes into the world.

¹⁰ He was in the world, and the world was made by Him, yet the world did not know Him.

¹¹ He came to His own, and His own did not receive Him.

¹² But as many as received Him, to them He gave authority to become the sons of God, *even* to those who believe on His name:

¹³ who were born, not of blood, nor of the will of the flesh, nor of the will of man, but of God.

¹⁴ And the Word was made flesh and dwelt among us, and we beheld His glory, the glory as of the only begotten of the Father, full of grace and truth.

¹⁵ John bore witness of Him and shouted out, saying, "This was He of whom I said, 'He who comes after me is preferred before me, because He was before me.' "

¹⁶ And of His fullness we all have received, and grace for grace.

¹⁷ Because, the law was given through Moses, *but* grace and truth came by Jesus Christ.

¹⁸ No one has seen God at any time. The only begotten Son, who is in the bosom of the Father, He has declared *Him*.

¹⁹ Now this is the record of John, when the Jews sent priests and Levites from Jerusalem to ask him, "Who are you?"

²⁰ And he confessed, and did not deny, but confessed, "I am not the Christ."

²¹ And they asked him, "What then? Are you Elijah?" And he said, "I am not." "Are you the Prophet?" And he answered, "No."

²² Then they said to him, "Who are you, that we may give an answer to those who sent us? What do you say about yourself?"

²³ He said: "I *am* 'the voice of one shouting out in the wilderness: "Make straight the way of the

LORD,'" as the prophet Isaiah said.

²⁴ Now those who were sent were of the Pharisees.

²⁵ And they asked him, and said to him, "Why then do you baptize if you are not the Christ, nor Elijah, nor the Prophet?"

²⁶ John answered them, saying, "I baptize with water, but there stands One among you whom you do not know.

²⁷ It is He who, coming after me, is preferred before me, whose sandal strap I am not worthy to unloose."

²⁸ These things were done in Bethabara beyond Jordan, where John was baptizing.

²⁹ The next day John saw Jesus coming to him, and said, "Behold the Lamb of God, who takes away the sin of the world!

³⁰ This is He of whom I said, 'After me comes a Man who is preferred before me, because He was before me.'

³¹ And I did not know Him; but that He should be revealed to Israel, therefore I came baptizing with water."

³² And John bore record, saying, "I saw the Spirit descending from heaven like a dove, and it remained upon Him.

³³ And I did not know Him, but He who sent me to baptize with water, the same said to me, 'Upon whom you will see the Spirit descending, and remaining on Him, this is He who baptizes with the Holy Spirit.'

³⁴ And I have seen and bare record that this is the Son of God."

³⁵ Again, the next day, after John stood with two of his disciples,

³⁶ looking upon Jesus as He walked, he said, "Behold the Lamb of God!"

³⁷ And the two disciples heard him speak, and they followed Jesus.

³⁸ Then Jesus turned, and saw them following, said to them, "What do you seek?" They said to Him, "Rabbi," (which is to say, when translated, Teacher), "where are You staying?"

³⁹ He said to them, "Come and see." They came and saw where He was staying, and remained with Him that day (because it was about the tenth hour).

⁴⁰ One of the two who heard John *speak*, and followed Him, was Andrew, Simon Peter's brother.

⁴¹ He first found his own brother Simon, and said to him, "We have found the Messiah" (which is translated, the Christ).

⁴² And he brought him to Jesus. And when Jesus looked at him, He said, "You are Simon the son of Jonah. You will be called Cephas," (which is translated, A Stone).

⁴³ The following day Jesus wanted to go to Galilee, and He found Philip, and said to him, "Follow Me."

⁴⁴ Now Philip was of Bethsaida, the city of Andrew and Peter.

⁴⁵ Philip found Nathanael and said to him, "We have found Him, of whom Moses in the law, and the prophets, wrote, Jesus of Nazareth,

the son of Joseph."

⁴⁶ And Nathanael said to him, "Can anything good come out of Nazareth?" Philip said to him, "Come and see."

⁴⁷ Jesus saw Nathanael coming to Him, and said of him, "Behold an Israelite indeed, in whom is no deceit!"

⁴⁸ Nathanael said to Him, "How do You know me?" Jesus answered and said to him, "Before Philip called you, when you were under the fig tree, I saw you."

⁴⁹ Nathanael replied and said to Him, "Rabbi, You are the Son of God! You are the King of Israel!"

⁵⁰ Jesus replied and said to him, "Because I said to you, 'I saw you under the fig tree,' do you believe? You will see greater things than these."

⁵¹ And He said to him, "Truly, truly, I say to you, after this you all will see heaven open, and the angels of God ascending and descending upon the Son of Man."

CHAPTER 2

¹ On the third day there was a wedding in Cana of Galilee, and the mother of Jesus was there.

² Now both Jesus and His disciples were invited to the wedding.

³ And when they ran out of grape juice, the mother of Jesus said to Him, "They have no grape juice."

⁴ Jesus said to her, "Woman, what does your concern have to do with Me? My hour has not yet come."

⁵ His mother said to the servants, "Whatever He says to you, do *it*."

⁶ Now there were set there six waterpots of stone, according to the manner of purification of the Jews, containing two or three measures each.

⁷ Jesus said to them, "Fill the waterpots with water." And they filled them up to the brim.

⁸ And He said to them, "Draw some out now, and take it to the master of the feast." And they took it.

⁹ When the master of the feast had tasted the water that was made grape juice, and did not know where it came from (but the servants who had drawn the water knew), the master of the feast called the bridegroom.

¹⁰ And said to him, "Every man at the beginning sets out the good grape juice, and when the guests fully drink that, then the inferior. *But* you have kept the good grape juice until now!"

¹¹ This beginning of miracles Jesus did in Cana of Galilee, and manifested His glory; and His disciples believed on Him.

¹² After this He went down to Capernaum, He, His mother, His brethren, and His disciples; and they did not stay there many days.

¹³ Now the Passover of the Jews was at hand, and Jesus went up to Jerusalem,

¹⁴ and found in the temple those who sold oxen and sheep and doves, and the money changers

sitting. ¹⁵ And when He had made a whip of small cords, He drove them all out of the temple, with the sheep and the oxen, and poured out the changers' money and overturned the tables.

¹⁶ And He said to those who sold doves, "Take these things away! Do not make My Father's house a house of merchandise!"

¹⁷ Then His disciples remembered that it was written, "The zeal for Your house has eaten Me up."

¹⁸ So the Jews responded and said to Him, "What sign do You show to us, seeing that You do these things?"

¹⁹ Jesus answered and said to them, "Destroy this temple, and in three days I will raise it up."

²⁰ Then the Jews said, "It has taken forty six years to build this temple, and will You raise it up in three days?"

²¹ But He was speaking of the temple of His body.

²² Therefore, when He had risen from the dead, His disciples remembered that He had said this to them; and they believed the Scripture and the word which Jesus had said.

²³ Now when He was in Jerusalem at the Passover, during the feast *day*, many believed in His name when they saw the miracles which He did.

²⁴ But Jesus did not commit Himself to them, because He knew all *men*,

²⁵ and had no need that anyone should testify of man, because He knew what was in man.

CHAPTER 3

¹ There was a man of the Pharisees named Nicodemus, a ruler of the Jews.

² This man came to Jesus by night and said to Him, "Rabbi, we know that You are a teacher come from God; because, no one can do these miracles that You do unless God is with him."

³ Jesus replied and said to him, "Truly, truly, I say to you, unless a man is born again, he cannot see the kingdom of God."

⁴ Nicodemus said to Him, "How can a man be born when he is old? Can he enter a second time into his mother's womb and be born?"

⁵ Jesus answered, "Truly, truly, I say to you, unless a man is born of water and of the Spirit, he cannot enter into the kingdom of God.

⁶ That which is born of the flesh is flesh, and that which is born of the Spirit is spirit.

⁷ Do not marvel that I said to you, 'You all must be born again.'

⁸ The wind blows where it wishes, and you hear the sound of it, but cannot tell where it comes from and where it goes. So is everyone who is born of the Spirit."

⁹ Nicodemus replied and said to Him, "How can these things be?"

¹⁰ Jesus answered and said to him, "Are you the teacher of Israel, and do not know these things?

¹¹ Truly, truly, I say to you, We

speak what We know and testify what We have seen, and you all do not receive Our witness.

¹² If I have told you earthly things and you do not believe, how will you believe if I tell you of heavenly things?

¹³ And no man has ascended up to heaven but He who came down from heaven, *that is*, the Son of Man who is in heaven.

¹⁴ And as Moses lifted up the serpent in the wilderness, even so must the Son of Man be lifted up,

¹⁵ that whoever believes in Him should not perish but have eternal life.

¹⁶ Because God loved the world so much He gave His only begotten Son, that whoever believes in Him would not perish but have everlasting life.

¹⁷ Because, God did not send His Son into the world to condemn the world, but that the world through Him might be saved.

¹⁸ "He who believes on Him is not condemned; but he who does not believe is condemned already, because he has not believed in the name of the only begotten Son of God.

¹⁹ And this is the condemnation, that the light came into the world, and men loved darkness rather than light, because their deeds were evil.

²⁰ Because, everyone who does evil hates the light and does not come to the light, lest his deeds should be exposed.

²¹ But he who does the truth comes to the light, that his deeds may be clearly seen, that they have been done in God."

²² After these things Jesus and His disciples came into the land of Judea, and there He remained with them and baptized.

²³ Now John also was baptizing in Aenon near Salim, because there was a lot of water there. And they came and were baptized.

²⁴ Because John had not yet been thrown into prison.

²⁵ Then there arose a dispute between *some* of John's disciples and the Jews about purification.

²⁶ And they came to John and said to him, "Rabbi, He who was with you beyond the Jordan, to whom you have witnessed of, look, He is baptizing, and everyone is coming to Him!"

²⁷John answered and said, "A man can receive nothing unless it has been given to him from heaven.

²⁸ You yourselves bear me witness, that I said, 'I am not the Christ,' but that, 'I have been sent before Him.'

²⁹ He who has the bride is the bridegroom; but the friend of the bridegroom, who stands and hears him, rejoices greatly because of the bridegroom's voice. Therefore this joy of mine is fulfilled.

³⁰ He must increase, but I *must* decrease.

³¹ He who comes from above is above all; he who is of the earth is

earthly and speaks of the earth. He who comes from heaven is above all.

³² And what He has seen and heard, that He testifies; and no one receives His testimony.

³³ He who has received His testimony has certified that God is true.

³⁴ Because, He whom God has sent speaks the words of God, because God does not give the Spirit by measure to *Him*.

³⁵ The Father loves the Son, and has given all things into His hand.

³⁶ He who believes on the Son has everlasting life; and he who does not believe the Son will not see life, but the wrath of God abides on him."

CHAPTER 4

¹ Therefore, when the Lord knew that the Pharisees had heard that Jesus made and baptized more disciples than John

² (though Jesus Himself did not baptize, but His disciples),

³ He left Judea and departed again to Galilee.

⁴ But He needed to go through Samaria.

⁵ So He came to a city of Samaria which is called Sychar, near the plot of ground that Jacob gave to his son Joseph.

⁶ Now Jacob's well was there. Jesus therefore, being wearied from *His* journey, sat thus on the well. *Now* it was about the sixth hour.

⁷ A woman of Samaria came there to draw water. Jesus said to her, "Give Me a drink."

⁸ Because His disciples had gone away into the city to buy food.

⁹ Then the woman of Samaria said to Him, "How is it that You, being a Jew, ask a drink from me, that is a Samaritan woman?" Because Jews have no dealings with Samaritans.

¹⁰ Jesus answered and said to her, "If you knew the gift of God, and who it is who says to you, 'Give Me a drink,' you would have asked Him, and He would have given you living water."

¹¹ The woman said to Him, "Sir, You have nothing to draw with, and the well is deep. Where then do You get that living water?

¹² Are You greater than our father Jacob, who gave us the well, and drank from it himself, as well as his children and his livestock?"

¹³ Jesus answered and said to her, "Whoever drinks of this water will thirst again,

¹⁴ but whoever drinks of the water that I will give him will never thirst. But the water that I will give him will be in him a fountain of water springing up into everlasting life."

¹⁵ The woman said to Him, "Sir, give me this water, that I may not thirst, nor come here to draw."

¹⁶ Jesus said to her, "Go, call your husband, and come here."

¹⁷ The woman replied and said, "I have no husband." Jesus said to her, "You have said rightly, 'I have no

husband,'
¹⁸ because, you have had five husbands, and the one whom you now have is not your husband; in that you spoke truly."
¹⁹ The woman said to Him, "Sir, I perceive that You are a prophet.
²⁰ Our fathers worshiped on this mountain, and you all say that in Jerusalem is the place where one ought to worship."
²¹ Jesus said to her, "Woman, believe Me, the hour is coming when you will neither on this mountain, nor in Jerusalem, worship the Father.
²² You worship what you do not know; we know what we worship, because salvation is of the Jews.
²³ But the hour is coming, and now is, when the true worshipers will worship the Father in spirit and truth; because the Father is seeking such to worship Him.
²⁴ God *is* a Spirit, and those who worship Him must worship *Him* in spirit and in truth."
²⁵ The woman said to Him, "I know that Messiah is coming who is called Christ. When He comes, He will tell us all things."
²⁶ Jesus said to her, "I who speak to you am He."
²⁷ And at this point His disciples came, and they marveled that He talked with the woman; yet no one said, "What do You seek?" or, "Why are You talking with her?"
²⁸ The woman then left her waterpot, went her way into the city, and said to the men,
²⁹ "Come, see a Man who told me everything that I ever did. Is this not the Christ?"
³⁰ Then they went out of the city and came to Him.
³¹ In the meantime His disciples urged Him, saying, "Teacher, eat."
³² But He said to them, "I have food to eat of which you do not know about."
³³ Therefore the disciples said to one another, "Has anyone brought Him *anything* to eat?"
³⁴ Jesus said to them, "My food is to do the will of Him who sent Me, and to finish His work.
³⁵ Do you not say, 'There are still four months and *then* comes the harvest'? Behold, I say to you, lift up your eyes and look at the fields, because they are already white for harvest!
³⁶ And he who reaps receives wages, and gathers fruit for eternal life, that both he who sows and he who reaps may rejoice together.
³⁷ Because in this the saying is true: 'One sows and another reaps.'
³⁸ I sent you to reap that for which you have not labored; others have labored, and you have entered into their labors."
³⁹ And many of the Samaritans of that city believed on Him because of the word of the woman who testified, "He told me everything that I ever did."
⁴⁰ So when the Samaritans had come to Him, they urged Him to

stay with them; and He stayed there two days.

⁴¹ And many more believed because of His own word.

⁴² Then they said to the woman, "Now we believe, not because of what you said, *but* because we have heard *Him* ourselves and we know that this is indeed the Christ, the Savior of the world."

⁴³ Now after the two days He departed from there and went to Galilee.

⁴⁴ Because, Jesus Himself testified that a prophet has no honor in his own region.

⁴⁵ Then when He came to Galilee, the Galileans received Him, having seen all the things He did in Jerusalem at the feast; because they also had gone to the feast.

⁴⁶ So Jesus came again to Cana of Galilee where He had made the water grape juice. And there was a certain nobleman whose son was sick at Capernaum.

⁴⁷ When he heard that Jesus had come out of Judea into Galilee, he went to Him and implored Him to come down and heal his son, because he was at the point of death.

⁴⁸ Then Jesus said to him, "Unless you see signs and wonders, you all will not believe."

⁴⁹ The nobleman said to Him, "Sir, come down before my child dies!"

⁵⁰ Jesus said to him, "Go your way; your son lives." So the man believed the word that Jesus spoke to him, and he went his way.

⁵¹ And as he was now going down, his servants met him and told *him*, saying, "Your son lives!"

⁵² Then he inquired of them the hour when he began to get better. And they said to him, "Yesterday at the seventh hour the fever left him."

⁵³ So the father knew that *it was* at the same hour in which Jesus said to him, "Your son lives." And he himself believed, and his entire household.

⁵⁴ This again *is* the second miracle *that* Jesus did when He had come out of Judea into Galilee.

CHAPTER 5

¹ After this there was a feast of the Jews, and Jesus went up to Jerusalem.

² Now there is in Jerusalem by the Sheep *Gate* a pool, which is called in the Hebrew language, *Bethesda*, having five porches.

³ In these lay a large crowd of sick people, blind, lame, paralyzed, waiting for the moving of the water.

⁴ Because, an angel went down at a certain time into the pool and stirred up the water; then whoever stepped in first, after the stirring of the water, was made well of whatever disease he had.

⁵ Now a certain man was there who had an infirmity thirty eight years.

⁶ When Jesus saw him lying there, and knew that he already had been

in that condition a long time, He said to him, "Do you want to be made well?"

⁷ The sick man answered Him, "Sir, I have no man to put me into the pool when the water is stirred up; but while I am coming, another steps down before me."

⁸ Jesus said to him, "Rise, take up your bed and walk."

⁹ And immediately the man was made well, took up his bed, and walked. And on the same day was the Sabbath.

¹⁰ The Jews therefore said to him who was cured, "It is the Sabbath day; it is not lawful for you to carry *your* bed."

¹¹ He replied to them, "He who made me well, He said to me, 'Take up your bed and walk.' "

¹² Then they asked him, "Who is the Man who said to you, 'Take up your bed and walk'?"

¹³ But the one who was healed did not know who it was, because Jesus had withdrawn, a crowd being in *that* place.

¹⁴ Afterward Jesus found him in the temple, and said to him, "See, you have been made well. Sin no more, lest a worse thing come upon you."

¹⁵ The man departed and told the Jews that it was Jesus who had made him well.

¹⁶ So therefore the Jews persecuted Jesus, and sought to kill Him, because He had done these things on the Sabbath day.

¹⁷ But Jesus responded to them, "My Father has been working until now, and I work."

¹⁸ Therefore the Jews sought all the more to kill Him, because He not only broke the Sabbath, but also said that God was His Father, making Himself equal with God.

¹⁹ Then Jesus responded and said to them, "Truly, truly, I say to you, the Son can do nothing of Himself, but what He sees the Father do; because whatever He does, the Son also does in like manner.

²⁰ Because, the Father loves the Son, and shows Him all things that He Himself does; and He will show Him greater works than these, that you may marvel.

²¹ Because, as the Father raises the dead and gives life *to them*, even so the Son gives life to whom He will.

²² Because, the Father judges no one, but has committed all judgment to the Son,

²³ that everyone should honor the Son just as they honor the Father. He who does not honor the Son does not honor the Father who sent Him.

²⁴ "Truly, truly, I say to you, he who hears My word and believes on Him who sent Me has everlasting life, and will not come into condemnation, but has passed from death into life.

²⁵ Truly, truly, I say to you, the hour is coming, and now is, when the dead will hear the voice of the Son of God; and those who hear will live.

²⁶ Because, as the Father has life in

Himself, so He has granted the Son to have life in Himself,

²⁷ and has given Him authority to execute judgment also, because He is the Son of Man.

²⁸ Do not marvel at this; because, the hour is coming in which all who are in the graves will hear His voice

²⁹ and will come forth; those who have done good, to the resurrection of life, and those who have done evil, to the resurrection of damnation.

³⁰ I can of Myself do nothing. As I hear, I judge; and My judgment is righteous, because I do not seek My own will but the will of the Father who has sent Me.

³¹ "If I bear witness of Myself, My witness is not true.

³² There is another who bears witness of Me, and I know that the witness which He witnesses of Me is true.

³³ You sent to John, and he has borne witness to the truth.

³⁴ Yet I do not receive testimony from man, but I say these things that you may be saved.

³⁵ He was the burning and shining lamp, and you were willing for a time to rejoice in his light.

³⁶ But I have a greater witness than John's; because, the works which the Father has given Me to finish, the same works that I do, bear witness of Me, that the Father has sent Me.

³⁷ And the Father Himself, who has sent Me, has testified of Me. You have neither heard His voice at any time, nor seen His form.

³⁸ And you do not have His word abiding in you, because whom He sent, Him you do not believe.

³⁹ Search the Scriptures, because in them you think you have eternal life; and these are they which testify of Me.

⁴⁰ But you are not willing to come to Me that you may have life.

⁴¹ "I do not receive honor from men.

⁴² But I know you, that you do not have the love of God in you.

⁴³ I have come in My Father's name, and you do not receive Me; if another comes in his own name, him you will receive.

⁴⁴ How can you believe, who receive honor from one another, and do not seek the honor that *comes* from God alone?

⁴⁵ Do not think that I will accuse you to the Father; there is *one* who accuses you, *that is* Moses, in whom you trust.

⁴⁶ Because, if you believed Moses, you would believe Me; because he wrote about Me.

⁴⁷ But if you do not believe his writings, how shall you believe My words?"

CHAPTER 6

¹ After these things Jesus went over the Sea of Galilee, which is *the* Sea of Tiberias.

² Then a large crowd followed Him, because they saw His miracles

which He performed on those who were diseased.

³ And Jesus went up on the mountain, and there He sat with His disciples.

⁴ Now the Passover, a feast of the Jews, was near.

⁵ Then Jesus lifted up *His* eyes, and seeing a large crowd coming toward Him, He said to Philip, "Where shall we buy bread, that these may eat?"

⁶ But this He said to test him, because He Himself knew what He would do.

⁷ Philip answered Him, "Two hundred denarii worth of bread is not sufficient for them, that every one of them may have a little."

⁸ One of His disciples, Andrew, Simon Peter's brother, said to Him,

⁹ "There is a boy here who has five barley loaves and two small fish, but what are they among so many?"

¹⁰ Then Jesus said, "Make the men sit down." Now there was a lot of grass in the place. So the men sat down, in number about five thousand.

¹¹ And Jesus took the loaves, and when He had given thanks He distributed them to the disciples, and the disciples to those who were sitting down; and likewise of the fish, as much as they wanted.

¹² So when they were filled, He said to His disciples, "Gather up the fragments that remain, so that nothing is lost."

¹³ Therefore they gathered *them* up, and filled twelve baskets with the fragments of the five barley loaves which were left over by those who had eaten.

¹⁴ Then those men, when they had seen the miracle that Jesus did, said, "This is truly that Prophet who is to come into the world."

¹⁵ Therefore when Jesus perceived that they were about to come and take Him by force to make Him king, He departed again to the mountain by Himself alone.

¹⁶ Now when evening came, His disciples went down to the sea,

¹⁷ got into a boat, and went over the sea toward Capernaum. And it was already dark, and Jesus had not come to them.

¹⁸ Then the sea arose because a great wind was blowing.

¹⁹ So when they had rowed about twenty or thirty stadiums they saw Jesus walking on the sea and drawing near the boat; and they were afraid.

²⁰ But He said to them, "It is Me; do not be afraid."

²¹ Then they willingly received Him into the boat, and immediately the boat was at the land where they were going.

²² On the following day, when the people who were standing on the other side of the sea saw that there was no other boat there, except that one which His disciples had entered, and that Jesus had not entered the boat with His disciples, but *that* His disciples had gone away

alone;

²³ (however, other boats came from Tiberias, near the place where they ate bread after the Lord had given thanks)

²⁴ therefore when the people saw that Jesus was not there, nor His disciples, they also got into boats and came to Capernaum, seeking Jesus.

²⁵ And when they found Him on the other side of the sea, they said to Him, "Rabbi, when did You come here?"

²⁶ Jesus answered them and said, "Truly, truly, I say to you, you seek Me, not because you saw the miracles, but because you ate of the loaves and were filled.

²⁷ Do not labor for the food which perishes, but for the food which endures to everlasting life, which the Son of Man will give you, because God the Father has set His seal on Him."

²⁸ Then they said to Him, "What shall we do, that we may work the works of God?"

²⁹ Jesus answered and said to them, "This is the work of God, that you believe on Him whom He has sent."

³⁰ Therefore they said to Him, "What sign shall You perform then, that we may see it and believe You? What work shall You do?

³¹ Our fathers ate the manna in the desert; as it is written, 'He gave them bread from heaven to eat.' "

³² Then Jesus said to them, "Truly, truly, I say to you, Moses did not give you the bread from heaven, but My Father gives you the true bread from heaven.

³³ Because, the bread of God is He who comes down from heaven and gives life to the world."

³⁴ Then they said to Him, "Lord, give us this bread always."

³⁵ And Jesus said to them, "I am the bread of life. He who comes to Me will never hunger, and he who believes on Me will never thirst.

³⁶ But I said to you that you have seen Me and yet do not believe.

³⁷ All that the Father gives Me will come to Me, and the one who comes to Me I will by no means cast out.

³⁸ Because, I came down from heaven, not to do My own will, but the will of Him who sent Me.

³⁹ And this is the will of the Father who sent Me, that of all He has given Me I should lose nothing, but should raise it up again at the last day.

⁴⁰ And this is the will of Him who sent Me, that everyone who sees the Son and believes on Him may have everlasting life; and I will raise him up at the last day."

⁴¹ The Jews then complained about Him, because He said, "I am the bread which came down from heaven."

⁴² And they said, "Is not this Jesus, the son of Joseph, whose father and mother we know? How is it then that He says, 'I came down from heaven'?"

⁴³ Jesus therefore responded and

said to them, "Do not murmur among yourselves.

⁴⁴ No one can come to Me unless the Father who sent Me draws him; and I will raise him up at the last day.

⁴⁵ It is written in the prophets, 'And they will all be taught by God.' Therefore everyone who has heard and learned from the Father comes to Me.

⁴⁶ Not that anyone has seen the Father, except He who is from God; He has seen the Father.

⁴⁷ Truly, truly, I say to you, he who believes on Me has everlasting life.

⁴⁸ I am the bread of life.

⁴⁹ Your fathers ate the manna in the wilderness, and are dead.

⁵⁰ This is the bread which comes down from heaven, that one may eat of it and not die.

⁵¹ I am the living bread which came down from heaven. If anyone eats of this bread, he will live forever; and the bread that I will give is My flesh, which I will give for the life of the world."

⁵² The Jews therefore disputed among themselves, saying, "How can this Man give us His flesh to eat?"

⁵³ Then Jesus said to them, "Truly, truly, I say to you, unless you eat the flesh of the Son of Man and drink His blood, you have no life in you.

⁵⁴ Whoever eats My flesh and drinks My blood has eternal life, and I will raise him up at the last day.

⁵⁵ Because My flesh is food indeed, and My blood is drink indeed.

⁵⁶ He who eats My flesh and drinks My blood abides in Me, and I in him.

⁵⁷ As the living Father has sent Me, and I live because of the Father, so he who eats Me will live because of Me.

⁵⁸ This is the bread which came down from heaven; not as your fathers ate the manna, and are dead. He who eats this bread will live forever."

⁵⁹ These things He said in the synagogue as He taught in Capernaum.

⁶⁰ Therefore many of His disciples, when they heard *this*, said, "This is a hard saying; who can understand it?"

⁶¹ When Jesus knew in Himself that His disciples complained about this, He said to them, "Does this offend you?

⁶² *What* then if you should see the Son of Man ascend up where He was before?

⁶³ It is the Spirit who gives life; the flesh profits nothing. The words that I speak to you, *they* are spirit, and *they* are life.

⁶⁴ But there are some of you who do not believe." Because, Jesus knew from the beginning who they were who did not believe, and who would betray Him.

⁶⁵ And He said, "Therefore I have said to you that no one can come to Me unless it has been granted to him by My Father."

⁶⁶ From that *time* many of His disciples went back and walked with Him no longer.

⁶⁷ Then Jesus said to the twelve, "Do you also want to go away?"

⁶⁸ But Simon Peter answered Him, "Lord, to whom shall we go? You have the words of eternal life.

⁶⁹ Also we believe and are convinced that You are the Christ, the Son of the living God."

⁷⁰ Jesus replied to them, "Did I not choose you twelve, and one of you is a devil?"

⁷¹ He spoke of Judas Iscariot, *the son* of Simon, because it was he who would betray Him, being one of the twelve.

CHAPTER 7

¹ After these things Jesus walked in Galilee; because, He did not want to walk in Judea, because the Jews sought to kill Him.

² Now the Jews' Feast of Tabernacles was at hand.

³ His brethren therefore said to Him, "Depart from here and go into Judea, that Your disciples also may see the works that You are doing.

⁴ Because, no one does anything in secret while he himself seeks to be known openly. If You do these things, show Yourself to the world."

⁵ Because even His brethren did not believe in Him.

⁶ Then Jesus said to them, "My time has not yet come, but your time is always ready.

⁷ The world cannot hate you, but it hates Me because I testify of it that its works are evil.

⁸ You go up to this feast. I am not going up to this feast yet, because My time has not yet fully come."

⁹ When He had said these words to them, He remained in Galilee.

¹⁰ But when His brethren had gone up, then He also went up to the feast, not openly, but as it were in secret.

¹¹ Then the Jews sought Him at the feast, and said, "Where is He?"

¹² And there was much murmuring among the people concerning Him. Because, some said, "He is a good Man"; others said, "No, but He deceives the people."

¹³ However, no one spoke openly of Him for fear of the Jews.

¹⁴ Now about the middle of the feast Jesus went up into the temple and taught.

¹⁵ And the Jews marveled, saying, "How does this Man know letters, having never studied?"

¹⁶ Jesus answered them and said, "My doctrine is not Mine, but His who sent Me.

¹⁷ If anyone will do His will, he will know concerning the doctrine, whether it is from God or *whether* I speak from Myself.

¹⁸ He who speaks from himself seeks his own glory; but He who seeks the glory of the One who sent Him is true, and no unrighteousness is in Him.

¹⁹ Did not Moses give you the law,

and yet none of you keeps the law? Why do you seek to kill Me?"

²⁰ The people answered and said, "You have a demon. Who is seeking to kill You?"

²¹ Jesus answered and said to them, "I did one work, and you all marvel.

²² Moses therefore gave you circumcision (not that it is from Moses, but from the fathers), and you circumcise a man on the Sabbath day.

²³ If a man receives circumcision on the Sabbath day, so that the law of Moses should not be broken, are you angry with Me because I made a man completely well on the Sabbath day?

²⁴ Do not judge according to appearance, but judge with righteous judgment."

²⁵ Now some of them from Jerusalem said, "Is this not He whom they seek to kill?

²⁶ But look! He speaks boldly, and they say nothing to Him. Do the rulers actually know that this is truly the Christ?

²⁷ However, we know where this Man is from; but when the Christ comes, no one knows where He is from."

²⁸ Then Jesus shouted out, as He taught in the temple, saying, "You both know Me, and you know where I am from; and I have not come of Myself, but He who sent Me is true, whom you do not know.

²⁹ But I know Him, because I am from Him, and He sent Me."

³⁰ Therefore they sought to take Him; but no one laid hands on Him, because His hour had not yet come.

³¹ And many of the people believed on Him, and said, "When the Christ comes, will He do more miracles than these which this *Man* has done?"

³² The Pharisees heard the people murmuring these things concerning Him, and the Pharisees and the chief priests sent officers to take Him.

³³ Then Jesus said to them, "I will be with you a little while longer, and *then* I go to Him who sent Me.

³⁴ You will seek Me and not find *Me*, and where I am, there you cannot come."

³⁵ Then the Jews said among themselves, "Where does He intend to go that we will not find Him? Does He intend to go to the Dispersion among the Gentiles and teach the Gentiles?

³⁶ What is this thing that He said, 'You shall seek Me and not find *Me*, and where I am, *there* you cannot come'?"

³⁷ During the last day, that great day of the feast, Jesus stood and shouted out saying, "If anyone thirsts, let him come to Me and drink.

³⁸ He who believes on Me, as the Scripture has said, out of his belly will flow rivers of living water."

³⁹ But this He spoke concerning the Spirit, whom those believing on Him would receive; because, the

Holy Spirit was not yet *given*, because Jesus was not yet glorified.

⁴⁰ Therefore many from the people, when they heard this saying, said, "Truly this is the Prophet."

⁴¹ Others said, "This is the Christ." But some said, "Shall the Christ come out of Galilee?

⁴² Has not the Scripture said that the Christ comes from the seed of David and from the town of Bethlehem, where David was?"

⁴³ So there was a division among the people because of Him.

⁴⁴ Now some of them wanted to take Him, but no one laid hands on Him.

⁴⁵ Then the officers came to the chief priests and Pharisees, and they said to them, "Why have you not brought Him?"

⁴⁶ The officers answered, "No man ever spoke like this Man!"

⁴⁷ Then the Pharisees replied to them, "Are you also deceived?

⁴⁸ Have any of the rulers or the Pharisees believed on Him?

⁴⁹ But these people that do not know the law are accursed."

⁵⁰ Nicodemus (he who came to Jesus by night, being one of them) said to them,

⁵¹ "Does our law judge a man before it hears him and knows what he is doing?"

⁵² They answered and said to him, "Are you also from Galilee? Search and look, because no prophet has arisen out of Galilee."

⁵³ And everyone went to his own house.

CHAPTER 8

¹ Jesus went to the Mount of Olives.

² Now early in the morning He came again into the temple, and all the people came to Him; and He sat down and taught them.

³ Then the scribes and Pharisees brought to Him a woman caught in adultery. And when they had set her in the midst,

⁴ they said to Him, "Teacher, this woman was caught in adultery, in the very act.

⁵ Now Moses, in the law, commanded us that such should be stoned. But what do You say?"

⁶ This they said, testing Him, that they might have something of which to accuse Him. But Jesus stooped down and wrote on the ground with *His* finger, as though He did not hear them.

⁷ So when they continued asking Him, He raised Himself up and said to them, "He who is without sin among you, let him throw a stone at her first."

⁸ And again He stooped down and wrote on the ground.

⁹ Then those who heard it, being convicted by *their own* conscience, went out one by one, beginning with the oldest *even* to the last. And Jesus was left alone, and the woman standing in the midst.

¹⁰ When Jesus had lifted Himself up and saw no one but the woman, He said to her, "Woman, where are

those accusers of yours? Has no one condemned you?"

¹¹ She said, "No one, Lord." And Jesus said to her, "Neither do I condemn you; go and sin no more."

¹² Then Jesus spoke to them again, saying, "I am the light of the world. He who follows Me will not walk in darkness, but will have the light of life."

¹³ The Pharisees therefore said to Him, "You bear record of Yourself; Your record is not true."

¹⁴ Jesus replied and said to them, "Though I bear record of Myself, *yet* My record is true, because, I know where I came from and where I am going; but you do not know where I come from and where I am going.

¹⁵ You judge according to the flesh; I judge no one.

¹⁶ And yet if I judge, My judgment is true; because I am not alone, but I and the Father who sent Me.

¹⁷ It is also written in your law that the testimony of two men is true.

¹⁸ I am One who bears witness of Myself, and the Father who sent Me bears witness of Me."

¹⁹ Then they said to Him, "Where is Your Father?" Jesus answered, "You know neither Me nor My Father. If you had known Me, you would have known My Father also."

²⁰ These words Jesus spoke in the treasury, as He taught in the temple; and no one laid hands on Him, because His hour had not yet come.

²¹ The Jesus said to them again, "I am going my way, and you will seek Me, and will die in your sins. Where I go you cannot come."

²² So the Jews said, "Shall He kill Himself, because He says, 'Where I go you cannot come'?"

²³ And He said to them, "You are from beneath; I am from above. You are of this world; I am not of this world.

²⁴ Therefore I said to you that you will die in your sins; because, if you do not believe that I am *He*, you will die in your sins."

²⁵ Then they said to Him, "Who are You?" And Jesus said to them, "Just what I have been saying to you from the beginning.

²⁶ I have many things to say and to judge concerning you, but He who sent Me is true; and I speak to the world those things which I heard from Him."

²⁷ They did not understand that He spoke to them of the Father.

²⁸ Then Jesus said to them, "When you lift up the Son of Man, then you will know that I am *He*, and *that* I do nothing of Myself; but as My Father has taught Me, I speak these things.

²⁹ And He who sent Me is with Me. The Father has not left Me alone, because I always do those things that please Him."

³⁰ As He spoke these words, many believed on Him.

³¹ Then Jesus said to those Jews who believed on Him, "If you continue in My word, *then* you are My disciples indeed.

³² And you will know the truth, and the truth will make you free."

³³ They replied to Him, "We are Abraham's descendants, and have never been in bondage to anyone. How can You say, 'You will be made free'?"

³⁴ Jesus answered them, "Truly, truly, I say to you, whoever commits sin is a servant of sin.

³⁵ And a servant does not abide in the house forever, *but* the Son abides forever.

³⁶ Therefore if the Son makes you free, you will be free indeed.

³⁷ "I know that you are Abraham's seed, but you seek to kill Me, because My word has no place in you.

³⁸ I speak what I have seen with My Father, and you do what you have seen with your father."

³⁹ They replied and said to Him, "Abraham is our father." Jesus said to them, "If you were Abraham's children, you would do the works of Abraham.

⁴⁰ But now you seek to kill Me, a Man who has told you the truth which I heard from God. Abraham did not do this.

⁴¹ You do the deeds of your father." Then they said to Him, "We were not born of fornication; we have one Father, *even* God."

⁴² Jesus said to them, "If God were your Father, you would love Me, because, I proceeded forth and came from God; nor have I come of Myself, but He sent Me.

⁴³ Why do you not understand My speech? *That is* because you are not able to hear My word.

⁴⁴ You are of *your* father the devil, and the desires of your father you will do. He was a murderer from the beginning, and did not abide in the truth, because there is no truth in him. When he speaks a lie, he speaks from his own resources, because he is a liar and the father of it.

⁴⁵ And because I tell *you* the truth, you do not believe Me.

⁴⁶ Which of you convicts Me of sin? And if I tell the truth, why do you not believe Me?

⁴⁷ He who is of God hears God's words; therefore you do not hear *them*, because you are not of God."

⁴⁸ Then the Jews replied and said to Him, "Do we not say rightly that You are a Samaritan and have a demon?"

⁴⁹ Jesus answered, "I do not have a demon; but I honor My Father, and you dishonor Me.

⁵⁰ And I do not seek My own glory; there is One who seeks and judges.

⁵¹ Truly, truly, I say to you, if anyone keeps My word he will never see death."

⁵² Then the Jews said to Him, "Now we know that You have a demon! Abraham is dead, and the prophets; and You say, 'If anyone keeps My word he will never taste death.'

⁵³ Are You greater than our father Abraham, who is dead? And the prophets are dead. Who do You

make Yourself out to be?"

⁵⁴ Jesus answered, "If I honor Myself, My honor is nothing. It is My Father who honors Me, of whom you say that He is your God.

⁵⁵ Yet you have not known Him, but I know Him. And if I should say, 'I do not know Him,' I would be a liar like you; but I do know Him and keep His word.

⁵⁶ Your father Abraham rejoiced to see My day, and he saw *it* and was glad."

⁵⁷ Then the Jews said to Him, "You are not yet fifty years old, and have You seen Abraham?"

⁵⁸ Jesus said to them, "Truly, truly, I say to you, before Abraham was, I AM."

⁵⁹ Then they took up stones to throw at Him; but Jesus hid Himself and went out of the temple, going through the midst of them, and so passed by.

CHAPTER 9

¹ Now as *Jesus* passed by, He saw a man who was blind from *his* birth.

² And His disciples asked Him, saying, "Teacher, who sinned, this man or his parents, that he was born blind?"

³ Jesus answered, "Neither this man nor his parents sinned, but that the works of God should be revealed in him.

⁴ I must work the works of Him who sent Me while it is day; the night is coming when no one can work.

⁵ As long as I am in the world, I am the light of the world."

⁶ When He had said these things, He spat on the ground and made clay with the saliva; and He anointed the eyes of the blind man with the clay.

⁷ And He said to him, "Go, wash in the pool of Siloam" (which is translated, Sent). So he went and washed, and returned seeing.

⁸ Therefore the neighbors and those who previously had seen that he was blind said, "Is not this he who sat and begged?"

⁹ Some said, "This is he." Others *said*, "He is like him." *But* he said, "I am he."

¹⁰ Therefore they said to him, "How were your eyes opened?"

¹¹ He answered and said, "A Man who is called Jesus made clay and anointed my eyes and said to me, 'Go to the pool of Siloam and wash.' So I went and washed, and I received sight."

¹² Then they said to him, "Where is He?" He said, "I do not know."

¹³ They brought him who formerly was blind to the Pharisees.

¹⁴ Now it was a Sabbath day when Jesus made the clay and opened his eyes.

¹⁵ Then the Pharisees also asked him again how he had received his sight. He said to them, "He put clay on my eyes, and I washed, and I see."

¹⁶ Therefore some of the Pharisees said, "This Man is not from God, because He does not keep the Sabbath day." Others said, "How

can a man who is a sinner do such miracles?" And there was a division among them.

¹⁷ They said to the blind man again, "What do you say about Him because He opened your eyes?" He said, "He is a prophet."

¹⁸ But the Jews did not believe concerning him, that he had been blind and received his sight, until they called the parents of him who had received his sight.

¹⁹ And they asked them, saying, "Is this your son, who you say was born blind? How then does he now see?"

²⁰ His parents answered them and said, "We know that this is our son, and that he was born blind;

²¹ but by what means he now sees we do not know, or who opened his eyes we do not know. He is of age; ask him. He will speak for himself."

²² His parents said these *things* because they feared the Jews, because, the Jews had agreed already that if anyone confessed that He was Christ, he would be put out of the synagogue.

²³ Therefore his parents said, "He is of age; ask him."

²⁴ So they again called the man who was blind, and said to him, "Give God the praise! We know that this Man is a sinner."

²⁵ He replied and said, "Whether He is a sinner *or not* I do not know. One thing I know: that though I was blind, now I see."

²⁶ Then they said to him again, "What did He do to you? How did He open your eyes?"

²⁷ He answered them, "I have told you already, and you did not listen. Why do you want to hear it again? Do you also want to become His disciples?"

²⁸ Then they reviled him and said, "You are His disciple, but we are Moses' disciples.

²⁹ We know that God spoke to Moses; *as* for this *fellow*, we do not know where He is from."

³⁰ The man responded and said to them, "Why, this is a marvelous thing, that you do not know where He is from; and *yet* He has opened my eyes!

³¹ Now we know that God does not hear sinners; but if anyone is a worshiper of God and does His will, He hears him.

³² Since the world began it has been unheard of that anyone opened the eyes of one who was born blind.

³³ If this Man were not from God, He could do nothing."

³⁴ They replied and said to him, "You were completely born in sins, and are you teaching us?" And they threw him out.

³⁵ Jesus heard that they had thrown him out; and when He had found him, He said to him, "Do you believe on the Son of God?"

³⁶ He answered and said, "Who is He, Lord, that I may believe on Him?"

³⁷ And Jesus said to him, "You have both seen Him and it is He who is talking with you."

[38] Then he said, "Lord, I believe!" And he worshiped Him.

[39] And Jesus said, "For judgment I have come into this world, that those who do not see may see, and that those who see may be made blind."

[40] Then *some* of the Pharisees who were with Him heard these words, and said to Him, "Are we blind also?"

[41] Jesus said to them, "If you were blind, you would have no sin; but now you say, 'We see.' Therefore your sin remains."

CHAPTER 10

[1] "Truly, truly, I say to you, he who does not enter the sheepfold by the door, but climbs up some other way, the same is a thief and a robber.

[2] But he who enters by the door is the shepherd of the sheep.

[3] To him the doorkeeper opens, and the sheep hear his voice; and he calls his own sheep by name and leads them out.

[4] And when he brings out his own sheep, he goes before them; and the sheep follow him, because they know his voice.

[5] Yet they will not follow a stranger, but will flee from him, because they do not know the voice of strangers."

[6] Jesus spoke this parable to them, but they did not understand those things which He spoke to them.

[7] Then Jesus said to them again, "Truly, truly, I say to you, I am the door of the sheep.

[8] All who ever came before Me are thieves and robbers, but the sheep did not hear them.

[9] I am the door. If anyone enters by Me, he will be saved, and will go in and out and find pasture.

[10] The thief does not come except to steal, and to kill, and to destroy. I have come that they may have life, and that they may have *it* more abundantly.

[11] "I am the good shepherd. The good shepherd gives His life for the sheep.

[12] But he who is a hireling, and is not the shepherd, who does not own the sheep, sees the wolf coming and leaves the sheep and flees; and the wolf catches them and scatters the sheep.

[13] The hireling flees because he is a hireling and does not care for the sheep.

[14] I am the good shepherd; and know My *sheep*, and am known by My own.

[15] As the Father knows Me, even so I know the Father; and I lay down My life for the sheep.

[16] And other sheep I have which are not of this fold; them also I must bring, and they will hear My voice; and there will be one fold *and* one shepherd.

[17] "Therefore My Father loves Me, because I lay down My life that I may take it again.

[18] No one takes it from Me, but I lay

it down of Myself. I have authority to lay it down, and I have authority to take it again. This command I have received from My Father."

¹⁹ Therefore there was a division again among the Jews because of these sayings.

²⁰ And many of them said, "He has a demon and is mad. Why do you listen to Him?"

²¹ Others said, "These are not the words of one who has a demon. Can a demon open the eyes of the blind?"

²² Now it was the Feast of Dedication in Jerusalem, and it was winter.

²³ And Jesus walked in the temple, in Solomon's porch.

²⁴ Then the Jews surrounded Him and said to Him, "How long do You keep us in doubt? If You are the Christ, tell us plainly."

²⁵ Jesus answered them, "I told you, and you do not believe. The works that I do in My Father's name, they bear witness of Me.

²⁶ But you do not believe, because you are not of My sheep, as I said to you.

²⁷ My sheep hear My voice, and I know them, and they follow Me.

²⁸ And I give them eternal life, and they will never perish; neither will anyone snatch them out of My hand.

²⁹ My Father, who has given *them* to Me, is greater than all; and no *one* is able to snatch *them* out of My Father's hand.

³⁰ I and My Father are one."

³¹ Then the Jews took up stones again to stone Him.

³² Jesus responded to them, "Many good works I have shown you from My Father. For which of those works do you stone Me?"

³³ The Jews answered Him, saying, "For a good work we do not stone You, but for blasphemy, and because You, being a Man, make Yourself God."

³⁴ Jesus replied to them, "Is it not written in your law, 'I said, "You are gods" '?

³⁵ If He called them gods, to whom the word of God came, and the Scripture cannot be broken,

³⁶ do you say of Him whom the Father has sanctified and sent into the world, 'You are blaspheming,' because I said, 'I am the Son of God'?

³⁷ If I do not do the works of My Father, do not believe Me;

³⁸ but if I do, though you do not believe Me, believe the works, that you may know and believe that the Father is in Me, and I in Him."

³⁹ Therefore they sought again to seize Him, but He escaped out of their hand.

⁴⁰ And He went away again beyond the Jordan to the place where John was baptizing at first, and there He stayed.

⁴¹ Then many came to Him and said, "John performed no miracle, but all the things that John spoke about this Man are true."

⁴² And many believed on Him there.

CHAPTER 11

¹ Now a certain *man* was sick, *named* Lazarus, of Bethany, the town of Mary and her sister Martha.

² It was that Mary who anointed the Lord with fragrant oil and wiped His feet with her hair, whose brother Lazarus was sick.

³ Therefore the sisters sent to Him, saying, "Lord, behold, he whom You love is sick."

⁴ When Jesus heard *that*, He said, "This sickness is not to death, but for the glory of God, that the Son of God may be glorified through it."

⁵ Now Jesus loved Martha and her sister and Lazarus.

⁶ So, when He heard that he was sick, He stayed two more days in the place where He was.

⁷ Then after this He said to *His* disciples, "Let us go to Judea again."

⁸ *His* disciples said to Him, "Teacher, lately the Jews sought to stone You, and are You going there again?"

⁹ Jesus answered, "Are there not twelve hours in the day? If anyone walks in the day, he does not stumble, because he sees the light of this world.

¹⁰ But if one walks in the night, he stumbles, because the light is not in him."

¹¹ These things He said, and after that He said to them, "Our friend Lazarus sleeps, but I go that I may wake him out of sleep."

¹² Then His disciples said, "Lord, if he sleeps he will recover."

¹³ However, Jesus spoke of his death, but they thought that He was speaking about taking rest in sleep.

¹⁴ Then Jesus said to them plainly, "Lazarus is dead.

¹⁵ And I am glad for your sakes that I was not there, that you may believe. Nevertheless let us go to him."

¹⁶ Then Thomas, who is called Didymus, said to his fellow disciples, "Let us also go, that we may die with Him."

¹⁷ So when Jesus came, He found that he had already been *laid* in the tomb four days.

¹⁸ Now Bethany was near Jerusalem, about fifteen stadiums away.

¹⁹ And many of the Jews came to Martha and Mary, to comfort them concerning their brother.

²⁰ Now Martha, as soon as she heard that Jesus was coming, went and met Him, but Mary was *still* sitting in the house.

²¹ Then Martha said to Jesus, "Lord, if You had been here, my brother would not have died.

²² But even now I know that whatever You ask of God, God will give You."

²³ Jesus said to her, "Your brother will rise again."

²⁴ Martha said to Him, "I know that he will rise again in the resurrection at the last day."

²⁵ Jesus said to her, "I am the resur-

rection and the life. He who believes in Me, though he may die, yet he will live.

²⁶ And whoever lives and believes in Me will never die. Do you believe this?"

²⁷ She said to Him, "Yes, Lord, I believe that You are the Christ, the Son of God, who would come into the world."

²⁸ And when she had said these things, she went her way and secretly called Mary her sister, saying, "The Teacher has come and is calling for you."

²⁹ As soon as she heard *that*, she arose quickly and came to Him.

³⁰ Now Jesus had not yet come into the town, but was in the place where Martha met Him.

³¹ Then the Jews who were with her in the house, and comforting her, when they saw that Mary rose up quickly and went out, followed her, saying, "She is going to the tomb to weep there."

³² Then, when Mary came where Jesus was, and saw Him, she fell down at His feet, saying to Him, "Lord, if You had been here, my brother would not have died."

³³ Therefore, when Jesus saw her weeping, and the Jews who came with her weeping, He groaned in the spirit and was troubled,

³⁴ and said, "Where have you laid him?" They said to Him, "Lord, come and see."

³⁵ Jesus wept.

³⁶ Then the Jews said, "See how He loved him!"

³⁷ And some of them said, "Could not this Man, who opened the eyes of the blind, also have kept this man from dying?"

³⁸ Then Jesus, again groaning in Himself, came to the tomb. It was a cave, and a stone lay on it.

³⁹ Jesus said, "Take away the stone." Martha, the sister of him who was dead, said to Him, "Lord, by this time he smells, because he has been *dead* four days."

⁴⁰ Jesus said to her, "Did I not say to you that if you would believe you would see the glory of God?"

⁴¹ Then they took away the stone *from the place* where the dead man was lying. And Jesus lifted up *His* eyes and said, "Father, I thank You that You have heard Me.

⁴² And I know that You always hear Me, but because of the people who are standing by I said *this*, that they may believe that You sent Me."

⁴³ Now when He had spoken these things, He shouted out with a loud voice, "Lazarus, come forth!"

⁴⁴ And he who had died came out bound hand and foot with graveclothes, and his face was wrapped with a cloth. Jesus said to them, "Loose him, and let him go."

⁴⁵ Then many of the Jews who had come to Mary, and had seen the things Jesus did, believed on Him.

⁴⁶ But some of them went away to the Pharisees and told them the things Jesus had done.

⁴⁷ Then the chief priests and the

Pharisees gathered a council and said, "What shall we do? Because this Man does many miracles.

⁴⁸ If we leave Him alone like this, everyone will believe on Him, and the Romans will come and take away both our place and nation."

⁴⁹ And one of them, *named* Caiaphas, being the high priest that year, said to them, "You know nothing at all,

⁵⁰ nor do you consider that it is expedient for us that one man should die for the people, and not that the entire nation should perish."

⁵¹ Now this he did not say from himself; but being high priest that year he prophesied that Jesus would die for the nation,

⁵² and not for that nation only, but also that He would gather together in one the children of God who were scattered abroad.

⁵³ Then, from that day on, they plotted to put Him to death.

⁵⁴ Therefore Jesus no longer walked openly among the Jews, but went from there into the countryside near the wilderness, to a city called Ephraim, and there remained with His disciples.

⁵⁵ And the Passover of the Jews was soon at hand, and many went from the countryside up to Jerusalem before the Passover, to purify themselves.

⁵⁶ Then they sought Jesus, and spoke among themselves as they stood in the temple, "What do you think, that He will not come to the feast?"

⁵⁷ Now both the chief priests and the Pharisees had given a command, that if anyone knew where He was, he should report *it*, that they might seize Him.

CHAPTER 12

¹ Then, six days before the Passover, Jesus came to Bethany, where Lazarus was who had been dead, whom He had raised from the dead.

² There they made Him a supper; and Martha served, but Lazarus was one of those who sat at the table with Him.

³ Then Mary took a pound of very costly oil of spikenard, anointed the feet of Jesus, and wiped His feet with her hair. And the house was filled with the fragrance of the oil.

⁴ But one of His disciples, Judas Iscariot, Simon's *son*, who would betray Him, said,

⁵ "Why was this fragrant oil not sold for three hundred denarii and given to the poor?"

⁶ This he said, not that he cared for the poor, but because he was a thief, and had the money bag; and carried what was put in it.

⁷ But Jesus said, "Leave her alone; she has kept this for the day of My burial.

⁸ Because, the poor you have with you always, but Me you do not have always."

⁹ Now a great many of the Jews

knew that He was there; and they came, not for Jesus' sake only, but that they might also see Lazarus, whom He had raised from the dead.
¹⁰ But the chief priests plotted to put Lazarus to death also,
¹¹ because on account of him many of the Jews went away and believed on Jesus.
¹² On the next day many people who had come to the feast, when they heard that Jesus was coming to Jerusalem,
¹³ took branches of palm trees and went out to meet Him, and shouted out: "Hosanna! Blessed *is* the King of Israel who comes in the name of the LORD!"
¹⁴ Then Jesus, when He had found a young donkey, sat on it; as it is written:
¹⁵ "Fear not, daughter of Zion; behold, your King is coming, sitting on a donkey's colt."
¹⁶ His disciples did not understand these things at first; but when Jesus was glorified, then they remembered that these things were written about Him and *that* they had done these things to Him.
¹⁷ Therefore the people, who were with Him when He called Lazarus out of his tomb and raised him from the dead, bore record.
¹⁸ For this reason the people also met Him, because they heard that He had done this miracle.
¹⁹ The Pharisees therefore said among themselves, "You see that you are accomplishing nothing. Look, the world has gone after Him!"
²⁰ Now there were certain Greeks among those who came up to worship at the feast.
²¹ So they came to Philip, who was from Bethsaida of Galilee, and asked him, saying, "Sir, we desire to see Jesus."
²² Philip came and told Andrew, and in turn Andrew and Philip told Jesus.
²³ But Jesus replied to them, saying, "The hour has come that the Son of Man should be glorified.
²⁴ Truly, truly, I say to you, unless a grain of wheat falls into the ground and dies, it remains alone; but if it dies, it produces much grain.
²⁵ He who loves his life will lose it, and he who hates his life in this world will keep it for eternal life.
²⁶ If anyone serves Me, let him follow Me; and where I am, there My servant will be also. If anyone serves Me, him *My* Father will honor.
²⁷ "Now My soul is troubled, and what shall I say? 'Father, save Me from this hour'? But for this purpose I came to this hour.
²⁸ Father, glorify Your name." Then a voice came from heaven, *saying*, "I have both glorified *it* and will glorify it again."
²⁹ Therefore the people who stood by and heard *it* said that it had thundered. Others said, "An angel has spoken to Him."
³⁰ Jesus responded and said, "This

voice did not come because of Me, but for your sake.

³¹ Now is the judgment of this world; now the ruler of this world will be cast out.

³² And I, if I am lifted up from the earth, will draw all men to Me."

³³ This He said, signifying by what death He would die.

³⁴ The people responded to Him, "We have heard from the law that the Christ remains forever; and how can You say, 'The Son of Man must be lifted up'? Who is this Son of Man?"

³⁵ Then Jesus said to them, "A little while longer the light is with you. Walk while you have the light, lest darkness overtake you; because he who walks in darkness does not know where he is going.

³⁶ While you have the light, believe in the light, that you may be children of light." These things Jesus spoke, and departed, and hid Himself from them.

³⁷ But although He had done so many miracles before them, they did not believe in Him,

³⁸ that the word of Isaiah the prophet might be fulfilled, which he spoke: "Lord, who has believed our report? And to whom has the arm of the LORD been revealed?"

³⁹ Therefore they could not believe, because Isaiah said again:

⁴⁰ "He has blinded their eyes and hardened their hearts, lest they should see with *their* eyes, lest they should understand with *their* hearts and be converted, so that I should heal them."

⁴¹ These things Isaiah said when he saw His glory and spoke of Him.

⁴² Nevertheless even among the rulers many believed on Him, but because of the Pharisees they did not confess *Him*, lest they should be put out of the synagogue;

⁴³ because they loved the praise of men more than the praise of God.

⁴⁴ Jesus shouted out and said, "He who believes on Me, believes not on Me but on Him who sent Me.

⁴⁵ And he who sees Me sees Him who sent Me.

⁴⁶ I have come as a light into the world, that whoever believes on Me should not abide in darkness.

⁴⁷ And if anyone hears My words and does not believe, I do not judge him; because I did not come to judge the world but to save the world.

⁴⁸ He who rejects Me, and does not receive My words, has that which judges him, the word that I have spoken, that will judge him in the last day.

⁴⁹ Because, I have not spoken from Myself; but the Father who sent Me gave Me a commandment, what I should say and what I should speak.

⁵⁰ And I know that His command is everlasting life. Therefore, whatever I speak, just as the Father said to Me, so I speak."

CHAPTER 13

¹ Now before the Feast of the Pass-

over, when Jesus knew that His hour had come that He should depart from this world to the Father, having loved His own who were in the world, He loved them to the end.

² And supper being ended, the devil having already put it into the heart of Judas Iscariot, Simon's *son*, to betray Him,

³ Jesus, knowing that the Father had given all things into His hands, and that He had come from God and was going to God,

⁴ He rose from supper and laid aside His clothes, took a towel and tied it around his waist.

⁵ After that, He poured water into a basin and began to wash the disciples' feet, and to wipe *them* with the towel with which He wrapped around Himself.

⁶ Then He came to Simon Peter. And Peter said to Him, "Lord, are You washing my feet?"

⁷ Jesus answered and said to him, "What I am doing you do not understand now, but you will know after this."

⁸ Peter said to Him, "You shall never wash my feet!" Jesus replied to him, "If I do not wash you, you have no part with Me."

⁹ Simon Peter said to Him, "Lord, not my feet only, but also *my* hands and *my* head!"

¹⁰ Jesus said to him, "He who is washed needs only to wash *his* feet, but is completely clean; and you are clean, but not all of you."

¹¹ Because, He knew who would betray Him; therefore He said, "You are not all clean."

¹² So when He had washed their feet, taken His clothes, and sat down again, He said to them, "Do you know what I have done to you?

¹³ You call Me Teacher and Lord, and you say well, because *so* I am.

¹⁴ If I then, *your* Lord and Teacher, have washed your feet, you also ought to wash one another's feet.

¹⁵ Because, I have given you an example, that you should do as I have done to you.

¹⁶ Truly, truly, I say to you, a servant is not greater than his master; nor is he who is sent greater than he who sent him.

¹⁷ If you know these things, blessed are you if you do them.

¹⁸ "I do not speak concerning all of you. I know whom I have chosen; but that the Scripture may be fulfilled, 'He who eats bread with Me has lifted up his heel against Me.'

¹⁹ Now I tell you before it comes, that when it does come to pass, you may believe that I am *He*.

²⁰ Truly, truly, I say to you, he who receives whomever I send receives Me; and he who receives Me receives Him who sent Me."

²¹ When Jesus had said these things, He was troubled in spirit, and testified and said, "Truly, truly, I say to you, one of you will betray Me."

²² Then the disciples looked at one

another, dubious about whom He spoke.

²³ Now there was leaning on Jesus' bosom one of His disciples, whom Jesus loved.

²⁴ Simon Peter therefore motioned to him to ask who it was of whom He spoke.

²⁵ Then, leaning back on Jesus' breast, he said to Him, "Lord, who is it?"

²⁶ Jesus answered, "It is he to whom I will give a piece of bread when I have dipped it." And having dipped the bread, He gave *it* to Judas Iscariot, *the son* of Simon.

²⁷ Now after the piece of bread, Satan entered him. Then Jesus said to him, "What you do, do quickly."

²⁸ But no one at the table knew for what reason He said this to him.

²⁹ Because, some of *them* thought, because Judas had the money bag, that Jesus had said to him, "Buy *those things* we need for the feast," or that he should give something to the poor.

³⁰ Having received the piece of bread, he then went out immediately. And it was night.

³¹ So, when he had gone out, Jesus said, "Now the Son of Man is glorified, and God is glorified in Him.

³² If God is glorified in Him, God will also glorify Him in Himself, and will glorify Him immediately.

³³ Little children, I will be with you a little while longer. You will seek Me; and as I said to the Jews, 'Where I am going, you cannot come,' so now I say to you.

³⁴ A new commandment I give to you, that you love one another; as I have loved you, that you also love one another.

³⁵ By this everyone will know that you are My disciples, if you have love for one another."

³⁶ Simon Peter said to Him, "Lord, where are You going?" Jesus answered him, "Where I am going you cannot follow Me now, but you will follow Me afterward."

³⁷ Peter said to Him, "Lord, why can I not follow You now? I will lay down my life for Your sake."

³⁸ Jesus answered him, "Will you lay down your life for My sake? Truly, truly, I say to you, the rooster will not crow until you have denied Me three times.

CHAPTER 14

¹ "Let not your heart be troubled; you believe in God, believe also in Me.

² In My Father's house are many mansions; if *it were* not so, I would have told you. I go to prepare a place for you.

³ And if I go and prepare a place for you, I will come again and receive you to Myself; that where I am, *there* you may be also.

⁴ And where I go you know, and the way you know."

⁵ Thomas said to Him, "Lord, we do not know where You are going, and how can we know the way?"

⁶ Jesus said to him, "I am the way, the truth, and the life. No one comes to the Father except through Me.

⁷ "If you had known Me, you would have known My Father also; and from now on you know Him and have seen Him."

⁸ Philip said to Him, "Lord, show us the Father, and it is enough for us."

⁹ Jesus said to him, "Have I been with you for such a long a time, and yet you have not known Me, Philip? He who has seen Me has seen the Father; so how can you say, 'Show us the Father'?

¹⁰ Do you not believe that I am in the Father, and the Father in Me? The words that I speak to you I do not speak from Myself; but the Father who dwells in Me, He does the works.

¹¹ Believe Me that I *am* in the Father and the Father in Me, or else believe Me for the sake of the works themselves.

¹² "Truly, truly, I say to you, he who believes on Me, the works that I do he will do also; and greater *works* than these he will do, because I go to My Father.

¹³ And whatever you ask in My name, that I will do, that the Father may be glorified in the Son.

¹⁴ If you shall ask anything in My name, I will do *it*.

¹⁵ "If you love Me, keep My commandments.

¹⁶ And I will pray the Father, and He will give you another Comforter, that He may abide with you forever;

¹⁷ *that is* the Spirit of truth, whom the world cannot receive, because it neither sees Him nor knows Him; but you know Him, because He dwells with you and will be in you.

¹⁸ I will not leave you comfortless; I will come to you.

¹⁹ "Yet a little while longer and the world will see Me no more, but you see Me. Because I live, you will live also.

²⁰ At that day you will know that I *am* in My Father, and you in Me, and I in you.

²¹ He who has My commandments and keeps them, it is he who loves Me. And he who loves Me will be loved by My Father, and I will love him and will manifest Myself to him."

²² Judas (not Iscariot) said to Him, "Lord, how is it that You will manifest Yourself to us, and not to the world?"

²³ Jesus answered and said to him, "If anyone loves Me, he will keep My words; and My Father will love him, and We will come to him and make Our home with him.

²⁴ He who does not love Me does not keep My words; and the word which you hear is not Mine but the Father's who sent Me.

²⁵ "These things I have spoken to you while being present with you.

²⁶ But the Comforter, *who is* the Holy Spirit, whom the Father will send in My name, He will teach you all things, and bring all things to

your remembrance, whatever I have said to you.

²⁷ Peace I leave with you, My peace I give to you; not as the world gives do I give to you. Do not let your heart to be troubled, neither let it be afraid.

²⁸ You have heard Me say to you, 'I am going away and coming *back* to you.' If you loved Me, you would rejoice because I said, 'I am going to the Father,' because My Father is greater than I.

²⁹ "And now I have told you before it comes to pass, that when it does come to pass, you may believe.

³⁰ I will no longer talk much with you, because the ruler of this world is coming, and he has nothing in Me.

³¹ But that the world may know that I love the Father, and just as the Father gave Me commandment, so I do. Arise, let us go from here.

CHAPTER 15

¹ "I am the true vine, and My Father is the vinedresser.

² Every branch in Me that does not bear fruit He takes away; and every *branch* that bears fruit He prunes, that it may bear more fruit.

³ Now you are clean because of the word which I have spoken to you.

⁴ Abide in Me, and I in you. As the branch cannot bear fruit of itself, unless it abides in the vine, neither can you, unless you abide in Me.

⁵ "I am the vine, you *are* the branches. He who abides in Me, and I in him, the same bears much fruit; because without Me you can do nothing.

⁶ If anyone does not abide in Me, he is cast out as a branch and is withered; and people gather them and throw *them* into the fire, and they are burned.

⁷ If you abide in Me, and My words abide in you, you will ask what you desire, and it will be done to you.

⁸ By this My Father is glorified, that you bear much fruit; so you will be My disciples.

⁹ "As the Father has loved Me, I also have loved you; continue in My love.

¹⁰ If you keep My commandments, you will abide in My love, just as I have kept My Father's commandments and abide in His love.

¹¹ "These things I have spoken to you, that My joy may remain in you, and *that* your joy may be full.

¹² This is My commandment, that you love one another as I have loved you.

¹³ No one has greater love than this, that a man lay down his life for his friends.

¹⁴ You are My friends if you do whatever I command you.

¹⁵ No longer do I call you servants, because a servant does not know what his master is doing; but I have called you friends, because all things that I have heard from My Father I have made known to you.

¹⁶ You did not choose Me, but I chose you and ordained you that

you should go and bear fruit, and *that* your fruit should remain, that whatever you ask the Father in My name He may give you.

¹⁷ These things I command you, that you love one another.

¹⁸ "If the world hates you, you know that it hated Me before *it hated* you. ¹⁹ If you were of the world, the world would love its own. But because you are not of the world, but I chose you out of the world, therefore the world hates you. ²⁰ Remember the word that I said to you, 'A servant is not greater than his master.' If they persecuted Me, they will also persecute you. If they kept My word, they will keep yours also.

²¹ But all these things they will do to you for My name's sake, because they do not know Him who sent Me.

²² If I had not come and spoken to them, they would have no sin, but now they have no excuse for their sin.

²³ He who hates Me hates My Father also.

²⁴ If I had not done among them the works which no one else did, they would have no sin; but now they have both seen and hated both Me and My Father.

²⁵ But *this happened* that the word might be fulfilled which is written in their law, 'They hated Me without a reason.'

²⁶ "But when the Comforter comes, whom I will send to you from the Father, *that is* the Spirit of truth who proceeds from the Father, He will testify of Me.

²⁷ And you also will bear witness, because you have been with Me from the beginning.

CHAPTER 16

¹ "These things I have spoken to you, that you should not be made to stumble.

² They will put you out of the synagogues; yes, the time is coming that whoever kills you will think that he offers God service.

³ And these things they will do to you because they have not known the Father nor Me.

⁴ But these things I have told you, that when the time comes, you may remember that I told you of them. And these things I did not say to you at the beginning, because I was with you.

⁵ "But now I go away to Him who sent Me, and none of you asks Me, 'Where are You going?'

⁶ But because I have said these things to you, sorrow has filled your heart.

⁷ Nevertheless I tell you the truth. It is to your advantage that I go away; because, if I do not go away, the Comforter will not come to you; but if I depart, I will send Him to you.

⁸ And when He has come, He will convict the world of sin, and of righteousness, and of judgment:

⁹ of sin, because they do not believe on Me;

¹⁰ of righteousness, because I go to My Father and you see Me no more; ¹¹ of judgment, because the ruler of this world is judged.

¹² "I still have many things to say to you, but you cannot bear them now. ¹³ However, when He, the Spirit of truth, has come, He will guide you into all truth; because, He will not speak on from Himself, but whatever He hears He will speak; and He will show you things to come.

¹⁴ He will glorify Me, because He will take of what is Mine and declare it to you.

¹⁵ All things that the Father has are Mine. Therefore I said that He will take of Mine and declare *it* to you.

¹⁶ "A little while, and you will not see Me; and again a little while, and you will see Me, because I go to the Father."

¹⁷ Then *some* of His disciples said among themselves, "What is this that He says to us, 'A little while, and you will not see Me; and again a little while, and you will see Me'; and, 'because I go to the Father'?"

¹⁸ They said therefore, "What is this that He says, 'A little while'? We do not know what He is saying."

¹⁹ Now Jesus knew that they desired to ask Him, and He said to them, "Are you inquiring among yourselves about what I said, 'A little while, and you will not see Me; and again a little while, and you will see Me'?

²⁰ Truly, truly, I say to you that you will weep and lament, but the world will rejoice; and you will be sorrowful, but your sorrow will be turned into joy.

²¹ A woman, when she is in labor, has sorrow because her hour has come; but as soon as she has given birth to the child, she no longer remembers the anguish, for joy that a human being has been born into the world.

²² Therefore you now have sorrow; but I will see you again and your heart will rejoice, and your joy no one will take from you.

²³ "And in that day you will ask Me nothing. Truly, truly, I say to you, whatever you ask the Father in My name He will give you.

²⁴ Until now you have asked nothing in My name. Ask, and you will receive, that your joy may be full.

²⁵ "These things I have spoken to you in proverbs; but the time is coming when I will no longer speak to you in proverbs, but I will tell you plainly about the Father.

²⁶ In that day you will ask in My name, and I do not say to you that I will pray the Father for you;

²⁷ because the Father Himself loves you, because you have loved Me, and have believed that I came forth from God.

²⁸ I came forth from the Father and have come into the world. Again, I leave the world and go to the Father."

²⁹ His disciples said to Him, "See, now You are speaking plainly, and

using no proverb!
³⁰ Now we are sure that You know all things, and have no need that anyone should question You. By this we believe that You came forth from God."
³¹ Jesus replied to them, "Do you now believe?
³² Behold, the hour is coming, yes, has now come, that you will be scattered, each to his own, and will leave Me alone. And yet I am not alone, because the Father is with Me.
³³ These things I have spoken to you, that in Me you may have peace. In the world you will have tribulation; but be of good cheer, I have overcome the world."

CHAPTER 17

¹ Jesus spoke these words, and lifted up His eyes to heaven, saying: "Father, the hour has come. Glorify Your Son, that Your Son also may glorify You,
² as You have given Him authority over all flesh, that He should give eternal life to as many as You have given Him.
³ And this is eternal life, that they may know You, the only true God, and Jesus Christ whom You have sent.
⁴ I have glorified You on the earth. I have finished the work which You have given Me to do.
⁵ And now, O Father, glorify Me together with Yourself, with the glory which I had with You before the world was.
⁶ "I have manifested Your name to the men whom You have given Me out of the world. They were Yours, You gave them to Me, and they have kept Your word.
⁷ Now they have known that all things which You have given Me are from You.
⁸ Because, I have given to them the words which You have given Me; and they have received *them*, and have known surely that I came forth from You; and they have believed that You sent Me.
⁹ "I pray for them. I do not pray for the world but for those whom You have given Me, because they are Yours.
¹⁰ And all Mine are Yours, and Yours are Mine, and I am glorified in them.
¹¹ and now I am no longer in the world, but these are in the world, and I come to You. Holy Father, keep through Your own name those whom You have given Me, that they may be one as We *are*.
¹² While I was with them in the world, I kept them in Your name. Those whom You gave Me I have kept; and none of them is lost except the son of perdition, that the Scripture might be fulfilled.
¹³ But now I come to You, and these things I speak in the world, that they may have My joy fulfilled in themselves.
¹⁴ I have given them Your word; and the world has hated them

because they are not of the world, just as I am not of the world.

¹⁵ I do not pray that You should take them out of the world, but that You should keep them from the evil.

¹⁶ They are not of the world, just as I am not of the world.

¹⁷ Sanctify them through Your truth. Your word is truth.

¹⁸ Just as You have sent Me into the world, I also have sent them into the world.

¹⁹ And for their sakes I sanctify Myself, that they also may be sanctified through the truth.

²⁰ "I do not pray for these only, but also for those who will believe on Me through their word;

²¹ that they all may be one, as You, Father, *are* in Me, and I in You; that they also may be one in Us, that the world may believe that You have sent Me.

²² And the glory which You gave Me I have given them, that they may be one just as We are one:

²³ I in them, and You in Me; that they may be made perfect in one, and that the world may know that You have sent Me, and have loved them as You have loved Me.

²⁴ "Father, I desire that they also whom You have given Me may be with Me where I am, that they may behold My glory which You have given Me; because You loved Me before the foundation of the world.

²⁵ O righteous Father! The world has not known You, but I have known You; and these have known that You sent Me.

²⁶ And I have declared to them Your name, and will declare *it*, that the love with which You loved Me may be in them, and I in them."

CHAPTER 18

¹ When Jesus had spoken these words, He went out with His disciples over the Brook Kidron, where there was a garden, which He and His disciples entered into.

² And Judas, who betrayed Him, also knew the place; because Jesus often met there with His disciples.

³ Then Judas, having received a detachment of *men*, and officers from the chief priests and Pharisees, came there with lanterns, torches, and weapons.

⁴ Jesus therefore, knowing all things that would come upon Him, went forward and said to them, "Whom are you seeking?"

⁵ They answered Him, "Jesus of Nazareth." Jesus said to them, "I am *He*." And Judas, who betrayed Him, also stood with them.

⁶ Now when He said to them, "I am He," they drew back and fell to the ground.

⁷ Then He asked them again, "Whom are you seeking?" And they said, "Jesus of Nazareth."

⁸ Jesus answered, "I have told you that I am *He*. Therefore, if you seek Me, let these go their way,"

⁹ that the saying might be fulfilled which He spoke, "Of those whom

You gave Me I have lost none."

¹⁰ Then Simon Peter, having a sword, drew it and struck the high priest's servant, and cut off his right ear. The servant's name was Malchus.

¹¹ So Jesus said to Peter, "Put your sword into the sheath. The cup which My Father has given Me, should I not drink it?"

¹² Then the detachment of troops and the captain and the officers of the Jews arrested Jesus and bound Him.

¹³ And they led Him away to Annas first, because he was the father in law of Caiaphas who was high priest that year.

¹⁴ Now it was Caiaphas who advised the Jews that it was expedient that one man should die for the people.

¹⁵ And Simon Peter followed Jesus, and *so did* another disciple. Now that disciple was known to the high priest, and went with Jesus into the courtyard of the high priest.

¹⁶ But Peter stood at the door outside. Then the other disciple, who was known to the high priest, went out and spoke to her who kept the door, and brought Peter in.

¹⁷ Then the servant girl who kept the door said to Peter, "You are not also *one* of this Man's disciples, are you?" He said, "I am not."

¹⁸ Now the servants and officers who had made a fire of coals stood there, because it was cold, and they warmed themselves. And Peter stood with them and warmed himself.

¹⁹ The high priest then asked Jesus about His disciples and of His doctrine.

²⁰ Jesus answered him, "I spoke openly to the world. I always taught in synagogue and in the temple, where the Jews always meet, and in secret I have said nothing.

²¹ Why do you ask Me? Ask those who have heard Me what I said to them. Indeed they know what I said."

²² And when He had said these things, one of the officers who stood by struck Jesus with the palm of his hand, saying, "Do You answer the high priest like that?"

²³ Jesus answered him, "If I have spoken evil, bear witness of the evil; but if well, why do you strike Me?"

²⁴ Now Annas had sent Him bound to Caiaphas the high priest.

²⁵ Now Simon Peter stood and warmed himself. Therefore they said to him, "Are you not also *one* of His disciples?" He denied *it* and said, "I am not!"

²⁶ One of the servants of the high priest, being a relative *of him* whose ear Peter cut off, said, "Did I not see you in the garden with Him?"

²⁷ Peter then denied again; and immediately the rooster crowed.

²⁸ Then they led Jesus from Caiaphas to the judgment hall, and it was early. But they themselves did not go into the judgment hall, lest they should be defiled, but that they might eat the Passover.

²⁹ Pilate then went out to them and said, "What accusation do you bring against this Man?"
³⁰ They answered and said to him, "If He were not an evildoer, we would not have delivered Him up to you."
³¹ Then Pilate said to them, "You take Him and judge Him according to your law." Therefore the Jews said to him, "It is not lawful for us to put anyone to death,"
³² that the saying of Jesus might be fulfilled which He spoke, signifying by what death He would die.
³³ Then Pilate entered the judgment hall again, called Jesus, and said to Him, "Are You the King of the Jews?"
³⁴ Jesus answered him, "Are you speaking for yourself about this, or did others tell you this concerning Me?"
³⁵ Pilate answered, "Am I a Jew? Your own nation and the chief priests have delivered You to me. What have You done?"
³⁶ Jesus answered, "My kingdom is not of this world. If My kingdom were of this world, My servants would fight, so that I would not be delivered to the Jews; but now My kingdom is not from here."
³⁷ Pilate therefore said to Him, "Are You a king then?" Jesus answered, "You say rightly that I am a king. For this reason I was born, and for this reason I have come into the world, that I should bear witness to the truth. Everyone who is of the truth hears My voice."
³⁸ Pilate said to Him, "What is truth?" And when he had said this, he went out again to the Jews, and said to them, "I find no fault in Him *at all*.
³⁹ "But you have a custom that I should release someone to you at the Passover. Do you therefore want me to release to you the King of the Jews?"
⁴⁰ Then they all shouted out again, saying, "Not this Man, but Barabbas!" Now Barabbas was a robber.

CHAPTER 19

¹ So then Pilate took Jesus and scourged *Him*.
² And the soldiers twisted a crown of thorns and put *it* on His head, and they put a purple robe on Him.
³ Then they said, "Hail, King of the Jews!" And they struck Him with their hands.
⁴ Then Pilate then went out again, and said to them, "Behold, I am bringing Him out to you, that you may know that I find no fault in Him."
⁵ Then Jesus came out, wearing the crown of thorns and the purple robe. And *Pilate* said to them, "Behold the Man!"
⁶ Therefore, when the chief priests and officers saw Him, they shouted out, saying, "Crucify *Him*, crucify *Him!*" Pilate said to them, "You take Him and crucify *Him*, because I find no fault in Him."
⁷ The Jews replied to him, "We have

a law, and according to our law He ought to die, because He made Himself the Son of God."

⁸ Therefore, when Pilate heard that saying, he was the more afraid,

⁹ and went again into the judgment hall, and said to Jesus, "Where are You from?" But Jesus gave him no answer.

¹⁰ Then Pilate said to Him, "Are You not speaking to me? Do You not know that I have authority to crucify You, and have authority to release You?"

¹¹ Jesus answered, "You could have no authority *at all* against Me unless it had been given you from above. Therefore the one who delivered Me to you has the greater sin."

¹² From then on Pilate sought to release Him, but the Jews shouted out, saying, "If you let this Man go, you are not Caesar's friend. Whoever makes himself a king speaks against Caesar."

¹³ When Pilate therefore heard that saying, he brought Jesus out and sat down in the judgment seat in a place that is called The Pavement, but in the Hebrew, Gabbatha.

¹⁴ Now it was the Preparation Day of the Passover, and about the sixth hour. And he said to the Jews, "Behold your King!"

¹⁵ But they shouted out, "Away with *Him*, away with *Him*! Crucify *Him*!" Pilate said to them, "Shall I crucify your King?" The chief priests answered, "We have no king but Caesar!"

¹⁶ Then therefore, he delievered Him to them to be crucified. So they took Jesus and led *Him* away.

¹⁷ And He, bearing His cross, went out to a place called *the Place* of a Skull, which is called in the Hebrew, Golgotha,

¹⁸ where they crucified Him, and two others with Him, one on either side, and Jesus in the middle.

¹⁹ Now Pilate wrote a title and put *it* on the cross. And the writing was: JESUS OF NAZARETH, THE KING OF THE JEWS.

²⁰ Then many of the Jews read this title, because, the place where Jesus was crucified was near the city; and it was written in Hebrew, Greek, *and* Latin.

²¹ So the chief priests of the Jews said to Pilate, "Do not write, 'The King of the Jews,' but, 'He said, "I am the King of the Jews." ' "

²² Pilate replied, "What I have written, I have written."

²³ Then the soldiers, when they had crucified Jesus, took His clothes and made four parts, to each soldier a part, and also *His* coat. Now the coat was without seam, woven from the top in one piece.

²⁴ Therefore they said among themselves, "Let us not tear it, but cast lots for it, whose it shall be," that the Scripture might be fulfilled which says: "They divided My clothes among them, and for My coat they cast lots." Therefore the soldiers did these things.

²⁵ Now there stood by the cross of

Jesus His mother, and His mother's sister, Mary the *wife* of Clopas, and Mary Magdalene.

²⁶ Therefore, when Jesus saw His mother, and the disciple whom He loved standing by, He said to His mother, "Woman, behold your son!"

²⁷ Then He said to the disciple, "Behold your mother!" And from that hour that disciple took her to his own *home*.

²⁸ After this, Jesus, knowing that all things were now accomplished, that the Scripture might be fulfilled, said, "I thirst!"

²⁹ Now a vessel full of vinegar was sitting there; and they filled a sponge with vinegar, put *it* on hyssop, and put it to His mouth.

³⁰ So when Jesus had received the vinegar, He said, "It is finished!" He bowed His head, and gave up His spirit.

³¹ Then since it was the Preparation Day, that the bodies should not remain on the cross on the Sabbath day (because that Sabbath was a high day), the Jews asked Pilate that their legs might be broken, and *that* they might be taken away.

³² Then the soldiers came and broke the legs of the first and of the other who was crucified with Him

³³ But when they came to Jesus and saw that He was already dead, they did not break His legs.

³⁴ But one of the soldiers pierced His side with a spear, and blood and water came out straight away.

³⁵ And he who saw *it* bare record, and his record is true; and he knows that he is speaking the truth, so that you may believe.

³⁶ Because these things were done that the Scripture should be fulfilled, "Not one of His bones will be broken."

³⁷ And again another Scripture says, "They will look on Him whom they pierced."

³⁸ After this, Joseph of Arimathea, being a disciple of Jesus, but secretly, for fear of the Jews, asked Pilate that he might take away the body of Jesus; and Pilate gave *him* permission. So he came and took the body of Jesus.

³⁹ And Nicodemus, who at first came to Jesus by night, also came, bringing a mixture of myrrh and aloes, *weighing* about a hundred pounds.

⁴⁰ Then they took the body of Jesus, and bound it in strips of linen with the spices, as the custom of the Jews is to bury.

⁴¹ Now in the place where He was crucified there was a garden, and in the garden a new tomb in which no one had yet been laid.

⁴² So there they laid Jesus, because of the Jews' Preparation *Day*, because the tomb was nearby.

CHAPTER 20

¹ The first *day* of the week Mary Magdalene came to the tomb early, while it was still dark, and saw that the stone had been taken away

from the tomb.

² Then she ran and came to Simon Peter, and to the other disciple, whom Jesus loved, and said to them, "They have taken away the Lord out of the tomb, and we do not know where they have laid Him."

³ Peter therefore went out, and the other disciple, and came to the tomb.

⁴ So they both ran together, and the other disciple outran Peter and came to the tomb first.

⁵ And he, stooping down *and looking in*, saw the linen cloths lying there; yet he did not go in.

⁶ Then Simon Peter came, following him, and went into the tomb; and he saw the linen cloths lying there, ⁷ and the handkerchief that had been around His head, not lying with the linen cloths, but folded together in a place by itself.

⁸ Then the other disciple, who came to the tomb first, went in also; and he saw and believed.

⁹ Because, as yet they did not know the Scripture, that He must rise again from the dead.

¹⁰ Then the disciples went away again to their own homes.

¹¹ But Mary stood outside by the tomb weeping, and as she wept she stooped down *and looked* into the tomb.

¹² And she saw two angels in white sitting, one at the head and the other at the feet, where the body of Jesus had laid.

¹³ Then they said to her, "Woman, why are you weeping?" She said to them, "Because they have taken away my Lord, and I do not know where they have laid Him."

¹⁴ Now when she had said this, she turned around and saw Jesus standing there, and did not know that it was Jesus.

¹⁵ Jesus said to her, "Woman, why are you weeping? Whom are you seeking?" She, supposing Him to be the gardener, said to Him, "Sir, if You have carried Him away, tell me where You have laid Him, and I will take Him away."

¹⁶ Jesus said to her, "Mary!" She turned and said to Him, "Rabboni!" (which is to say, Teacher).

¹⁷ Jesus said to her, "Do not cling to Me, because, I have not yet ascended to My Father; but go to My brethren and say to them, 'I am ascending to My Father and your Father, and *to* My God and your God.' "

¹⁸ Mary Magdalene came and told the disciples that she had seen the Lord, and that He had spoken these things to her.

¹⁹ Then, the same day at evening, being the first *day* of the week, when the doors were shut where the disciples were assembled, for fear of the Jews, Jesus came and stood in the midst, and said to them, "Peace *be* with you."

²⁰ And when He had said this, He showed them *His* hands and His side. Then the disciples rejoiced when they saw the Lord.

²¹ So Jesus said to them again, "Peace *be* to you! As *My* Father has sent Me, so I also send you."
²² And when He had said this, He breathed on *them*, and said to them, "Receive the Holy Spirit.
²³ If you forgive the sins of any, they are forgiven them; *and* if you retain the *sins* of any, they are retained."
²⁴ Now Thomas, called Didymus, one of the twelve, was not with them when Jesus came.
²⁵ The other disciples therefore said to him, "We have seen the Lord." But he said to them, "Unless I see in His hands the print of the nails, and put my finger into the print of the nails, and put my hand into His side, I will not believe."
²⁶ And after eight days His disciples were again inside, and Thomas with them. *Then* Jesus came, the doors being shut, and stood in the midst, and said, "Peace *be* to you!"
²⁷ Then He said to Thomas, "Reach your finger here, and look at My hands; and reach your hand here, and put *it* into My side. Do not be faithless, but believing."
²⁸ And Thomas replied and said to Him, "My Lord and my God!"
²⁹ Jesus said to him, "Thomas, because you have seen Me, you have believed. Blessed *are* those who have not seen and *yet* have believed."
³⁰ And truly Jesus did many other signs in the presence of His disciples, which are not written in this book;
³¹ but these are written that you may believe that Jesus is the Christ, the Son of God, and that believing you may have life through His name.

CHAPTER 21

¹ After these things Jesus showed Himself again to the disciples at the Sea of Tiberias, and in this way He showed *Himself*.
² Simon Peter, Thomas called Didymus, Nathanael of Cana in Galilee, *the sons* of Zebedee, and two others of His disciples were together.
³ Simon Peter said to them, "I am going fishing." They said to him, "We are going with you also." They went out and immediately got into the boat, and that night they caught nothing.
⁴ But when the morning had now come, Jesus stood on the shore; but the disciples did not know that it was Jesus.
⁵ Then Jesus said to them, "Children, have you any food?" They answered Him, "No."
⁶ And He said to them, "Cast the net on the right side of the boat, and you will find some." So they cast, and now they were not able to draw it in because of the multitude of fish.
⁷ Therefore that disciple whom Jesus loved said to Peter, "It is the Lord!" Now when Simon Peter heard that it was the Lord, he put on *his* fisherman's coat (because he

had removed it), and plunged himself into the sea.

⁸ But the other disciples came in the little boat (because they were not far from land, but about two hundred cubits), dragging the net with fish.

⁹ Then, as soon as they had come to land, they saw a fire of coals there, and fish laid on it, and bread.

¹⁰ Jesus said to them, "Bring some of the fish which you have just caught."

¹¹ Simon Peter went up and dragged the net to land, full of large fish, one hundred and fifty three; and although there were so many, the net was not broken.

¹² Jesus said to them, "Come and eat." Yet none of the disciples dared ask Him, "Who are You?" Knowing that it was the Lord.

¹³ Jesus then came and took the bread and gave it to them, and likewise the fish.

¹⁴ This is now the third time Jesus showed Himself to His disciples after He was risen from the dead.

¹⁵ So when they had eaten, Jesus said to Simon Peter, "Simon, *son* of Jonah, do you love Me more than these?" He said to Him, "Yes, Lord; You know that I love You." He said to him, "Feed My lambs."

¹⁶ He said to him again a second time, "Simon, *son* of Jonah, do you love Me?" He said to Him, "Yes, Lord; You know that I love You." He said to him, "Feed My sheep."

¹⁷ He said to him the third time, "Simon, *son* of Jonah, do you love Me?" Peter was grieved because He said to him the third time, "Do you love Me?" And he said to Him, "Lord, You know all things; You know that I love You." Jesus said to him, "Feed My sheep.

¹⁸ Truly, truly, I say to you, when you were younger, you girded yourself and walked where you desired; but when you are old, you will stretch out your hands, and another will gird you and carry *you* where you do not desire."

¹⁹ This He spoke, signifying by what death he would glorify God. And when He had spoken this, He said to him, "Follow Me."

²⁰ Then Peter, turning around, saw the disciple whom Jesus loved following, who also had leaned on His breast at the supper, and said, "Lord, who is the one who betrays You?"

²¹ Peter, seeing him, said to Jesus, "Lord, what *shall* this man do?"

²² Jesus said to him, "If I will that he remains until I come, what *is that* to you? You follow Me."

²³ Then this saying went out among the brethren that this disciple would not die. Yet Jesus did not say to him that he would not die, but, "If I will that he remain until I come, what *is that* to you?"

²⁴ This is the disciple who testifies of these things, and wrote these things; and we know that his testimony is true.

²⁵ And there are also many other

things that Jesus did, which if every one was written, I suppose that even the world itself could not contain the books that would be written. Amen.

THE ACTS OF THE APOSTLES

CHAPTER 1

¹ The former account I made, O Theophilus, of all that Jesus began both to do and teach,

² until the day in which He was taken up, after He through the Holy Spirit had given commandments to the apostles whom He had chosen,

³ to whom He also presented Himself alive after His passion by many infallible proofs, being seen by them for forty days and speaking of the things pertaining to the kingdom of God.

⁴ And being assembled together with *them*, commanded them that they should not depart from Jerusalem, but to wait for the Promise of the Father, "which," *He said,* "you have heard from Me;

⁵ because, John truly baptized with water, but you will be baptized with the Holy Spirit not many days from now."

⁶ Therefore, when they had come together, they asked Him, saying, "Lord, will You at this time restore again the kingdom to Israel?"

⁷ And He said to them, "It is not for you to know the times or the seasons which the Father has put in His own authority.

⁸ But you will receive power when the Holy Spirit has come upon you; and you will be witnesses to Me in Jerusalem, and also in all Judea and Samaria, and to the end of the earth."

⁹ Now when He had spoken these things, while they watched, He was taken up, and a cloud received Him out of their sight.

¹⁰ And while they looked stedfastly toward heaven as He went up, behold, two men stood by them in white clothing,

¹¹ who also said, "You men of Galilee, why do you stand gazing up into heaven? This same Jesus, who is taken up from you into heaven, will so come in like manner as you saw Him go into heaven."

¹² Then they returned to Jerusalem from the mount called Olivet, which is near Jerusalem, a Sabbath day's journey.

¹³ And when they had entered, they went up into an upper room where, Peter, James, John, and Andrew; Philip and Thomas; Bartholomew and Matthew; James *the son* of Alphaeus and Simon Zelotes, and Judas *the brother* of James, were staying.

¹⁴ These all continued with one accord in prayer and supplication, with the women and Mary the mother of Jesus, and with His brethren.

¹⁵ And in those days Peter stood up in the midst of the disciples (altogether the number of names

was about a hundred and twenty), and said,

¹⁶ "Men *and* brethren, this Scripture had to be fulfilled, which the Holy Spirit spoke beforehand through the mouth of David concerning Judas, who became a guide to those who arrested Jesus;

¹⁷ because he was numbered with us and obtained a part in this ministry.

¹⁸ Now this man purchased a field with the wages of iniquity; and falling headlong, he burst open in the middle and all his entrails gushed out.

¹⁹ And it became known to all those dwelling in Jerusalem; so that field is called in their own language, Akeldama, that is to say, The Field of Blood.

²⁰ Because, it is written in the Book of Psalms: 'Let his dwelling place be desolate, and let no one live in it'; and, 'Let another take his position.'

²¹ Therefore, of these men who have accompanied us the entire time that the Lord Jesus went in and out among us,

²² beginning from the baptism of John to that day when He was taken up from us, one of these must be ordained to be a witness with us of His resurrection."

²³ And they proposed two: Joseph called Barsabas, who was surnamed Justus, and Matthias.

²⁴ And they prayed and said, "You, O Lord, who know the hearts of all *men*, show which of these two You have chosen,

²⁵ that he may take part in this ministry and apostleship from which Judas by transgression fell, that he might go to his own place."

²⁶ And they put forward their lots, and the lot fell on Matthias. And he was numbered with the eleven apostles.

CHAPTER 2

¹ Now when the Day of Pentecost had fully come, they were all with one accord in one place.

² And suddenly there came a sound from heaven, as of a rushing mighty wind, and it filled the entire house where they were sitting.

³ Then there appeared to them divided tongues like as of fire, and it sat upon each of them.

⁴ And they were all filled with the Holy Spirit and began to speak with other tongues, as the Spirit gave them utterance.

⁵ And there were dwelling in Jerusalem Jews, devout men, from every nation under heaven.

⁶ And when this sound occurred, the crowd came together, and were confused, because everyone heard them speak in his own language.

⁷ Then they were all amazed and marveled, saying to one another, "Look, are not all these who speak Galileans?

⁸ And how *is it that* we hear, each man in our own language in which we were born?

⁹ Parthians and Medes and Elam-

ites, those dwelling in Mesopotamia, in Judea and Cappadocia, in Pontus and Asia,

[10] Phrygia and Pamphylia, in Egypt and in the parts of Libya adjoining Cyrene, visitors from Rome, Jews and proselytes,

[11] Cretans and Arabs, we hear them speaking in our own languages the wonderful works of God."

[12] So they were all amazed and in doubt, saying to one another, "Whatever could this mean?"

[13] Others mocking said, "They are full of new wine."

[14] But Peter, standing up with the eleven, raised his voice and said to them, "You men of Judea and all of you who dwell in Jerusalem, let this be known to you, and heed my words.

[15] Because, these are not drunk, as you suppose, since it is *only* the third hour of the day.

[16] But this is what was spoken through the prophet Joel:

[17] 'And it will come to pass in the last days, says God, I will pour out of My Spirit on all flesh, and your sons and your daughters will prophesy, your young men will see visions, and your old men will dream dreams.

[18] And on My menservants and on My maidservants I will pour out of My Spirit in those days; and they will prophesy.

[19] I will show wonders in heaven above and signs in the earth beneath: Blood and fire and vapor of smoke.

[20] The sun will be turned into darkness, and the moon into blood, before the coming of the great and awesome day of the LORD comes.

[21] And it will come to pass *that* whoever calls on the name of the name of the LORD will be saved.'

[22] "You men of Israel, hear these words: Jesus of Nazareth, a Man approved by God among you by miracles, wonders, and signs which God did by Him in your midst, as you yourselves also know:

[23] Him, being delivered by the determined purpose and foreknowledge of God, you have taken, and by wicked hands, have crucified, and put to death;

[24] whom God raised up, having loosed the pains of death, because it was not possible that He should be held by it.

[25] Because, David says concerning Him: 'I foresaw the LORD always before my face, because, He is at my right hand, that I may not be shaken.

[26] Therefore my heart rejoiced, and my tongue was glad; moreover my flesh also will rest in hope.

[27] Because, You will not leave my soul in the abode of the dead, nor will You allow Your Holy One to see corruption.

[28] You have made known to me the ways of life; You will make me full of joy in Your presence.'

[29] "Men *and* brethren, let me speak freely to you of the patriarch David,

that he is both dead and buried, and his tomb is with us to this day.

³⁰ Therefore, being a prophet, and knowing that God had sworn with an oath to him that of the fruit of his body, according to the flesh, He would raise up the Christ to sit on his throne,

³¹ he, foreseeing this, spoke concerning the resurrection of the Christ, that His soul was not left in the abode of the dead, nor did His flesh see corruption.

³² This Jesus God has raised up, of which we are all witnesses.

³³ Therefore being exalted to the right hand of God, and having received from the Father the promise of the Holy Spirit, He poured out this which you now see and hear.

³⁴ "Because, David did not ascend into the heavens, but he says himself: 'The Lord said to my Lord, "Sit at My right hand,

³⁵ until I make Your enemies Your footstool."'

³⁶ "Therefore let all the house of Israel know with certainty that God has made this same Jesus, whom you have crucified, both Lord and Christ."

³⁷ Now when they heard *this*, they were cut to the heart, and said to Peter and the rest of the apostles, "Men *and* brethren, what shall we do?"

³⁸ Then Peter said to them, "Repent, and let every one of you be baptized in the name of Jesus Christ for the remission of sins; and you will receive the gift of the Holy Spirit.

³⁹ Because, the promise is to you and to your children, and to all who are afar off, *that is to* as many as the Lord our God will call."

⁴⁰ And with many other words he testified and exhorted them, saying, "Save yourselves from this perverse generation."

⁴¹ Then those who gladly received his word were baptized; and that day about three thousand souls were added *to them*.

⁴² And they continued steadfastly in the apostles' doctrine and fellowship, in the breaking of bread, and in prayers.

⁴³ Then reverence came upon every soul, and many wonders and signs were done by the apostles.

⁴⁴ Now all who believed were together, and had all things in common,

⁴⁵ and sold their possessions and goods, and divided them among all the people, as anyone had need.

⁴⁶ So continuing daily with one accord in the temple, and breaking bread from house to house, they ate their food with gladness and simplicity of heart,

⁴⁷ praising God and having favor with all the people. And the Lord added to the church daily those who were being saved.

CHAPTER 3

¹ Now Peter and John went up to-

gether into the temple at the hour of prayer, *being* the ninth hour.

² And a certain man lame from his mother's womb was carried, whom they laid daily at the gate of the temple which is called Beautiful, to ask for charitable gifts from those who entered the temple;

³ who, seeing Peter and John about to go into the temple, asked for charitable gifts.

⁴ And fixing his eyes on him, with John, Peter said, "Look at us."

⁵ So he gave them his attention, expecting to receive something from them.

⁶ Then Peter said, "I do not have any silver and gold, but what I do have I give to you: In the name of Jesus Christ of Nazareth, rise up and walk."

⁷ And he took him by the right hand and lifted *him* up, and immediately his feet and ankle bones received strength.

⁸ So he, leaping up, stood and walked and entered the temple with them, walking, leaping, and praising God.

⁹ And all the people saw him walking and praising God.

¹⁰ Then they knew that it was he who sat begging for charitable gifts at the Beautiful Gate of the temple; and they were filled with wonder and amazement at what had happened to him.

¹¹ Now as the lame man who was healed held on to Peter and John, all the people ran together to them in the porch which is called Solomon's, greatly amazed.

¹² So when Peter saw *it*, he responded to the people: "You men of Israel, why do you marvel at this? Or why look so intently at us, as though by our own power or holiness we had made this man walk?

¹³ The God of Abraham, Isaac, and Jacob, the God of our fathers, glorified His Son Jesus, whom you delivered up and rejected Him in the presence of Pilate, when he was determined to let *Him* go.

¹⁴ But you rejected the Holy One and the Just, and desired a murderer to be granted to you,

¹⁵ and killed the Prince of life, whom God has raised from the dead, of which we are witnesses.

¹⁶ And His name, through faith in His name, has made this man strong, whom you see and know. Yes, the faith which comes by Him has given him this perfect soundness in the presence of you all.

¹⁷ "Yet now, brethren, I know that you did *it* in ignorance, as *did* also your rulers.

¹⁸ But those things which God foretold by the mouth of all His prophets, that Christ would suffer, He has likewise fulfilled.

¹⁹ Therefore repent and be converted, that your sins may be blotted out, so that times of refreshing may come from the presence of the Lord,

²⁰ and He will send Jesus Christ,

who was preached to you beforehand,

²¹ whom the heaven must receive until the times of restoration of all things, which God has spoken by the mouth of all His holy prophets since the world began.

²² Because, Moses truly said to the fathers, 'The LORD your God will raise up for you a Prophet like me from your brethren. Him you will hear in all things, whatever He says to you.

²³ And it will be *that* every soul who shall not hear that Prophet will be utterly destroyed from among the people.'

²⁴ Yes, and all the prophets, from Samuel and those who followed later, as many as have spoken, have also foretold these days.

²⁵ You are the children of the prophets, and of the covenant which God made with our fathers, saying to Abraham, 'And in your seed all the families of the earth will be blessed.'

²⁶ To you first, God, having raised up His Son Jesus, sent Him to bless you, in turning away every one of you from your iniquities."

CHAPTER 4

¹ Now as they spoke to the people, the priests, the captain of the temple, and the Sadducees came upon them,

² being greatly disturbed that they taught the people and preached through Jesus the resurrection from the dead.

³ And they laid hands on *them*, and put them in custody until the next day, because it was already evening.

⁴ However, many of those who heard the word believed; and the number of the men was about five thousand.

⁵ And it came to pass, on the next day, that their rulers, elders, and scribes,

⁶ and Annas the high priest, Caiaphas, John, and Alexander, and as many as were of the family of the high priest, were gathered together at Jerusalem.

⁷ And when they had set them in the midst, they asked, "By what authority or by what name have you done this?"

⁸ Then Peter, filled with the Holy Spirit, said to them, "You rulers of the people and elders of Israel:

⁹ If we this day are examined for the good deed done to the helpless man, by what means he has been made well,

¹⁰ let it be known to you all, and to all the people of Israel, that by the name of Jesus Christ of Nazareth, whom you crucified, whom God raised from the dead, *that* by Him this man stands here before you whole.

¹¹ This is the 'stone which was rejected by you builders, which has become the chief cornerstone.'

¹² Nor is there salvation in any other, because, there is no other

name under heaven given among men by which we must be saved."

¹³ Now when they saw the boldness of Peter and John, and perceived that they were uneducated and untrained men, they marveled. And they recognized them, that they had been with Jesus.

¹⁴ And looking at the man who had been healed standing with them, they could say nothing against it.

¹⁵ But when they had commanded them to go aside out of the council, they conferred among themselves,

¹⁶ saying, "What shall we do to these men? Because, indeed, that a notable miracle has been done by them *is* evident to all who dwell in Jerusalem, and we cannot deny *it*.

¹⁷ But so that it spreads no further among the people, let us severely threaten them, that from now on they speak to no one in this name."

¹⁸ So they called them and commanded them not to speak at all nor teach in the name of Jesus.

¹⁹ But Peter and John replied and said to them, "Whether it is right in the sight of God to listen to you more than to God, you judge.

²⁰ Because we cannot but speak the things which we have seen and heard."

²¹ So when they had further threatened them, they let them go, finding no way of punishing them, because of the people, since they all glorified God for what had been done.

²² Because, the man was over forty years old on whom this miracle of healing had been performed.

²³ And being let go, they went to their own companions and reported all that the chief priests and elders had said to them.

²⁴ So when they heard that, they raise their voice to God with one accord and said: "Lord, You *are* God who made heaven and earth and the sea, and everything that is in them,

²⁵ who by the mouth of Your servant David have said: 'Why did the nations rage, and the people plot vain things?

²⁶ The kings of the earth took their stand, and the rulers were gathered together against the LORD and against His Christ.'

²⁷ "Because, truly against Your holy Child Jesus, whom You have anointed, both Herod and Pontius Pilate, with the Gentiles and the people of Israel, were gathered together

²⁸ to do whatever Your hand and Your purpose determined beforehand to be done.

²⁹ And now Lord, look on their threats, and grant to Your servants that with boldness they may speak your word.

³⁰ by stretching out Your hand to heal, and that signs and wonders may be done by the name of Your holy Child Jesus."

³¹ And when they had prayed, the place where they were assembled together was shaken, and they were

all filled with the Holy Spirit, and they spoke the word of God with boldness.

[32] Now the multitude of those who believed were of one heart and one soul; neither did anyone say that any of the things he possessed was his own, but they had all things in common.

[33] And with great power the apostles gave witness to the resurrection of the Lord Jesus. And great grace was upon them all.

[34] Nor was there anyone among them who lacked; because, all who were possessors of lands or houses sold them, and brought the proceeds of the things that were sold,

[35] and laid *them* down at the apostles' feet. And distribution was made to everyone as they had need.

[36] And Joses, who was surnamed Barnabas by the apostles (which is translated The Son of Encouragement), a Levite, *and* of the country of Cyprus,

[37] having land, sold *it*, and brought the money and laid *it* at the apostles' feet.

CHAPTER 5

[1] But a certain man named Ananias, with Sapphira his wife, sold a possession,

[2] and kept back *part* of the proceeds, his wife also being aware *of it*, and brought a certain part and laid *it* at the apostles' feet.

[3] But Peter said, "Ananias, why has Satan filled your heart to lie to the Holy Spirit and keep back *part* of the price of the land?

[4] While it remained, was it not your own? And after it was sold, was it not in your own control? Why have you conceived this thing in your heart? You have not lied to men but to God."

[5] Then Ananias, hearing these words, fell down and gave up the spirit. So great fear came upon all those who heard these things.

[6] And the young men arose and wrapped him up, carried *him* out, and buried *him*.

[7] Now it was about three hours later when his wife came in, not knowing what had happened.

[8] And Peter responded to her, "Tell me whether you sold the land for so much?" And she said, "Yes, for so much."

[9] Then Peter said to her, "How is it that you have agreed together to test the Spirit of the Lord? Look, the feet of those who have buried your husband *are* at the door, and they will carry you out."

[10] Then immediately she fell down at his feet and gave up the spirit. And the young men came in and found her dead, and carrying *her* out, buried *her* by her husband.

[11] So great fear came upon all the church and upon all who heard these things.

[12] And by the hands of the apostles many signs and wonders were done among the people. And they were

all with one accord in Solomon's Porch.

¹³ Yet none of the rest dared join them, but the people esteemed them highly.

¹⁴ And believers were increasingly added to the Lord, multitudes of both men and women,

¹⁵ so that they brought the sick out into the streets and laid *them* on beds and couches, that at least the shadow of Peter passing by might fall on some of them.

¹⁶ Also a multitude came *out* from the surrounding cities to Jerusalem, bringing sick people and those who were tormented by unclean spirits, and they were all healed.

¹⁷ Then the high priest rose up, and all those who were with him (which is the sect of the Sadducees), and they were filled with indignation,

¹⁸ and laid their hands on the apostles and put them in the common prison.

¹⁹ But at night an angel of the Lord opened the prison doors and brought them out, and said,

²⁰ "Go, stand in the temple and speak to the people all the words of this life."

²¹ And when they heard *that*, they entered into the temple early in the morning and taught. But the high priest and those with him came and called the council together, with all the elders of the children of Israel, and sent to the prison to have them brought.

²² But when the officers came and did not find them in the prison, they returned and reported,

²³ saying, "Indeed we found the prison shut securely, and the guards standing outside before the doors; but when we opened them, we found no one inside!"

²⁴ Now when the high priest, the captain of the temple, and the chief priests heard these things, they wondered what the outcome would be concerning them.

²⁵ So one came and told them, saying, "Look, the men whom you put in prison are standing in the temple and teaching the people!"

²⁶ Then the captain went with the officers and brought them without violence, because they feared the people, lest they should be stoned.

²⁷ And when they had brought them, they *set them* before the council. And the high priest asked them,

²⁸ saying, "Did we not strictly command you that you should not teach in this name? And look, you have filled Jerusalem with your doctrine, and intend to bring this Man's blood on us!"

²⁹ But Peter and the *other* apostles answered and said: "We ought to obey God rather than men.

³⁰ The God of our fathers raised up Jesus whom you murdered and hung on a tree.

³¹ Him God has exalted to His right hand *to be* Prince and Savior, to give repentance to Israel and forgiveness of sins.

³² And we are His witnesses to these things, and *so* also *is* the Holy Spirit whom God has given to those who obey Him."

³³ When they heard *this*, they were cut *to the heart*, and plotted to kill them.

³⁴ Then one in the council stood up, a Pharisee named Gamaliel, a teacher of the law held in respect by all the people, and commanded them to put the apostles outside in every house, they did not for a little while.

³⁵ And he said to them: "You men of Israel, take heed to yourselves what you intend to do regarding these men.

³⁶ Because, some time ago Theudas rose up, claiming to be somebody. A number of men, about four hundred, joined him. He was slain, and all who obeyed him were scattered and came to nothing.

³⁷ After this man, Judas of Galilee rose up in the days of the registration, and drew away many people after him. He also perished, and everyone who obeyed him was dispersed.

³⁸ And now I say to you, keep away from these men and leave them alone; because, if this plan or this work is of men, it will come to nothing;

³⁹ but if it is of God, you cannot overthrow it, lest you even be found to fight against God."

⁴⁰ And they agreed with him, and when they had called for the apostles and beaten *them*, they commanded that they should not speak in the name of Jesus, and let them go.

⁴¹ So they departed from the presence of the council, rejoicing that they were counted worthy to suffer shame for His name.

⁴² And daily in the temple, and in every house, they did not cease teaching and preaching Jesus Christ.

CHAPTER 6

¹ Now in those days, when the number of the disciples was multiplying, there arose a complaint against the Hebrews by the Hellenists, because their widows were neglected in the daily distribution.

² Then the twelve summoned the multitude of the disciples to them and said, "It is not desirable that we should leave the word of God and serve tables.

³ Therefore, brethren, seek out from among you seven men of good reputation, full of the Holy Spirit and wisdom, whom we may appoint over this business;

⁴ but we will give ourselves continually to prayer and to the ministry of the word."

⁵ And the saying pleased the entire multitude. And they chose Stephen, a man full of faith and the Holy Spirit, and Philip, Prochorus, Nicanor, Timon, Parmenas, and Nicolas, a proselyte from Antioch,

⁶ whom they set before the apost-

les; and when they had prayed, they laid *their* hands on them.

⁷ Then the word of God spread, and the number of the disciples multiplied greatly in Jerusalem, and a large company of the priests were obedient to the faith.

⁸ And Stephen, full of faith and power, did great wonders and miracles among the people.

⁹ Then there arose some from what is called *the Synagogue* of the Libertines (Cyrenians, Alexandrians, and those from Cilicia and Asia), disputing with Stephen.

¹⁰ And they were not able to resist the wisdom and the Spirit by which he spoke.

¹¹ Then they secretly induced men to say, "We have heard him speak blasphemous words against Moses and *against* God."

¹² And they stirred up the people, the elders, and the scribes; and they came upon him, seized *him*, and brought *him* to the council.

¹³ They also set up false witnesses who said, "This man does not cease to speak blasphemous words against this holy place and the law;

¹⁴ because, we have heard him say that this Jesus of Nazareth will destroy this place and change the customs which Moses delivered to us."

¹⁵ And all who sat in the council, looking steadfastly at him, saw his face as though it was the face of an angel.

CHAPTER 7

¹ Then the high priest said, "Are these things so?"

² And he said, "Men, brethren, and fathers, listen: The God of glory appeared to our father Abraham when he was in Mesopotamia, before he dwelt in Haran,

³ and said to him, 'Get out of your country and from your relatives, and come into the land that I will show you.'

⁴ Then he came out of the land of the Chaldeans and dwelt in Haran. And from there, when his father was dead, He moved him to this land in which you now dwell.

⁵ And He gave him no inheritance in it, not *even enough* to set his foot on. But even when he had no child, He promised to give it to him for a possession, and to his seed after him.

⁶ But God spoke in this way: that his seed would dwell in a foreign land, and that they would bring them into bondage and oppress them four hundred years.

⁷ 'And the nation to whom they will be in bondage I will judge,' said God, 'and after that, they will come out and serve Me in this place.'

⁸ Then He gave him the covenant of circumcision; and so *Abraham* begot Isaac and circumcised him *on* the eighth day; and Isaac *begot* Jacob, and Jacob *begot* the twelve patriarchs.

⁹ "And the patriarchs, becoming envious, sold Joseph into Egypt. But

God was with him

¹⁰ and delivered him out of all his afflictions, and gave him favor and wisdom in the presence of Pharaoh, king of Egypt; and he made him governor over Egypt and all his house.

¹¹ Now a famine and great affliction came over all the land of Egypt and Canaan, and our fathers found no sustenance.

¹² But when Jacob heard that there was grain in Egypt, he sent out our fathers first.

¹³ And during the second *occasion* Joseph was made known to his brethren, and Joseph's family became known to the Pharaoh.

¹⁴ Then Joseph sent and called his father Jacob and all his relatives to *him*, seventy five people.

¹⁵ So Jacob went down to Egypt; and died, he and our fathers.

¹⁶ And they were carried back to Shechem and laid in the tomb that Abraham bought for a sum of money from the sons of Hamor, *the father* of Shechem.

¹⁷ "But when the time of the promise drew near which God had sworn to Abraham, the people grew and multiplied in Egypt

¹⁸ until another king arose who did not know Joseph.

¹⁹ This one dealt treacherously with our people, and oppressed our forefathers, making them throw out their babes, so that they would not live.

²⁰ During this time Moses was born, and was very beautiful; and *he was* brought up in his father's house for three months.

²¹ But when he was thrown out, Pharaoh's daughter took him away and brought him up as her own son.

²² And Moses was learned in all the wisdom of the Egyptians, and was mighty in words and deeds.

²³ "Now when he was forty years old, it came into his heart to visit his brethren, the children of Israel.

²⁴ And seeing one *of them* suffer wrongfully, he defended *him*, and avenged him who was oppressed, and struck down the Egyptian.

²⁵ Because, he supposed that his brethren would have understood that God would deliver them by his hand, but they did not understand.

²⁶ And the next day he appeared to two of them as they were fighting, and tried to reconcile them, saying, 'Men, you are brethren; why do you do wrong one to another?'

²⁷ But he who did his neighbor wrong pushed him away, saying, 'Who made you a ruler and a judge over us?

²⁸ Will you kill me as you did the Egyptian yesterday?'

²⁹ Then, at this saying, Moses fled and became a foreigner in the land of Midian, where he begot two sons.

³⁰ "And when forty years had passed, an Angel of the Lord appeared to him in a flame of fire in a bush, in the wilderness of Mount Sinai.

³¹ When Moses saw *it*, he marveled

at the sight; and as he drew near to observe *it*, the voice of the Lord came to him,

³² *saying*, 'I am the God of your fathers, the God of Abraham, the God of Isaac, and the God of Jacob.' And Moses trembled and dared not look.

³³ 'Then the LORD said to him, "Take your sandals off your feet, because the place where you stand is holy ground.

³⁴ I have seen, I have seen the oppression of My people who are in Egypt; I have heard their groaning and have come down to deliver them. And now come, I will send you to Egypt."'

³⁵ "This Moses whom they rejected, saying, 'Who made you a ruler and a judge?' is the one God sent *to be* a ruler and a deliverer by the hand of the Angel who appeared to him in the bush.

³⁶ He brought them out, after he had shown wonders and signs in the land of Egypt, and in the Red Sea, and in the wilderness forty years.

³⁷ "This is that Moses who said to the children of Israel, 'The LORD your God will raise up for you a Prophet like me from your brethren. Him you will hear.'

³⁸ "This is he who was in the congregation in the wilderness with the Angel who spoke to him on Mount Sinai, and *with* our fathers, who received the living oracles to give to us,

³⁹ whom our fathers would not obey, but rejected Him. And in their hearts they returned back to Egypt,

⁴⁰ saying to Aaron, 'Make us gods to go before us; *as for* this Moses who brought us out of the land of Egypt, we do not know what has become of him.'

⁴¹ And they made a calf in those days, offered sacrifices to the idol, and rejoiced in the works of their own hands.

⁴² Then God turned and gave them up to worship the army of heaven, as it is written in the book of the Prophets: 'Did you offer Me slaughtered animals and sacrifices *during the* forty years in the wilderness, O house of Israel?

⁴³ But you took up the tabernacle of Moloch, and the star of your god Remphan, images which you made to worship them; and I will carry you away beyond Babylon.'

⁴⁴ "Our fathers had the tabernacle of witness in the wilderness, as He had appointed, speaking to Moses, that he should make it according to the pattern that he had seen,

⁴⁵ which our fathers also, who came afterwards, brought in with Joshua into the possession of the Gentiles, whom God drove out before the face of our fathers until the days of David,

⁴⁶ who found favor before God and asked to find a tabernacle for the God of Jacob.

⁴⁷ But Solomon built Him a house.

⁴⁸ "However, the Most High does

not dwell in temples made with hands, as the prophet says:

⁴⁹ 'Heaven *is* My throne, and earth *is* My footstool. What house will you build for Me? says the LORD, or what is the place of My rest?

⁵⁰ Has My hand not made all these things?'

⁵¹ "You stiff necked and uncircumcised in heart and ears! You always resist the Holy Spirit; as your fathers *did*, so *do* you.

⁵² Which of the prophets did your fathers not persecute? And they have killed those who foretold the coming of the Just One, of whom you now have become the betrayers and murderers,

⁵³ who have received the law by the direction of angels and have not kept *it*."

⁵⁴ when they heard these things they were cut to the heart, and they gnashed at him with *their* teeth.

⁵⁵ But he, being full of the Holy Spirit, looked up gazing into heaven and saw the glory of God, and Jesus standing at the right hand of God,

⁵⁶ and said, "Behold! I see the heavens opened and the Son of Man standing at the right hand of God!"

⁵⁷ Then they shouted out with a loud voice, stopped their ears, and ran at him with one accord;

⁵⁸ and threw *him* out of the city and stoned *him*. And the witnesses laid down their clothes at the feet of a young man named Saul.

⁵⁹ And they stoned Stephen *as he was* calling on *God* and saying, "Lord Jesus, receive my spirit."

⁶⁰ Then he knelt down and shouted out with a loud voice, "Lord, do not charge them with this sin." And when he had said this, he fell asleep.

CHAPTER 8

¹ Now Saul was consenting to his death. And at that time there was a great persecution against the church which was at Jerusalem; and they were all scattered throughout the regions of Judea and Samaria, except the apostles.

² And devout men carried Stephen *to his burial*, and made great lamentation over him.

³ As for Saul, he made havoc of the church, entering into every house, and dragging men and women away, committing *them* to prison.

⁴ Therefore those who were scattered went everywhere preaching the word.

⁵ Then Philip went down to the city of Samaria and preached Christ to them.

⁶ And the people with one accord heeded the things spoken by Philip, hearing and seeing the miracles which he did.

⁷ Because, unclean spirits, shouting out with a loud voice, came out of many who were possessed *with them*; and many who were paralyzed and lame were healed.

⁸ And there was great joy in that city.

⁹ But there was a certain man called

Simon, who previously practiced sorcery in the same city and seduced the people of Samaria, claiming that he was some great one,

10 to whom they all gave heed, from the least to the greatest, saying, "This man is the great power of God."

11 And they heeded him because he had seduced them with his sorceries for a long time.

12 But when they believed Philip as he preached the things concerning the kingdom of God and the name of Jesus Christ, both men and women were baptized.

13 Then Simon himself also believed; and when he was baptized he continued with Philip, and was amazed, seeing the miracles and signs which were done.

14 Now when the apostles who were at Jerusalem heard that Samaria had received the word of God, they sent Peter and John to them,

15 who, when they had come down, prayed for them that they might receive the Holy Spirit.

16 Because as yet He had fallen upon none of them. They had only been baptized in the name of the Lord Jesus.

17 Then they laid *their* hands on them, and they received the Holy Spirit.

18 And when Simon saw that through the laying on of the apostles' hands the Holy Spirit was given, he offered them money,

19 saying, "Give me this authority also, that whoever I lay hands upon, they may receive the Holy Spirit."

20 But Peter said to him, "Your money perish with you, because you thought that the gift of God could be purchased with money!

21 You have neither part nor portion in this matter, because your heart is not right in the sight of God.

22 Therefore repent of this your wickedness, and ask God if perhaps the thought of your heart may be forgiven you.

23 Because I perceive that you are poisoned by bitterness and bound by iniquity."

24 Then Simon replied and said, "Pray to the Lord for me, that none of the things which you have spoken should come upon me."

25 So when they had testified and preached the word of the Lord, they returned to Jerusalem, and preached the gospel in many villages of the Samaritans.

26 Now an angel of the Lord spoke to Philip, saying, "Arise and go toward the south along the road which goes down from Jerusalem to Gaza, which is desert."

27 So he arose and went. And behold, a man of Ethiopia, a eunuch of great authority under Candace the queen of the Ethiopians, who had charge of all her treasury, and had come to Jerusalem to worship,

28 was returning, and sitting in his

chariot, *was* reading Isaiah the prophet.

²⁹ Then the Spirit said to Philip, "Go near and join yourself to this chariot."

³⁰ So Philip ran over to *him*, and heard him reading the prophet Isaiah, and said, "Do you understand what you are reading?"

³¹ And he said, "How can I, unless someone guides me?" And he wanted Philip to come up and sit with him.

³² The place in the Scripture which he read was this: "He was led as a sheep to the slaughter; and as a lamb before its shearer is silent, so He did not open His mouth.

³³ In His humiliation His justice was taken away, and who shall declare His generation? Because His life is taken from the earth."

³⁴ So the eunuch replied to Philip and said, "I ask you, of whom does the prophet say this, of himself or of some other man?"

³⁵ Then Philip opened his mouth, and beginning at this Scripture, preached Jesus to him.

³⁶ Now as they went on their way, they came to some water. And the eunuch said, "Look, *here* is water. What hinders me from being baptized?"

³⁷ Then Philip said, "If you believe with all your heart, you may." And he replied and said, "I believe that Jesus Christ is the Son of God."

³⁸ So he commanded the chariot to stand still. And they went down into the water, both Philip and the eunuch, and he baptized him.

³⁹ Now when they came up out of the water, the Spirit of the Lord caught Philip away, so that the eunuch did not see him any longer; and he went on his way rejoicing.

⁴⁰ But Philip was found at Azotus. And passing through, he preached in all the cities until he came to Caesarea.

CHAPTER 9

¹ Then Saul, still breathing threats and murder against the disciples of the Lord, went to the high priest

² and requested letters from him to the synagogues of Damascus, so that if he found any who were of the Way, whether men or women, he might bring them bound to Jerusalem.

³ As he journeyed he came near Damascus, and suddenly a light shone around him from heaven.

⁴ Then he fell to the ground, and heard a voice saying to him, "Saul, Saul, why are you persecuting Me?"

⁵ And he said, "Who are You, Lord?" Then the Lord said, "I am Jesus, whom you are persecuting. It is hard for you to kick against the prods."

⁶ So he, trembling and astonished, said, "Lord, what do You want me to do?" Then the Lord *said* to him, "Arise and go into the city, and you will be told what you must do."

⁷ And the men who journeyed with him stood speechless, hearing a

voice but seeing no one.

⁸ Then Saul arose from the ground, and when his eyes were opened he saw no one. But they led him by the hand and brought *him* into Damascus.

⁹ And he was without sight for three days, and neither ate nor drank.

¹⁰ Now there was a certain disciple at Damascus named Ananias; and to him the Lord said in a vision, "Ananias." And he said, "Behold, I am here, Lord."

¹¹ So the Lord *said* to him, "Arise and go to the street which is called Straight, and inquire at the house of Judas for *one* called Saul of Tarsus, because behold, he is praying.

¹² And in a vision he has seen a man named Ananias coming in and putting *his* hand on him, so that he might receive his sight."

¹³ Then Ananias replied, "Lord, I have heard from many about this man, how much evil he has done to Your saints in Jerusalem.

¹⁴ And here he has authority from the chief priests to bind all who call on Your name."

¹⁵ But the Lord said to him, "Go your way, because, he is a chosen vessel of Mine to bear My name before the Gentiles, kings, and the children of Israel.

¹⁶ Because, I will show him how many things he must suffer for My name's sake."

¹⁷ And Ananias went his way and entered into the house; and putting his hands on him he said, "Brother Saul, the Lord, *even* Jesus who appeared to you on the road as you came, has sent me that you may receive your sight and be filled with the Holy Spirit."

¹⁸ And immediately there fell from his eyes something like scales, and he received his sight at once; and he arose and was baptized.

¹⁹ So when he had received food, he was strengthened. Then Saul spent some days with the disciples at Damascus.

²⁰ And immediately he preached the Christ in the synagogues, that He is the Son of God.

²¹ Then all who heard *him* were amazed, and said, "Is this not he who destroyed those who called on this name in Jerusalem, and has come here for that purpose, so that he might bring them bound to the chief priests?"

²² But Saul increased all the more in strength, and confounded the Jews who dwelt in Damascus, proving that this truly is the Christ.

²³ Now after many days were past, the Jews plotted to kill him.

²⁴ But their plot became known to Saul. And they watched the gates day and night, to kill him.

²⁵ Then the disciples took him by night and let *him* down by the wall in a basket.

²⁶ And when Saul had come to Jerusalem, he tried to join himself to the disciples; but they were all

afraid of him, and did not believe that he was a disciple.

²⁷ But Barnabas took him and brought him to the apostles. And he declared to them how he had seen the Lord on the road, and that He had spoken to him, and how he had preached boldly at Damascus in the name of Jesus.

²⁸ So he was with them at Jerusalem, coming in and going out.

²⁹ And he spoke boldly in the name of the Lord Jesus and disputed against the Hellenists, but they attempted to kill him.

³⁰ Which when the brethren found out, they brought him down to Caesarea and sent him out to Tarsus.

³¹ Then the churches throughout all Judea, Galilee, and Samaria had rest and were edified. And walking in the reverence of the Lord and in the comfort of the Holy Spirit, they were multiplied.

³² Now it came to pass, as Peter went through every *corner of the country*, that he also came down to the saints who dwelt in Lydda.

³³ There he found a certain man named Aeneas, who had been bedridden eight years and was paralyzed.

³⁴ And Peter said to him, "Aeneas, Jesus Christ makes you whole. Arise and make your bed." Then he arose immediately.

³⁵ So all who dwelt at Lydda and Sharon saw him and turned to the Lord.

³⁶ Now at Joppa there was a certain disciple named Tabitha, which is translated Dorcas. This woman was full of good works and charitable deeds which she did.

³⁷ But it happened in those days that she became sick and died. When they had washed her, they laid *her* in an upper room.

³⁸ And since Lydda was near Joppa, and the disciples had heard that Peter was there, they sent two men to him, imploring *him* not to delay in coming to them.

³⁹ Then Peter arose and went with them. When he had come, they brought him into the upper room. And all the widows stood by him weeping, showing the coats and garments which Dorcas had made while she was with them.

⁴⁰ But Peter put them all out, and knelt down and prayed. And turning *himself* toward the body he said, "Tabitha, arise." And she opened her eyes, and when she saw Peter she sat up.

⁴¹ Then he gave her *his* hand and lifted her up; and when he had called the saints and widows, he presented her alive.

⁴² And it became known throughout all Joppa, and many believed in the Lord.

⁴³ So it was that he stayed many days in Joppa with Simon, a tanner.

CHAPTER 10

¹ There was a certain man in Caesarea called Cornelius, a cen-

turion of the regiment called the Italian Regiment,

² a devout *man* and one who reverenced God with all his household, who gave many charitable gifts to the people, and prayed to God always.

³ About the ninth hour of the day he saw clearly in a vision an angel of God coming in to him, and saying to him, "Cornelius!"

⁴ And when he looked at him, he was afraid, and said, "What is it, Lord?" So he said to him, "Your prayers and your charitable gifts have come up as a memorial before God.

⁵ And now send men to Joppa, and call for *one* Simon whose surname is Peter.

⁶ He is lodging with Simon, a tanner, whose house is beside the sea. He will tell you what you must do."

⁷ And when the angel who spoke to him had departed, Cornelius called two of his household servants and a devout soldier from among those who waited on him continually.

⁸ So when he had explained all *these* things to them, he sent them to Joppa.

⁹ On the next day, as they went on their journey and drew near the city, Peter went up on the housetop to pray, about the sixth hour.

¹⁰ Then he became very hungry and wanted to eat; but while they were preparing, he fell into a trance

¹¹ and saw heaven opened and a certain object just like a great sheet bound at the four corners, descending to him and let down to the earth.

¹² In it were all kinds of four footed animals of the earth, wild beasts, creeping things, and birds of the air.

¹³ And a voice came to him, "Rise, Peter; kill and eat."

¹⁴ But Peter said, "Not so, Lord! Because I have never eaten anything that is common or unclean."

¹⁵ And a voice *spoke* to him again the second time, "What God has cleansed you must not call common."

¹⁶ This was done three times. And the object was taken up into heaven again.

¹⁷ Now while Peter wondered within himself what this vision which he had seen meant, behold, the men who had been sent from Cornelius had made inquiry for Simon's house, and stood before the gate.

¹⁸ And they called and asked whether Simon, whose surname was Peter, was lodging there.

¹⁹ While Peter thought about the vision, the Spirit said to him, "Behold, three men are seeking you.

²⁰ Therefore arise, go down and go with them, doubting nothing; because I have sent them."

²¹ Then Peter went down to the men who had been sent to him from Cornelius, and said, "Behold, I am

he whom you seek. What *is* the reason then you have come?"

²² And they said, "Cornelius the centurion, a just man, one who reverences God and has a good reputation among all the nation of the Jews, was advised from God through a holy angel to summon you to his house, and to hear words from you."

²³ Then he invited them in and lodged *them*. On the next day Peter went away with them, and some brethren from Joppa accompanied him.

²⁴ And the following day they entered into Caesarea. Now Cornelius was waiting for them, and had called together his relatives and close friends.

²⁵ As Peter was coming in, Cornelius met him and fell down at his feet and worshiped *him*.

²⁶ But Peter lifted him up, saying, "Stand up; I myself am also a man."

²⁷ And as he talked with him, he went in and found many who had come together.

²⁸ Then he said to them, "You know how unlawful it is for someone who is a Jew to keep company with or go to one of another nation. But God has shown me that I should not call any man common or unclean.

²⁹ Therefore I came *to you* without objection as soon as I was sent for. I ask, then, for what reason have you sent for me?"

³⁰ So Cornelius said, "Four days ago I was fasting until this hour; and at the ninth hour I prayed in my house, and behold, a man stood before me in bright clothing,

³¹ and said, 'Cornelius, your prayer has been heard, and your charitable gifts are remembered in the sight of God.

³² Therefore send away to Joppa and call Simon here, whose surname is Peter. He is lodging in the house of *one* Simon, a tanner, beside the sea. When he comes, he will speak to you.'

³³ So I sent to you immediately, and you have done well that you came. Now therefore, we are all present before God, to hear all the things commanded you from God."

³⁴ Then Peter opened *his* mouth and said: "In truth I perceive that God shows no personal favoritism.

³⁵ But in every nation whoever reverences Him and works righteousness is accepted by Him.

³⁶ The word which *God* sent to the children of Israel, preaching peace through Jesus Christ, He is Lord of all,

³⁷ that word *I speak of,* you know, which was proclaimed throughout all Judea, and began from Galilee after the baptism which John preached:

³⁸ how God anointed Jesus of Nazareth with the Holy Spirit and with power, who went about doing good and healing all who were oppressed by the devil, because God was with Him.

³⁹ And we are witnesses of all things

which He did both in the land of the Jews and in Jerusalem, whom they murdered and hung on a tree.

⁴⁰ Him God raised up on the third day, and showed Him openly,

⁴¹ not to all the people, but to witnesses chosen before by God, *even* to us who ate and drank with Him after He arose from the dead.

⁴² And He commanded us to preach to the people, and to testify that it is He who was ordained by God *to be* the Judge of the living and the dead.

⁴³ To Him all the prophets give witness that, through His name, whoever believes in Him will receive remission of sins."

⁴⁴ While Peter was still speaking these words, the Holy Spirit fell upon all those who heard the word.

⁴⁵ And those of the circumcision who believed were astonished, as many as came with Peter, because the gift of the Holy Spirit had been poured out on the Gentiles also.

⁴⁶ Because they heard them speak with tongues and magnify God. *Then* they responded to Peter,

⁴⁷ "Can anyone forbid water, that these should not be baptized who have received the Holy Spirit just as we *have*?"

⁴⁸ And he commanded them to be baptized in the name of the Lord. Then they asked him to stay a few days.

CHAPTER 11

¹ Now the apostles and brethren who were in Judea heard that the Gentiles had also received the word of God.

² And when Peter came up to Jerusalem, those who were of the circumcision contended with him,

³ saying, "You went in to uncircumcised men and ate with them!"

⁴ But Peter explained *the issue* from the beginning, describing *it* to them in sequence, saying:

⁵ "I was in the city of Joppa praying; and in a trance I saw a vision, an object descending just like a great sheet, let down from heaven by four corners; and it came to me.

⁶ On which, when I observed it intently and considered, I saw four footed animals of the earth, wild beasts, creeping things, and birds of the air.

⁷ And I heard a voice saying to me, 'Rise, Peter; kill and eat.'

⁸ But I said, 'Not so, Lord! Because nothing common or unclean has at any time entered my mouth.'

⁹ But the voice replied to me again from heaven, 'What God has cleansed you must not call *that* common .'

¹⁰ Now this was done three times, and all were drawn up again into heaven.

¹¹ And, behold, immediately there were three men already standing before the house where I was, having been sent to me from Caesarea.

¹² Then the Spirit told me to go with them, doubting nothing. Moreover

these six brethren accompanied me, and we entered the man's house.

¹³ And he told us how he had seen an angel standing in his house, who said to him, 'Send men to Joppa, and call for Simon whose surname is Peter,

¹⁴ who will tell you words by which you and all your household will be saved.'

¹⁵ And as I began to speak, the Holy Spirit fell upon them, as upon us at the beginning.

¹⁶ Then I remembered the word of the Lord, how He said, 'John indeed baptized with water, but you will be baptized with the Holy Spirit.'

¹⁷ If therefore God gave them the same gift as *He did* to us when we believed on the Lord Jesus Christ, who was I that I could withstand God?"

¹⁸ When they heard these things they held their peace; and they glorified God, saying, "Then God has also granted to the Gentiles repentance to life."

¹⁹ Now those who were scattered after the persecution that arose over Stephen traveled as far as Phoenicia, Cyprus, and Antioch, preaching the word to no one but the Jews only.

²⁰ But some of them were men from Cyprus and Cyrene, who, when they had come to Antioch, spoke to the Hellenists, preaching the Lord Jesus.

²¹ And the hand of the Lord was with them, and a great number believed and turned to the Lord.

²² Then news of these things came to the ears of the church that was in Jerusalem, and they sent out Barnabas to go as far as Antioch.

²³ Who when he came and had seen the grace of God, was glad, and encouraged them all that with purpose of heart they should continue with the Lord.

²⁴ Because, he was a good man, full of the Holy Spirit and of faith. And many people were added to the Lord.

²⁵ Then Barnabas departed for Tarsus to seek for Saul.

²⁶ And when he had found him, he brought him to Antioch. So it was that for an entire year they assembled with the church and taught many people. And the disciples were first called Christians in Antioch.

²⁷ And in these days prophets came from Jerusalem to Antioch.

²⁸ Then one of them, named Agabus, stood up and signified by the Spirit that there was going to be a great famine throughout all the world, which occurred in the days of Claudius Caesar.

²⁹ Then the disciples, each according to his ability, determined to send relief to the brethren dwelling in Judea.

³⁰ This they also did, and sent it to the elders by the hands of Barnabas and Saul.

CHAPTER 12

¹ Now about that time Herod the king stretched out *his* hand to harass some from the church.

² Then he killed James the brother of John with the sword.

³ And because he saw that it pleased the Jews, he proceeded further to seize Peter also. These were the Days of Unleavened Bread.

⁴ So when he had arrested him, he put *him* in prison, and delivered *him* to four squads of soldiers to keep him, intending after Easter to bring him before the people.

⁵ Therefore Peter was kept in prison, but constant prayer was offered to God for him by the church.

⁶ And when Herod was about to bring him out, that same night Peter was sleeping, bound with two chains between two soldiers; and the guards before the door were guarding the prison.

⁷ Now behold, the angel of the Lord stood over *him*, and a light shone in the prison; and he struck Peter on the side and raised him up, saying, "Rise up quickly!" And his chains fell off from *his* hands.

⁸ Then the angel said to him, "Gird yourself and tie on your sandals"; and so he did. And he said to him, "Put on your clothes and follow me."

⁹ So he went out and followed him, and did not know that what was done by the angel was real, but thought he saw a vision.

¹⁰ When they were past the first and the second guard posts, they came to the iron gate that leads to the city, which opened to them of its own accord; and they went out and went down through one street, and immediately the angel departed from him.

¹¹ And when Peter had come to himself, he said, "Now I know for certain that the Lord has sent His angel, and has delivered me from the hand of Herod and *from* all the expectation of the Jewish people."

¹² So, when he had considered *the matter*, he came to the house of Mary, the mother of John whose surname was Mark, where many were gathered together praying.

¹³ And as Peter knocked at the door of the gate, a girl named Rhoda came to answer.

¹⁴ When she recognized Peter's voice, because of gladness she did not open the gate, but ran in and announced that Peter stood before the gate.

¹⁵ But they said to her, "You are mad!" Yet she kept insisting that it was so. So they said, "It is his angel."

¹⁶ Now Peter continued knocking; and when they opened *the door* and saw him, they were astonished.

¹⁷ But motioning to them with his hand to keep silent, he declared to them how the Lord had brought him out of the prison. And he said, "Go, tell these things to James and to the brethren." And he departed

and went to another place.

¹⁸ Then, as soon as it was day, there was no small stir among the soldiers about what had become of Peter.

¹⁹ But when Herod had searched for him and did not find him, he examined the guards and commanded that *they* should be put to death. And he went down from Judea to Caesarea, and stayed *there*.

²⁰ Now Herod had been very displeased with the people of Tyre and Sidon; but they came to him with one accord, and having made Blastus the king's personal aide their friend, they desired peace, because their country was supplied with food by the king's *country*.

²¹ So on a set day Herod, arrayed in royal apparel, sat upon his throne and gave a speech to them.

²² And the people shouted out, *saying*, "It *is* the voice of a god and not of a man!"

²³ Then immediately an angel of the Lord struck him, because he did not give glory to God. So he became eaten by worms and gave up the spirit.

²⁴ But the word of God grew and multiplied.

²⁵ And Barnabas and Saul returned from Jerusalem when they had fulfilled *their* ministry, and they also took with them John whose surname was Mark.

CHAPTER 13

¹ Now in the church that was at Antioch there were certain prophets and teachers: Barnabas, Simeon who was called Niger, Lucius of Cyrene, Manaen who had been brought up with Herod the tetrarch, and Saul.

² As they ministered to the Lord and fasted, the Holy Spirit said, "Now separate to Me Barnabas and Saul for the work to which I have called them."

³ Then, when they had fasted and prayed, and laid *their* hands on them, they sent *them* away.

⁴ So, being sent out by the Holy Spirit, they departed to Seleucia, and from there they sailed to Cyprus.

⁵ And when they arrived in Salamis, they preached the word of God in the synagogues of the Jews. They also had John as *their* assistant.

⁶ Now when they had gone through the island to Paphos, they found a certain sorcerer, a false prophet, a Jew whose name *was* Barjesus,

⁷ who was with the proconsul of the country, Sergius Paulus, a prudent man. This man called for Barnabas and Saul and sought to hear the word of God.

⁸ But Elymas the sorcerer (for so his name is translated) opposed them, seeking to turn the proconsul away from the faith.

⁹ Then Saul (who also *is called* Paul), filled with the Holy Spirit, looked intently at him

¹⁰ and said, "O full of all deceit and all fraud, *you* child of the devil, *you*

enemy of all righteousness, will you not cease perverting the right ways of the Lord?

¹¹ And now, behold, the hand of the Lord *is* upon you, and you will be blind, not seeing the sun for a season." And immediately a mist fell on him and darkness, and he went around seeking someone to lead him by the hand.

¹² Then the proconsul believed, when he saw what had been done, being astonished at the doctrine of the Lord.

¹³ Now when Paul and his company set sail from Paphos, they came to Perga in Pamphylia; and John, departing from them, returned to Jerusalem.

¹⁴ But when they departed from Perga, they came to Antioch in Pisidia, and went into the synagogue on the Sabbath day and sat down.

¹⁵ And after the reading of the Law and the Prophets, the rulers of the synagogue sent to them, saying, "*You* men *and* brethren, if you have any word of exhortation for the people, say on."

¹⁶ Then Paul stood up, and motioning with *his* hand said, "Men of Israel, and you who reverence God, pay attention:

¹⁷ The God of this people Israel chose our fathers, and lifted up the people when they dwelt as foreigners in the land of Egypt, and with an uplifted arm He brought them out of it.

¹⁸ Now for a time of about forty years He endured with their ways in the wilderness.

¹⁹ And when He had destroyed seven nations in the land of Canaan, He distributed their land to them by allotment.

²⁰ "And after that He gave judges *to them* for the period of four hundred and fifty years, until Samuel the prophet.

²¹ And afterward they desired a king; so God gave them Saul the son of Kish, a man of the tribe of Benjamin, for the period of forty years.

²² And when He had removed him, He raised up for them David to be their king, to whom also He gave testimony and said, 'I have found David the *son* of Jesse, a man after My own heart, who will fulfill all My will.'

²³ From this man's seed, according to *His* promise, has God raised up for Israel a Savior, Jesus;

²⁴ after John had first preached, before His coming, the baptism of repentance to all the people of Israel.

²⁵ And as John fulfilled his course, he said, 'Who do you think I am? I am not *He*. But behold, there comes One after me, the sandals of *His* feet I am not worthy to loose.'

²⁶ "Men *and* brethren, children of the family of Abraham, and those among you who reverence God, to you the word of this salvation has been sent.

²⁷ Because, those who dwell in Jeru-

salem, and their rulers, since they did not know Him, nor even the voices of the Prophets which are read every Sabbath day, have fulfilled *them* in condemning *Him*.

²⁸ And though they found no reason for death *in Him*, they asked Pilate that He should be killed.

²⁹ Now when they had fulfilled all that was written concerning Him, they took *Him* down from the tree and laid *Him* in a tomb.

³⁰ But God raised Him from the dead.

³¹ He was seen for many days by those who came up with Him from Galilee to Jerusalem, who are His witnesses to the people.

³² And we declare to you glad tidings; how that promise which was made to the fathers,

³³ God has fulfilled this for us their children, in that He has raised up Jesus again. As it is also written in the second Psalm: 'You are My Son, today I have begotten You.'

³⁴ And concerning how He raised Him from the dead, *now* no more to return to corruption, He has spoken in this way: 'I will give you the sure mercies of David.'

³⁵ Therefore He also says in another *Psalm*: 'You will not allow Your Holy One to see corruption.'

³⁶ "Because David, after he had served his own generation by the will of God, fell asleep, was placed with his fathers, and saw corrupttion;

³⁷ but He whom God raised up saw no corruption.

³⁸ Therefore let it be known to you, men *and* brethren, that through this Man is preached to you the forgiveness of sins;

³⁹ and by Him everyone who believes is justified from all things from which you could not be justified by the law of Moses.

⁴⁰ Beware therefore, lest what has been spoken in the prophets come upon you:

⁴¹ 'Behold, you despisers, marvel and perish! Because, I work a work in your days, a work which you will by no means believe, though one were to declare it to you.' "

⁴² So when the Jews had gone out of the synagogue, the Gentiles begged that these words might be preached to them the next Sabbath.

⁴³ Now when the congregation had broken up, many of the Jews and devout proselytes followed Paul and Barnabas, who, speaking to them, persuaded them to continue in the grace of God.

⁴⁴ And the next Sabbath day almost the entire city came together to hear the word of God.

⁴⁵ But when the Jews saw the crowds, they were filled with envy; and contradicting and blaspheming, they spoke against the things spoken by Paul.

⁴⁶ Then Paul and Barnabas grew bold and said, "It was necessary that the word of God should be spoken to you first; but since you reject it, and judge yourselves un-

worthy of everlasting life, behold, we turn to the Gentiles.

⁴⁷ Because, so has the Lord commanded us, *saying* 'I have set you as a light to the Gentiles, that you should exist for salvation to the ends of the earth.' "

⁴⁸ Now when the Gentiles heard this, they were glad and glorified the word of the Lord. And as many as were ordained to eternal life believed.

⁴⁹ And the word of the Lord was being spread throughout the entire region.

⁵⁰ But the Jews stirred up the devout and prominent women and the chief men of the city, raised up persecution against Paul and Barnabas, and expelled them from their region.

⁵¹ But they shook off the dust from their feet against them, and came to Iconium.

⁵² And the disciples were filled with joy and with the Holy Spirit.

CHAPTER 14

¹ Now it happened in Iconium that they both went together to the synagogue of the Jews, and spoke in such a way that a large crowd both of the Jews and of the Greeks believed.

² But the unbelieving Jews stirred up the Gentiles and poisoned their minds against the brethren.

³ Therefore they stayed there a long time, speaking boldly in the Lord, who gave testimony to the word of His grace, and granted signs and wonders to be done by their hands.

⁴ But the population of the city was divided: part sided with the Jews, and part with the apostles.

⁵ And when a violent attempt was made by both the Gentiles and Jews, with their rulers, to abuse them, and to stone them,

⁶ they were aware of *it* and fled to Lystra and Derbe, cities of Lycaonia, and to the surrounding region.

⁷ And they preached the gospel there.

⁸ And in Lystra a certain man without strength in his feet was sitting, being a cripple from his mother's womb, who had never walked.

⁹ *This* man heard Paul speaking, who observing him intently and seeing that he had faith to be healed,

¹⁰ said with a loud voice, "Stand up straight on your feet!" And he leaped and walked.

¹¹ Now when the people saw what Paul had done, they raised their voices, saying in the Lycaonian language, "The gods have come down to us in the likeness of men!"

¹² And Barnabas they called Jupiter, and Paul, Mercurius, because he was the chief speaker.

¹³ Then the priest of Jupiter, who was in front of their city, brought oxen and garlands to the gates, intending to do sacrifice with the people.

¹⁴ *But* when the apostles Barnabas and Paul heard this, they tore their clothes and ran in among the people, shouting out
¹⁵ and saying, "Men, why are you doing these things? We also are men with similar desires to you, and preach to you that you should turn from these useless things to the living God, who made the heaven, the earth, the sea, and all things that are in them,
¹⁶ who in times past allowed all nations to walk in their own ways.
¹⁷ Nevertheless He did not leave Himself without witness, in that He did good, gave us rain from heaven and fruitful seasons, filling our hearts with food and gladness."
¹⁸ And with these sayings they could barely restrain the people from sacrificing to them.
¹⁹ Then *certain* Jews from Antioch and Iconium came there; who persuaded the people, and having stoned Paul, dragged *him* out of the city, supposing him to be dead.
²⁰ However, when the disciples gathered around him, he rose up and went into the city. And the next day he departed with Barnabas to Derbe.
²¹ And when they had preached the gospel to that city and taught many, they returned to Lystra, Iconium, and Antioch,
²² strengthening the souls of the disciples, exhorting them to continue in the faith, and that through many tribulations we must enter the kingdom of God.
²³ So when they had ordained elders in every church, and prayed with fasting, they commended them to the Lord in whom they had believed.
²⁴ And after they had passed through Pisidia, they came to Pamphylia.
²⁵ Now when they had preached the word in Perga, they went down into Attalia.
²⁶ From there they sailed to Antioch, where they had been commended to the grace of God for the work which they had completed.
²⁷ Now when they had come and gathered the church together, they reported all that God had done with them, and how He had opened the door of faith to the Gentiles.
²⁸ So they stayed there a long time with the disciples.

CHAPTER 15

¹ And certain men who came down from Judea taught the brethren, *and said* "Unless you are circumcised according to the custom of Moses, you cannot be saved."
² Therefore, when Paul and Barnabas had no small dissension and dispute with them, they determined that Paul and Barnabas and certain others of them should go up to Jerusalem, to the apostles and elders, about this question.
³ So, being sent on their way by the church, they passed through Phoenicia and Samaria, describing the

conversion of the Gentiles; and they caused great joy to all the brethren.

⁴ And when they had come to Jerusalem, they were received by the church and *by* the apostles and the elders; and they declared everything that God had done with them.

⁵ But some of the sect of the Pharisees who believed rose up, saying, "It is necessary to circumcise them, and to command them to keep the law of Moses."

⁶ Now the apostles and elders came together to consider this matter.

⁷ And when there had been a great disputation, Peter rose up and said to them: "Men *and* brethren, you know that a good while ago God chose among us, that by my mouth the Gentiles should hear the word of the gospel and believe.

⁸ So God, who knows the heart, bore witness to them by giving them the Holy Spirit, just as *He* did to us,

⁹ and made no distinction between us and them, purifying their hearts by faith.

¹⁰ Now therefore, why do you test God by putting a yoke on the neck of the disciples which neither our fathers nor we were able to bear?

¹¹ But we believe that through the grace of the Lord Jesus Christ we will be saved in the same manner as they."

¹² Then all the multitude kept silent and listened to Barnabas and Paul declaring what miracles and wonders God had worked through them among the Gentiles.

¹³ And after they had become silent, James replied, saying, "Men *and* brethren, listen to me:

¹⁴ Simon has declared how God at the first visited the Gentiles to take out of them a people for His name.

¹⁵ And with this the words of the prophets agree, as it is written:

¹⁶ 'After this I will return and will rebuild the tabernacle of David, which has fallen down; I will rebuild its ruins, and I will set it up;

¹⁷ So that the remainder of the people may seek the Lord, and all the Gentiles who are called by My name, says the Lord who does all these things.'

¹⁸ "Known to God are all His works from the beginning of the world.

¹⁹ Therefore my judgment is that we should not trouble those from among the Gentiles who have turned to God,

²⁰ but that we write to them that they abstain from things polluted by idols, *from* sexual immorality, from things strangled, and *from* blood.

²¹ Because, Moses has those who preach him in every city from old times, being read in the synagogues every Sabbath day."

²² Then it pleased the apostles and elders, with the entire church, to send chosen men of their own company to Antioch with Paul and Barnabas, *namely*, Judas surnamed Barsabas, and Silas, leading men

among the brethren.

²³ They wrote letters by them according to this manner: The apostles, the elders, and the brethren, send greetings to the brethren who are of the Gentiles in Antioch, Syria, and Cilicia.

²⁴ Since we have heard that some who went out from us have troubled you with words, unsettling your souls, saying, "*You must* be circumcised and keep the law," to whom we gave no *such* commandment ,

²⁵ it seemed good to us, being assembled with one accord, to send chosen men to you with our beloved Barnabas and Paul,

²⁶ men who have endangered their lives for the name of our Lord Jesus Christ.

²⁷ We have therefore sent Judas and Silas, who will also tell *you* the same things by mouth.

²⁸ Because, it seemed good to the Holy Spirit, and to us, to lay upon you no greater burden than these necessary things:

²⁹ that you abstain from food offered to idols, from blood, from things strangled, and from sexual immorality. If you keep yourselves from these, you will do well. Farewell.

³⁰ So when they were dismissed, they came to Antioch; and when they had gathered the multitude together, they delivered the letter.

³¹ Which when they had read, they rejoiced over its encouragement.

³² Now Judas and Silas, themselves being prophets also, exhorted the brethren with many words and confirmed *them.*

³³ And after they had stayed there for a time, they were let go in peace from the brethren to the apostles.

³⁴ However, it seemed good to Silas to remain there.

³⁵ Paul and Barnabas also remained in Antioch, teaching and preaching the word of the Lord, with many others also.

³⁶ Then after some days Paul said to Barnabas, "Let us now go back and visit our brethren in every city where we have preached the word of the Lord, *and see* how they are doing."

³⁷ Now Barnabas was determined to take with them John whose surname was Mark.

³⁸ But Paul did not think it good to take him with them, who had departed from them in Pamphylia, and had not gone with them to the work.

³⁹ Then the contention became so sharp that they parted from one another. And so Barnabas took Mark and sailed to Cyprus;

⁴⁰ but Paul chose Silas and departed, being commended by the brethren to the grace of God.

⁴¹ And he went through Syria and Cilicia, strengthening the churches.

CHAPTER 16

¹ Then he came to Derbe and Lystra. And behold, a certain dis-

ciple was there, named Timothy, the son of a certain Jewish woman who believed, but his father *was a* Greek.

² He was well reported of by the brethren who were at Lystra and Iconium.

³ Paul wanted to have him go on with him. And he took *him* and circumcised him because of the Jews who were in that region, because they all knew that his father was a Greek.

⁴ And as they went through the cities, they delivered to them the decrees to keep, which were determined by the apostles and elders who were at Jerusalem.

⁵ And so the churches were established in the faith, and increased in number daily.

⁶ Now when they had gone throughout Phrygia and the region of Galatia, they were forbidden by the Holy Spirit to preach the word in Asia.

⁷ After they had come to Mysia, they tried to go into Bithynia, but the Spirit did not permit them.

⁸ So passing by Mysia, they came down to Troas.

⁹ And a vision appeared to Paul in the night. A man of Macedonia stood and pleaded with him, saying, "Come over to Macedonia and help us."

¹⁰ Now after he had seen the vision, immediately we sought to go to Macedonia, concluding that the Lord had called us to preach the gospel to them.

¹¹ Therefore, untying from Troas, we ran a straight course to Samothrace, and the next *day* to Neapolis,

¹² and from there to Philippi, which is the foremost city of that part of Macedonia and a colony. And we were staying in that city for some days.

¹³ And on the Sabbath we went out of the city to the riverside, where prayer was customarily made; and we sat down and spoke to the women who met *there*.

¹⁴ Now a certain woman named Lydia heard *us*. She was a seller of purple from the city of Thyatira, who worshiped God. The Lord opened her heart to heed the things that were spoken by Paul.

¹⁵ And when she and her household were baptized, she begged *us*, saying, "If you have judged me to be faithful to the Lord, come to my house and stay *there*." So she persuaded us.

¹⁶ Now it happened, as we went to prayer, that a certain girl possessed with a spirit of divination met us, who brought her masters much profit by fortune telling.

¹⁷ This girl followed Paul and us, and shouted out, saying, "These men are the servants of the Most High God, who proclaim to us the way of salvation."

¹⁸ And this she did for many days. But Paul, being grieved, turned and said to the spirit, "I command you

in the name of Jesus Christ to come out of her." And he came out that very hour.

¹⁹ But when her masters saw that their hope of profit was gone, they seized Paul and Silas and dragged *them* into the marketplace to the authorities.

²⁰ And they brought them to the magistrates, and said, "These men, being Jews, greatly trouble our city; ²¹ and they teach customs which are not lawful for us to receive or to observe being Romans."

²² Then the crowd rose up together against them; and the magistrates tore off their clothes and commanded *them* to beat them.

²³ And when they had laid many stripes on them, they threw *them* into prison, commanding the jailer to keep them securely.

²⁴ Who Having received such an order, put them into the inner prison and fastened their feet in the stocks.

²⁵ But at midnight Paul and Silas were praying and singing praises to God, and the prisoners listened to them.

²⁶ Then suddenly there was a great earthquake, so that the foundations of the prison were shaken; and immediately all the doors were opened and everyone's chains were loosed.

²⁷ And the keeper of the prison, awaking from sleep and seeing the prison doors open, supposing the prisoners had fled, drew his sword and would have killed himself.

²⁸ But Paul shouted out with a loud voice, saying, "Do yourself no harm, because we are all here."

²⁹ Then he called for a light, ran in, and fell down trembling before Paul and Silas.

³⁰ And he brought them out and said, "Men, what must I do to be saved?"

³¹ So they said, "Believe on the Lord Jesus Christ, and you shall be saved, likewise your household."

³² Then they spoke the word of the Lord to him and to all who were in his house.

³³ And he took them the same hour of the night and washed *their* stripes. And immediately he and all his family were baptized.

³⁴ Now when he had brought them into his house, he set food before them; and he rejoiced, having believed in God with his entire household.

³⁵ And when it was day, the magistrates sent the officers, saying, "Let those men go."

³⁶ So the keeper of the prison reported these words to Paul, saying, "The magistrates have sent to let you go. Now therefore depart, and go in peace."

³⁷ But Paul said to them, "They have beaten us openly, being uncondemned Romans, and have thrown *us* into prison. And now do they put us out secretly? No indeed! But let them come themselves and get us out."

³⁸ And the officers told these words to the magistrates, and they were afraid when they heard that they were Romans.

³⁹ Then they came and pleaded with them and brought *them* out, and asked *them* to depart from the city.

⁴⁰ So they went out of the prison and entered *the house* of Lydia; and when they had seen the brethren, they encouraged them and departed.

CHAPTER 17

¹ Now when they had passed through Amphipolis and Apollonia, they came to Thessalonica, where there was a synagogue of the Jews.

² Then Paul, as his custom was, went in to them, and for three Sabbath days reasoned with them from the Scriptures,

³ explaining and demonstrating that Christ had to suffer and rise again from the dead, and saying, "This Jesus whom I preach to you is Christ."

⁴ And some of them believed; and a large multitude of the devout Greeks, and not a few of the leading women, joined Paul and Silas.

⁵ But the Jews who did not believe, becoming envious, took some of the wicked men of a vulgar sort, and gathering a mob, set the entire city in an uproar and attacked the house of Jason, and sought to bring them out to the people.

⁶ But when they did not find them, they dragged Jason and some brethren to the rulers of the city, shouting out, "These who have turned the world upside down have come here also,

⁷ Jason has harbored them, and these are all acting contrary to the decrees of Caesar, saying there is another king, *one* Jesus."

⁸ And they troubled the people and the rulers of the city when they heard these things.

⁹ So when they had taken *enough* security from Jason and from the rest, they let them go.

¹⁰ Then the brethren immediately sent Paul and Silas away by night to Berea. When they arrived, they went into the synagogue of the Jews.

¹¹ These were more noble than those in Thessalonica, in that they received the word with all readiness of mind, and searched the Scriptures daily whether these things were so.

¹² Therefore many of them believed, and also not a few of the Greeks, prominent women as well as men.

¹³ But when the Jews from Thessalonica learned that the word of God was preached by Paul at Berea, they came there also and stirred up the people.

¹⁴ And then immediately the brethren sent Paul away, to go as it were to the sea; but both Silas and Timothy remained there.

¹⁵ So those who escorted Paul brou-

ght him to Athens; and receiving a command for Silas and Timothy to come to him as soon as possible, they departed.

16 Now while Paul waited for them at Athens, his spirit was stirred within him when he saw that the city was entirely given over to idolatry.

17 Therefore he disputed in the synagogue with the Jews and with the devout people, and in the marketplace daily with those who met with him.

18 Then some of the Epicurean and of the Stoic philosophers encountered him. And some said, "What does this babbler say?" Others said, "He seems to be a proclaimer of foreign gods," because he preached to them Jesus and the resurrection.

19 And they took him and brought him to the Areopagus, saying, "May we know what this new doctrine is of which you speak?

20 Because, you are bringing some strange things to our ears. Therefore we want to know what these things mean."

21 Because, all the Athenians and the foreigners who were there spent their time in nothing else except to tell or to hear something new.

22 Then Paul stood in the midst of the Mars' Hill and said, "*You* men of Athens, I perceive that in all things you are too superstitious;

23 because, as I was passing by and considering the objects of your worship, I found an altar with this inscription: TO THE UNKNOWN GOD. Therefore, the One whom you ignorantly worship, Him I proclaim to you:

24 "God, who made the world and everything in it, since He is Lord of heaven and earth, does not dwell in temples made with hands.

25 Nor is He worshiped with men's hands, as though He needed anything, since He gives to all life, breath, and all things.

26 And He has made from one blood every nation of men to dwell on all the face of the earth, and has determined their preappointed times and the boundaries of their dwellings,

27 so that they should seek the Lord, in the hope that they might seek for Him and find Him, though He is not far from each one of us;

28 because in Him we live and move and have our being, as also some of your own poets have said, 'because we are also His offspring.'

29 Therefore, since we are the offspring of God, we ought not to think that the Godhead is like gold or silver or stone, something shaped by art and man's devising.

30 And, these times of such ignorance God overlooked, but now commands all men everywhere to repent,

31 because He has appointed a day on which He will judge the world in righteousness by *that* Man whom He has ordained. He has given as-

surance of this to all *people* by raising Him from the dead."

³² And when they heard of the resurrection of the dead, some mocked, while others said, "We will hear you again on this *matter*."

³³ So Paul departed from among them.

³⁴ However, some men joined him and believed, among them *was* Dionysius the Areopagite, a woman named Damaris, and others with them.

CHAPTER 18

¹ After these things Paul departed from Athens and came to Corinth.

² And he found a certain Jew named Aquila, born in Pontus, who had recently come from Italy with his wife Priscilla (because Claudius had commanded all the Jews to depart from Rome); and he came to them.

³ So, because he was of the same trade, he stayed with them and worked; because by occupation they were tentmakers.

⁴ And he reasoned in the synagogue every Sabbath, and persuaded both Jews and Greeks.

⁵ And when Silas and Timothy had come from Macedonia, Paul was compelled by the Spirit, and testified to the Jews *that* Jesus *is* the Christ.

⁶ But when they opposed themselves and blasphemed, he shook *his* clothes and said to them, "Your blood *be* upon your own heads; I *am* clean. From now on I will go to the Gentiles."

⁷ And he departed from there and entered the house of a certain *man* named Justus, one who worshiped God, whose house was next door to the synagogue.

⁸ Then Crispus, the ruler of the synagogue, believed on the Lord with his entire household. And many of the Corinthians, hearing, believed and were baptized.

⁹ Now the Lord spoke to Paul in the night by a vision, "Do not be afraid, but speak, and do not keep silent;

¹⁰ because I am with you, and no one will attack you to hurt you; because I have many people in this city."

¹¹ And he continued *there* a year and six months, teaching the word of God among them.

¹² When Gallio was proconsul of Achaia, the Jews with one accord rose up against Paul and brought him to the judgment seat,

¹³ saying, "This *man* persuades men to worship God contrary to the law."

¹⁴ And when Paul was about to open *his* mouth, Gallio said to the Jews, "If it were a matter of wrongdoing or wicked crimes, O Jews, there would be reason why I should bear with you.

¹⁵ But if it is a question of words and names and your own law, look *to it* yourselves; because I do not want to be a judge of such *matters*."

¹⁶ And he drove them from the judgment seat.

¹⁷ Then all the Greeks took Sosthenes, the ruler of the synagogue, and beat *him* before the judgment seat. But Gallio took no notice of these things.

¹⁸ So *after this* Paul still remained there a good while. Then he took leave of the brethren and sailed there into Syria, and Priscilla and Aquila were with him; having shaved *his* head at Cenchrea, because he had taken a vow.

¹⁹ And he came to Ephesus, and left them there; but he himself entered the synagogue and reasoned with the Jews.

²⁰ when they asked *him* to stay a longer time with them, he did not consent,

²¹ but bid them goodbye, saying, "I must by all means keep this coming feast in Jerusalem; but I will return again to you, God willing." And he sailed from Ephesus.

²² And when he had landed at Caesarea, and gone up and greeted the church, he went down to Antioch.

²³ After he had spent some time *there*, he departed and went over the *entire* region of Galatia and Phrygia in order, strengthening all the disciples.

²⁴ Now a certain Jew named Apollos, born at Alexandria, an eloquent man and mighty in the Scriptures, came to Ephesus.

²⁵ This man had been instructed in the way of the Lord; and being fervent in spirit, he spoke and taught diligently the things of the Lord, though he knew only the baptism of John.

²⁶ So he began to speak boldly in the synagogue. When Aquila and Priscilla heard him, they took him aside and explained to him the way of God more exactly.

²⁷ And when he desired to cross to Achaia, the brethren wrote, exhorting the disciples to receive him; and when he arrived, he greatly helped those who had believed through grace;

²⁸ because he effectively refuted the Jews, *doing* so publicly, showing from the Scriptures that Jesus is the Christ.

CHAPTER 19

¹ And it happened, while Apollos was at Corinth, that Paul, having passed through the upper regions, came to Ephesus. And finding certain disciples

² he said to them, "Have you received the Holy Spirit since you believed?" But they said to him, "We have not so much as heard whether there is a Holy Spirit."

³ And he said to them, "Into what then were you baptized?" And they said, "Into John's baptism."

⁴ Then Paul said, "John indeed baptized with a baptism of repentance, saying to the people that they should believe on Him who would come after him, that is, on Christ Jesus."

⁵ When they heard *this*, they were

baptized in the name of the Lord Jesus.

⁶ And when Paul had laid his hands on them, the Holy Spirit came upon them, and they spoke with tongues and prophesied.

⁷ Now the men were about twelve in all.

⁸ And he went into the synagogue and spoke boldly for the space of three months, disputing and persuading the things concerning the kingdom of God.

⁹ But when some were hardened and did not believe, but spoke evil of the Way before the crowd, he departed from them and withdrew the disciples, reasoning daily in the school of one Tyrannus.

¹⁰ And this continued for the space of two years, so that all those who dwelt in Asia heard the word of the Lord Jesus, both Jews and Greeks.

¹¹ Now God worked unusual miracles by the hands of Paul,

¹² so that handkerchiefs or aprons were brought from his body to the sick, and the diseases left them and the evil spirits went out of them.

¹³ Then some of the itinerant Jewish exorcists took it upon themselves to call the name of the Lord Jesus over those who had evil spirits, saying, "We exorcise you by Jesus whom Paul preaches."

¹⁴ And there were seven sons of one Sceva, a Jew and chief priest, who did so.

¹⁵ And the evil spirit replied and said, "Jesus I know, and Paul I know; but who are you?"

¹⁶ Then the man in whom the evil spirit was leaped on them, overpowered them, and prevailed against them, so that they fled out of that house naked and wounded.

¹⁷ This became known both to all Jews and Greeks dwelling in Ephesus; and fear fell on them all, and the name of the Lord Jesus was magnified.

¹⁸ And many who had believed came confessing and telling their deeds.

¹⁹ Also, many of those who had practiced magic brought their books together and burned them in the sight of everyone. And they counted up the value of them, and *it* totaled fifty thousand *pieces* of silver.

²⁰ So the word of God grew mightily and prevailed.

²¹ When these things were accomplished, Paul purposed in the Spirit, when he had passed through Macedonia and Achaia, to go to Jerusalem, saying, "After I have been there, I must also see Rome."

²² So he sent into Macedonia two of those who ministered to him, Timothy and Erastus, but he himself stayed in Asia for a season.

²³ And about that time there arose no small commotion about the Way.

²⁴ Because, a certain *man* named Demetrius, a silversmith, who made silver shrines of Diana, brought no small profit to the craftsmen,

²⁵ whom he called together with the workers of similar occupation, and said: "Men, you know that we have our wealth by this trade.

²⁶ Moreover you see and hear that not only at Ephesus, but throughout almost all Asia, this Paul has persuaded and turned away many people, saying that they are not gods which are made with hands.

²⁷ So that not only is this trade of ours in danger of becoming disgraced, but also the temple of the great goddess Diana may be despised and her magnificence shall be destroyed, whom all Asia and the world worship."

²⁸ Now when they heard *these words*, they were full of wrath and shouted out, saying, "Great *is* Diana of the Ephesians!"

²⁹ So the entire city was filled with confusion, and having seized Gaius and Aristarchus, Macedonians, Paul's travel companions, they rushed into the theater with one accord.

³⁰ And when Paul wanted to go in to the people, the disciples would not allow him.

³¹ Then some of the officials of Asia, who were his friends, sent to him begging *him* that he himself would not venture into the theater.

³² Some therefore shouted out one thing and some another, because the assembly was confused, and most of them did not know why they had come together.

³³ And they drew Alexander out of the crowd, the Jews putting him forward. And Alexander motioned with his hand, and wanted to make his defense to the people.

³⁴ But when they found out that he was a Jew, all with one voice shouted out *for* about the space of two hours, "Great *is* Diana of the Ephesians!"

³⁵ And when the city clerk had quieted the crowd, he said: "You men of Ephesus, what man is there who does not know that the city of the Ephesians is a worshipper of the great goddess Diana, and of the *image* which fell down from Jupiter?

³⁶ Therefore, since these things cannot be denied, you ought to be quiet and do nothing rashly.

³⁷ Because, you have brought these men here who are neither robbers of churches nor blasphemers of your goddess.

³⁸ Therefore, if Demetrius and his fellow craftsmen who are with him, have a case against anyone, the courts are open and there are proconsuls. Let them bring charges against one another.

³⁹ But if you inquire anything concerning other matters, it should be determined in a lawful assembly.

⁴⁰ Because, we are in danger of being called in question for today's uproar, there being no reason which we may give to account for this commotion."

⁴¹ And when he had said these things, he dismissed the assembly.

CHAPTER 20

¹ After the uproar had ceased, Paul called the disciples to *himself*, embraced *them*, and departed to go to Macedonia.

² Now when he had gone over that region and encouraged them with many words, he came into Greece

³ and stayed *there* three months. And when the Jews plotted against him as he was about to sail to Syria, he decided to return through Macedonia.

⁴ And Sopater of Berea accompanied him to Asia, also Aristarchus and Secundus of the Thessalonians, and Gaius of Derbe, and Timothy, and of Asia Tychicus and Trophimus.

⁵ These, going ahead, waited for us at Troas.

⁶ But we sailed away from Philippi after the Days of Unleavened Bread, and in five days joined them at Troas, where we stayed seven days.

⁷ Now on the first *day* of the week, when the disciples came together to break bread, Paul, ready to depart the next day, preached to them and continued his message until midnight.

⁸ There were many lamps in the upper room where they were gathered together.

⁹ And in a window sat a certain young man named Eutychus, who was falling into a deep sleep. He was overcome by sleep; and as Paul continued preaching, he fell down from the third story and was taken up dead.

¹⁰ But Paul went down, fell on him, and embracing *him* said, "Do not trouble yourselves, because his life is in him."

¹¹ Now when he had come up again, had broken bread and eaten, and talked a long while, even until daybreak, he departed.

¹² And they brought the young man in alive, and they were not a little comforted.

¹³ Then we went ahead to the ship and sailed to Assos, there intending to take Paul on board; because he had given orders, intending himself to go on foot.

¹⁴ And when he met us at Assos, we took him on board and came to Mitylene.

¹⁵ We sailed from there, and the next *day* came opposite Chios. The following *day* we arrived at Samos and stayed at Trogyllium. The next *day* we came to Miletus.

¹⁶ Because, Paul had determined to sail past Ephesus, so that he would not have to spend time in Asia; because he was hurrying to be at Jerusalem, if possible, on the Day of Pentecost.

¹⁷ From Miletus he sent to Ephesus and called for the elders of the church.

¹⁸ And when they had come to him, he said to them: "You know, from the first day that I came to Asia, in what manner I always lived among you, in every season

¹⁹ serving the Lord with all humility

of mind, with many tears and trials which happened to me by the plotting of the Jews;

²⁰ *and* how I kept back nothing that was helpful *to* you, but have shown you, and taught you publicly and from house to house,

²¹ testifying both to Jews, and also to Greeks, repentance toward God and faith toward our Lord Jesus Christ.

²² And behold, now I go bound in the spirit to Jerusalem, not knowing the things that shall happen to me there,

²³ except that the Holy Spirit witnesses in every city, saying that chains and afflictions await me.

²⁴ But none of these things move me; nor do I count my life dear to myself, so that I may finish my race with joy, and the ministry which I received from the Lord Jesus, to testify the gospel of the grace of God.

²⁵ "And indeed, now I know that you all, among whom I have gone preaching the kingdom of God, will see my face no longer.

²⁶ Therefore I want you to record this day that I am innocent of the blood of all *people*.

²⁷ Because I have not shunned to declare to you the entire counsel of God.

²⁸ Therefore take heed to yourselves and to all the flock, among whom the Holy Spirit has made you overseers, to feed the church of God which He purchased with His own blood.

²⁹ Because I know this, that after my departure savage wolves will come in among you, not sparing the flock.

³⁰ Also from among yourselves men will rise up, speaking perverse things, to draw away disciples after themselves.

³¹ Therefore watch, and remember that for the space of three years I did not cease to warn everyone night and day with tears.

³² "So now, brethren, I commend you to God and to the word of His grace, which is able to build you up and give you an inheritance among all those who are sanctified.

³³ I have coveted no one's silver or gold or apparel.

³⁴ Yes, you yourselves know that these hands have provided for my necessities, and for those who were with me.

³⁵ I have shown you in everything, by laboring like this, that you must support the weak. And remember the words of the Lord Jesus, that He said, 'It is more blessed to give than to receive.' "

³⁶ And when he had said these things, he knelt down and prayed with them all.

³⁷ Then they all wept freely, and fell on Paul's neck and kissed him,

³⁸ sorrowing most of all for the words which he spoke, that they would see his face no longer. And they accompanied him to the ship.

CHAPTER 21

¹ Now it came to pass, that when we had departed from them and set sail, running a straight course we came to Cos, the following *day* to Rhodes, and from there to Patara.

² And finding a ship sailing over to Phoenicia, we went aboard and set sail.

³ When we had sighted Cyprus, we passed it on the left, sailed to Syria, and landed at Tyre; because there the ship was to unload her cargo.

⁴ And finding disciples, we stayed there seven days. They told Paul through the Spirit that he should not go up to Jerusalem.

⁵ And when we had come to the end of those days, we departed and went on our way; and they all accompanied us, with wives and children, until *we were* out of the city. And we knelt down on the shore and prayed.

⁶ When we had taken our leave of one another, we boarded the ship, and they returned home again.

⁷ And when we had finished *our* voyage from Tyre, we came to Ptolemais, greeted the brethren, and stayed with them one day.

⁸ On the next *day* we who were Paul's companions departed and came to Caesarea, and entered the house of Philip the evangelist, who was *one* of the seven, and stayed with him.

⁹ Now this man had four virgin daughters who prophesied.

¹⁰ And as we stayed *there* several days, a certain prophet named Agabus came down from Judea.

¹¹ When he had come to us, he took Paul's belt, bound his own hands and feet, and said, "Thus says the Holy Spirit, 'So will the Jews at Jerusalem bind the man who owns this belt, and will deliver *him* into the hands of the Gentiles.' "

¹² Now when we heard these things, both we and those from that place pleaded with him not to go up to Jerusalem.

¹³ Then Paul replied, "What do you mean by weeping and breaking my heart? Because I am ready not only to be bound, but also to die at Jerusalem for the name of the Lord Jesus."

¹⁴ So when he would not be persuaded, we ceased, saying, "The will of the Lord be done."

¹⁵ And after those days we took up our belongings and went up to Jerusalem.

¹⁶ Also *some* of the disciples from Caesarea went with us and brought with them one Mnason of Cyprus, an early disciple, with whom we were to lodge.

¹⁷ And when we had come to Jerusalem, the brethren received us gladly.

¹⁸ On the following *day* Paul went in with us to James, and all the elders were present.

¹⁹ When he had greeted them, he told in detail those things which God had done among the Gentiles through his ministry.

²⁰ And when they heard *it*, they glorified the Lord. And they said to him, "You see, brother, how many thousands of Jews there are who believe, and they are all zealous for the law; ²¹ but they have been informed about you that you teach all the Jews who are among the Gentiles to forsake Moses, saying that they ought not to circumcise *their* children nor to walk according to the customs. ²² What is it then? The assembly must certainly meet, because they will hear that you have come. ²³ Therefore do what we tell you: We have four men who have taken a vow upon themselves. ²⁴ Take them and purify yourself with them, and pay their expenses so that they may shave *their* heads, and that all may know that those things of which they were informed concerning you are nothing, but *that* you yourself also walk orderly and keep the law. ²⁵ But concerning the Gentiles who believe, we have written *and* concluded that they should observe no such thing, except that they should keep themselves from *things* offered to idols, from blood, from things strangled, and from sexual immorality." ²⁶ Then Paul took the men, and the next day, purifying himself with them, entered into the temple to signify the conclusion of the days of purification, at which time an offering should be made for each one of them.

²⁷ Now when the seven days were almost ended, the Jews from Asia, when they saw him in the temple, stirred up all the people and laid hands on him, ²⁸ shouting out, "Men of Israel, help! This is the man who teaches all *men* everywhere against the people, the law, and this place; and furthermore he also brought Greeks into the temple and has defiled this holy place." ²⁹ (Because, they had previously seen Trophimus the Ephesian with him in the city, whom they supposed that Paul had brought into the temple.) ³⁰ And all the city was disturbed; and the people ran together, seized Paul, and dragged him out of the temple; and immediately the doors were shut. ³¹ Now as they were seeking to kill him, news came to the commander of the garrison that all Jerusalem was in an uproar. ³² He immediately took soldiers and centurions, and ran down to them. And when they saw the commander and the soldiers, they stopped beating Paul. ³³ Then the commander came near and took him, and commanded *him* to be bound with two chains; and he asked who he was and what he had done. ³⁴ And some among the crowd shouted out one thing and some

another. So when he could not be certain of the truth because of the tumult, he commanded him to be carried into the barracks.

³⁵ when he reached the stairs, it happened that he had to be carried by the soldiers because of the violence of the mob.

³⁶ Because the crowd of the people followed after, shouting out, "Away with him!"

³⁷ Then as Paul was about to be led into the barracks, he said to the commander, "May I speak to you?" He replied, "Can you speak Greek?

³⁸ Are you not the Egyptian who some time ago stirred up a rebellion and led the four thousand assassins out into the wilderness?"

³⁹ But Paul said, "I am a man *who is* a Jew from Tarsus, in Cilicia, a citizen of no obscure city; and I implore you, permit me to speak to the people."

⁴⁰ So when he had given him permission, Paul stood on the stairs and motioned with his hand to the people. And when there was a great silence, he spoke to *them* in the Hebrew language, saying,

CHAPTER 22

¹ "Men, brethren, and fathers, hear my defense *which I make* before you now."

² And when they heard that he spoke to them in the Hebrew language, they kept all the more silent. Then he said:

³ "I am indeed a man *who is* a Jew, born in Tarsus *a city* in Cilicia, but brought up in this city at the feet of Gamaliel, taught according to the perfect method of our fathers' law, and was zealous toward God as you all are today.

⁴ And I persecuted this Way to the death, binding and delivering into prisons both men and women,

⁵ as also the high priest bears me witness, and all the council of the elders, from whom I also received letters to the brethren, and went to Damascus to bring those who were there in chains to Jerusalem to be punished.

⁶ "Now it happened, as I journeyed and came near Damascus at about noon, suddenly a great light from heaven shone around me.

⁷ And I fell to the ground and heard a voice saying to me, 'Saul, Saul, why are you persecuting Me?'

⁸ So I replied, 'Who are You, Lord?' And He said to me, 'I am Jesus of Nazareth, whom you are persecuting.'

⁹ "And those who were with me indeed saw the light and were afraid, but they did not hear the voice of Him who spoke to me.

¹⁰ So I said, 'What shall I do, Lord?' And the Lord said to me, 'Arise and go into Damascus, and there you will be told all things which are appointed for you to do.'

¹¹ And since I could not see because of the glory of that light, being led by the hand of those who were with me, I came into Damascus.

¹² "Then a certain Ananias, a devout man according to the law, having a good testimony with all the Jews who dwelt *there*,
¹³ came to me; and he stood and said to me, 'Brother Saul, receive your sight.' And at that same hour I looked up at him.
¹⁴ Then he said, 'The God of our fathers has chosen you that you should know His will, and see the Just One, and hear the voice of His mouth.
¹⁵ Because, you will be His witness to all people of what you have seen and heard.
¹⁶ And now why are you waiting? Arise and be baptized, and wash away your sins, calling on the name of the Lord.'
¹⁷ "Now it happened, when I returned to Jerusalem and was praying in the temple, that I was in a trance
¹⁸ and saw Him saying to me, 'Make haste and get out of Jerusalem quickly, because they will not receive your testimony concerning Me.'
¹⁹ So I said, 'Lord, they know that in every synagogue I imprisoned and beat those who believe on You.
²⁰ And when the blood of Your martyr Stephen was shed, I also was standing by consenting to his death, and guarding the clothes of those who were killing him.'
²¹ Then He said to me, 'Depart, because I will send you far from here to the Gentiles.'"
²² And they listened to him until this word, and *then* they raised their voices and said, "Away with such a *man* from the earth, because he is not fit to live!"
²³ Then, as they shouted out and tore off *their* clothes and threw dust into the air,
²⁴ the commander ordered him to be brought into the barracks, and said that he should be examined under scourging, so that he might know why they shouted out like this against him.
²⁵ And as they bound him with thongs, Paul said to the centurion who stood by, "Is it lawful for you to scourge a man who is a Roman, and uncondemned?"
²⁶ When the centurion heard that, he went and told the commander, saying, "Take care what you do, because this man is a Roman."
²⁷ Then the commander came and said to him, "Tell me, are you a Roman?" He said, "Yes."
²⁸ The commander replied, "With a large sum I obtained this freedom." And Paul said, "But I was born free."
²⁹ Then immediately those who were about to examine him withdrew from him; and the commander was also afraid after he found out that he was a Roman, and because he had bound him.
³⁰ The next day, because he wanted to know for certain why he was accused by the Jews, he released him from *his* bonds, and commanded the chief priests and all

their council to appear, and brought Paul down and set him before them.

CHAPTER 23

¹ Then Paul, looking earnestly at the council, said, "Men *and* brethren, I have lived in all good conscience before God until this day."

² And the high priest Ananias commanded those who stood by him to strike him on the mouth.

³ Then Paul said to him, "God will strike you, *you* whitewashed wall! Because, you sit to judge me according to the law, and do you command me to be struck contrary to the law?"

⁴ And those who stood by said, "Do you revile God's high priest?"

⁵ Then Paul said, "I did not know, brethren, that he was the high priest; because it is written, 'You shall not speak evil of a ruler of your people.'"

⁶ But when Paul perceived that one part were Sadducees and the other Pharisees, he shouted out in the council, "Men *and* brethren, I am a Pharisee, the son of a Pharisee; concerning the hope and resurrection of the dead I am being questioned!"

⁷ And when he had said this, a dissension arose between the Pharisees and the Sadducees; and the assembly was divided.

⁸ Because, Sadducees say that there is no resurrection, nor angel, nor spirit; but the Pharisees confess both.

⁹ Then there arose a loud uproar. And the scribes *who were* of the Pharisees' company arose and protested, saying, "We find no evil in this man; but if a spirit or an angel has spoken to him, let us not fight against God."

¹⁰ Now when there arose a great dissension, the commander, fearing lest Paul might be pulled to pieces by them, commanded the soldiers to go down and take him by force from among them, and bring *him* into the barracks.

¹¹ But the following night the Lord stood by him and said, "Be of good cheer Paul; because, as you have testified of Me in Jerusalem, so you must also bear witness at Rome."

¹² And when it was day, some of the Jews banded together and bound themselves under an oath, saying that they would neither eat nor drink until they had killed Paul.

¹³ Now there were more than forty who had formed this conspiracy.

¹⁴ They came to the chief priests and elders, and said, "We have bound ourselves under a great oath that we will eat nothing until we have killed Paul.

¹⁵ Now you, therefore, together with the council, suggest to the commander that he be brought down to you tomorrow, as though you were going to make further inquiries concerning him; but we are ready to kill him before he

comes near."

¹⁶ So when Paul's sister's son heard of their ambush, he went and entered the barracks and told Paul.

¹⁷ Then Paul called one of the centurions to *him* and said, "Take this young man to the commander, because he has something to tell him."

¹⁸ So he took him and brought *him* to the commander and said, "Paul the prisoner called me to *him* and asked me to bring this young man to you. He has something to say to you."

¹⁹ Then the commander took him by the hand, went aside *with him*, and asked *him* privately, "What is it that you have to tell me?"

²⁰ And he said, "The Jews have agreed to ask that you bring Paul down to the council tomorrow, as though they were going to inquire more fully about him.

²¹ But do not yield to them, because more than forty of them lie in wait for him, men who have bound themselves by an oath that they will neither eat nor drink until they have killed him; and now they are ready, waiting for the promise from you."

²² So then the commander let the young man depart, and commanded *him*, "*See that you* tell no one that you have revealed these things to me."

²³ And he called two centurions to *himself*, saying, "Prepare two hundred soldiers, seventy horsemen, and two hundred spearmen to go to Caesarea at the third hour of the night;

²⁴ and provide *for them* animals to set Paul upon, and bring *him* safely to Felix the governor."

²⁵ Then he wrote a letter in the following manner:

²⁶ Claudius Lysias, to the most excellent governor Felix: *I send* Greetings.

²⁷ This man was seized by the Jews and would have been killed by them. Then I came with the troops and rescued him, having learned that he was a Roman.

²⁸ And when I wanted to know the reason they accused him, I brought him before their council.

²⁹ I perceived that he was accused concerning questions of their law, but had nothing charged against him deserving of death or chains.

³⁰ And when it was told me that the Jews lay in wait for the man, I sent him immediately to you, and also commanded his accusers to state before you the charges *they had* against him. Farewell.

³¹ Then the soldiers, as they were commanded, took Paul and brought *him* by night to Antipatris.

³² On the next day, they left the horsemen to go on with him, and returned to the barracks.

³³ Who when they came to Caesarea and had delivered the letter to the governor, they also presented Paul to him.

³⁴ And when the governor had read

the letter, he asked what province he was from. And when he understood that he was from Cilicia,

³⁵ he said, "I will hear you when your accusers also have come." And he commanded him to be kept in Herod's judgment hall.

CHAPTER 24

¹ Now after five days Ananias the high priest came down with the elders and *with* a certain orator *named* Tertullus, who gave evidence to the governor against Paul.
² And when he was called upon, Tertullus began to accuse *him*, saying: "Seeing that through you we enjoy great peace, and very admirable deeds are done to this nation by your foresight,
³ we accept *it* always and in all places, most noble Felix, with all thankfulness.
⁴ Nevertheless, not to be tedious to you any further, I beg you to hear, by your courtesy, a few words from us.
⁵ Because, we have found this man a plague, a creator of dissension among all the Jews throughout the world, and a ringleader of the cult of the Nazarenes.
⁶ He even tried to profane the temple, and we seized him, and wanted to judge him according to our law.
⁷ But the commander Lysias went above us and with great violence took *him* out of our hands,
⁸ commanding his accusers to come to you. By examining him yourself you may ascertain all these things of which we accuse him."
⁹ And the Jews also assented, maintaining that these things were so.
¹⁰ Then Paul, after the governor had motioned to him to speak, replied: "Inasmuch as I know that you have been for many years a judge of this nation, I do the more cheerfully answer for myself,
¹¹ because, you may ascertain that it is no more than twelve days since I went up to Jerusalem to worship.
¹² And they neither found me in the temple disputing with anyone nor inciting the people, either in the synagogues or in the city.
¹³ Nor can they prove the things of which they now accuse me.
¹⁴ But this I confess to you, that according to the Way which they call heresy, so I worship the God of my fathers, believing all things which are written in the Law and in the Prophets.
¹⁵ I have hope in God, which they themselves also accept, that there will be a resurrection of the dead, both of the just and *the* unjust.
¹⁶ And in this I always strive to have a conscience without offense toward God and *towards* men.
¹⁷ "Now after many years I came to bring charitable gifts and offerings to my nation,
¹⁸ in the midst of which some Jews from Asia found me purified in the temple, neither with a mob nor

with tumult.

¹⁹ They ought to have been here before you to object if they had anything against me.

²⁰ Or else let these people *here* say if they found any wrongdoing in me while I stood before the council,

²¹ unless it is for this one statement which I shouted out, standing among them, 'Concerning the resurrection of the dead I am being judged by you this day.'"

²² But when Felix heard these things, having more accurate knowledge of *that* Way, he deferred them and said, "When Lysias the commander comes down, I will make a decision on your case."

²³ So he commanded the centurion to guard Paul and to let him have liberty, and that he should not forbid any of his friends to provide for or visit him.

²⁴ And after some days, when Felix came with his wife Drusilla, who was Jewish, he sent for Paul and heard him concerning the faith in Christ.

²⁵ Now as he reasoned about righteousness, self control, and judgment to come, Felix was afraid and replied, "Go away for now; when I have a convenient time I will call for you."

²⁶ He also hoped that money would be given him by Paul, that he might release him. Therefore he sent for him more often and conversed with him.

²⁷ But after two years Porcius Festus succeeded Felix' office; and Felix, wanting to do the Jews a favor, left Paul bound.

CHAPTER 25

¹ Now when Festus had come into the province, after three days he went up from Caesarea to Jerusalem.

² Then the high priest and the chief men of the Jews informed him against Paul; and they petitioned him,

³ asking a favor against him, that he would summon him to Jerusalem, while *they* lay in ambush along the road to kill him.

⁴ But Festus replied that Paul should be kept at Caesarea, and that he himself was going *there* shortly.

⁵ "Therefore," he said, "let those who are able among you go down with *me* and accuse this man, to see if there is any fault in him."

⁶ And when he had remained among them more than ten days, he went down to Caesarea. And the next day, sitting on the judgment seat, he commanded Paul to be brought.

⁷ When he had come, the Jews who had come down from Jerusalem stood about and laid many serious complaints against Paul, which they could not prove,

⁸ while he answered for himself, "Neither against the law of the Jews, nor against the temple, nor even against Caesar have I offended in anything at all."

⁹ But Festus, wanting to do the Jews a favor, replied to Paul and said, "Are you willing to go up to Jerusalem and there be judged before me concerning these things?"

¹⁰ So Paul said, "I stand at Caesar's judgment seat, where I ought to be judged. To the Jews I have done no wrong, as you very well know.

¹¹ Because if I am an offender, or have committed anything deserving of death, I do not object to dying; but if there is nothing in these things of which these men accuse me, no one can deliver me to them. I appeal to Caesar."

¹² Then Festus, when he had conferred with the council, replied, "You have appealed to Caesar? To Caesar you will go!"

¹³ And after some days King Agrippa and Bernice came to Caesarea to greet Festus.

¹⁴ And when they had been there many days, Festus laid Paul's case before the king, saying: "There is a certain man left a prisoner by Felix,

¹⁵ about whom the chief priests and the elders of the Jews informed *me*, when I was in Jerusalem, asking *to have* judgment against him.

¹⁶ To them I replied, 'It is not the custom of the Romans to deliver any man to die before the accused meets the accusers face to face, and has opportunity to answer for himself concerning the charge against him.'

¹⁷ Therefore when they had come here, without any delay, the next day I sat on the judgment seat and commanded the man to be brought in.

¹⁸ When the accusers stood up, they brought no accusation against him of such things as I supposed,

¹⁹ but had some questions against him about their own superstition and about a certain Jesus, who had died, whom Paul affirmed to be alive.

²⁰ And because I was uncertain of such questions, I asked *him* whether he was willing to go to Jerusalem and there be judged concerning these matters.

²¹ But when Paul appealed to be reserved for the decision of Augustus, I commanded him to be kept until I could send him to Caesar."

²² Then Agrippa said to Festus, "I also would like to hear the man myself." "Tomorrow," he said, "you will hear him."

²³ So on the next day, when Agrippa and Bernice had come with great fanfare, and had entered the auditorium with the commanders and the prominent men of the city, at Festus' command Paul was brought in.

²⁴ And Festus said: "King Agrippa and all the men who are here present with us, you see this man about whom the entire assembly of the Jews petitioned me, both at Jerusalem and *also* here, shouting out that he was not fit to live any longer.

²⁵ But when I found that he had

committed nothing deserving of death, and that he himself had appealed to Augustus, I decided to send him.

²⁶ I have nothing certain to write to my lord concerning him. Therefore I have brought him out before you, and especially before you, King Agrippa, so that after the examination has taken place I may have something to write.

²⁷ Because, it seems to me unreasonable to send a prisoner and not to specify the charges *laid* against him."

CHAPTER 26

¹ Then Agrippa said to Paul, "You are permitted to speak for yourself." So Paul stretched out his hand and answered for himself:

² "I think myself happy, King Agrippa, because today I will answer for myself before you concerning all the things of which I am accused by the Jews,

³ especially *because I know* that you are an expert in all customs and questions which have to do with the Jews. Therefore I beg you to hear me patiently.

⁴ "My manner of life from my youth, which was spent from the beginning among my own nation at Jerusalem, all the Jews know.

⁵ Who knew me from the beginning, if they were willing to testify, that according to the strictest sect of our religion I lived a Pharisee.

⁶ And now I stand and am judged for the hope of the promise made by God to our fathers.

⁷ To this *promise* our twelve tribes, earnestly serving *God* night and day, hope to attain. For this hope's sake, King Agrippa, I am accused by the Jews.

⁸ Why should it be thought an improbable thing by you that God raises the dead?

⁹ "Truly, I myself thought I must do many things contrary to the name of Jesus of Nazareth.

¹⁰ This I also did in Jerusalem, and many of the saints I shut up in prison, having received authority from the chief priests; and when they were put to death, I cast my voice against *them*.

¹¹ And I punished them often in every synagogue and compelled *them* to blaspheme; and being exceedingly enraged against them, I persecuted *them* even to foreign cities.

¹² "Being preoccupied with this, as I journeyed to Damascus with authority and commission from the chief priests,

¹³ at midday, O king, along the road I saw a light from heaven, brighter than the sun, shining around me and those who journeyed with me.

¹⁴ And when we all had fallen to the ground, I heard a voice speaking to me and saying in the Hebrew language, 'Saul, Saul, why are you persecuting Me? *It is* hard for you to kick against the prods.'

¹⁵ So I said, 'Who are You, Lord?'

And He said, 'I am Jesus, whom you are persecuting.

¹⁶ But rise and stand on your feet; because I have appeared to you for this reason, to make you a minister and a witness both of the things which you have seen and of the things which I will yet reveal to you.

¹⁷ Delivering you from the people, and *from* the Gentiles, to whom I now send you,

¹⁸ to open their eyes, to turn them from darkness to light, and *from* the power of Satan to God, that they may receive forgiveness of sins and an inheritance among those who are sanctified by faith that is in Me.'

¹⁹ "Therefore, King Agrippa, I was not disobedient to the heavenly vision,

²⁰ but declared first to those in Damascus and in Jerusalem, and throughout all the region of Judea, and *then* to the Gentiles, that they should repent, turn to God, and do works befitting repentance.

²¹ For these reasons the Jews seized me in the temple and tried to kill *me*.

²² Therefore, having obtained help from God, to this day I stand, witnessing both to small and great, saying no other things than those which the prophets and Moses said would come;

²³ that Christ would suffer, that He would be the first to rise from the dead, and would show light to the people and to the Gentiles."

²⁴ Now as he spoke for himself like this, Festus said with a loud voice, "Paul, you are beside yourself! Much learning is driving you mad!"

²⁵ But he said, "I am not mad, most noble Festus, but speak the words of truth and reason.

²⁶ Because the king, before whom I also speak freely, knows these things; because, I am convinced that none of these things are hidden from him, since this thing was not done in a corner.

²⁷ King Agrippa, do you believe the prophets? I know that you do believe."

²⁸ Then Agrippa said to Paul, "You almost persuade me to become a Christian."

²⁹ And Paul said, "I would to God that not only you, but also all who hear me today, might become both almost and altogether such as I am, except for these chains."

³⁰ When he had said these things, the king stood up, as well as the governor and Bernice and those who sat with them;

³¹ and when they had gone aside, they talked among themselves, saying, "This man is doing nothing deserving of death or chains."

³² Then Agrippa said to Festus, "This man might have been set free if he had not appealed to Caesar."

CHAPTER 27

¹ And when it was determined that we should sail to Italy, they delivered Paul and some other pris-

oners to *one* named Julius, a centurion of the Augustan Regiment.

² So, entering into a ship of Adramyttium, we launched, meaning to sail along the coasts of Asia. *One* Aristarchus, a Macedonian of Thessalonica, was with us.

³ And the next *day* we landed at Sidon. And Julius treated Paul kindly and gave *him* liberty to go to his friends and refresh himself.

⁴ When we had launched from there, we sailed under Cyprus, because the winds were contrary.

⁵ And when we had sailed over the sea which is off Cilicia and Pamphylia, we came to Myra, *a city* of Lycia.

⁶ And there the centurion found an Alexandrian ship sailing to Italy, and he put us on board.

⁷ And when we had sailed slowly many days, and arrived with difficulty off Cnidus, the wind not permitting us to proceed, we sailed under Crete off Salmone.

⁸ And passing it with difficulty, we came to a place called The Fair Havens; nearby was the city *of* Lasea.

⁹ Now when much time had been spent, and sailing was now dangerous because the Fast was already over, Paul advised *them*,

¹⁰ and said to them, "Men, I perceive that this voyage will end with disaster and much loss, not only of the cargo and ship, but also our lives."

¹¹ Nevertheless the centurion believed the helmsman and the owner of the ship than those things which were spoken by Paul.

¹² And because the harbor was not suitable to winter in, the majority advised to set sail from there also, if by any means they might reach Phoenix, *which is* a harbor of Crete opening toward the southwest and northwest, *and* winter *there.*

¹³ And when the south wind blew softly, supposing that they had obtained *their* desire, leaving *there*, they sailed close by Crete.

¹⁴ But not long after, a tempestuous wind arose against it, called Euroclydon.

¹⁵ So when the ship was caught, and could not head into the wind, we let *her* drive.

¹⁶ And running underneath an island which is called Clauda, we secured the *smaller* boat with difficulty.

¹⁷ Which, when they had taken it on board, they used cables to undergird the ship; and fearing lest they should run aground on the sandbanks, they struck sail and so were driven.

¹⁸ And because we were exceedingly tossed with a tempest, the next *day* they lightened the ship.

¹⁹ And on the third *day* we threw the ship's tackle overboard with our own hands.

²⁰ Now when neither sun nor stars appeared for many days, and no small tempest beat on *us*, all hope

that we would be saved was finally gone.

²¹ But after long abstinence from food, then Paul stood in the midst of them and said, "Men, you should have listened to me, and not have untied from Crete and incurred this disaster and loss.

²² And now I urge you to be optimistic, because there will be no loss of *any man's* life among you, but only of the ship.

²³ Because, there stood by me this night the angel of the God to whom I belong and whom I serve,

²⁴ saying, 'Do not be afraid, Paul; you must be brought before Caesar; and indeed God has granted you all those who sail with you.'

²⁵ Therefore men, take heart, because I believe God that it will be just as it was told me.

²⁶ However, we must run aground on a certain island."

²⁷ Now when the fourteenth night had come, as we were driven up and down in the Adriatic Sea, about midnight the sailors sensed that they were drawing near some land.

²⁸ And they took soundings and found it to be twenty fathoms; and when they had gone a little farther, they took soundings again and found *it* to be fifteen fathoms.

²⁹ Then, fearing lest we should run aground on the rocks, they dropped four anchors from the stern, and wished for day to come.

³⁰ And as the sailors were seeking to escape from the ship, when they had let down the *small* boat into the sea, pretending to be about to cast out anchors from the front of the ship,

³¹ Paul said to the centurion and the soldiers, "Unless these men stay in the ship, you cannot all be saved."

³² Then the soldiers cut away the ropes of the *small* boat and let it fall off.

³³ And as day was about to dawn, Paul implored *them* all to take food, saying, "Today is the fourteenth day you have waited and continued fasting, and eaten nothing.

³⁴ Therefore I urge you to take *some* food, because this is for your survival, because not a hair will fall from the head of any of you."

³⁵ And when he had said these things, he took bread and gave thanks to God in the presence of them all; and when he had broken *it* he began to eat.

³⁶ Then they were all encouraged, and they also took *some* food.

37 And in all we were two hundred and seventy six persons on the ship.

³⁸ So when they had eaten enough, they lightened the ship and threw out the wheat into the sea.

³⁹ And when it was day, they did not recognize the land; but they observed a bay with a beach, onto which they planned to drive the ship if possible.

⁴⁰ And when they had taken up the anchors, they committed *themselves* to the sea, untied the rudder ropes, hoisted the mainsail to the wind,

and made for shore.

⁴¹ And striking a place where two seas met, they ran the ship aground; and the front stuck fast and remained immovable, but the back part was being broken up by the violence of the waves.

⁴² And the soldiers' instructions were to kill the prisoners, lest any of them should swim away and escape.

⁴³ But the centurion, wanting to save Paul, kept them from *their* purpose, and commanded that those who could swim should throw *themselves* first into the sea and get to land,

⁴⁴ and the rest, some on boards and some on *broken pieces* of the ship. And so it was that they all escaped safely to land.

CHAPTER 28

¹ Now when they had escaped, they then discovered that the island was called Malta.

² And the natives showed us no small amount of kindness; because, they kindled a fire and made us all welcome, because of the falling rain and because of the cold.

³ But when Paul had gathered a bundle of sticks and laid *them* on the fire, a viper came out because of the heat, and fastened on his hand.

⁴ So when the natives saw the *venomous* creature hanging on his hand, they said to one another, "No doubt this man is a murderer, whom, though he has escaped the sea, yet justice does not allow to live."

⁵ But he shook off the creature into the fire and felt no harm.

⁶ However, they were expecting that he would swell up or suddenly fall down dead. But after they had looked for a long time and saw no harm come to him, they changed their minds and said that he was a god.

⁷ In that region there was an estate of the leading citizen of the island, whose name was Publius, who received us and hosted us hospitably for three days.

⁸ And it happened that the father of Publius lay sick of a fever and dysentery. Paul went in to him and prayed, and he laid his hands on him and healed him.

⁹ So when this was done, the rest of those on the island who had diseases also came and were healed.

¹⁰ They also honored us in many ways; and when we departed, they provided *us with* such things as were necessary.

¹¹ After three months we sailed in an Alexandrian ship whose figurehead was Castor and Pollux, which had wintered at the island.

¹² And landing at Syracuse, we stayed *there for* three days.

¹³ From there we circled round and reached Rhegium. And after one day the south wind blew; and the next day we came to Puteoli,

¹⁴ where we found brethren, and were invited to stay with them

seven days. And so we went toward Rome.

¹⁵ And from there, when the brethren heard about us, they came to meet us as far as Appii Forum and Three Inns. When Paul saw them, he thanked God and took courage.

¹⁶ Now when we came to Rome, the centurion delivered the prisoners to the captain of the guard; but Paul was permitted to dwell by himself with the soldier who guarded him.

¹⁷ And it came to pass after three days that Paul called the leaders of the Jews together. So when they had come together, he said to them: "Men *and* brethren, though I have done nothing against our people or the customs of our fathers, yet I was delivered as a prisoner from Jerusalem into the hands of the Romans,

¹⁸ who, when they had examined me, wanted to let *me* go, because there were no grounds for putting me to death.

¹⁹ But when the Jews spoke against *it*, I was compelled to appeal to Caesar, not that I had anything of which to accuse my nation.

²⁰ For this reason therefore I have called for you, to see *you* and speak with *you*, because for the hope of Israel I am bound with this chain."

²¹ Then they said to him, "We neither received letters from Judea concerning you, nor have any of the brethren who came reported or spoken any evil of you.

²² But we desire to hear from you what you think; for concerning this sect, we know that it is spoken against everywhere."

²³ So when they had appointed him a day, many came to him at *his* lodging, to whom he explained and testified of the kingdom of God, persuading them concerning Jesus from both the Law of Moses and *out* of the Prophets, from morning until evening.

²⁴ And some were persuaded by the things which were spoken, and some disbelieved.

²⁵ So when they did not agree among themselves, they departed after Paul had said one word: "The Holy Spirit spoke rightly through Isaiah the prophet to our fathers,

²⁶ saying, 'Go to this people and say: "Hearing you will hear, and shall not understand; and seeing you will see, and not perceive;

²⁷ Because the hearts of this people have grown dull. Their ears are hard of hearing, and their eyes they have closed, lest they should see with *their* eyes, and hear with *their* ears, and should understand with *their* hearts, and be converted, then I could heal them." '

²⁸ "Therefore let it be known to you that the salvation of God has been sent to the Gentiles, and *they* will hear it!"

²⁹ And when he had said these words, the Jews departed and had a great dispute among themselves.

³⁰ Then Paul dwelt an entire two years in his own rented house, and

received all who came to him, ³¹ preaching the kingdom of God and teaching the things which concern the Lord Jesus Christ with all confidence, no one forbidding him.

THE LETTER OF PAUL THE APOSTLE TO THE

ROMANS

CHAPTER 1

¹ Paul, a servant of Jesus Christ, called *to be* an apostle, separated to the gospel of God,

² which He had promised beforehand through His prophets in the Holy Scriptures,

³ concerning His Son Jesus Christ our Lord, who was made of the seed of David according to the flesh,

⁴ and declared *to be* the Son of God with power according to the Spirit of holiness, by the resurrection from the dead.

⁵ By whom we have received grace and apostleship for obedience to the faith among all nations for His name,

⁶ among whom you also are the called of Jesus Christ;

⁷ To all who are in Rome, beloved of God, called *to be* saints: Grace to you and peace from God our Father, and the Lord Jesus Christ.

⁸ first, I thank my God through Jesus Christ for you all, that your faith is spoken of throughout the entire world.

⁹ Because, God is my witness, whom I serve with my spirit in the gospel of His Son, that without ceasing I make mention of you always in my prayers,

¹⁰ making request if, by some means, now at last I may have a prosperous journey by the will of God to come to you.

¹¹ Because, I long to see you, that I may impart to you some spiritual gift, so that you may be established;

¹² that is, that I may be encouraged together with you by the mutual faith both of you and me.

¹³ Now I do not want you to be unaware, brethren, that I often planned to come to you, (but was hindered until now), that I might have some fruit among you also, just as among other Gentiles.

¹⁴ I am a debtor both to the Greeks, and to the Barbarians, both to the wise, and to the unwise.

¹⁵ So, as much as is in me, I am ready to preach the gospel to you who are in Rome also.

¹⁶ Because, I am not ashamed of the gospel of Christ, because it is the power of God to salvation to everyone who believes, for the Jew first, and also for the Greek.

¹⁷ Because in it, the righteousness of God is revealed from faith to faith; as it is written, "The just will live by faith."

¹⁸ Because, the wrath of God is revealed from heaven against all ungodliness and unrighteousness of men, who suppress the truth in unrighteousness,

¹⁹ because what may be known of God is manifest in them, because God has shown *it* to them.

[20] Because, since the creation of the world His invisible attributes are clearly seen, being understood by the things that are made, *even* His eternal power and Godhead; so that they are without excuse,

[21] because although they knew God, they did not glorify *Him* as God, nor were thankful, but became vain in their imaginations, and their foolish hearts were darkened.

[22] Professing themselves to be wise, they became fools,

[23] and changed the glory of the uncorruptible God into an image made like to corruptible man, and to birds and four footed animals and creeping things.

[24] Therefore God also gave them up to uncleanness through the lusts of their own hearts, to dishonor their bodies among themselves,

[25] who changed the truth of God into lie, and worshiped and served the creature more than the Creator, who is blessed forever. Amen.

[26] For this reason God gave them over to vile passions. Because, even their women exchanged the natural use for what is against nature.

[27] And likewise also the men, leaving the natural use of the woman, burned in their lust for one another, men with men doing what is shameful, and receiving in themselves that penalty of their error which was due.

[28] And even as they did not like to retain God in *their* knowledge, God gave them over to a reprobate mind, to do those things which are not appropriate;

[29] being filled with all unrighteousness, sexual immorality, wickedness, covetousness, maliciousness; full of envy, murder, debate, deception, malignity; being whisperers,

[30] backbiters, haters of God, violent, proud, boasters, inventors of evil things, disobedient to parents,

[31] without understanding, covenant breakers, without natural affection, implacable, unmerciful;

[32] who knowing the judgment of God, that those who commit such things are worthy of death, not only do the same but approve those who do them.

CHAPTER 2

[1] Therefore you are inexcusable, O man, whoever you are who judge, because, in whatever you judge another you condemn yourself; because you who judge practice the same things.

[2] But we are certain that the judgment of God is according to truth against those who commit such things.

[3] And do you think this, O man, you who judge those who do such things, and doing the same, that you will escape the judgment of God?

[4] Or do you despise the riches of His goodness, forbearance, and longsuffering, not knowing that the goodness of God leads you to re-

pentance?

⁵ But according to your hardness and your impenitent heart you are treasuring up for yourself wrath in the day of wrath and revelation of the righteous judgment of God,

⁶ who "will render to each one according to his deeds":

⁷ eternal life to those who by patient continuance in doing good seek for glory, honor, and immortality;

⁸ but to those who are contentious and do not obey the truth, but obey unrighteousness, indignation and wrath,

⁹ tribulation and anguish, on every soul of man who does evil, of the Jew first and also of the Gentile;

¹⁰ but glory, honor, and peace to everyone who works what is good, to the Jew first and also to the Gentile.

¹¹ Because there is no personal favoritism with God.

¹² Because, as many as have sinned without law will also perish without law, and as many as have sinned in the law will be judged by the law

¹³ (because, not the hearers of the law *are* just in the sight of God, but the doers of the law will be justified;

¹⁴ because, when the Gentiles, who do not have the law, by nature do the things contained in the law, these, although not having the law, are a law to themselves,

¹⁵ who show the work of the law written in their hearts, their conscience also bearing witness, and between themselves *their* thoughts accusing or else excusing them)

¹⁶ in the day when God will judge the secrets of men by Jesus Christ, according to my gospel.

¹⁷ Indeed you are called a Jew, and rest in the law, and make your boast in God,

¹⁸ and know *His* will, and approve the things that are more excellent, being instructed out of the law,

¹⁹ and are confident that you yourself are a guide to the blind, a light to those who are in darkness,

²⁰ an instructor of the foolish, a teacher of babes, who has the form of knowledge and of the truth in the law.

²¹ You, therefore, who teach another, do you not teach yourself? You who preach that a man should not steal, do you steal?

²² You who say, "A man should not commit adultery," do you commit adultery? You who abhor idols, do you commit sacrilege?

²³ You who make your boast in the law, do you dishonor God through breaking the law?

²⁴ Because, "the name of God is blasphemed among the Gentiles because of you," as it is written.

²⁵ Because, circumcision is indeed profitable if you keep the law; but if you are a breaker of the law, your circumcision has become uncircumcision.

²⁶ Therefore, if an uncircumcised man keeps the righteous require-

ments of the law, will not his uncircumcision be counted as circumcision?

²⁷ And will not the physically uncircumcised, if he fulfills the law, judge you who, even with your written code and circumcision, are a transgressor of the law?

²⁸ Because, he is not a Jew who is one outwardly, nor *is that* circumcision that which is outward in the flesh;

²⁹ but he *is* a Jew who is one inwardly; and circumcision *is that* of the heart, in the Spirit, *and* not in the letter; whose praise *is* not from men but from God.

CHAPTER 3

¹ What advantage then has the Jew, or what *is the* profit of circumcision?

² Much in every way! Chiefly because to them were committed the oracles of God.

³ Because, what if some did not believe? Will their unbelief make the faith of God without effect?

⁴ God forbid! Indeed, let God be true but every man a liar. As it is written: "That You may be justified in Your words, and may overcome when You are judged."

⁵ But if our unrighteousness establishes the righteousness of God, what shall we say? Is God unjust who inflicts wrath? (I speak as a man.)

⁶ God forbid! Because then how will God judge the world?

⁷ Because, if the truth of God has increased through my lie to His glory, why am I also still judged as a sinner?

⁸ So *why* not *just say*, "Let us do evil that good may come," As we are slanderously reported and as some affirm that we say? Their damnation is just.

⁹ What then? Are we better *than they*? Not at all. Because we have previously charged both Jews and Greeks that they are all under sin.

¹⁰ As it is written: "There is none righteous, no, not one;

¹¹ There is none who understands; there is none who seeks after God.

¹² They have all turned aside; they have together become unprofitable; there is none who does good, no, not one."

¹³ "Their throat *is* an open tomb; with their tongues they have practiced deceit"; "The poison of asps *is* under their lips";

¹⁴ "Whose mouth is full of cursing and bitterness."

¹⁵ "Their feet *are* swift to shed blood;

¹⁶ destruction and misery *are* in their ways;

¹⁷ and the way of peace they have not known."

¹⁸ "There is no reverence of God before their eyes."

¹⁹ Now we know that whatever the law says, it says to those who are under the law, that every mouth may be stopped, and all the world may become guilty before God.

²⁰ Therefore by the deeds of the law no flesh will be justified in His sight, because by the law *is* the knowledge of sin.

²¹ But now the righteousness of God apart from the law is revealed, being witnessed by the Law and the Prophets,

²² even the righteousness of God, *which is* by the faith of Jesus Christ, to all and on all those who believe. Because there is no difference;

²³ because all have sinned and fall short of the glory of God,

²⁴ being justified freely by His grace through the redemption that is in Christ Jesus,

²⁵ whom God foreordained *to be* a propitiation through faith in His blood, to demonstrate His righteousness, for the remission of sins that were previously committed, through the forbearance of God;

²⁶ to demonstrate at the present time His righteousness, that He might be just and the justifier of the one who believes in Jesus.

²⁷ Where is boasting then? It is excluded. By what law? Of works? No, but by the law of faith.

²⁸ Therefore we conclude that a man is justified by faith without the deeds of the law.

²⁹ *Is He* the God of the Jews only? *Is He* not also the God of the Gentiles? Yes, of the Gentiles also,

³⁰ since there is one God who will justify the circumcised by faith and the uncircumcised through faith.

³¹ Do we then make void the law through faith? God forbid! On the contrary, we establish the law.

CHAPTER 4

¹ What then shall we say that Abraham our father has found according to the flesh?

² Because, if Abraham was justified by works, he has *something* to boast about, but not before God.

³ Because what does the Scripture say? "Abraham believed God, and it was accounted to him for righteousness."

⁴ Now to him who works, the wages are not counted as grace but as debt.

⁵ But to him who does not work but believes on Him who justifies the ungodly, his faith is accounted for righteousness,

⁶ just as David also describes the blessedness of the man to whom God imputes righteousness apart from works:

⁷ *Saying* "Blessed *are* those whose iniquities are forgiven, and whose sins are covered;

⁸ blessed is the man to whom the LORD will not impute sin."

⁹ Does this blessedness then *come* upon the circumcised *only*, or upon the uncircumcised also? Because we say that faith was accounted to Abraham for righteousness.

¹⁰ How then was it accounted? While he was circumcised, or uncircumcised? Not while circumcised, but while uncircumcised.

¹¹ And he received the sign of circumcision, a seal of the righteousness of the faith which *he had while* still uncircumcised, that he might be the father of all those who believe, though they are uncircumcised, that righteousness might be imputed to them also,

¹² and the father of circumcision to those who not only are of the circumcision, but who also walk in the steps of the faith of our father Abraham, which *he had* while still uncircumcised.

¹³ Because, the promise that he would be the heir of the world *was* not to Abraham or to his seed through the law, but through the righteousness of faith.

¹⁴ Because, if those who are of the law *are* heirs, faith is made void and the promise made of no effect,

¹⁵ because, the law brings about wrath; because where there is no law *there* is no transgression.

¹⁶ Therefore *it is* of faith that it might be by grace, so that the promise might be certain to all the seed, not only to those who are of the law, but also to those who are of the faith of Abraham, who is the father of us all

¹⁷ (as it is written, "I have made you a father of many nations") in the presence of Him whom he believed, *even* God, who gives life to the dead and calls those things which do not exist as though they did;

¹⁸ who, contrary to hope, in hope believed, so that he would become the father of many nations, according to what was spoken, "So will your seed be."

¹⁹ And not being weak in faith, he did not consider his own body, now dead (since he was about a hundred years old), nor the deadness of Sarah's womb.

²⁰ He did not waver at the promise of God through unbelief, but was strong in faith, giving glory to God,

²¹ and being fully persuaded that what He had promised He was also able to perform.

²² And therefore "it was imputed to him for righteousness."

²³ Now it was not written for his sake alone that it was imputed to him,

²⁴ but also for us. It will be imputed to us, if we believe in Him who raised up Jesus our Lord from the dead,

²⁵ who was delivered for our offenses, and was raised again for our justification.

CHAPTER 5

¹ Therefore, having been justified by faith, we have peace with God through our Lord Jesus Christ,

² by whom also we have access by faith into this grace in which we stand, and rejoice in hope of the glory of God.

³ And not only *that*, but we also glory in tribulations, knowing that tribulation produces perseverance;

⁴ and perseverance, character; and character, hope.

⁵ Now hope does not make us ashamed, because the love of God has been poured out in our hearts by the Holy Spirit who was given to us.

⁶ Because, when we were still without strength, in due time Christ died for the ungodly.

⁷ Because, scarcely for a righteous man will one die; yet perhaps for a good man someone would even dare to die.

⁸ But God confirms His own love toward us, in that while we were still sinners, Christ died for us.

⁹ Much more then, having now been justified by His blood, we will be saved from wrath through Him.

¹⁰ Because, if when we were enemies we were reconciled to God through the death of His Son, much more, having been reconciled, we will be saved by His life.

¹¹ And not only *that*, but we also rejoice in God through our Lord Jesus Christ, by whom we have now received the atonement.

¹² Therefore, just as by one man sin entered the world, and death by sin, and thus death spread to everyone, because all sinned:

¹³ (Because, until the law sin was in the world, but sin is not imputed when there is no law.

¹⁴ Nevertheless death reigned from Adam to Moses, even over those who had not sinned according to the likeness of the transgression of Adam, who is a type of Him who was to come.

¹⁵ But the free gift *is* not like the offense. Because, if through the one *man's* offense many died, much more the grace of God and the gift by grace, *which is* by one Man, Jesus Christ, has abounded to many.

¹⁶ And the gift *is* not *like that* which came through the one who sinned. Because the judgment *which came* from one offense resulted in condemnation, but the free gift which came from many offenses resulted in justification.

¹⁷ Because, if by the one man's offense death reigned by one, much more those who receive abundance of grace and of the gift of righteousness will reign in life by One, Jesus Christ.)

¹⁸ Therefore, as by one man's offense *judgment came* upon all mankind, resulting in condemnation, even so by one Man's righteous act *the free gift came* to all mankind, resulting in justification of life.

¹⁹ Because, as by one man's disobedience many were made sinners, so also by the obedience of One many will be made righteous.

²⁰ Moreover the law entered that the offense might abound. But where sin abounded, grace abounded much more,

²¹ so that as sin reigned in death, even so grace might reign through righteousness to eternal life through Jesus Christ our Lord.

CHAPTER 6

¹ What shall we say then? Shall we continue in sin that grace may abound?

² God forbid! How shall we who died to sin live any longer in it?

³ Or do you not know that as many of us as were baptized into Jesus Christ were baptized into His death?

⁴ Therefore we were buried with Him by baptism into death, that just as Christ was raised up from the dead by the glory of the Father, even so we also should walk in newness of life.

⁵ Because, if we have been planted together in the likeness of His death, we will be also *in the likeness* of His resurrection,

⁶ knowing this, that our old man was crucified with *Him*, that the body of sin might be destroyed, that we should no longer serve sin.

⁷ Because he who has died has been freed from sin.

⁸ Now if we died with Christ, we believe that we will also live with Him,

⁹ knowing that Christ, having been raised from the dead, dies no more. Death no longer has dominion over Him.

¹⁰ Because, in the death that He died, He died to sin once; but the life that He lives, He lives to God.

¹¹ Likewise you also, reckon yourselves to be dead indeed to sin, but alive to God in Jesus Christ our Lord.

¹² Therefore do not let sin reign in your mortal body, that you should obey it in its lusts.

¹³ And do not present your members *as* instruments of unrighteousness to sin, but present yourselves to God as those who are alive from the dead, and your members *as* instruments of righteoussness to God.

¹⁴ Because, sin will not have dominion over you, because you are not under law but under grace.

¹⁵ What then? Shall we sin because we are not under law but under grace? God forbid!

¹⁶ Do you not know that to whom you present yourselves servants to obey, you are that one's servant whom you obey, whether of sin leading to death, or of obedience leading to righteousness?

¹⁷ But God be thanked that though you were servants of sin, yet you obeyed from the heart that form of doctrine which was delivered to you.

¹⁸ And having been set free from sin, you became servants of righteousness.

¹⁹ I speak in human terms because of the weakness of your flesh. Because, just as you presented your members as servants of uncleanness, and of iniquity leading to more iniquity, so now present your members as servants of righteousness for holiness.

²⁰ Because when you were servants of sin, you were free from righteousness.

²¹ What fruit did you have then in the things of which you are now ashamed? Because the end of those things is death.

²² But now having been set free from sin, and having become servants of God, you have your fruit to holiness, and the end, everlasting life.

²³ Because, the wages of sin is death, but the gift of God is eternal life through Jesus Christ our Lord.

CHAPTER 7

¹ Or do you not know, brethren (because I speak to those who know the law), that the law has dominion over a man as long as he lives?

² Because, the woman who has a husband is bound by the law to *her* husband as long as he lives. But if the husband dies, she is released from the law of *her* husband.

³ So then if, while *her* husband lives, she marries another man, she will be called an adulteress; but if her husband dies, she is free from that law, so that she is no adulteress, though she has married another man.

⁴ Therefore, my brethren, you also have become dead to the law by the body of Christ, that you may be married to another, *even* to Him who was raised from the dead, that we should bear fruit to God.

⁵ Because, when we were in the flesh, the sinful passions which were through the law were at work in our members to bear fruit to death.

⁶ But now we have been delivered from the law, that which we were held by being dead, so that we should serve in the newness of the spirit and *not* in the oldness of the letter.

⁷ What shall we say then? *Is* the law sin? God forbid! On the contrary, I would not have known covetousness unless the law had said, "You shall not covet."

⁸ But sin, taking opportunity by the commandment, produced in me all manner of evil desire. Because apart from the law sin *was* dead.

⁹ Because, I was alive once without the law, but when the commandment came, sin revived and I died.

¹⁰ And the commandment, which was *ordained for* life, I found to *bring* death.

¹¹ Because sin, taking occasion by the commandment, deceived me, and by it killed *me*.

¹² Therefore the law *is* holy, and the commandment holy and just and good.

¹³ Has then what is good become death to me? God forbid! But sin, that it might appear sin, was producing death in me by what is good, so that sin through the commandment might become exceedingly sinful.

¹⁴ Because, we know that the law is spiritual, but I am carnal, sold under sin.

¹⁵ Because what I am doing, I do not approve. Because what I will to do,

that I do not do; but what I hate, that I do.

¹⁶ If, then, I do what I will not to do, I agree with the law that *it is* good.

¹⁷ But now, it is no longer I who do it, but sin that dwells in me.

¹⁸ Because, I know that in me (that is, in my flesh) nothing good dwells; because, to will is present with me, but *how* to perform what is good I do not find.

¹⁹ Because, the good that I will to do, I do not do; but the evil I will not to do, that I do.

²⁰ Now if I do what I will not to do, it is no longer I who do it, but sin that dwells in me.

²¹ I find then a law, that when I will to do good, evil is present with me.

²² Because, I delight in the law of God according to the inward man.

²³ But I see another law in my members, warring against the law of my mind, and bringing me into captivity to the law of sin which is in my members.

²⁴ O wretched man that I am! Who shall deliver me from the body of this death?

²⁵ I thank God through Jesus Christ our Lord! So then, with the mind I myself serve the law of God, but with the flesh the law of sin.

CHAPTER 8

¹ *There* is therefore now no condemnation to those who are in Christ Jesus, who do not walk according to the flesh, but according to the Spirit.

² Because, the law of the Spirit of life in Christ Jesus has made me free from the law of sin and death.

³ Because what the law could not do in that it was weak through the flesh, God did by sending His own Son in the likeness of sinful flesh, and for sin: condemned sin in the flesh,

⁴ that the righteous requirement of the law might be fulfilled in us who do not walk according to the flesh but according to the Spirit.

⁵ Because, those who live according to the flesh mind the things of the flesh, but those who live according to the Spirit, the things of the Spirit.

⁶ Because, to be carnally minded *is* death, but to be spiritually minded *is* life and peace.

⁷ Because, the carnal mind is enmity against God; because it is not subject to the law of God, nor indeed can *it* be.

⁸ So then, those who are in the flesh cannot please God.

⁹ But you are not in the flesh but in the Spirit, if indeed the Spirit of God dwells in you. Now if anyone does not have the Spirit of Christ, he is not His.

¹⁰ And if Christ *is* in you, the body *is* dead because of sin, but the Spirit *is* life because of righteousness.

¹¹ But if the Spirit of Him who raised up Jesus from the dead dwells in you, He who raised up Christ from the dead will also give life to your mortal bodies by His

Spirit who dwells in you.

¹² Therefore, brethren, we are debtors, not to the flesh, to live according to the flesh.

¹³ Because, if you live according to the flesh you will die; but if through the Spirit you put to death the deeds of the body, you will live.

¹⁴ Because, as many as are led by the Spirit of God, these are sons of God.

¹⁵ Because, you did not receive the spirit of bondage again to fear, but you have received the Spirit of adoption by whom we cry out, "Abba, Father."

¹⁶ The Spirit Himself bears witness with our spirit that we are children of God,

¹⁷ and if children, then heirs, heirs of God and joint heirs with Christ, providing we suffer with *Him*, that we may also be glorified together.

¹⁸ Because, I consider that the sufferings of this present time *are* not worthy *to be compared* with the glory which will be revealed in us.

¹⁹ Because, the earnest expectation of the creature waits for the revealing of the sons of God.

²⁰ Because, the creature was subjected to vanity, not willingly, but because of Him who subjected *it* in hope;

²¹ because, the creature itself also will be delivered from the bondage of corruption into the glorious liberty of the children of God.

²² Because, we know that the entire creation groans and labors with birth pangs together until now.

²³ And not only *they*, but we also who have the firstfruits of the Spirit, even we ourselves groan within ourselves, eagerly waiting for the adoption, *that is* the redemption of our body.

²⁴ Because, we were saved by hope, but hope that is seen is not hope; because why does one still hope for what he sees?

²⁵ But if we hope for what we do not see, *then* we eagerly wait for *it* with perseverance.

²⁶ Likewise the Spirit also helps in our weaknesses. Because, we do not know what we should pray for as we ought, but the Spirit Himself makes intercession for us with groanings which cannot be uttered.

²⁷ Now He who searches the hearts knows what the mind of the Spirit *is*, because He makes intercession for the saints according to *the will of* God.

²⁸ And we know that all things work together for good to those who love God, to those who are the called according to *His* purpose.

²⁹ Because, whom He foreknew, He also predestined *to be* conformed to the image of His Son, that He might be the firstborn among many brethren.

³⁰ Moreover whom He predestined, these He also called; whom He called, these He also justified; and whom He justified, these He also glorified.

³¹ What then shall we say to these

things? If God *is* for us, who *can be* against us?

³² He who did not spare His own Son, but delivered Him up for us all, how will He not with Him also freely give us all things?

³³ Who shall bring a charge against God's elect? It is God who justifies.

³⁴ Who *is* he who condemns? *It is* Christ who died, and furthermore is also risen, who is even at the right hand of God, who also makes intercession for us.

³⁵ Who shall separate us from the love of Christ? *Shall* tribulation, or distress, or persecution, or famine, or nakedness, or peril, or sword?

³⁶ As it is written: "For Your sake we are killed all day long; we are accountted as sheep for the slaughter."

³⁷ Yet in all these things we are more than conquerors through Him who loved us.

³⁸ Because, I am persuaded that neither death nor life, nor angels nor principalities nor powers, nor things present nor things to come,

³⁹ nor height nor depth, nor any other creature, will be able to separate us from the love of God which is in Christ Jesus our Lord.

CHAPTER 9

¹ I tell the truth in Christ, I am not lying, my conscience also bearing me witness in the Holy Spirit,

² that I have great heaviness and continual sorrow in my heart.

³ Because, I could wish that I myself were accursed from Christ for my brethren, my countrymen according to the flesh,

⁴ who are Israelites, to whom *pertain* the adoption, the glory, the covenants, the giving of the law, the service *of* God, and the promises;

⁵ of whom *are* the fathers and of whom, according to the flesh, Christ *came*, who is over all, God blessed forever. Amen.

⁶ But it is not that the word of God has taken no effect. Because, they *are* not all Israel who are of Israel,

⁷ nor are *they* all children because they are the seed of Abraham; but, "In Isaac your seed will be called."

⁸ That is, those who are the children of the flesh, these *are* not the children of God; but the children of the promise are counted as the seed.

⁹ Because, this *is* the word of promise: "At this time I will come and Sarah will have a son."

¹⁰ And not only *this*, but when Rebecca also had conceived by one man, *that is* by our father Isaac

¹¹ (because, the *children* being not yet born, nor having done any good or evil, that the purpose of God according to election might stand, not of works but of Him who calls),

¹² it was said to her, "The older will serve the younger."

¹³ As it is written, "Jacob I have loved, but Esau I have hated."

¹⁴ what shall we say then? *Is there* unrighteousness with God? God

forbid!

¹⁵ Because, He says to Moses, "I will have mercy on whomever I will have mercy, and I will have compassion on whomever I will have compassion."

¹⁶ So then *it is* not of him who wills, nor of him who runs, but of God who shows mercy.

¹⁷ Because, the Scripture says to the Pharaoh, "For this very purpose I have raised you up, that I may show My power in you, and that My name may be declared throughout all the earth."

¹⁸ Therefore He has mercy on whom He will have mercy, and whom He wills He hardens.

¹⁹ You will say to me then, "Why does He still find fault? Because who has resisted His will?"

²⁰ But indeed, O man, who are you to reply against God? Shall the thing formed say to him who formed *it*, "Why have you made me like this?"

²¹ Does not the potter have power over the clay, from the same lump to make one vessel for honor and another for dishonor?

²² *What if* God, wanting to show His wrath and to make His power known, endured with much longsuffering the vessels of wrath prepared for destruction,

²³ and that He might make known the riches of His glory on the vessels of mercy, which He had prepared beforehand for glory,

²⁴ even us whom He called, not of the Jews only, but also of the Gentiles?

²⁵ As He says also in Hosea: "I will call them My people, who were not My people, and her beloved, who was not beloved."

²⁶ "And it will come to pass *that* in the place where it was said to them, 'You *are* not My people,' There they will be called children of the living God."

²⁷ Isaiah also proclaims concerning Israel: "Though the number of the children of Israel be as the sand of the sea, a remnant will be saved.

²⁸ Because, He will finish the work and cut it short in righteousness, because the Lord will make a short work upon the earth."

²⁹ And as Isaiah said before: "Unless the Lord of Sabaoth had left us a seed, we would have become like Sodom, and we would have been made like Gomorrah."

³⁰ What shall we say then? That Gentiles, who did not pursue righteousness, have attained to righteousness, even the righteousness which is of faith;

³¹ but Israel, pursuing the law of righteousness, has not attained to the law of righteousness.

³² Why? Because, *they* did not *seek it* by faith, but as it were, by the works of the law. Because they stumbled at that stumbling stone.

³³ As it is written: "Behold, I lay in Zion a stumbling stone and rock of offense, and whoever believes on Him will not be put to shame."

CHAPTER 10

¹ Brethren, my heart's desire and prayer to God for Israel is that they might be saved.
² Because, I bear them record that they have a zeal for God, but not according to knowledge.
³ Because, they being ignorant of God's righteousness, and seeking to establish their own righteousness, have not submitted themselves to the righteousness of God.
⁴ Because Christ *is* the end of the law for righteousness to everyone who believes.
⁵ Because, Moses writes about the righteousness which is of the law, "That the man who does those things shall live by them."
⁶ But the righteousness that is of faith speaks in this way, "Do not say in your heart, 'Who shall ascend into heaven?' " (that is, to bring Christ down *from above*)
⁷ or, "'Who shall descend into the deep?' " (that is, to bring Christ up from the dead).
⁸ But what does it say? "The word is near you, *even* in your mouth and in your heart" (that is, the word of faith which we preach):
⁹ that if you confess with your mouth the Lord Jesus and will believe in your heart that God has raised Him from the dead, you will be saved.
¹⁰ Because, with the heart one believes to righteousness, and with the mouth confession is made to salvation.
¹¹ Because, the Scripture says, "Whoever believes on Him will not be put to shame."
¹² Because, there is no distinction between the Jew and the Greek, because the same Lord over all is rich to all who call upon Him.
¹³ Because "whoever calls on the name of the Lord will be saved."
¹⁴ How then shall they call on Him in whom they have not believed? And how shall they believe in Him of whom they have not heard? And how shall they hear without a preacher?
¹⁵ And how shall they preach unless they are sent? As it is written: "How beautiful are the feet of those who preach the gospel of peace, and bring glad tidings of good things!"
¹⁶ But they have not all obeyed the gospel. Because, Isaiah says, "LORD, who has believed our report?"
¹⁷ So then faith *comes* by hearing, and hearing by the word of God.
¹⁸ But I say, have they not heard? Yes indeed: "Their sound has gone out to all the earth, and their words to the ends of the world."
¹⁹ But I say, did Israel not know? First Moses says: "I will provoke you to jealousy by *those who are* not a people, *and* I will move you to anger by a foolish nation."
²⁰ But Isaiah is very bold and says: "I was found by those who did not seek Me; I was made manifest to those who did not ask for Me."
²¹ But to Israel he says: "All day long I have stretched out My hands to a

disobedient and contrary people."

CHAPTER 11

¹ I say then, has God cast away His people? God forbid! Because, I also am an Israelite, of the seed of Abraham, *of* the tribe of Benjamin.

² God has not cast away His people whom He foreknew. Or do you not know what the Scripture says of Elijah, how he makes intercession to God against Israel, saying,

³ "LORD, they have killed Your prophets and torn down Your altars, and I alone am left, and they seek my life"?

⁴ But what does God reply to him? "I have reserved for Myself seven thousand men who have not bowed the knee to *the image* of Baal."

⁵ Even so then, at this present time there is a remnant according to the election of grace.

⁶ And if by grace, then *it is* no longer of works; otherwise grace is no longer grace. But if *it is* of works, it is no longer grace; otherwise work is no longer work.

⁷ What then? Israel has not obtained what it seeks after; but the elect have obtained it, and the rest were blinded.

⁸ Just as it is written: "God has given them a spirit of slumber, eyes that they should not see and ears that they should not hear, to this very day."

⁹ And David says: "Let their table become a snare and a trap, a stumbling block and a retribution to them.

¹⁰ Let their eyes be darkened, so that they cannot see, and bow down their back always."

¹¹ I say then, have they stumbled that they should fall? God forbid! But *rather* through their fall, salvation *has come* to the Gentiles, to provoke them to jealousy,

¹² Now if their fall *became* riches of the world, and their failure the riches of the Gentiles, how much more their fullness!

¹³ Because, I speak to you Gentiles; inasmuch as I am an apostle to the Gentiles, I magnify my ministry,

¹⁴ if by any means I may provoke to jealousy *those who are* my flesh and might save some of them.

¹⁵ Because, if their rejection *is* the reconciling of the world, what *shall their* acceptance *be* but life from the dead?

¹⁶ Because, if the firstfruit *is* holy, the lump *is* also *holy*; and if the root is holy, so *are* the branches.

¹⁷ And if some of the branches were broken off, and you, being a wild olive tree, were grafted in among them, and with them became a partaker of the root and nourishment of the olive tree,

¹⁸ do not boast against the branches. But if you do boast, remember that you do not support the root, but the root supports you.

¹⁹ You will say then, "Branches were broken off that I might be grafted in."

²⁰ Well *said*. Because of unbelief

they were broken off, and you stand by faith. Do not be high-minded, but have reverence.

²¹ Because, if God did not spare the natural branches, He may not spare you either.

²² Therefore consider the goodness and severity of God: on those who fell, severity; but toward you, goodness, if you continue in *His* goodness. Otherwise you also will be cut off.

²³ And they also, if they do not continue in unbelief, will be grafted in, because God is able to graft them in again.

²⁴ Because, if you were cut out of the olive tree which is wild by nature, and were grafted contrary to nature into a good olive tree, how much more will these, who are natural *branches*, be grafted into their own olive tree?

²⁵ Because, I do not desire, brethren, that you should be ignorant of this mystery, lest you should be wise in your own opinion, that blindness in part has happened to Israel until the fullness of the Gentiles has come in.

²⁶ And so all Israel will be saved, as it is written: "The Deliverer will come out of Zion, and He will turn away ungodliness from Jacob;

²⁷ Because, this is My covenant with them, when I will take away their sins."

²⁸ Concerning the gospel *they are* enemies for your sake, but concerning the election *they are* beloved because of the fathers.

²⁹ Because the gifts and the calling of God *are* irrevocable.

³⁰ Because, as you previously did not believe God, yet have now obtained mercy through their unbelief,

³¹ even so these also have now not believed, that through the mercy shown you they also may obtain mercy.

³² Because, God has concluded them all in unbelief, that He might have mercy on all.

³³ oh, the depth of the riches both of the wisdom and knowledge of God! How unsearchable *are* His judgments and His ways past finding out!

³⁴ "Because, who has known the mind of the LORD? Or who has become His counselor?"

³⁵ "Or who has first given to Him and it will be repaid to him?"

³⁶ Because, of Him and through Him and to Him *are* all things, to whom *be* glory forever. Amen.

CHAPTER 12

¹ I urge you therefore, brethren, by the mercies of God, that you present your bodies a living sacrifice, holy, acceptable to God, *which* is your reasonable service.

² And do not be conformed to this world, but be transformed by the renewing of your mind, that you may prove what *is* that good and acceptable and perfect will of God.

³ Because I say, through the grace

given to me, to everyone who is among you, not to think *of himself* more highly than he ought to think, but to think soberly, just as God has dealt to everyone the measure of faith.

⁴ Because, as we have many members in one body, but all the members do not have the same function,

⁵ so we, *being* many, are one body in Christ, and individually members of one another.

⁶ Having then gifts differing according to the grace that is given to us: if prophecy, *let us prophesy* according to the proportion of faith;

⁷ or ministry, *let us use it* in *our* ministering; he who teaches, in teaching;

⁸ he who exhorts, in exhortation; he who gives, *let him* do it with liberality; he who leads, with diligence; he who shows mercy, with cheerfulness.

⁹ Let love be without hypocrisy. Abhor what is evil. Cling to what is good.

¹⁰ *Be* affectionate to one another as family with brotherly love, in honor giving preference to one another;

¹¹ not lagging in diligence, fervent in spirit, serving the Lord;

¹² rejoicing in hope, patient in tribulation, continuing steadfastly in prayer;

¹³ distributing to the needs of the saints, given to hospitality.

¹⁴ Bless those who persecute you; bless and do not curse.

¹⁵ Rejoice with those who rejoice, and weep with those who weep.

¹⁶ *Be* of the same mind toward one another. Do not set your mind on high things, but associate with the humble. Do not be wise in your own opinion.

¹⁷ Repay no one evil for evil. Provide things that are right in the sight of everyone.

¹⁸ If it is possible, as much as depends on you, live peaceably with everyone.

¹⁹ Beloved, do not avenge yourselves, but *rather* give place to wrath; because it is written, "Vengeance is Mine, I will repay," says the Lord.

²⁰ Therefore "If your enemy hungers, feed him; if he thirsts, give him a drink; because in so doing you will heap coals of fire on his head."

²¹ Do not be overcome by evil, but overcome evil with good.

CHAPTER 13

¹ Let every soul be subject to the governing authorities. Because, there is no authority except from God; the authorities that exist are ordained by God.

² Therefore whoever resists the authority resists the ordinance of God, and those who resist will bring damnation on themselves.

³ Because, rulers are not a terror to good conduct, but to evil. Do you want to be unafraid of the auth-

ority? Do what is good, and you will have praise from the same.

⁴ Because, he is God's minister to you for good. But if you do that which is evil, be afraid; because he does not bear the sword in vain; because he is God's minister, an avenger to *execute* wrath on him who does evil.

⁵ Therefore *you* must be subject, not only because of wrath but also for conscience' sake.

⁶ Because, for this reason you also pay taxes, because they are God's ministers attending continually to this very thing.

⁷ Render therefore to all their due: taxes to whom taxes *are due*, customs to whom customs, reverence to whom reverence, honor to whom honor.

⁸ Owe no one anything except to love one another, because he who loves another has fulfilled the law.

⁹ Because these, "You shall not commit adultery," "You shall not murder," "You shall not steal," "You shall not bear false witness," "You shall not covet," and if *there is* any other commandment, are all summed up in this saying, namely, "You shall love your neighbor as yourself."

¹⁰ Love does no harm to a neighbor; therefore love *is* the fulfillment of the law.

¹¹ And this, knowing the time, that now *it is* high time to awake out of sleep; because now our salvation *is* nearer than when we first believed.

¹² The night is well advanced, the day is at hand. Therefore let us cast off the works of darkness, and let us put on the armor of light.

¹³ Let us walk appropriately, as in the day, not in riotous behavior and drunkenness, not in lewdness and lust, not in strife and envy.

¹⁴ But you, put on the Lord Jesus Christ, and make no provision for the flesh, to *fulfill* its lusts.

CHAPTER 14

¹ Receive one who is weak in the faith, *but* not to disputes over doubtful things.

² Because, one believes he may eat all things, but he who is weak eats only vegetables.

³ Let not him who eats despise him who does not eat, and let not him who does not eat judge him who eats; because God has received him.

⁴ Who are you to judge another's servant? To his own master he stands or falls. Indeed, he will be able to stand, because God is able to make him stand.

⁵ One person esteems one day above another; another esteems every day *alike*. Let each be fully convinced in his own mind.

⁶ He who observes the day, observes *it* to the Lord; and he who does not observe the day, to the Lord he does not observe *it*. He who eats, eats to the Lord, because he gives God thanks; and he who does not eat, to the Lord he does not eat, and gives God thanks.

⁷ Because none of us lives to himself, and no one dies to himself.

⁸ Because, if we live, we live to the Lord; and if we die, we die to the Lord. So whether we live or die, we are the Lord's.

⁹ Because, for this purpose Christ both died, and rose, and revived, that He might be Lord of both the dead and the living.

¹⁰ But why do you judge your brother? Or why do you show contempt for your brother? Because we will all stand before the judgment seat of Christ.

¹¹ Because, it is written: "*As* I live, says the LORD, every knee will bow to Me, and every tongue will confess to God."

¹² So then each of us will give account of himself to God.

¹³ Therefore let us not judge one another anymore, but rather resolve this, not to put a stumbling block or a reason to fall in *his* brother's way.

¹⁴ I know and am convinced by the Lord Jesus that *there* is nothing unclean of itself; but to him who considers anything to be unclean, to him *it is* unclean.

¹⁵ But if your brother is grieved because of *your* food, you are no longer walking in love. Do not destroy with your food the one who Christ died for.

¹⁶ Therefore do not let your good be spoken of as evil;

¹⁷ because, the kingdom of God is not eating and drinking, but righteousness and peace and joy in the Holy Spirit.

¹⁸ Because, he who serves Christ in these things *is* acceptable to God and approved by men.

¹⁹ Therefore let us pursue the things which make for peace and the things by which one may edify another.

²⁰ Do not destroy the work of God for the sake of food. All things indeed *are* pure, but *it is* evil for the man who eats with offense.

²¹ *It is* good neither to eat meat nor drink grape juice nor do *anything* by which your brother stumbles or is offended or is made weak.

²² Do you have faith? Have *it* to yourself before God. Happy is he who does not condemn himself in those things which he approves.

²³ But he who doubts is damned if he eats, because *he* does not *eat* from faith; because whatever *is* not from faith is sin.

CHAPTER 15

¹ We then who are strong ought to bear with the failures of the weak, and not to please ourselves.

² Let each of us please *his* neighbor for *his* good, leading to edification.

³ Because, even Christ did not please Himself; but as it is written, "The reproaches of those who reproached You fell on Me."

⁴ Because, whatever things were written beforehand were written for our learning, that we through the patience and comfort of the

Scriptures might have hope.

⁵ Now may the God of patience and comfort grant you to be like minded toward one another, according to Christ Jesus,

⁶ that you may with one mind *and* one mouth glorify God, *even* the Father of our Lord Jesus Christ.

⁷ You therefore, receive one another, just as Christ also received us, to the glory of God.

⁸ Now I say that Jesus Christ has become a servant to the circumcision for the truth of God, to confirm the promises *made* to the fathers,

⁹ and that the Gentiles might glorify God for *His* mercy, as it is written: "For this reason I will confess to You among the Gentiles, and sing to Your name."

¹⁰ And again he says: "Rejoice, O Gentiles, with His people!"

¹¹ And again: "Praise the LORD, all you Gentiles! Laud Him, all you people!"

¹² And again, Isaiah says: "There will be a root of Jesse; and He who will rise to reign over the Gentiles, in Him the Gentiles will trust."

¹³ Now may the God of hope fill you with all joy and peace in believing, that you may abound in hope through the power of the Holy Spirit.

¹⁴ Now I myself am persuaded concerning you, my brethren, that you also are full of goodness, filled with all knowledge, able also to admonish one another.

¹⁵ Nevertheless, brethren, I have written more boldly to you on some points, as reminding you, because of the grace given to me by God,

¹⁶ that I might be a minister of Jesus Christ to the Gentiles, ministering the gospel of God, that the offering up of the Gentiles might be acceptable, being sanctified by the Holy Spirit.

¹⁷ Therefore I have reason to glory through Jesus Christ in those things which pertain to God.

¹⁸ Because, I will not dare to speak of any of those things which Christ has not accomplished through me, in word and deed, to make the Gentiles obedient,

¹⁹ in mighty signs and wonders, by the power of the Spirit of God, so that from Jerusalem and round about to Illyricum I have fully preached the gospel of Christ.

²⁰ Yes, so I have striven to preach the gospel, not where Christ was named, lest I should build on another man's foundation,

²¹ but as it is written: "To whom He was not announced, they will see; and those who have not heard will understand."

²² For this reason I also have been often hindered from coming to you.

²³ But now no longer having a place in these parts, and having a great desire these many years to come to you,

²⁴ whenever I take my journey to Spain, I will come to you. Because, I hope to see you on my journey, and to be helped on my way there by

you, once I have enjoyed your *company* for a while.

²⁵ But now I am going to Jerusalem to minister to the saints.

²⁶ Because, it pleased those from Macedonia and Achaia to make a certain contribution for the poor among the saints who are in Jerusalem.

²⁷ It has pleased them indeed, and they are their debtors. Because, if the Gentiles have been partakers of their spiritual things, their duty is also to minister to them in material things.

²⁸ Therefore, when I have performed this and have sealed to them this fruit, I will come via you into Spain.

²⁹ But I know that when I come to you, I will come in the fullness of the blessing of the gospel of Christ.

³⁰ Now I urge you, brethren, for *the* sake *of* the Lord Jesus Christ, and for the love of the Spirit, that you strive together with me in prayers to God for me,

³¹ that I may be delivered from those in Judea who do not believe, and that my service which *I have* for Jerusalem may be accepted by the saints,

³² that I may come to you with joy by the will of God, and may be refreshed together with you.

³³ Now the God of peace *be* with you all. Amen.

CHAPTER 16

¹ I commend to you Phoebe our sister, who is a servant of the church in Cenchrea,

² that you may receive her in the Lord in a manner worthy of the saints, and that you assist her in whatever business she has need of you; because she has been a helper of many and of myself also.

³ Greet Priscilla and Aquila, my helpers in Christ Jesus,

⁴ who risked their own necks for my life, to whom not only I give thanks, but also all the churches of the Gentiles.

⁵ Likewise *greet* the church that is in their house. Greet my beloved Epaenetus, who is the firstfruits of Achaia to Christ.

⁶ Greet Mary, who labored much for us.

⁷ Greet Andronicus and Junia, my countrymen and my fellow prisoners, who are of note among the apostles, who also were in Christ before me.

⁸ Greet Amplias, my beloved in the Lord.

⁹ Greet Urbanus, our helper in Christ, and Stachys, my beloved.

¹⁰ Greet Apelles, approved in Christ. Greet those who are of the *household* of Aristobulus.

¹¹ Greet Herodion, my countryman. Greet those who are of the *household* of Narcissus who are in the Lord.

¹² Greet Tryphena and Tryphosa, who labor in the Lord. Greet the beloved Persis, who labored much

in the Lord.

¹³ Greet Rufus, chosen in the Lord, and his mother and mine.

¹⁴ Greet Asyncritus, Phlegon, Hermas, Patrobas, Hermes, and the brethren who are with them.

¹⁵ Greet Philologus and Julia, Nereus and his sister, and Olympas, and all the saints who are with them.

¹⁶ Greet one another with a holy kiss. The churches of Christ greet you.

¹⁷ Now I urge you, brethren, note those who cause divisions and offenses, contrary to the doctrine which you learned, and avoid them.

¹⁸ Because, those who are such do not serve our Lord Jesus Christ, but their own belly, and by smooth words and flattering speech deceive the hearts of the simple.

¹⁹ Because, your obedience has become known to everyone. Therefore I am glad on your behalf; but I want you to be wise in what is good, and simple concerning evil.

²⁰ And the God of peace will crush Satan under your feet shortly. The grace of our Lord Jesus Christ *be* with you. Amen.

²¹ Timothy, my fellow worker, and Lucius, Jason, and Sosipater, my countrymen, greet you.

²² I, Tertius, who wrote *this* letter, greet you in the Lord.

²³ Gaius, my host and *the host* of the entire church, greets you. Erastus, the treasurer of the city, greets you, and Quartus, a brother.

²⁴ The grace of our Lord Jesus Christ *be* with you all. Amen.

²⁵ Now to Him who is mighty to establish you according to my gospel and the preaching of Jesus Christ, according to the revelation of the mystery kept secret since the ages began

²⁶ but is now made manifest, and by the scriptures of the prophets, made known to all nations, according to the commandment of the everlasting God, for obedience to the faith,

²⁷ to God, alone wise, be glory through Jesus Christ forever. Amen.

Written to the Romans from Corinth, and *sent by* Phoebe, the servant of the church at Cenchrea.

THE FIRST LETTER OF PAUL THE APOSTLE TO THE
CORINTHIANS

CHAPTER 1

¹ Paul, called *to be* an apostle of Jesus Christ through the will of God, and Sosthenes *our* brother,

² To the church of God which is at Corinth, to those who are sanctified in Christ Jesus, called *to be* saints, with all who in every place call on the name of Jesus Christ our Lord, both theirs and ours:

³ Grace *be* to you and peace from God our Father and *from* the Lord Jesus Christ.

⁴ I thank my God always concerning you for the grace of God which was given to you by Jesus Christ,

⁵ that you are enriched in everything by Him in all utterance and *in* all knowledge,

⁶ even as the testimony of Christ was confirmed in you,

⁷ so that you come short in no gift, waiting for the coming of our Lord Jesus Christ,

⁸ who will also confirm you to the end, *that you may be* blameless in the day of our Lord Jesus Christ.

⁹ God is faithful, by whom you were called into the fellowship of His Son, Jesus Christ our Lord.

¹⁰ Now I plead with you, brethren, by the name of our Lord Jesus Christ, that you all speak the same thing, and that there be no divisions among you, but *that* you be perfectly joined together in the same mind and in the same judgment.

¹¹ Because, it has been declared to me concerning you, my brethren, by those *of* Chloe's *household*, that there are contentions among you.

¹² Now I say this, that each of you says, "I am of Paul," or "I am of Apollos," or "I am of Cephas," or "I am of Christ."

¹³ Is Christ divided? Was Paul crucified for you? Or were you baptized in the name of Paul?

¹⁴ I thank God that I baptized none of you except Crispus and Gaius,

¹⁵ lest anyone should say that I had baptized in my own name.

¹⁶ And, I also baptized the household of Stephanas. Besides, I do not know whether I baptized any other.

¹⁷ Because, Christ did not send me to baptize, but to preach the gospel, not with wisdom of words, lest the cross of Christ should be made of no effect.

¹⁸ Because, the preaching of the cross is foolishness to those who perish, but to us who are saved it is the power of God.

¹⁹ Because it is written: "I will destroy the wisdom of the wise, and bring to nothing the understanding of the prudent."

²⁰ Where is the wise? Where is the scribe? Where is the disputer of this age? Has not God made foolish the

wisdom of this world?

²¹ Because since, in the wisdom of God, the world by wisdom did not know God, it pleased God through the foolishness of preaching to save those who believe.

²² Because, Jews request a sign, and Greeks seek after wisdom;

²³ but we preach Christ crucified, to the Jews a stumbling block and to the Greeks foolishness,

²⁴ but to those who are called, both Jews and Greeks, Christ the power of God and the wisdom of God.

²⁵ Because, the foolishness of God is wiser than men, and the weakness of God is stronger than men.

²⁶ Because, you see your calling, brethren, that not many wise according to the flesh, not many mighty, not many noble, *are called.*

²⁷ But God has chosen the foolish things of the world to put to shame the wise, and God has chosen the weak things of the world to put to shame the things which are mighty;

²⁸ and the base things of the world and the things which are despised God has chosen, *yes* and the things which are not, to bring to nothing the things that are,

²⁹ that no flesh should glory in His presence.

³⁰ But of Him you are in Christ Jesus, who, from God, became for us wisdom and righteousness and sanctification and redemption,

³¹ that, according to as it is written, "He who glories, let him glory in the Lord."

CHAPTER 2

¹ And I, brethren, when I came to you, did not come with excellence of speech or of wisdom declaring to you the testimony of God.

² Because, I determined not to know anything among you except Jesus Christ and Him crucified.

³ And I was with you in weakness, in fear, and in much trembling.

⁴ And my speech and my preaching was not with persuasive words of human wisdom, but in demonstration of the Spirit and of power,

⁵ that your faith should not stand in the wisdom of men but in the power of God.

⁶ However, we speak wisdom among those who are perfect, yet not the wisdom of this age, nor of the rulers of this age, who come to nothing.

⁷ But we speak the wisdom of God in a mystery, *even* the hidden *wisdom* which God ordained before the ages for our glory,

⁸ which none of the rulers of this age knew; because, had they known *it,* they would not have crucified the Lord of glory.

⁹ But as it is written: "Eye has not seen, nor ear heard, nor have entered into the heart of man the things which God has prepared for those who love Him."

¹⁰ But God has revealed *them* to us by His Spirit. Because, the Spirit searches all things, yes, the deep things of God.

¹¹ Because, what man knows the

things of a man except the spirit of the man which is in him? Even so no one knows the things of God except the Spirit of God.

¹² Now we have received, not the spirit of the world, but the Spirit who is from God, that we might know the things that have been freely given to us from God.

¹³ These things we also speak, not in words which man's wisdom teaches but which the Holy Spirit teaches, comparing spiritual things with spiritual.

¹⁴ But the natural man does not receive the things of the Spirit of God, because they are foolishness to him; nor can he know *them*, because they are spiritually discerned.

¹⁵ But he who is spiritual judges all things, yet he himself is judged by no one.

¹⁶ Because, "who has known the mind of the Lord that he may instruct Him?" But we have the mind of Christ.

CHAPTER 3

¹ And I, brethren, could not speak to you as to spiritual people but as to carnal, *even* as to babes in Christ.

² I have fed you with milk and not with solid food; because until now you were not able to *receive it*, and even now you are still not able;

³ because you are still carnal. Because where *there is* envy, strife, and divisions among you, are you not carnal and walk like men?

⁴ Because when one says, "I am of Paul," and another, "I *am* of Apollos," are you not carnal?

⁵ Who then is Paul, and who is Apollos, but ministers by whom you believed, as the Lord gave to each person?

⁶ I have planted, Apollos watered, but God gave the increase.

⁷ So then neither he who plants is anything, nor he who waters, but God who gives the increase.

⁸ Now he who plants and he who waters are one, and each one will receive his own reward according to his own labor.

⁹ Because, we are God's coworkers; you are God's field, *you are* God's building.

¹⁰ According to the grace of God which was given to me, as a wise master builder I have laid the foundation, and another builds on it. But let each one take heed how he builds on it.

¹¹ Because no other foundation can anyone lay than that which is laid, which is Jesus Christ.

¹² Now if anyone builds on this foundation with gold, silver, precious stones, wood, hay, straw,

¹³ each one's work will be revealed; because the Day will declare it, because it will be revealed by fire; and the fire will test each one's work, of what sort it is.

¹⁴ If anyone's work which he has built on it endures, he will receive a reward.

¹⁵ If anyone's work is burned, he

will suffer loss; but he himself will be saved, yet so as through fire.

¹⁶ Do you not know that you are the temple of God and that the Spirit of God dwells in you?

¹⁷ If anyone defiles the temple of God, God will destroy him. Because the temple of God is holy, which temple you are.

¹⁸ Let no one deceive himself. If anyone among you seems to be wise in this age, let him become a fool that he may be wise.

¹⁹ Because the wisdom of this world is foolishness with God. Because it is written, "He traps the wise in their own craftiness";

²⁰ and again, "The LORD knows the thoughts of the wise, that they are vain."

²¹ Therefore let no one boast in men. Because all things are yours:

²² whether Paul or Apollos or Cephas, or the world or life or death, or things present or things to come; all are yours.

²³ And you are Christ's, and Christ *is* God's.

CHAPTER 4

¹ Let a man so consider us, as servants of Christ and stewards of the mysteries of God.

² Moreover it is required in stewards that one be found faithful.

³ But with me it is a very small thing that I should be judged by you or by a man's judgment. In fact, I do not even judge myself.

⁴ Because, I know of nothing against myself, yet I am not justified by this; but He who judges me is the Lord.

⁵ Therefore judge nothing before the time, until the Lord comes, who will both bring to light the hidden things of darkness and reveal the counsels of the hearts. And then each one's praise will come from God.

⁶ Now these things, brethren, I have figuratively transferred to myself and Apollos for your sakes, that you may learn in us not to think *about people* beyond what is written, that none of you may be puffed up on behalf of one against the other.

⁷ Because who makes you differ *from another*? And what do you have that you did not receive? Now if you did indeed receive it, why do you boast as if you had not received *it*?

⁸ You are already full! You are already rich! You have reigned as kings without us; and indeed, I could wish you did reign, that we also might reign with you!

⁹ Because, I think that God has displayed us, the apostles, last, as men condemned to death; because we have been made a spectacle to the world, to angels and to men.

¹⁰ We *are* fools for Christ's sake, but you *are* wise in Christ! We *are* weak, but you *are* strong! You are honorable, but we *are* despised!

¹¹ Even to the present hour we both hunger and thirst, and we are unclothed, and beaten, and have no

permanent home.

¹² And we labor, working with our own hands. Being reviled, we bless; being persecuted, we endure;

¹³ being defamed, we entreat. We have been made as the scum of the earth, and are the offscouring of all things to this day.

¹⁴ I do not write these things to shame you, but as my beloved sons I warn *you*.

¹⁵ Because, though you might have ten thousand instructors in Christ, yet *you* do not *have* many fathers; because in Christ Jesus I have begotten you through the gospel.

¹⁶ Therefore I urge you all, be followers of me.

¹⁷ For this reason I have sent Timothy to you, who is my beloved and faithful son in the Lord, who will remind you of my ways which are in Christ, as I teach everywhere in every church.

¹⁸ Now some are puffed up, as though I were not coming to you.

¹⁹ But I will come to you shortly, if the Lord wills, and I will know, not the speech of those who are puffed up, but the power.

²⁰ Because the kingdom of God is not in word but in power.

²¹ what do you want? Shall I come to you with a rod, or in love and *in* the spirit of meekness?

CHAPTER 5

¹ It is commonly reported *that there is* sexual immorality among you, and such sexual immorality as is not even named among the Gentiles, that a man has his father's wife!

² And you are puffed up, and have not rather mourned, that he who has done this deed might be taken away from among you.

³ Because, I indeed, as absent in body but present in spirit, have already judged (as though I were present) *concerning* him who has so done this deed,

⁴ in the name of our Lord Jesus Christ, when you are gathered together, along with my spirit, with the power of our Lord Jesus Christ,

⁵ to deliver such a one to Satan for the destruction of the flesh, that his spirit may be saved in the day of the Lord Jesus.

⁶ Your glorying *is* not good. Do you not know that a little leaven leavens the entire lump?

⁷ Therefore purge out the old leaven, that you may be a new lump, since you truly are unleavened. Because, even Christ, our Passover, was sacrificed for us.

⁸ Therefore let us keep the feast, not with old leaven, nor with the leaven of malice and wickedness, but with the unleavened *bread* of sincerity and truth.

⁹ I wrote to you in a letter not to keep company with sexually immoral people.

¹⁰ Yet I certainly did not mean with the sexually immoral people of this world, or with the covetous, or extortioners, or idolaters, since then

you would need to go out of the world.

¹¹ But now I have written to you not to keep company with anyone that is named a brother, who is sexually immoral, or covetous, or an idolater, or a reviler, or a drunkard, or an extortioner; not even to eat with such a person.

¹² Because, what have I to do with judging those also who are outside? Do you not judge those who are inside?

¹³ But those who are outside God judges. Therefore "put away from yourselves that evil person."

CHAPTER 6

¹ Dare any of you, having a matter against another, go to law before the unrighteous, and not before the saints?

² Do you not know that the saints will judge the world? And if the world will be judged by you, are you unworthy to judge the smallest matters?

³ Do you not know that we will judge angels? How much more, things that pertain to this life?

⁴ If then you have judgments concerning things pertaining to this life, appoint those who are least esteemed in the church to judge!

⁵ I say this to your shame. Is it so, that there is not a wise man among you, not even one, who will be able to judge between his brethren?

⁶ But brother goes to law against brother, and that before the unbelievers!

⁷ Now therefore, it is already an utter failure for you, because you go to law against one another. Why do you not rather accept wrong? Why do you not rather *allow* yourselves be defrauded?

⁸ No, you do wrong and defraud, and that *to your* brethren!

⁹ Do you not know that the unrighteous will not inherit the kingdom of God? Do not be deceived. Neither fornicators, nor idolaters, nor adulterers, nor effeminate, nor abusers of themselves with mankind,

¹⁰ nor thieves, nor covetous, nor drunkards, nor revilers, nor extortioners will inherit the kingdom of God.

¹¹ And such were some of you. But you are washed, but you are sanctified, but you are justified in the name of the Lord Jesus and by the Spirit of our God.

¹² All things are lawful for me, but all things are not helpful. All things are lawful for me, but I will not be brought under the authority of any.

¹³ Foods for the stomach and the stomach for foods, but God will destroy both it and them. Now the body *is* not for sexual immorality but for the Lord, and the Lord for the body.

¹⁴ And God has both raised up the Lord and will also raise us up by His own power.

¹⁵ Do you not know that your bodies

are members of Christ? Shall I then take the members of Christ and make *them* the members of a harlot? God forbid!

[16] Or do you not know that he who is joined to a harlot is one body with her? Because "the two," He says, "will be one flesh."

[17] But he who is joined to the Lord is one spirit with Him.

[18] Flee sexual immorality. Every sin that a man does is outside the body, but he who commits sexual immorality sins against his own body.

[19] Or do you not know that your body is the temple of the Holy Spirit *who is* in you, whom you have from God, and you are not your own?

[20] Because, you were bought at a price; therefore glorify God in your body and in your spirit, which are God's.

CHAPTER 7

[1] Now concerning the things of which you wrote to me: *It is* good for a man not to touch a woman.

[2] Nevertheless, *to avoid* sexual immorality, let each man have his own wife, and let each woman have her own husband.

[3] Let the husband render to his wife the affection due her, and likewise also the wife to her husband.

[4] The wife does not have authority over her own body, but the husband does. And likewise the husband does not have authority over his own body, but the wife does.

[5] Do not deprive one another except *it be* with consent for a time, that you may give yourselves to fasting and prayer; and come together again so that Satan does not tempt you because of your lack of self control.

[6] But I say this by permission, *and* not as a commandment.

[7] Because I wish that all men were even as I myself. But each one has his own gift from God, one in this manner and another in that.

[8] Therefore, I say to the unmarried and to the widows: It is good for them if they remain even as I am;

[9] but if they cannot exercise self control, let them marry. Because it is better to marry than to burn *with passion.*

[10] Now to the married I command, *yet* not I but the Lord: A wife is not to depart from *her* husband.

[11] But even if she does depart, let her remain unmarried or be reconciled to *her* husband. And do not let a husband divorce *his* wife.

[12] But to the rest I, not the Lord, say: If any brother has a wife who does not believe, and she is willing to live with him, let him not divorce her.

[13] And a woman who has a husband who does not believe, if he is willing to live with her, let her not divorce him.

[14] Because, the unbelieving husband is sanctified by the wife, and the unbelieving wife is sanctified by the husband; otherwise your children would be unclean, but now

they are holy.

¹⁵ But if the unbeliever departs, let him depart; a brother or a sister is not under bondage in such *cases*. But God has called us to peace.

¹⁶ Because, how do you know, O wife, whether you will save your husband? Or how do you know, O husband, whether you will save *your* wife?

¹⁷ But as God has distributed to each one, as the Lord has called each one, so let him walk. And so I ordain in all the churches.

¹⁸ Was anyone called while circumcised? Let him not become uncircumcised. Was anyone called while uncircumcised? Let him not be circumcised.

¹⁹ Circumcision is nothing and uncircumcision is nothing, but keeping the commandments of God.

²⁰ Let each one remain in the same calling in which he was called.

²¹ Were you called *while* a servant? Do not be concerned about it; but if you can be made free, rather use *it*.

²² Because he who is called in the Lord *while* a servant is the Lord's freedman. Likewise he who is called while *free* is Christ's servant.

²³ You were bought with a price; do not become servants of men.

²⁴ Brethren, let each one remain with God in that state in which he was called.

²⁵ Now concerning virgins: I have no commandment from the Lord; yet I give my judgment as one who has received mercy from the Lord to be faithful.

²⁶ I suppose therefore that this is good because of the present distress, *I say* that it is good for a man to remain as he is:

²⁷ Are you bound to a wife? Do not seek to be loosed. Are you loosed from a wife? Do not seek a wife.

²⁸ But even if you do marry, you have not sinned; and if a virgin marries, she has not sinned. Nevertheless such will have trouble in the flesh, but I would spare you that.

²⁹ But this I say, brethren, the time *is* short, so that from now on even those who have wives should be as though they had none,

³⁰ those who weep as though they did not weep, those who rejoice as though they did not rejoice, those who buy as though they did not possess,

³¹ and those who use this world as not misusing *it*. Because the form of this world is passing away.

³² But I want you to be without worry. He who is unmarried cares for the things that pertain to the Lord, how he may please the Lord.

³³ But he who is married cares about the things that are of the world, how he may please *his* wife.

³⁴ There is also a difference between a wife and a virgin. The unmarried woman cares about the things of the Lord, that she may be holy both in body and in spirit. But she who is married cares about the

things of the world, how she may please *her* husband.

³⁵ And this I say for your own profit, not that I may put a snare on you, but for what is proper, and that you may serve the Lord without distraction.

³⁶ But if any man thinks he is behaving improperly toward his virgin, if she is past the flower of *her* age, and thus it must be, let him do what he wishes. He does not sin; let them marry.

³⁷ Nevertheless he who stands steadfast in his heart, having no necessity, but has power over his own will, and has so determined in his heart that he will keep his virgin, does well.

³⁸ So then he who gives *her* in marriage does well, but he who does not give *her* in marriage does better.

³⁹ A wife is bound by law as long as her husband lives; but if her husband dies, she is at liberty to be married to whom she wills, only in the Lord.

⁴⁰ But she is happier if she remains as she is, according to my judgment; and I think also that I have the Spirit of God.

CHAPTER 8

¹ Now concerning things offered to idols: We know that we all have knowledge. Knowledge puffs up, but love edifies.

² And if anyone thinks that he knows anything, he knows nothing yet as he ought to know.

³ But if anyone loves God, this one is known of Him.

⁴ Therefore concerning the eating of things that are offered in sacrifice to idols, we know that an idol *is* nothing in the world, and that *there is* no other God but one.

⁵ Because, even if there are so called gods, whether in heaven or on earth (as there are many gods and many lords),

⁶ yet for us *there* is *only* one God, the Father, of whom *are* all things, and we in Him; and one Lord Jesus Christ, by whom *are* all things, even ourselves by Him.

⁷ However, not everyone possesses that knowledge; but some, with consciousness of the idol, until now eat *it* as a thing offered to an idol; and their conscience, being weak, is defiled.

⁸ But food does not commend us to God; because neither if we eat are we better off, nor if we do not eat are we worse off.

⁹ But beware lest somehow this liberty of yours becomes a stumbling block to those who are weak.

¹⁰ Because, if anyone sees you who have knowledge eating in an idol's temple, shall not the conscience of him who is weak be emboldened to eat those things offered to idols?

¹¹ And because of your knowledge shall the weak brother perish, for whom Christ died?

¹² But when you all sin like this against the brethren, and wound

their weak conscience, you all sin against Christ.

¹³ Therefore, if food makes my brother stumble, I will never eat meat while the world stands, lest I make my brother stumble.

CHAPTER 9

¹ Am I not an apostle? Am I not free? Have I not seen Jesus Christ our Lord? Are you not my work in the Lord?

² If I am not an apostle to others, yet doubtless I am to you. Because, you are the seal of my apostleship in the Lord.

³ My defense to those who examine me is this:

⁴ Do we have no right to eat and drink?

⁵ Do we have no right to take along a sister, a wife, as do also the other apostles, the brethren of the Lord, and Cephas?

⁶ Or is it only Barnabas and I who have no right to refrain from working?

⁷ Who ever goes to war at his own expense? Who plants a vineyard and does not eat of its fruit? Or who tends a flock and does not drink of the milk of the flock?

⁸ Do I say these things as a *mere* man? Or does not the law say the same also?

⁹ Because, it is written in the law of Moses, "You shall not muzzle an ox while it treads out the grain." Is it oxen God is concerned about?

¹⁰ Or does He say *it* entirely for our sakes? No doubt, *this* is written for our sakes, that he who plows should plow in hope, and he who threshes in hope should be partaker of his hope.

¹¹ If we have sown spiritual things for you, *is it* a great thing if we reap your material things?

¹² If others are partakers of *this* authority over you, *are* we not even more? Nevertheless we have not used this authority, but endure all things lest we hinder the gospel of Christ.

¹³ Do you not know that those who minister the holy things eat *of the things* of the temple, and those who serve at the altar partake of the altar?

¹⁴ Even so the Lord has ordained that those who preach the gospel should live from the gospel.

¹⁵ But I have used none of these things, nor have I written these things that it should be done so to me; because *it would be* better for me to die than that anyone should make my boasting empty.

¹⁶ Because, though I preach the gospel, I have nothing to boast about, because necessity is laid upon me; yes, woe is me if I do not preach the gospel!

¹⁷ Because, if I do this thing willingly, I have a reward; but if against my will, I have been entrusted with a stewardship *of the gospel*.

¹⁸ What is my reward then? *Truly,* that when I preach the gospel, I

may present the gospel of Christ free of charge, that I may not abuse my authority in the gospel.

¹⁹ Because, though I am free from all *men*, I have made myself a servant to all, that I might win the more;

²⁰ and to the Jews I became as a Jew, that I might win Jews; to those who are under the law, as under the law, that I might win those who are under the law;

²¹ to those who are without law, as without law (not being without law toward God, but under the law toward Christ), that I might win those who are without law;

²² to the weak I became as weak, that I might win the weak. I have become all things to all *men*, that I might by all means save some.

²³ Now this I do for the gospel's sake, that I may be partaker of it with *you*.

²⁴ Do you not know that those who run in a race all run, but one receives the prize? Run in such a way that you may obtain it.

²⁵ And everyone who strives for dominance has self control in all things. Now they *do it* to obtain a perishable crown, but we *for* the imperishable.

²⁶ Therefore I do not run with uncertainty. So I do not fight as one who beats the air.

²⁷ But I discipline my body and bring *it* into subjection, lest in any way when I have preached to others, I myself should become an outcast.

CHAPTER 10

¹ Moreover, brethren, I do not want you to be ignorant that all our fathers were under the cloud, all passed through the sea,

² all were baptized under Moses in the cloud and in the sea,

³ all ate the same spiritual food,

⁴ and all drank the same spiritual drink. Because, they drank of that spiritual Rock that followed them, and that Rock was Christ.

⁵ But with most of them God was not well pleased, because they were overthrown in the wilderness.

⁶ Now these things became our examples, to the intent that we should not lust after evil things as they also lusted.

⁷ And do not become idolaters as *were* some of them. As it is written, "The people sat down to eat and drink, and rose up to play."

⁸ Nor let us commit sexual immorality, as some of them committed, and in one day twenty three thousand fell;

⁹ nor let us tempt Christ, as some of them also tempted, and were destroyed by serpents;

¹⁰ nor complain, as some of them also complained, and were destroyed by the destroyer.

¹¹ Now all these things happened to them as examples, and they were written for our admonition, upon whom the ends of the ages have come.

¹² Therefore let him who thinks he stands take heed lest he fall.

¹³ There is no temptation that has come upon you except such as is common to everyone; but God is faithful, who will not allow you to be tempted beyond what you are able, but with the temptation will also make the way of escape, that you may be able to endure it.

¹⁴ Therefore, my beloved, flee from idolatry.

¹⁵ I speak as to wise men; judge for yourselves what I say.

¹⁶ The cup of blessing which we bless, is it not the communion of the blood of Christ? The bread which we break, is it not the communion of the body of Christ?

¹⁷ Because we, though many, are one bread and one body; because we all partake of that one bread.

¹⁸ Observe Israel according to the flesh: Are not those who eat of the sacrifices partakers of the altar?

¹⁹ What am I saying then? That an idol is anything, or what is offered in sacrifice to idols is anything?

²⁰ Rather, *I am saying* that the things which the Gentiles sacrifice they sacrifice to demons and not to God, and I do not want that you would have fellowship with demons.

²¹ You cannot drink the cup of the Lord and the cup of demons; you cannot partake of the Lord's table and of the table of demons.

²² Or do we provoke the Lord to jealousy? Are we stronger than He?

²³ All things are lawful for me, but not all things are helpful; all things are lawful for me, but not all things edify.

²⁴ Let no one seek his own, but each one the other's well being.

²⁵ Eat whatever is sold in the meat market, asking no questions for conscience' sake;

²⁶ because "the earth is the LORD'S, and all its fullness."

²⁷ If any of those who do not believe invites you *to a meal*, and you desire to go, eat whatever is set before you, asking no question for conscience' sake.

²⁸ But if anyone says to you, "This was offered to idols," do not eat it for the sake of the one who told you, and for conscience' sake; because "the earth is the LORD'S, and all its fullness."

²⁹ I do not say your own conscience, but that of the others. Because why is my liberty judged by another man's conscience?

³⁰ But if I partake with thanks, why am I evil spoken of for that over which I give thanks?

³¹ Therefore, whether you eat or drink, or whatever you do, do all to the glory of God.

³² Give no offense, either to the Jews or to the Gentiles or to the church of God,

³³ just as I also please all *men* in all *things*, not seeking my own profit, but the *profit* of many, that they may be saved.

CHAPTER 11

¹ Be followers of me, just as I also am of Christ.

² Now I praise you, brethren, that you remember me in all things and keep the traditions just as I delivered *them* to you.

³ But I want you to know that the head of every man is Christ, the head of the woman *is* man, and the head of Christ *is* God.

⁴ Every man praying or prophesying, having *his* head covered, dishonors his head.

⁵ But every woman who prays or prophesies with *her* head uncovered dishonors *her* head, because, that is one and the same as if her head were shaved.

⁶ Because, if a woman is not covered, let her also be shorn. But if it is shameful for a woman to be shorn or shaved, let her be covered.

⁷ Because, a man indeed ought not to cover *his* head, since he is the image and glory of God; but woman is the glory of man.

⁸ Because, the man is not from the woman, but the woman from the man.

⁹ Nor was man created for the woman, but woman for the man.

¹⁰ For this reason the woman ought to have a symbol of authority on *her* head, because of the angels.

¹¹ Nevertheless, neither is man independent of woman, nor woman independent of man, in the Lord.

¹² Because, as woman *came* from man, even so man also comes through woman; but all things are from God.

¹³ Judge among yourselves. Is it proper for a woman to pray to God uncovered?

¹⁴ Does not even nature itself teach you that if a man has long hair, it is a dishonor to him?

¹⁵ But if a woman has long hair, it is a glory to her; because her hair is given to her for a covering.

¹⁶ But if anyone seems to be contentious, we have no such custom, nor do the churches of God.

¹⁷ Now in giving these instructions *to you* I do not praise *you*, since you come together not for the better but for the worse.

¹⁸ Because, first of all, when you come together in the church, I hear that there are divisions among you, and in part I believe it.

¹⁹ Because, there must also be heresies among you, that those who are approved may be identified among you.

²⁰ Therefore when you come together into one place, *this is* not to eat the Lord's Supper.

²¹ Because, in eating, each one takes his own supper ahead of *others*; and one is hungry and another drinks to the full.

²² What! Do you not have houses to eat and drink in? Or do you despise the church of God and shame those who have nothing? What shall I say to you? Shall I praise you in this? I do not praise *you*.

²³ Because, I received from the Lord that which I also delivered to you:

that the Lord Jesus on the *same* night in which He was betrayed took bread;

²⁴ and when He had given thanks, He broke *it* and said, "Take, eat; this is My body which is broken for you; do this in remembrance of Me."

²⁵ In the same manner *He* also *took* the cup after supper, saying, "This cup is the new testament in My blood. This do, each time you drink *it*, in remembrance of Me."

²⁶ Because, every time you eat this bread and drink this cup, you proclaim the Lord's death until He comes.

²⁷ Therefore whoever eats this bread or drinks this cup of the Lord in an unworthy manner will be guilty of the body and blood of the Lord.

²⁸ But let a man examine himself, and so let him eat of *the* bread and drink of *the* cup.

²⁹ Because, he who eats and drinks in an unworthy manner eats and drinks damnation to himself, not discerning the Lord's body.

³⁰ For this reason many *are* weak and sick among you, and many sleep.

³¹ Because if we would judge ourselves, we would not be judged.

³² But when we are judged, we are chastened by the Lord, that we may not be condemned with the world.

³³ Therefore, my brethren, when you come together to eat, wait for one another.

³⁴ But if anyone is hungry, let him eat at home, lest you come together for condemnation. And the rest I will set in order when I come.

CHAPTER 12

¹ Now concerning spiritual *gifts*, brethren, I do not want you to be ignorant:

² You know that you were Gentiles, carried away to these mute idols, however you were led.

³ Therefore I make known to you that no one speaking by the Spirit of God calls Jesus accursed, and *that* no one can say that Jesus is the Lord except by the Holy Spirit.

⁴ Now there are diversities of gifts, but the same Spirit.

⁵ And there are differences of ministries, but the same Lord.

⁶ And there are diversities of activities, but it is the same God who empowers them all in everyone.

⁷ But the manifestation of the Spirit is given to each one for everyone's benefit.

⁸ Because, to one is given the word of wisdom by the Spirit, to another the word of knowledge by the same Spirit,

⁹ to another faith by the same Spirit, to another gifts of healing by the same Spirit,

¹⁰ to another the working of miracles, to another prophecy, to another discerning of spirits, to another *different* kinds of tongues, to another the interpretation of tongues.

¹¹ But these are empowered by one and the same Spirit, distributing to each one individually as He wills.

¹² Because, as the body is one and has many members, but all the members of that one body, being many, are one body, so also *is* Christ.

¹³ Because, by one Spirit we were all baptized into one body, whether *we are* Jews or Greeks, whether *we are* slaves or free, and have all been made to drink into one Spirit.

¹⁴ Because the body is not one member but many.

¹⁵ If the foot should say, "Because I am not a hand, I am not of the body," is it therefore not of the body?

¹⁶ And if the ear should say, "Because I am not an eye, I am not of the body," is it therefore not of the body?

¹⁷ If the whole body *were* an eye, where *would be* the hearing? If the whole *were* hearing, where *would be* the smelling?

¹⁸ But now God has arranged the members, each one of them, in the body just as He pleased.

¹⁹ And if they were all one member, where *would* the body *be*?

²⁰ But now indeed *there are* many members, yet one body.

²¹ And the eye cannot say to the hand, "I have no need of you"; nor again the head to the feet, "I have no need of you."

²² No, on the contrary, those members of the body which seem to be weaker are necessary.

²³ And those *members* of the body which we think to be less honorable, on these we bestow more abundant honor; and our unpresentable *parts* have more abundant modesty,

²⁴ but our presentable *parts* have no lack. But God assembled together the body, having given more abundant honor to that *part* which lacked,

²⁵ that there should be no division in the body, but that the members should have the same care for one another.

²⁶ And if one member suffers, all the members suffer with it; or if one member is honored, all the members rejoice with it.

²⁷ Now you are the body of Christ, and members individually.

²⁸ And God has arranged these in the church: first apostles, second prophets, third teachers, after that miracles, then gifts of healings, helps, administrations, varieties of tongues.

²⁹ *Are* all apostles? *Are* all prophets? *Are* all teachers? *Are* all workers of miracles?

³⁰ Do all have gifts of healing? Do all speak with tongues? Do all interpret?

³¹ But earnestly desire the best gifts. And yet I show you a more excellent way.

CHAPTER 13

¹ Though I speak with the tongues

of men and of angels, but do not have love, I have become *as* sounding brass or a clanging cymbal.

² And though I have *the gift of* prophecy, and understand all mysteries and all knowledge, and though I have all faith, so that I could remove mountains, but do not have love, I am nothing.

³ And though I give all my goods to feed *the poor*, and though I give my body to be burned, but have not love, it profits me nothing.

⁴ Love suffers long *and* is kind; love does not envy; love does not parade itself, is not puffed up;

⁵ does not behave rudely, does not seek its own, is not easily provoked, thinks no evil;

⁶ does not rejoice in iniquity, but rejoices in the truth;

⁷ bears all things, believes all things, hopes all things, endures all things.

⁸ Love never fails. But if *there are* prophecies, they will fail; if *there are* tongues, they will cease; if *there is* knowledge, it will vanish away.

⁹ Because, we know in part and we prophesy in part.

¹⁰ But when that which is perfect has come, then that which is in part will be done away.

¹¹ When I was a child, I spoke as a child, I understood as a child, I thought as a child; but when I became a man, I put away childish things.

¹² Because, now we see in a mirror, dimly, but then face to face. Now I know in part, but then I will know just as I also am known.

¹³ So now faith, hope, *and* love, abide, these three; but the greatest of these *is* love.

CHAPTER 14

¹ Pursue love, and desire spiritual *gifts*, but especially that you may prophesy.

² Because, he who speaks in an *unknown* tongue does not speak to men but to God, because no one understands *him*; however, in the spirit he speaks mysteries.

³ But he who prophesies speaks edification and exhortation and comfort *to* men.

⁴ He who speaks in an *unknown* tongue edifies himself, but he who prophesies edifies the church.

⁵ I wish you all spoke with tongues, but even more that you prophesied; because, he who prophesies *is* greater than he who speaks with tongues, unless he interprets, that the church may receive edification.

⁶ Now, brethren, if I come to you speaking with tongues, what shall I profit you unless I speak to you either by revelation, by knowledge, by prophesying, or by doctrine?

⁷ Even things without life, whether flute or harp, when they make a sound, unless they make a distinction in the notes, how will it be known what is piped or played?

⁸ Because, if the trumpet makes an uncertain sound, who will prepare

themselves for battle?

⁹ So likewise you, unless you utter by the tongue words easy to understand, how will it be known what is spoken? Because you will speak into the air.

¹⁰ There are, it may be, so many kinds of languages in the world, and none of them *is* without significance.

¹¹ Therefore, if I do not know the meaning of the language, I will be a foreigner to him who speaks, and he who speaks *will be* a foreigner to me.

¹² Even so you, since you are zealous for spiritual *gifts*, seek that you may excel for the edification of the church.

¹³ Therefore let him who speaks in an *unknown* tongue pray that he may interpret.

¹⁴ Because, if I pray in an unknown tongue, my spirit prays, but my understanding is unfruitful.

¹⁵ What is *the conclusion* then? I will pray with the spirit, and I will also pray with the understanding. I will sing with the spirit, and I will also sing with the understanding.

¹⁶ otherwise, if you bless with the spirit, how will he who occupies the place of the uninformed say "Amen" at your giving of thanks, since he does not understand what you say?

¹⁷ Because, you indeed give thanks well, but the other is not edified.

¹⁸ I thank my God I speak with tongues more than you all;

¹⁹ yet in the church I would rather speak five words with my understanding, that *by my voice* I may teach others also, than ten thousand words in an *unknown* tongue.

²⁰ Brethren, do not be children in understanding; however, in malice be children, but in understanding be mature.

²¹ In the law it is written: "With *people* of other tongues and other lips I will speak to this people; and yet, for all that, they will not hear Me," says the Lord.

²² Therefore tongues are for a sign, not to those who believe but to unbelievers; but prophesying *is* not for unbelievers but serves for those who believe.

²³ Therefore if the entire church comes together in one place, and all speak with tongues, and there come in *those who are* uninformed or unbelievers, will they not say that you are crazy?

²⁴ But if all prophesy, and an unbeliever or *an* uninformed person comes in, he is convinced by all, he is convicted by all.

²⁵ And so the secrets of his heart are revealed; and so, falling down on *his* face, he will worship God and report that God is truly among you.

²⁶ How is it then, brethren? Whenever you come together, each of you has a psalm, has a doctrine, has a tongue, has a revelation, has an interpretation. Let all things be done for edification.

²⁷ If anyone speaks in an *unknown*

tongue, *let there be* two or at the most three, each in turn, and let one interpret.

²⁸ But if there is no interpreter, let him keep silent in church, and let him speak to himself and to God.

²⁹ Let two or three prophets speak, and let the others judge.

³⁰ But if *anything* is revealed to another who sits by, let the first keep silent.

³¹ Because, you can all prophesy one by one, that all may learn and all may be encouraged.

³² And the spirits of the prophets are subject to the prophets.

³³ Because, God is not *the author* of confusion but of peace, as in all the churches of the saints.

³⁴ Let your women keep silent in the churches, because they are not permitted to speak; but *they are commanded* to be submissive, as the law also says.

³⁵ And if they want to learn something, let them ask their husbands at home; because it is shameful for women to speak in the church.

³⁶ What? Did the word of God *originate* from you? Or was it to you only that it has come?

³⁷ If anyone thinks himself to be a prophet or spiritual, let him acknowledge that the things which I write to you are the commandments of the Lord.

³⁸ But if anyone is ignorant, let him be ignorant.

³⁹ Therefore, brethren, desire earnestly to prophesy, and do not forbid to speak with tongues.

⁴⁰ Let all things be done decently and in order.

CHAPTER 15

¹ Moreover, brethren, I declare to you the gospel which I preached to you, which
also you received and in which you stand,

² by which also you are saved, if you keep in memory that which I preached to you, unless you have believed in vain.

³ Because, I delivered to you first of all that which I also received: how Christ died for our sins according to the Scriptures,

⁴ and that He was buried, and that He rose again the third day according to the Scriptures,

⁵ and that He was seen by Cephas, then by the twelve.

⁶ After that He was seen by over five hundred brethren at once, of whom the greater part remain to the present, but some have fallen asleep.

⁷ After that He was seen by James, then by all the apostles.

⁸ Then last of all He was seen by me also, as by one born out of due time.

⁹ Because, I am the least of the apostles, who am not worthy to be called an apostle, because I persecuted the church of God.

¹⁰ But by the grace of God I am what I am, and His grace which *was imparted* to me was not in vain; but

I labored more abundantly than they all, yet not I, but the grace of God which was with me.

¹¹ Therefore, whether it *was* I or they, so we preach and so you believed.

¹² Now if Christ is preached that He rose from the dead, how do some among you say that there is no resurrection of the dead?

¹³ But if there is no resurrection of the dead, then Christ is not risen.

¹⁴ And if Christ is not risen, then our preaching is in vain and your faith is also in vain.

¹⁵ Yes, and we are found *to be* false witnesses of God, because we have testified of God that He raised up Christ, whom He did not raise up, if in fact the dead do not rise.

¹⁶ Because, if the dead do not rise, then Christ is not risen.

¹⁷ And if Christ is not risen, your faith *is* vain; you are still in your sins!

¹⁸ Then also those who have fallen asleep in Christ have perished.

¹⁹ If in this life only we have hope in Christ, we are of all men the most to be pitied.

²⁰ But now Christ is risen from the dead, *and has* become the firstfruits of those who sleep.

²¹ Because, since by man *came* death, by Man also *came* the resurrection of the dead.

²² Because as in Adam all die, even so in Christ all will be made alive.

²³ But each one in his own order: Christ the first fruits, afterward those who are Christ's at His coming.

²⁴ Then *comes* the end, when He will have delivered the kingdom to God, even the Father, when He puts down all rule and all authority and power.

²⁵ Because, He must reign until He has put all enemies under His feet.

²⁶ The last enemy *that* will be destroyed *is* death.

²⁷ Because "He has put all things under His feet." But when He says "all things are put under *Him*," *it is* evident that He who put all things under Him is the exception.

²⁸ Now when all things are made subject to Him, then the Son Himself will also be subject to Him who put all things under Him, that God may be all in all.

²⁹ Otherwise, what shall they do who are baptized for the dead, if the dead do not rise at all? Why then are they baptized for the dead?

³⁰ And why do we stand in danger every hour?

³¹ I affirm, by your boasting which I have in Christ Jesus our Lord, I die daily.

³² If, in the manner of men, I have fought with beasts at Ephesus, what advantage is it to me? If the dead do not rise, "Let us eat and drink, because tomorrow we die!"

³³ Do not be deceived: "Evil company corrupts good morals."

³⁴ Awake to righteousness, and do not sin; because some do not have the knowledge of God. I speak *this* to

your shame.

³⁵ But someone will say, "How are the dead raised up? And with what body do they come?"

³⁶ Foolish *one*, what you sow is not made alive unless it dies.

³⁷ And what you sow, you do not sow that body that will be, but mere grain, perhaps wheat or some other *grain*.

³⁸ But God gives it a body as it has pleased Him, and to each seed its own body.

³⁹ All flesh *is* not the same flesh, but *there* is one *kind of* flesh of men, another flesh of animals, another of fish, *and* another of birds.

⁴⁰ *There are* also celestial bodies and terrestrial bodies; but the glory of the celestial *is* one, and the *glory* of the terrestrial *is* another.

⁴¹ *There is* one glory of the sun, another glory of the moon, and another glory of the stars; because *one* star differs from *another* star in glory.

⁴² So also *is* the resurrection of the dead. The body is sown in corruption, it is raised in incurruption.

⁴³ It is sown in dishonor, it is raised in glory. It is sown in weakness, it is raised in power.

⁴⁴ It is sown a natural body, it is raised a spiritual body. There is a natural body, and there is a spiritual body.

⁴⁵ And so it is written, "The first man Adam became a living soul." The last Adam became a life giving spirit.

⁴⁶ However, the spiritual is not first, but the natural, and afterward that which is spiritual.

⁴⁷ The first man *was* of the earth, made of dust; the second Man *is* the Lord from heaven.

⁴⁸ As *was* the man of dust, so also *are* those who are made of dust; and as *is* the heavenly Man, so also *are* those who are heavenly.

⁴⁹ And as we have borne the image of the man of dust, we will also bear the image of the Heavenly

⁵⁰ Now this I say, brethren, that flesh and blood cannot inherit the kingdom of God; nor does corruption inherit incorruption.

⁵¹ Behold, I show you a mystery: We will not all sleep, but we will all be changed,

⁵² in a moment, in the twinkling of an eye, at the last trumpet. Because, the trumpet will sound, and the dead will be raised incorruptible, and we will be changed.

⁵³ Because, this corruptible must put on incorruption, and this mortal *must* put on immortality.

⁵⁴ So when this corruptible has put on incorruption, and this mortal has put on immortality, then will be brought to pass the saying that is written: "Death is swallowed up in victory."

⁵⁵ "O Death, where *is* your sting? O grave, where *is* your victory?"

⁵⁶ The sting of death *is* sin, and the strength of sin *is* the law.

⁵⁷ But thanks *be* to God, who gives us the victory through our Lord

Jesus Christ.

⁵⁸ Therefore, my beloved brethren, be steadfast, immovable, always abounding in the work of the Lord, knowing that your labor is not in vain in the Lord.

CHAPTER 16

¹ Now concerning the collection for the saints, as I have directed the churches of Galatia, so you must do also:

² On the first *day* of the week let each one of you lay something aside, storing up as *God* has prospered him, that there be no collections when I come.

³ And when I come, whomever you approve by *your* letters I will send to bear your gift to Jerusalem.

⁴ But if it is fitting that I go also, they will go with me.

⁵ Now I will come to you when I pass through Macedonia (because I am passing through Macedonia).

⁶ And it may be that I will remain, or even spend the winter with you, that you may send me on my journey, wherever I go.

⁷ Because, I do not wish to see you now along the way; but I hope to stay a while with you, if the Lord permits.

⁸ But I will stay in Ephesus until Pentecost.

⁹ Because, a great and effective door has opened to me, and *there are* many adversaries.

¹⁰ Now if Timothy comes, see that he may be with you without fear; because, he does the work of the Lord, as I also *do*.

¹¹ Therefore let no one despise him. But send him on his journey in peace, that he may come to me; because I am expecting him with the brethren.

¹² Now concerning *our* brother Apollos, I strongly urged him to come to you with the brethren, but he was quite unwilling to come at this time; however, he will come when he has a convenient time.

¹³ Watch, stand fast in the faith, act like men, be strong.

¹⁴ Let all that you do be done with love.

¹⁵ I urge you, brethren, you know the household of Stephanas, that it is the firstfruits of Achaia, and *that* they have devoted themselves to the ministry of the saints,

¹⁶ that you also submit to such, and to everyone who works and labors with *us*.

¹⁷ I am glad about the coming of Stephanas, Fortunatus, and Achaicus, because what was lacking on your part they supplied.

¹⁸ Because they refreshed my spirit and yours. Therefore acknowledge such people.

¹⁹ The churches of Asia greet you. Aquila and Priscilla greet you heartily in the Lord, with the church that is in their house.

²⁰ All the brethren greet you. Greet one another with a holy kiss.

²¹ The salutation from *me* Paul with my own hand.

²² If anyone does not love the Lord Jesus Christ, let him be Anathema Maranatha!

²³ The grace of our Lord Jesus Christ *be* with you.

²⁴ My love *be* with you all in Christ Jesus. Amen.

The first letter to the Corinthians was written from Philippi by Stephanas, Fortunatus, Achaicus, and Timothy.

THE SECOND LETTER OF PAUL THE APOSTLE TO THE
CORINTHIANS

CHAPTER 1

¹ Paul, an apostle of Jesus Christ by the will of God, and Timothy *our* brother, to the church of God which is at Corinth, with all the saints who are in all Achaia:

² Grace *be* to you and peace from God our Father and *from* the Lord Jesus Christ.

³ Blessed *be* the God and Father of our Lord Jesus Christ, the Father of mercies and God of all comfort,

⁴ who comforts us in all our tribulation, that we may be able to comfort those who are in any trouble, with the comfort with which we ourselves are comforted by God.

⁵ Because, as the sufferings of Christ abound in us, so our consolation also abounds by Christ.

⁶ Now if we are afflicted, *it is* for your consolation and salvation, which is effective for enduring the same sufferings which we also suffer. Or if we are comforted, *it is* for your consolation and salvation.

⁷ And our hope for you *is* unshaken, because, we know that as you are partakers of the sufferings, so also *you will* also *be* of the consolation.

⁸ Because, we do not want you to be ignorant, brethren, of our trouble which came to us in Asia: that we were burdened beyond measure, above strength, so that we despaired even of life.

⁹ But we had the sentence of death in ourselves, that we should not trust in ourselves but in God who raises the dead,

¹⁰ who delivered us from so great a death, and does deliver us; in whom we trust that He will still deliver,

¹¹ you also helping together in prayer for us, that thanks may be given by the means of many people on our behalf for the gift *granted* to us through many.

¹² Because our rejoicing is this: the testimony of our conscience that we conducted ourselves in the world in simplicity and godly sincerity, not with fleshly wisdom but by the grace of God, and more abundantly toward you.

¹³ Because, we are not writing any other things to you than what you read or acknowledge, and I trust you will acknowledge, even to the end

¹⁴ as also you have acknowledged us partially, that we are your rejoicing, just as you also *are* ours, in the day of the Lord Jesus.

¹⁵ And in this confidence I intended to come to you before, that you might have a second benefit;

¹⁶ to visit you on the way to Macedonia, to return again from Macedonia to you, and be brought on my way toward Judea.

¹⁷ Therefore, when I was planning this, did I do it lightly? Or the things I plan, do I plan according to the flesh, that with me there should be Yes, Yes, and No, No?

¹⁸ But *as* God *is* true, our word to you was not Yes and No.

¹⁹ Because, the Son of God, Jesus Christ, who was preached among you by us, even by me, Silvanus, and Timothy, was not Yes and No, but in Him was Yes.

²⁰ Because, all the promises of God in Him *are* Yes, and in Him Amen, to the glory of God by us.

²¹ Now He who establishes us with you in Christ and has anointed us *is* God,

²² who also has sealed us and given us the Spirit in our hearts as a guarantee.

²³ Moreover I call God to record against my soul, that to spare you I have not yet come to Corinth.

²⁴ Not that we have dominion over your faith, but are helpers for your joy; because by faith you stand.

CHAPTER 2

¹ But I determined this within myself, that I would not come again to you in sorrow.

² Because, if I make you sorrowful, then who is he who makes me glad but the one who is made sorrowful by me?

³ And I wrote this very thing to you, lest, when I came, I should have sorrow from those of whom I ought to rejoice, having confidence in you all that my joy is *the joy* of you all.

⁴ Because, out of much affliction and anguish of heart I wrote to you, with many tears, not that you should be grieved, but that you might know the love which I have so abundantly for you.

⁵ But if anyone has caused grief, he has not grieved me, except partially; so that I may not be harsh to you all.

⁶ This punishment which *was inflicted* by many *is* sufficient for such a man,

⁷ so that, on the contrary, you *ought* rather to forgive him, and comfort him, lest perhaps such a one should be swallowed up with too much sorrow.

⁸ Therefore I urge you to reaffirm *your* love to him.

⁹ Because, this is why I also wrote, that I might put you to the test, whether you are obedient in all things.

¹⁰ To whom you forgive anything, I also *forgive*. Because, if I have forgiven anything, to whom I forgive *it*, *I have forgiven it* for your sakes in the person of Christ,

¹¹ lest Satan should get a favorable position over us; because we are not ignorant of his devices.

¹² Furthermore, when I came to Troas to *preach* Christ's gospel, and a door was opened to me by the Lord,

¹³ I had no rest in my spirit, because I did not find Titus my brother; but taking my leave of them, I departed

from there into Macedonia.

¹⁴ Now thanks *be* to God who always causes us to triumph in Christ, and makes manifest the fragrance of His knowledge in every place through us.

¹⁵ Because, we are to God the sweet fragrance of Christ among those who are saved and among those who are perishing.

¹⁶ To the one *we are* the aroma of death leading to death, and to the other the aroma of life leading to life. And who *is* sufficient for these things?

¹⁷ Because, we are not, like so many, who corrupt the word of God; but as of sincerity, but as from God, in the sight of God we speak in Christ.

CHAPTER 3

¹ Do we begin again to commend ourselves? Or do we need, as some *others*, letters of commendation to you or *letters* of commendation from you?

² You are our letter written in our hearts, known and read by everyone;

³ *in as much as you are* clearly declared to be a letter of Christ, delivered by us, written not with ink but by the Spirit of the living God, not on tablets of stone but on tablets of flesh, that is, of the heart.

⁴ And we have such confidence through Christ toward God.

⁵ Not that we are sufficient of ourselves to think of anything as *originating* from ourselves, but our sufficiency *is* from God,

⁶ who also has made us competent ministers of the new testament, not of the letter but of the Spirit; because the letter kills, but the Spirit gives life.

⁷ But if the ministry of death, written *and* engraved on stones, was glorious, so that the children of Israel could not look steadfastly at Moses' face because of the glory of his countenance, which *glory* was passing away,

⁸ how will the ministry of the Spirit not be more glorious?

⁹ Because, if the ministry of condemnation *is* glory, the ministry of righteousness exceeds much more in glory.

¹⁰ Because, even what was made glorious had no glory in this respect, because of the glory that excels.

¹¹ Because, if what is passing away *was* glorious, what remains *is* much more glorious.

¹² Therefore, seeing we have such hope, we use much freedom of speech;

¹³ unlike Moses, who put a veil over his face so that the children of Israel could not look steadfastly at the outcome of what was passing away.

¹⁴ But their minds were blinded. Because, until this day the same veil remains un lifted in the reading of the Old Testament. This *veil* is taken away in Christ.

¹⁵ But even to this day, when Moses

is read, a veil is upon their heart.

¹⁶ Nevertheless when it shall turn to the Lord, the veil will be taken away.

¹⁷ Now the Lord is the Spirit; and where the Spirit of the Lord *is*, there *is* liberty.

¹⁸ But we all, with unveiled face, beholding as in a mirror the glory of the Lord, are changed into the same image from glory to glory, *just* as by the Spirit of the Lord.

CHAPTER 4

¹ Therefore, seeing we have this ministry, as we have received mercy, we do not lose heart.

² But we have renounced the hidden things of dishonesty, not walking in craftiness nor handling the word of God deceitfully, but by the manifestation of the truth commending ourselves to every man's conscience in the sight of God.

³ But even if our gospel is veiled, it is veiled to those who are perishing,

⁴ whose minds the god of this age has blinded, who do not believe, lest the light of the glorious gospel of Christ, who is the image of God, should shine on them.

⁵ Because, we do not preach ourselves, but Christ Jesus the Lord, and ourselves your servants for Jesus' sake.

⁶ Because God, who commanded light to shine out of darkness, has shone in our hearts to *give* the light of the knowledge of the glory of God in the face of Jesus Christ.

⁷ But we have this treasure in earthen vessels, that the excellence of the power may be of God and not of us.

⁸ We *are* troubled on every side, yet not distressed; *we are* perplexed, but not in despair;

⁹ persecuted, but not forsaken; struck down, but not destroyed;

¹⁰ always carrying about in the body the dying of the Lord Jesus, that the life of Jesus also may be manifested in our body.

¹¹ Because, we who live are always delivered to death for Jesus' sake, that the life of Jesus also may be manifested in our mortal flesh.

¹² So then death is working in us, but life in you.

¹³ We having the same spirit of faith, according to what is written, "I believed and therefore I spoke," we also believe and therefore speak,

¹⁴ knowing that He who raised up the Lord Jesus will also raise us up by Jesus, and will present *us* with you.

¹⁵ Because, all things *are* for your sakes, that the abundant grace may through the thanksgiving of many, abound to the glory of God.

¹⁶ Therefore we do not lose heart. Even though our outward man is perishing, yet the inward *man* is being renewed day by day.

¹⁷ Because, our light affliction, which is only for a moment, is working for us a far more exceeding

and eternal weight of glory,

¹⁸ while we do not look at the things which are seen, but at the things which are not seen. Because, the things which *are* seen are temporary, but the things which are not seen are eternal.

CHAPTER 5

¹ Because, we know that if our earthly house, *this* tent, is destroyed, we have a building from God, a house not made with hands, eternal in the heavens.

² Because, in this we groan, earnestly desiring to be clothed with our habitation which is from heaven,

³ if indeed, having been clothed, we will not be found naked.

⁴ Because, we who are in *this* tent groan, being burdened, not because we want to be unclothed, but further clothed, that mortality may be swallowed up by life.

⁵ Now He who has prepared us for this very thing *is* God, who also has given us the Spirit as a guarantee.

⁶ Therefore *we are* always confident, knowing that while we are at home in the body we are absent from the Lord.

⁷ Because we walk by faith, not by sight.

⁸ We are confident, *I proclaim*, and willing rather to be absent from the body and to be present with the Lord.

⁹ Therefore we labor, so that whether present or absent, we may be accepted of Him.

¹⁰ Because, we must all appear before the judgment seat of Christ, that each one may receive the things *done* in the body, according to what he has done, whether *it is* good or bad.

¹¹ Knowing, therefore, the terror of the Lord, we persuade men; but we are made manifest to God, and I also trust are made manifest in your consciences.

¹² Because, we do not commend ourselves again to you, but give you opportunity to boast on our behalf, that you may have something to *answer* them who boast in appearance and not in heart.

¹³ Because, if we are beside ourselves, *it is* for God; or if we are sober, *it is* for you.

¹⁴ Because, the love of Christ compels us, because we have judged thus: that if One died for all, then all died;

¹⁵ and *that* He died for all, that those who live should live no longer for themselves, but for Him who died for them and rose again.

¹⁶ Therefore, from now on, we regard no one according to the flesh. Even though we have known Christ according to the flesh, yet from now on we know *Him like this* no longer.

¹⁷ Therefore, if anyone *is* in Christ, *he* is a new creature; old things have passed away; behold, all things have become new.

¹⁸ Now all these things *are* from

God, who has reconciled us to Himself by Jesus Christ, and has given us the ministry of reconciliation,

[19] that is, that God was in Christ reconciling the world to Himself, not imputing their trespasses to them, and has committed to us the word of reconciliation.

[20] Now then, we are ambassadors for Christ, as though God were pleading *to you* through us: we urge *you* on Christ's behalf, be reconciled to God.

[21] Because, He made Him who knew no sin to *be* sin for us, that we might be made the righteousness of God in Him.

CHAPTER 6

[1] We then, as workers together *with Him* also urge *you* not to receive the grace of God in vain.

[2] Because, He says: "In an acceptable time I have heard you, and in the day of salvation I have helped you." Behold, now *is* the accepted time; behold, now *is* the day of salvation.

[3] Giving no offense in anything, that the ministry may not be faulted.

[4] But in all *things* we commend ourselves as the ministers of God: in much patience, in afflictions, in needs, in distresses,

[5] in stripes, in imprisonments, in riots, in labors, in sleeplessness, in fastings;

[6] by purity, by knowledge, by longsuffering, by kindness, by the Holy Spirit, by genuine love,

[7] by the word of truth, by the power of God, by the armor of righteousness on the right hand and on the left,

[8] by honor and dishonor, by evil report and good report; as deceivers, and *yet* true;

[9] as unknown, and *yet* well known; as dying, and behold we live; as chastened, and yet not killed;

[10] as sorrowful, yet always rejoicing; as poor, yet making many rich; as having nothing, and *yet* possessing all things.

[11] O *you* Corinthians! Our mouth is open to you, our heart is wide open.

[12] You are not restricted by us, but you are restricted by your own affections.

[13] Now in return for the same (I speak as to *my* children), you also be open.

[14] Do not be unequally yoked together with unbelievers. Because, what fellowship has righteousness with unrighteousness? And what communion has light with darkness?

[15] And what accord has Christ with Belial? Or what part has he who believes with an infidel?

[16] And what agreement has the temple of God with idols? Because, you are the temple of the living God. As God has said: "I will dwell in them and walk in *them*. And I will be their God, and they will be My people."

[17] Therefore "Come out from

among them and be separate, says the Lord. Do not touch what is unclean, and I will receive you."

¹⁸ "I will be a Father to you, and you will be My sons and daughters, says the LORD Almighty."

CHAPTER 7

¹ Therefore, having these promises, greatly beloved, let us cleanse ourselves from all filthiness of the flesh and spirit, perfecting holiness in the reverence of God.

² Receive us. We have wronged no one, we have corrupted no one, we have cheated no one.

³ I do not say *this* to condemn *you*; because I have said before that you are in our hearts, to die together and to live together with *you*.

⁴ Great *is* my boldness of speech toward you, great *is* my boasting on your behalf. I am filled with comfort. I am exceedingly joyful in all our tribulation.

⁵ Because, when we came to Macedonia, our bodies had no rest, but we were troubled on every side. Outside *were* conflicts, inside *were* fears.

⁶ Nevertheless God, who comforts the downcast, comforted us by the coming of Titus,

⁷ and not only by his coming, but also by the consolation with which he was comforted in you, when he told us of your earnest desire, your mourning, your fervent mind towards me, so that I rejoiced even more.

⁸ Because, even though I made you sorry with my letter, I do not regret it; though I did regret it. Because, I perceive that the same letter made you sorry, though only for a season.

⁹ Now I rejoice, not that you were made sorry, but that your sorrow led to repentance. Because you were made sorry in a godly manner, that you might suffer loss from us in nothing.

¹⁰ Because, godly sorrow produces repentance leading to salvation, not to be regretted; but the sorrow of the world produces death.

¹¹ Because, observe this very thing, that you sorrowed in a godly manner: yes what diligence it produced in you, yes *what* clearing of yourselves, yes *what* indignation, yes *what* fear, *what* vehement desire, *what* zeal, *what* vindication! In all *things* you have proven yourselves to be clear in this matter.

¹² Therefore, although I wrote to you, *I did* not do *it* because of him who had done the wrong, nor because of him who suffered wrong, but that our care for you in the sight of God might appear to you.

¹³ Therefore we have been comforted in your comfort. And we rejoiced exceedingly more for the joy of Titus, because his spirit was refreshed by you all.

¹⁴ Because, if in anything I have boasted to him about you, I am not ashamed. But as we spoke all things to you in truth, even so our

boasting which *I made* before Titus was found true.

¹⁵ And his inner affections are greater for you as he remembers the obedience of you all, how with reverence and trembling you received him.

¹⁶ Therefore I rejoice that I have confidence in you in all *things*.

CHAPTER 8

¹ Moreover, brethren, we make known to you the grace of God bestowed on the churches of Macedonia:

² how that in a great trial of affliction the abundance of their joy and their extreme poverty abounded in the riches of their liberality.

³ Because, I bear record that according to *their* ability, yes, and beyond their ability, *they were* freely willing,

⁴ urging us with many requests that we would receive the gift and *take on us* the fellowship of the ministering to the saints.

⁵ And *this they did*, not just as we hoped, but they first gave themselves to the Lord, and then to us by the will of God.

⁶ So that we urged Titus, that as he had begun, so he would also complete this grace in you also.

⁷ Therefore, as you abound in everything, *in* faith, in speech, in knowledge, and *in* all diligence, and *in* your love for us, *see* that you abound in this grace also.

⁸ I speak not by commandment, but I am testing the sincerity of your love by the diligence of others.

⁹ Because, you know the grace of our Lord Jesus Christ, that though He was rich, yet for your sakes He became poor, that you through His poverty might be rich.

¹⁰ And in this I give *my* advice: Since it is to your advantage not only to be doing what you began beforehand and were desiring to do a year ago;

¹¹ but now you also must complete the doing *of it*; that as *there was* a readiness to desire it, so *there* also *may be* a completion out of what you have.

¹² Because, if there is first a willing mind, *it is* accepted according to what one has, *and* not according to what he does not have.

¹³ Because, *I* do not *mean* that others should be eased and you burdened;

¹⁴ but by an equality, *that* now at this time your abundance *may be a* supply for their lack, that their abundance also may be *a supply* for your lack, that there may be equality.

¹⁵ As it is written, "He who *gathered* much had nothing left over, and he who *gathered* little had no lack."

¹⁶ But thanks *be* to God who put the same earnest care for you into the heart of Titus.

¹⁷ Because, he not only accepted the exhortation, but being more diligent, he went to you of his own accord.

[18] And we have sent with him the brother whose praise *is* in the gospel throughout all the churches,
[19] and not only *that*, but who was also chosen by the churches to travel with us with this grace, which is administered by us to the glory of the Lord Himself and *to show* your ready mind,
[20] avoiding this: that anyone should blame us in this abundance which is administered by us,
[21] providing for honorable things, not only in the sight of the Lord, but also in the sight of men.
[22] And we have sent with them our brother whom we have often proved diligent in many things, but now much more diligent, because of the great confidence which *I have* in you.
[23] If *anyone inquires* about Titus, he is my partner and fellow worker concerning you. Or if our brethren *are inquired about, they are* messengers of the churches, *and* the glory of Christ.
[24] Therefore show to them, and before the churches, the proof of your love and of our boasting on your behalf.

CHAPTER 9

[1] Now concerning the ministering to the saints, it is superfluous for me to write to you;
[2] Because, I know your willingness, about which I boast of you to the Macedonians, that Achaia was ready a year ago; and your zeal has stirred up the majority.
[3] Yet I have sent the brethren, lest our boasting of you should be in vain in this respect, that, you may be ready, as I said;
[4] lest if some Macedonians come with me and find you unprepared, we (that we do not mention you) should be ashamed of this confident boasting.
[5] Therefore I thought it necessary to exhort the brethren to go to you ahead of time, and prepare your generous gift beforehand, of which you had previous notification, that it may be ready as *a matter* of generosity and not as a grudging obligation.
[6] But this I say: He who sows sparingly will also reap sparingly, and he who sows bountifully will also reap bountifully.
[7] *So let each one give*, according as he purposes in his heart, not grudgingly or of necessity; because, God loves a cheerful giver.
[8] And God *is* able to make all grace abound toward you, that you, always having all sufficiency in all *things*, may have an abundance for every good work.
[9] As it is written: "He has dispersed abroad, he has given to the poor; his righteousness endures forever."
[10] Now He who supplies seed to the sower, also supply bread for *your* food, multiply your seed sown, and increase the fruits of your righteousness,
[11] being enriched in everything for

all abundance, which causes thanksgiving through us to God.

¹² Because, the administration of this service not only supplies the needs of the saints, but also is abounding through many thanksgivings to God,

¹³ while, through the proof of this ministry, they glorify God for the obedience of your confession to the gospel of Christ, and for *your* liberal distribution to them and all *people*,

¹⁴ and by their prayer for you, who long for you because of the exceeding grace of God in you.

¹⁵ Thanks *be* to God for His indescribable gift!

CHAPTER 10

¹ Now I, Paul, myself urge with you by the meekness and gentleness of Christ, who in presence *am* lowly among you, but being absent am bold toward you.

² But I urge *you* that when I am present I may not be bold with that confidence by which I intend to be bold against some, who think of us as if we walked according to the flesh.

³ Because, though we walk in the flesh, we do not war according to the flesh.

⁴ Because, the weapons of our warfare are not carnal but mighty through God for the pulling down of strongholds,

⁵ casting down imaginations and every high thing that exalts itself against the knowledge of God, bringing every thought into captivity to the obedience of Christ,

⁶ and being ready to punish all disobedience when your obedience is fulfilled.

⁷ Do you look at things according to the outward appearance? If anyone is convinced in himself that he is Christ's, let him again consider this in himself, that just as he *is* Christ's, even so we *are* Christ's.

⁸ Because, even if I should boast somewhat more about our authority, which the Lord gave us for edification and not for your destruction, I will not be ashamed,

⁹ lest I seem as if I would to terrify you by letters.

¹⁰ "Because, *his* letters," they say, "*are* weighty and powerful, but *his* bodily presence *is* weak, and *his* speech contemptible."

¹¹ Let such a person consider this, that what we are in word by letters when we are absent, such *we will* also *be* in deed when we are present.

¹² Because, we dare not classify ourselves or compare ourselves with those who commend themselves. But they, measuring themselves by themselves, and comparing themselves among themselves, are not wise.

¹³ We, however, will not boast of things beyond *our* measure, but according to the measure of the influence which God has distributed to us, a measure to reach to you also.

¹⁴ Because, we do not stretch ourselves beyond *our measure*, as though we did not extend to you, because, we have come as far as to you also with the *preaching* of the gospel of Christ;

¹⁵ not boasting of things beyond *our* influence, *that is*, in other men's labors, but having hope, when your faith is increased, that we shall be enlarged abundantly by you according to our influence,

¹⁶ to preach the gospel in the *regions* beyond you, *and* not to boast in another man's area of influence already accomplished.

¹⁷ But "he who glories, let him glory in the LORD."

¹⁸ Because, not he who commends himself is approved, but whom the Lord commends.

CHAPTER 11

¹ Oh, that you would bear with me in a little in *my* folly, and indeed you do bear with me.

² Because, I am jealous for you with godly jealousy. Because, I have betrothed you to one husband, that I may present *you as* a pure virgin to Christ.

³ But I fear, lest somehow, as the serpent deceived Eve by his craftiness, so your minds may be corrupted from the simplicity that is in Christ.

⁴ Because, if he who comes preaches another Jesus whom we have not preached, or *if* you receive a different spirit which you have not received, or a different gospel which you have not accepted, you may well put up with *him*!

⁵ Because, I consider that I am not at all inferior to the most eminent apostles.

⁶ Even though *I am* untrained in speech, yet I am not in knowledge. But we have been thoroughly manifested among you in all things.

⁷ Did I commit sin in humbling myself that you might be exalted, because I have preached the gospel of God to you free of charge?

⁸ I took from other churches, taking wages *from them* to minister to you.

⁹ And when I was present with you, and in need, I was a burden to no one, because, what I lacked the brethren who came from Macedonia supplied. And in all *things* I kept myself from being burdensome to you, and *so* I will keep *myself*.

¹⁰ As the truth of Christ is in me, no one will stop me from this boasting in the regions of Achaia.

¹¹ Why? Because I do not love you? God knows!

¹² But what I do, I will also continue to do, that I may cut off the opportunity from those who desire an opportunity to be regarded just as we are in the things of which they boast.

¹³ Because, such *are* false apostles, deceitful workers, transforming themselves into apostles of Christ.

¹⁴ And no wonder! Because, Satan himself is transformed into an

angel of light.

¹⁵ Therefore *it is* no great thing if his ministers also are transformed into ministers of righteousness, whose end will be according to their works.

¹⁶ I say again, let no one think me a fool. If otherwise, at least receive me as a fool, that I also may boast a little.

¹⁷ What I speak, I speak not according to the Lord, but as it were, foolishly, in this confidence of boasting.

¹⁸ Seeing that many boast according to the flesh, I also will boast.

¹⁹ Because, you put up with fools gladly, since you *yourselves* are wise!

²⁰ because, you put up with it if one brings you into bondage, if one devours *you*, if one takes *from you*, if one exalts himself, if one strikes you on the face.

²¹ To our shame I say that we were too weak for that! But in whatever anyone is bold, I speak foolishly, I am bold also.

²² Are they Hebrews? So *am* I. Are they Israelites? So *am* I. Are they the seed of Abraham? So *am* I.

²³ Are they ministers of Christ? I speak as a fool, I *am* more: in labors more abundant, in stripes above measure, in prisons more frequently, in deaths often.

²⁴ From the Jews five times I received forty *stripes* minus one.

²⁵ Three times I was beaten with rods; once I was stoned; three times I was shipwrecked; a night and a day I have been in the deep;

²⁶ *in* frequent journeys, in danger from waters, *in* danger from robbers, in danger from *my own* countrymen, *in* danger from the Gentiles, *in* danger in the city, *in* danger in the wilderness, *in* danger in the sea, in danger among false brethren;

²⁷ in weariness and toil, in sleeplessness often, in hunger and thirst, in fastings often, in cold and nakedness,

²⁸ besides those things that are external, what comes upon me daily: the concern for all the churches.

²⁹ Who is weak, and I am not weak? Who is offended, and I do not burn with *indignation*?

³⁰ If I must boast, I will boast in the things which concern my weakness.

³¹ The God and Father of our Lord Jesus Christ, who is blessed forever, knows that I am not lying.

³² In Damascus the governor, under Aretas the king, was guarding the city of the Damascenes with a garrison, desiring to arrest me;

³³ but I was let down in a basket through a window by the wall, and escaped from his hands.

CHAPTER 12

¹ It is obviously not profitable for me to boast. I will come to visions and revelations of the Lord:

² I knew a man in Christ who over

fourteen years ago (whether in the body I do not know, or whether out of the body I do not know, God knows) such a one was caught up to the third heaven.

³ And I knew such a man (whether in the body or out of the body I do not know, God knows)

⁴ how he was caught up into Paradise and heard inexpressible words, which it is not lawful for a man to utter.

⁵ Of such a one I will boast; yet of myself I will not boast, except in my weaknesses.

⁶ Because though I might desire to boast, I will not be a fool; because I will speak the truth. But *now* I refrain, lest anyone should think of me above what he sees me *to be* or *that* he hears from me.

⁷ And lest I should be exalted above measure by the abundance of the revelations, a thorn in the flesh was given to me, a messenger of Satan to wound me, lest I be exalted above measure.

⁸ Concerning this thing I sought the Lord three times that it might depart from me.

⁹ And He said to me, "My grace is sufficient for you, because My strength is made perfect in weakness." Therefore most gladly I will rather boast in my weaknesses, that the power of Christ may rest upon me.

¹⁰ Therefore I take pleasure in weaknesses, in reproaches, in needs, in persecutions, in distresses, for Christ's sake. Because when I am weak, then I am strong.

¹¹ I have become a fool in boasting; you have compelled me. Because, I ought to have been commended by you; because, in nothing was I behind the most eminent apostles, though I am nothing.

¹² Truly the signs of an apostle were accomplished among you with all perseverance, in signs and wonders and mighty deeds.

¹³ Because, what is it in which you were inferior to other churches, except *it is* that I myself was not burdensome to you? Forgive me this wrong!

¹⁴ Behold, the third time I am ready to come to you. And I will not be burdensome to you; because, I do not seek yours, but you. Because, the children ought not to lay up for the parents, but the parents for the children.

¹⁵ And I will very gladly spend and be spent for you; though the more abundantly I love you, the less I am loved.

¹⁶ But be that as it may, I did not burden you. Nevertheless, being crafty, I caught you with craftiness!

¹⁷ Did I take advantage of you by any of those whom I sent to you?

¹⁸ I urged Titus, and sent our brother with *him*. Did Titus take advantage of you? Did we not walk in the same spirit? Did *we* not walk in the same steps?

¹⁹ Again, do you think that we excuse ourselves to you? We speak

before God in Christ. But *we do* all things, beloved, for your edification.

²⁰ Because, I fear lest, when I come, I will not find you such as I wish, and *that* I will be found by you such as you do not wish; lest *there be* debates, jealousies, outbursts of wrath, selfish ambitions, backbitings, whisperings, puffed up pride, commotion;

²¹ *and* lest, when I come again, my God will humble me among you, and *that* I will mourn for many who have sinned already and have not repented of the uncleanness, fornication, and lewdness which they have committed.

CHAPTER 13

¹ This *is* the third *time* I am coming to you. "By the mouth of two or three witnesses shall every word be established."

² I have told you before, and foretell you, as if I were present the second time, and now being absent I write to those who have sinned already, and to all the rest, that if I come again I will not spare

³ since you seek a proof of Christ speaking in me, who is not weak toward you, but mighty in you.

⁴ Because, though He was crucified in weakness, yet He lives by the power of God. Because, we also are weak in Him, but we will live with Him by the power of God toward you.

⁵ Examine yourselves as to whether you are in the faith. Test yourselves. Do you not know yourselves, that Jesus Christ is in you? Unless indeed you are reprobates.

⁶ But I trust that you shall know that we are not reprobates.

⁷ Now I pray to God that you do no evil, not that we should appear approved, but that you should do what is honest, *even* though we are as reprobates.

⁸ Because, we can do nothing against the truth, but for the truth.

⁹ Because, we are glad when we are weak and you are strong. And this also we desire, *even* your perfection.

¹⁰ Therefore I write these things being absent, lest being present I should use sharpness, according to the authority which the Lord has given me for edification and not for destruction.

¹¹ Finally, brethren, farewell. Be perfect. Be of good comfort, be of one mind, live in peace; and the God of love and peace will be with you.

¹² Greet one another with a holy kiss.

¹³ All the saints greet you.

¹⁴ The grace of the Lord Jesus Christ, and the love of God, and the communion of the Holy Spirit *be* with you all. Amen.

The second letter to the Corinthians was written from Philippos, *a city* of Macedonia, by Titus and Lucas.

THE LETTER OF PAUL THE APOSTLE TO THE

GALATIANS

CHAPTER 1

¹ Paul, an apostle (not from men nor by man, but by Jesus Christ and God the Father who raised Him from the dead),

² and all the brethren who are with me, to the churches of Galatia:

³ *Grace be* to you and peace from God the Father and *from* our Lord Jesus Christ,

⁴ who gave Himself for our sins, that He might deliver us from this present evil age, according to the will of our God and Father,

⁵ to whom *be* glory forever and ever. Amen.

⁶ I marvel that you are turning away so soon from Him who called you into the grace of Christ, to another gospel,

⁷ which is not another; but there are some who trouble you and want to pervert the gospel of Christ.

⁸ But even if we, or an angel from heaven, preach any other gospel to you than what we have preached to you, let him be accursed.

⁹ As we have said before, so now I say again, if anyone preaches any other gospel to you than what you have received, let him be accursed.

¹⁰ So am I now persuading men, or God? Or do I seek to please men? Because if I still pleased men, I would not be the servant of Christ.

¹¹ But I make known to you, brethren, that the gospel which was preached by me is not according to man.

¹² Because, I neither received it from man, nor was I taught *it*, but *it came* by the revelation of Jesus Christ.

¹³ Because, you have heard of my former conduct in Judaism, how I persecuted the church of God beyond measure and destroyed it.

¹⁴ And I advanced in Judaism beyond many of my contemporaries in my own nation, being more exceedingly zealous for the traditions of my fathers.

¹⁵ But when it pleased God, who separated *me* from my mother's womb and called me by His grace,

¹⁶ to reveal His Son in me, that I might preach Him among the Gentiles, I did not immediately confer with flesh and blood,

¹⁷ nor did I go up to Jerusalem to those who were apostles before me; but I went to Arabia, and returned again to Damascus.

¹⁸ Then after three years I went up to Jerusalem to see Peter, and remained with him fifteen days.

¹⁹ But I saw none of the other apostles except James, the Lord's brother.

²⁰ (Now *concerning* the things which I write to you, indeed, before God, I do not lie.)

²¹ Afterward I came into the regions of Syria and Cilicia.
²² And I was unknown by face to the churches of Judea which were in Christ.
²³ But they had heard only, "He who formerly persecuted us now preaches the faith which he once destroyed."
²⁴ And they glorified God in me.

CHAPTER 2

¹ Then after fourteen years I went up again to Jerusalem with Barnabas, and took Titus with *me* also.
² And I went up by revelation, and communicated to them that gospel which I preach among the Gentiles, but privately to those who were of reputation, lest by any means I might run, or had run, in vain.
³ Yet not even Titus who was with me, being a Greek, was compelled to be circumcised.
⁴ And this *arose* because of false brethren secretly brought in (who came in secretly to spy out our liberty which we have in Christ Jesus, that they might bring us into bondage),
⁵ to whom we did not yield submission even for an hour, that the truth of the gospel might continue with you.
⁶ But from those who seemed to be something (whatever they were, it makes no difference to me; God shows personal favoritism to no man) because, those who seemed *to be something* added nothing to me.
⁷ But on the contrary, when they saw that the gospel for the uncircumcised had been committed to me, as *the gospel* for the circumcised *was* to Peter
⁸ because, He who worked effectively in Peter for the apostleship to the circumcised also worked effectively in me toward the Gentiles,
⁹ and when James, Cephas, and John, who seemed to be pillars, perceived the grace that had been given to me, they gave me and Barnabas the right hand of fellowship, that we *should go* to the Gentiles and they to the circumcised.
¹⁰ *Desiring* only that we should remember the poor, the very thing which I also was eager to do.
¹¹ But when Peter had come to Antioch, I withstood him to his face, because he was to be blamed;
¹² because, before certain men came from James, he would eat with the Gentiles; but when they came, he withdrew and separated himself, fearing those who were of the circumcision.
¹³ And the rest of the Jews also played the hypocrite with him, so that even Barnabas was carried away with their hypocrisy.
¹⁴ But when I saw that they were not straightforward about the truth of the gospel, I said to Peter before *them* all, "If you, being a Jew, live in the manner of Gentiles and not as the Jews, why do you compel

Gentiles to live as Jews?

¹⁵ We who *are* Jews by nature, and not sinners of the Gentiles,

¹⁶ knowing that a man is not justified by the works of the law but by the faith of Jesus Christ, even we have believed in Jesus Christ, that we might be justified by the faith of Christ and not by the works of the law; because by the works of the law no flesh will be justified.

¹⁷ "But if, while we seek to be justified by Christ, we ourselves also are found sinners, *is* Christ therefore a minister of sin? God forbid!

¹⁸ Because, if I build again those things which I destroyed, I make myself a transgressor.

¹⁹ Because, I through the law died to the law that I might live to God.

²⁰ I am crucified with Christ; nevertheless I live, yet not I but Christ lives in me; and the life which I now live in the flesh I live by the faith of the Son of God, who loved me and gave Himself for me.

²¹ I do not reject the grace of God; because, if righteousness *comes* through the law, then Christ died in vain."

CHAPTER 3

¹ O foolish Galatians! Who has bewitched you that you should not obey the truth, before whose eyes Jesus Christ was clearly portrayed among you as crucified?

² This only I want to learn from you: Did you receive the Spirit by the works of the law, or by the hearing of faith?

³ Are you so foolish? Having begun in the Spirit, are you now being made perfect by the flesh?

⁴ Have you suffered so many things in vain, if indeed *it* was in vain?

⁵ Therefore He who supplies the Spirit to you and works miracles among you, *does He* do it by the works of the law, or by the hearing of faith?

⁶ Just as Abraham "believed God, and it was accounted to him for righteousness."

⁷ Therefore know that those who are of faith, the same are children of Abraham.

⁸ And the Scripture, foreseeing that God would justify the Gentiles through faith, preached the gospel to Abraham beforehand, *saying*, "In you all the nations will be blessed."

⁹ So then those who are of faith are blessed with faithful Abraham.

¹⁰ Because, as many as are of the works of the law are under the curse; because it is written, "Cursed is everyone who does not continue in all things which are written in the book of the law, to do them."

¹¹ But that no one is justified by the law in the sight of God *is* evident, because "the just will live by faith."

¹² Yet the law is not of faith, but "the man who does them will live in them."

¹³ Christ has redeemed us from the curse of the law, having become a curse for us (because it is written,

"Cursed is everyone who hangs on a tree"),

¹⁴ that the blessing of Abraham might come upon the Gentiles through Christ Jesus, that we might receive the promise of the Spirit through faith.

¹⁵ Brethren, I speak in the manner of men: Though *it is* only a man's covenant, yet *if it is* confirmed, no one annuls or adds to it.

¹⁶ Now to Abraham and his Seed were the promises made. He does not say, "And to seeds," as of many, but as of one, "And to your Seed," who is Christ.

¹⁷ And this I say, *that* the law, which was four hundred and thirty years later, cannot annul the covenant that was confirmed before by God in Christ, that it should make the promise of no effect.

¹⁸ Because, if the inheritance *is* of the law, *it is* no longer of promise; but God gave *it* to Abraham by promise.

¹⁹ what purpose then *does* the law *serve*? It was added because of transgressions, until the Seed should come to whom the promise was made; *and it was* ordained through angels by the hand of a mediator.

²⁰ Now a mediator does not *mediate* for one *only*, but God is one.

²¹ *Is* the law then against the promises of God? God forbid! Because, if there had been a law given which could have given life, truly righteousness would have been by the law.

²² But the Scripture has concluded all under sin, that the promise by faith, of Jesus Christ, might be given to those who believe.

²³ But before faith came, we were preserved by the law, preserved for the faith which would afterward be revealed.

²⁴ Therefore the law was an instructor *to bring us* to Christ, that we might be justified by faith.

²⁵ But after faith has come, we are no longer under an instructor.

²⁶ Because, you are all sons of God by faith in Christ Jesus.

²⁷ Because, as many of you as have been baptized into Christ have put on Christ.

²⁸ There is neither Jew nor Greek, there is neither slave nor free, there is neither male nor female; because you are all one in Christ Jesus.

²⁹ And if you *are* Christ's, then you are Abraham's seed, and heirs according to the promise.

CHAPTER 4

¹ Now I say *that* the heir, as long as he is a child, does not differ at all from a servant, though he is master of all,

² but is under instructors and stewards until the time appointed by the father.

³ Even so we, when we were children, were in bondage under the elements of the world.

⁴ But when the fullness of the time

had come, God sent forth His Son, born of a woman, born under the law,

⁵ to redeem those who were under the law, that we might receive the adoption as sons.

⁶ And because you are sons, God has sent forth the Spirit of His Son into your hearts, crying, "Abba, Father!"

⁷ Therefore you are no longer a servant but a son, and if a son, then an heir of God through Christ.

⁸ But then, indeed, when you did not know God, you served those which by nature are not gods.

⁹ But now after you have known God, or rather are known by God, how *is it that* you turn again to the weak and beggarly elements, to which you desire again to be in bondage?

¹⁰ You observe days and months and seasons and years.

¹¹ I am afraid for you, lest I have labored for you in vain.

¹² Brethren, I urge you to be as I *am*, because I *am* as you are. You have not injured me at all.

¹³ You know that because of physical weakness I preached the gospel to you at the first.

¹⁴ And my trial which was in my flesh you did not despise or reject, but you received me as an angel of God, *even* as Christ Jesus.

¹⁵ What then was the blessing you spoke of? Because, I bear you witness that, if possible, you would have plucked out your own eyes and given them to me.

¹⁶ Have I therefore become your enemy because I tell you the truth?

¹⁷ They are zealous for you, *but* for no good; yes, they want to exclude you, that you may be zealous for them.

¹⁸ But *it is* good to be zealous in a good *thing* always, and not only when I am present with you.

¹⁹ My little children, for whom I labor in birth again until Christ is formed in you,

²⁰ I desire to be present with you now and to change my tone; because I stand in doubt concerning you.

²¹ Tell me, you who desire to be under the law, do you not hear the law?

²² Because, it is written that Abraham had two sons: the one by a bondwoman, the other by a freewoman.

²³ But he *who was* of the bondwoman was born according to the flesh, and he of the freewoman *was* by promise,

²⁴ which things are an allegory. Because, these are the two covenants: the one from Mount Sinai which gives birth to bondage, which is Hagar.

²⁵ Because, this Hagar is Mount Sinai in Arabia, and corresponds to Jerusalem which now is, and is in bondage with her children.

²⁶ But the Jerusalem above is free, which is the mother of us all.

²⁷ Because, it is written: "Rejoice, *you* barren, you who do not bear!

Break forth and cry, you who are not in labor! Because, the desolate has many more children than she who has a husband."

²⁸ Now we, brethren, as Isaac was, are children of promise.

²⁹ But, as he who was born according to the flesh then persecuted him *who was born* according to the Spirit, even so *it is* now.

³⁰ Nevertheless what does the Scripture say? "Cast out the bondwoman and her son, because, the son of the bondwoman will not be heir with the son of the freewoman."

³¹ So then, brethren, we are not children of the bondwoman but of the free.

CHAPTER 5

¹ Stand fast therefore in the liberty by which Christ has made us free, and do not be entangled again with a yoke of bondage.

² Behold I, Paul, say to you that if you become circumcised, Christ will profit you nothing.

³ And I testify again to every man who becomes circumcised that he is a debtor to keep the entire law.

⁴ Christ has become of no effect to you, those of you who are justified by law; you have fallen from grace.

⁵ Because, we through the Spirit wait for the hope of righteousness by faith.

⁶ Because, in Christ Jesus neither circumcision nor uncircumcision avails anything, but faith working through love.

⁷ You ran well. Who hindered you from obeying the truth?

⁸ This persuasion *does* not *come* from Him who calls you.

⁹ A little leaven leavens the entire lump.

¹⁰ I have confidence in you, through the Lord, that you will have no other mind; but he who troubles you will bear his judgment, whoever he is.

¹¹ And I, brethren, if I still preach circumcision, why do I still suffer persecution? Then the offense of the cross has ceased.

¹² I desire that those who trouble you were cut off.

¹³ Because you, brethren, have been called to liberty; only do not *use* liberty as an opportunity for the flesh, but through love serve one another.

¹⁴ Because all the law is fulfilled in one word, *even* in this: "You shall love your neighbor as yourself."

¹⁵ But if you bite and devour one another, beware that you are not consumed by one another!

¹⁶ This I say then: Walk in the Spirit, and you will not fulfill the lust of the flesh.

¹⁷ Because, the flesh lusts against the Spirit, and the Spirit against the flesh; and these are contrary to one another, so that you do not do the things that you want.

¹⁸ But if you are led by the Spirit, you are not under the law.

¹⁹ Now the works of the flesh are evident, which are *these*: adultery, fornication, uncleanness, lustfulness,
²⁰ idolatry, witchcraft, hatred, fights, jealousies, rage, selfish ambitions, rebellion, heresies,
²¹ envy, murders, drunkenness, partying, and the like; of which I tell you beforehand, just as I also told *you* in time past, that those who do such things will not inherit the kingdom of God.
²² But the fruit of the Spirit is love, joy, peace, longsuffering, kindness, goodness, faith,
²³ meekness, self control. Against such there is no law.
²⁴ And those who are Christ's have crucified the flesh with its passions and desires.
²⁵ If we live in the Spirit, let us also walk in the Spirit.
²⁶ Let us not desire vain glory, provoking one another, envying one another.

CHAPTER 6

¹ Brethren, if anyone is overtaken in any trespass, you who are spiritual restore such a one in a spirit of meekness, considering yourself lest you also be tempted.
² Bear one another's burdens, and so fulfill the law of Christ.
³ Because, if anyone thinks himself to be something, when he is nothing, he deceives himself.
⁴ But let each one examine his own work, and then he will have rejoicing in himself alone, and not in another.
⁵ Because each one shall bear his own load.
⁶ Let him who is taught the word communicate in every good thing with him who teaches.
⁷ Do not be deceived, God is not mocked; because whatever a man sows, that he will also reap.
⁸ Because, he who sows to his flesh will of the flesh reap corruption, but he who sows to the Spirit will of the Spirit reap everlasting life.
⁹ And let us not grow weary while doing good, because in due season we will reap if we do not lose heart.
¹⁰ Therefore, as we have opportunity, let us do good to everyone, especially to those who are of the household of faith.
¹¹ You see what a large letter I have written to you with my own hand!
¹² As many as desire to make a good showing in the flesh, these compel you to be circumcised, only lest they should suffer persecution for the cross of Christ.
¹³ Because, not even those who are circumcised keep the law, but they desire to have you circumcised that they may boast in your flesh.
¹⁴ But God forbid that I should boast except in the cross of our Lord Jesus Christ, by whom the world has been crucified to me and I to the world.
¹⁵ Because, in Christ Jesus neither circumcision nor uncircumcision avails anything, but a new creature.
¹⁶ And as many as walk according to

this rule, peace and mercy be upon them, and upon the Israel of God.

¹⁷ From now on let no one trouble me, because I bear in my body the marks of the Lord Jesus.

¹⁸ Brethren, the grace of our Lord Jesus Christ *be* with your spirit. Amen.

To the Galatians written from Rome.

THE LETTER OF PAUL THE APOSTLE TO THE

EPHESIANS

CHAPTER 1

¹ Paul, an apostle of Jesus Christ by the will of God, to the saints who are in Ephesus, and faithful in Christ Jesus:

² Grace *be* to you and peace from God our Father and *from* the Lord Jesus Christ.

³ Blessed *be* the God and Father of our Lord Jesus Christ, who has blessed us with every spiritual blessing in the heavenly *places* in Christ,

⁴ just as He has chosen us in Him before the foundation of the world, that we should be holy and without blame before Him in love,

⁵ having predestined us to adoption as children by Jesus Christ to Himself, according to the good pleasure of His will,

⁶ to the praise of the glory of His grace, by which He has made us accepted in the Beloved.

⁷ In Him we have redemption through His blood, the forgiveness of sins, according to the riches of His grace

⁸ which He made to abound toward us in all wisdom and prudence,

⁹ having made known to us the mystery of His will, according to His good pleasure which He has purposed in Himself,

¹⁰ that in the dispensation of the fullness of the times He might gather together in one all things in Christ, both which are in heaven and which are on earth, *even* in Him.

¹¹ In Him also we have obtained an inheritance, being predestined according to the purpose of Him who works all things according to the counsel of His own will,

¹² that we who first trusted in Christ should be to the praise of His glory.

¹³ In Him you also *trusted*, after you heard the word of truth, the gospel of your salvation; in whom also, after you believed, you were sealed with the Holy Spirit of promise,

¹⁴ who is the guarantee of our inheritance until the redemption of the purchased possession, to the praise of His glory.

¹⁵ Therefore I also, after I heard of your faith in the Lord Jesus and your love for all the saints,

¹⁶ do not cease to give thanks for you, making mention of you in my prayers:

¹⁷ that the God of our Lord Jesus Christ, the Father of glory, may give to you the spirit of wisdom and revelation in the knowledge of Him,

¹⁸ the eyes of your understanding being enlightened; that you may know what is the hope of His calling, what are the riches of the glory of His inheritance in the

saints,

¹⁹ and what *is* the exceeding greatness of His power toward us who believe, according to the working of His mighty power

²⁰ which He worked in Christ when He raised Him from the dead and seated *Him* at His own right hand in the heavenly *places*,

²¹ far above all principality and power and might and dominion, and every name that is named, not only in this age but also in that which is to come.

²² And has put all *things* under His feet, and gave Him *to be* the head over all *things* to the church,

²³ which is His body, the fullness of Him who fills all in all.

CHAPTER 2

¹ And you *He has made alive*, who were dead in trespasses and sins,

² in which you once walked according to the course of this world, according to the prince of the power of the air, the spirit who now works in the children of disobedience,

³ among whom also we all once conducted ourselves in the lusts of our flesh, fulfilling the desires of the flesh and of the mind, and were by nature children of wrath, just as the others.

⁴ But God, who is rich in mercy, because of His great love with which He loved us,

⁵ even when we were dead in sins, made us alive together with Christ (by grace you are saved),

⁶ and has raised *us* up together, and made *us* sit together in the heavenly *places* in Christ Jesus,

⁷ that in the ages to come He might show the exceeding riches of His grace in *His* kindness toward us through Christ Jesus.

⁸ Because, it is by grace you are saved through faith, and that not of yourselves; it is the gift of God,

⁹ not of works, lest anyone should boast.

¹⁰ Because, we are His workmanship, created in Christ Jesus for good works, which God prepared beforehand that we should walk in them.

¹¹ Therefore remember that you, once Gentiles in the flesh, who are called Uncircumcision by what is called the Circumcision made in the flesh by hands,

¹² that at that time you were without Christ, being aliens from the commonwealth of Israel and strangers from the covenants of promise, having no hope and without God in the world.

¹³ But now in Christ Jesus you who once were far off have been brought near by the blood of Christ.

¹⁴ Because, He is our peace, who has made both one, and has broken down the middle wall of separation *between* us,

¹⁵ having abolished in His flesh the enmity, *that is*, the law of commandments *contained* in ordinances, so as to make in Himself one new man from the two, *thus* making peace,

¹⁶ and that He might reconcile them both to God in one body by the cross, thereby putting to death the enmity.

¹⁷ And came and preached peace to you who were afar off and to those who were near.

¹⁸ Because, through Him we both have access by one Spirit to the Father.

¹⁹ Now, therefore, you are no longer strangers and foreigners, but fellow citizens with the saints and members of the household of God,

²⁰ and are built upon the foundation of the apostles and prophets, Jesus Christ Himself being the chief *cornerstone*,

²¹ in whom the entire building, being fitted together, grows into a holy temple in the Lord,

²² in whom you also are being built together for a dwelling place of God through the Spirit.

CHAPTER 3

¹ For this reason I, Paul, the prisoner of Jesus Christ for you Gentiles,

² if indeed you have heard of the dispensation of the grace of God which was given to me for you,

³ how that by revelation He made known to me the mystery (as I have briefly written already,

⁴ by which, when you read, you may understand my knowledge in the mystery of Christ),

⁵ which in other ages was not made known to the sons of men, as it has now been revealed by the Spirit to His holy apostles and prophets:

⁶ that the Gentiles should be fellow heirs, of the same body, and partakers of His promise in Christ through the gospel,

⁷ of which I became a minister according to the gift of the grace of God given to me by the effective working of His power.

⁸ To me, who am less than the least of all the saints, this grace was given, that I should preach among the Gentiles the unsearchable riches of Christ,

⁹ and to make all *people* see what *is* the fellowship of the mystery, which from the beginning of the ages has been hidden in God who created all things by Jesus Christ;

¹⁰ to the intent that now the manifold wisdom of God might be made known by the church to the principalities and powers in the heavenly *places*,

¹¹ according to the eternal purpose which He accomplished in Christ Jesus our Lord,

¹² in whom we have boldness and access with confidence by the faith of Him.

¹³ Therefore I ask that you do not grow weary at my tribulations for you, which is your glory.

¹⁴ For this reason I bow my knees to the Father of our Lord Jesus Christ,

¹⁵ from whom the whole family in heaven and earth is named,

¹⁶ that He would grant you, accord-

ing to the riches of His glory, to be strengthened with might by His Spirit in the inner man,

¹⁷ that Christ may dwell in your hearts by faith; that you, being rooted and grounded in love,

¹⁸ may be able to comprehend with all the saints what *is* the width and length and depth and height,

¹⁹ to know the love of Christ which passes knowledge; that you may be filled with all the fullness of God.

²⁰ Now to Him who is able to do exceedingly abundantly above all that we ask or think, according to the power that works in us,

²¹ to Him *be* glory in the church by Christ Jesus throughout all ages, forever and ever. Amen.

CHAPTER 4

¹ I, therefore, the prisoner of the Lord, urge you to walk worthy of the calling with which you were called,

² with all lowliness and meekness, with longsuffering, bearing with one another in love,

³ endeavoring to keep the unity of the Spirit in the bond of peace.

⁴ *There is* one body and one Spirit, just as you are called in one hope of your calling;

⁵ one Lord, one faith, one baptism;

⁶ one God and Father of all, who *is* above all, and through all, and in you all.

⁷ But to each one of us grace is given according to the measure of the gift of Christ.

⁸ Therefore He says: "When He ascended on high, He led captivity captive, and gave gifts to men."

⁹ (Now this, "He ascended," what does it mean but that He also first descended into the lower parts of earth?

¹⁰ He who descended is also the same who ascended up far above all the heavens, that He might fill all things.)

¹¹ And He gave some to be apostles, some prophets, some evangelists, and some pastors and teachers,

¹² for the perfecting of the saints, for the work of the ministry, for the edifying of the body of Christ,

¹³ until we all come to the unity of the faith and of the knowledge of the Son of God, to a perfect man, to the measure of the stature of the fullness of Christ;

¹⁴ that we *should no longer* be children, tossed to and fro and carried about with every wind of doctrine, by the trickery of men, *and* cunning craftiness, in which they make plans to deceive,

¹⁵ but, speaking the truth in love, may grow up in all things into Him who is the head, *who is* Christ,

¹⁶ from whom the entire body, joined and knit together by what every joint supplies, according to the effective working by which every part does its share, causes growth of the body for the edifying of itself in love.

¹⁷ This I say, therefore, and testify in the Lord, that you should no

longer walk as the rest of the Gentiles walk, in the vanity of their mind,

¹⁸ having their understanding darkened, being alienated from the life of God, through the ignorance that is in them, because of the blindness of their heart;

¹⁹ who, being past feeling, have given themselves over to filthiness, to work all uncleanness with greediness.

²⁰ But you have not so learned Christ,

²¹ if indeed you have heard Him and have been taught by Him, as the truth is in Jesus:

²² that you put off, concerning your former conduct, the old man which is corrupted according to the deceitful lusts,

²³ and be renewed in the spirit of your mind,

²⁴ and that you put on the new man which was created according to God, in righteousness and true holiness.

²⁵ Therefore, putting away lying, "every one speak truth with his neighbor," because we are members of one another.

²⁶ "Be angry, and do not sin": do not let the sun go down on your wrath,

²⁷ nor give place to the devil.

²⁸ Let him who stole steal no longer, but rather let him labor, working with *his* hands that which is good, that he may have something to give him who has need.

²⁹ Let no corrupt communication proceed out of your mouth, but what is good for necessary edification, that it may minister grace to the hearers.

³⁰ And do not grieve the Holy Spirit of God, by whom you were sealed for the day of redemption.

³¹ Let all bitterness, wrath, anger, clamor, and evil speaking be put away from you, with all malice.

³² And be kind to one another, tenderhearted, forgiving one another, just as God forgave you because of Christ.

CHAPTER 5

¹ You therefore be followers of God as dear children.

² And walk in love, as Christ also has loved us and given Himself for us, an offering and a sacrifice to God for a sweet smelling aroma.

³ But fornicators and all uncleanness or covetousness, let it not even be named among you, as is appropriate for saints;

⁴ neither filthiness, nor foolish talking, nor obscene jokes, which are not appropriate, but rather giving of thanks.

⁵ Because, you know this; that no fornicator, unclean person, nor covetous man, who is an idolater, has any inheritance in the kingdom of Christ and of God.

⁶ Let no one deceive you with vain words, for because of these things the wrath of God comes upon the children of disobedience.

⁷ Therefore do not be partakers

with them.

⁸ Because, you were once darkness, but now *you are* light in the Lord. Walk as children of light

⁹ (because, the fruit of the Spirit is in all goodness, righteousness, and truth),

¹⁰ finding out what is acceptable to the Lord.

¹¹ And have no fellowship with the unfruitful works of darkness, but rather reprove *them.*

¹² Because, it is shameful even to speak of those things which are done by them in secret.

¹³ But all things that are exposed are made manifest by the light, because whatever makes manifest is light.

¹⁴ Therefore He says: "Awake, you who sleep, arise from the dead, and Christ will give you light."

¹⁵ See then that you walk circumspectly, not as fools but as wise,

¹⁶ redeeming the time, because the days are evil.

¹⁷ Therefore do not be unwise, but understand what the will of the Lord *is.*

¹⁸ And do not be drunk with wine, in which is debauchery; but be filled with the Spirit,

¹⁹ speaking to yourselves in psalms and hymns and spiritual songs, singing and making melody in your heart to the Lord,

²⁰ giving thanks always for all things to God, even the Father in the name of our Lord Jesus Christ,

²¹ submitting yourselves to one another in the reverence of God.

²² Wives, submit yourselves to your own husbands, as to the Lord.

²³ Because, the husband is the head of the wife, just as Christ is head of the church; and He is the Savior of the body.

²⁴ Therefore, just as the church is subject to Christ, so *let* the wives be to their own husbands in everything.

²⁵ Husbands, love your wives, just as Christ also loved the church and gave Himself for her,

²⁶ that He might sanctify and cleanse her with the washing of water by the word,

²⁷ that He might present her to Himself a glorious church, not having spot or wrinkle or any such thing, but that she should be holy and without blemish.

²⁸ So husbands ought to love their wives as their own bodies; he who loves his wife loves himself.

²⁹ Because, no one ever hated his own flesh, but nourishes and cherishes it, just as the Lord *does* the church.

³⁰ Because, we are members of His body, of His flesh and of His bones.

³¹ "For this reason a man shall leave his father and mother and will be joined to his wife, and the two will become one flesh."

³² This is a great mystery, but I speak concerning Christ and the church.

³³ Nevertheless let each one of you in particular so love his own wife

just as himself, and let the wife *see* that she reverence *her* husband.

CHAPTER 6

¹ Children, obey your parents in the Lord, because this is right.

² "Honor your father and mother," which is the first commandment with promise:

³ "that it may be well with you and you may live long on the earth."

⁴ And you, fathers, do not provoke your children to wrath, but bring them up in the training and admonition of the Lord.

⁵ Servants, be obedient to those who are *your* masters according to the flesh, with reverence and trembling, in sincerity of your heart, as to Christ;

⁶ not with eye service, as men pleasers, but as servants of Christ, doing the will of God from the heart,

⁷ with goodwill doing service, as to the Lord, and not to men,

⁸ knowing that whatever good anyone does, he will receive the same from the Lord, whether *he is* a servant or free.

⁹ And you, masters, do the same things to them, giving up threatening, knowing that your own Master also is in heaven, and there is no personal favoritism with Him.

¹⁰ Finally, my brethren, be strong in the Lord and in the power of His might.

¹¹ Put on the whole armor of God, that you may be able to stand against the schemes of the devil.

¹² Because, we do not wrestle against flesh and blood, but against principalities, against powers, against the rulers of the darkness of this age, against spiritual wickedness in the heavenly *places*.

¹³ Therefore take up the whole armor of God, that you may be able to withstand in the evil day, and having done everything, to stand.

¹⁴ Stand therefore, having wrapped your waist with truth, having put on the breastplate of righteousness,

¹⁵ and shod your feet with the preparation of the gospel of peace;

¹⁶ above all, taking the shield of faith with which you will be able to quench all the fiery darts of the wicked.

¹⁷ And take the helmet of salvation, and the sword of the Spirit, which is the word of God;

¹⁸ praying always with all prayer and supplication in the Spirit, being watchful to this end with all perseverance and supplication for all the saints;

¹⁹ and for me, that utterance may be given to me, that I may open my mouth boldly to make known the mystery of the gospel,

²⁰ for which I am an ambassador in chains; that in it I may speak boldly, as I ought to speak.

²¹ But that you also may know my affairs *and* how I am doing, Tychicus, a beloved brother and faithful minister in the Lord, will make all things known to you;

²² whom I have sent to you for this very purpose, that you may know

our affairs, and *that* he may comfort your hearts.

²³ Peace *be* to the brethren, and love with faith, from God the Father and the Lord Jesus Christ.

²⁴ Grace *be* with all those who love our Lord Jesus Christ in sincerity. Amen.

To the Ephesians written from Rome, by Tychicus.

THE LETTERS OF PAUL THE APOSTLE TO THE

PHILIPPIANS

CHAPTER 1

¹ Paul and Timothy, the servants of Jesus Christ, to all the saints in Christ Jesus who are in Philippi, with the bishops and deacons:

² Grace *be* to you and peace from God our Father and *from* the Lord Jesus Christ.

³ I thank my God upon every remembrance of you,

⁴ always in every prayer of mine for you all, making request with joy,

⁵ for your fellowship in the gospel from the first day until now,

⁶ being confident of this very thing, that He who has begun a good work in you will perform *it* until the day of Jesus Christ;

⁷ just as it is right for me to think this of you all, because I have you in my heart, inasmuch as both in my chains and in the defense and confirmation of the gospel, you all are partakers of my grace.

⁸ Because, God is my record, how greatly I long for you all with the affection of Jesus Christ.

⁹ And this I pray, that your love may abound still more and more in knowledge and *in* all discernment,

¹⁰ that you may approve the things that are excellent, that you may be sincere and without offense until the day of Christ,

¹¹ being filled with the fruits of righteousness which are by Jesus Christ, to the glory and praise of God.

¹² But I want you to understand, brethren, that the things *which happened* to me have actually turned out for the furtherance of the gospel,

¹³ so that my chains in Christ have become evident to the entire palace, and in every other *place*;

¹⁴ and many of the brethren in the Lord, having become confident by my chains, are much more bold to speak the word without fear.

¹⁵ Some indeed preach Christ even from envy and strife, and some also from goodwill:

¹⁶ The former preach Christ from contention, not sincerely, supposing to add affliction to my chains;

¹⁷ but the other out of love, knowing that I am appointed for the defense of the gospel.

¹⁸ What then? Only that in every way, whether in pretence or in truth, Christ is preached; and in this I rejoice, yes, and will rejoice.

¹⁹ Because, I know that this will turn out for my deliverance through your prayer and the supply of the Spirit of Jesus Christ,

²⁰ according to my earnest expectation and *my* hope that in nothing I shall be ashamed, but *that* with all boldness, as always, *so* now also

Christ will be magnified in my body, whether *it be* by life or by death.

²¹ Because to me, to live *is* Christ, and to die is gain.

²² But if I live on in the flesh, this will mean fruit from my labor; yet what I shall choose I do not know.

²³ Because, I am hard pressed between the two, having a desire to depart and be with Christ, which is far better.

²⁴ Nevertheless to abide in the flesh *is* more needful for you.

²⁵ And being confident of this, I know that I will abide and continue with you all for your progress and joy of faith,

²⁶ that your rejoicing for me may be more abundant in Jesus Christ by my coming to you again.

²⁷ Only let your conduct be worthy of the gospel of Christ, so that whether I come and see you or am absent, I may hear of your affairs, that you stand fast in one spirit, with one mind striving together for the faith of the gospel,

²⁸ and not in any way terrified by your adversaries, which is to them a proof of perdition, but to you of salvation, and that from God.

²⁹ Because, to you it has been granted on behalf of Christ, not only to believe on Him, but also to suffer for His sake,

³⁰ having the same conflict which you saw in me and now hear *is* in me.

CHAPTER 2

¹ Therefore if *there is* any consolation in Christ, if any comfort of love, if any fellowship of the Spirit, if any affection and mercy,

² fulfill my joy by being likeminded, having the same love, *being* of one accord, of one mind.

³ Let nothing *be done* through strife or vain glory, but in lowliness of mind let each esteem others better than themselves.

⁴ Let each of you look out not only for his own interests, but each one also for the interests of others.

⁵ Let this mind be in you which was also in Christ Jesus,

⁶ who, being in the form of God, did not consider it robbery to be equal with God,

⁷ but made Himself of no reputation, and took on Himself the form of a servant, and was made in the likeness of men.

⁸ And being found in appearance as a man, He humbled Himself and became obedient to death, even the death of the cross.

⁹ Therefore God also has highly exalted Him and given Him a name which is above every name,

¹⁰ that at the name of Jesus every knee should bow, of *those* in heaven, and of *those* on earth, and of *those* under the earth,

¹¹ and *that* every tongue should confess that Jesus Christ *is* Lord, to the glory of God the Father.

¹² Therefore, my beloved, as you have always obeyed, not as in my presence only, but now much more

in my absence, work out your own salvation with reverence and trembling;
¹³ because, it is God who works in you both to will and to do for *His* good pleasure.
¹⁴ Do all things without complaining and disputing,
¹⁵ that you may be blameless and harmless, the sons of God without fault in the midst of a crooked and perverse generation, among whom you shine as lights in the world,
¹⁶ holding forth the word of life, so that I may rejoice in the day of Christ that I have not run in vain or labored in vain.
¹⁷ Yes, and if I am being offered on the sacrifice and service of your faith, I am glad and rejoice with you all.
¹⁸ For the same reason you also be glad and rejoice with me.
¹⁹ But I trust in the Lord Jesus to send Timothy to you shortly, that I also may be encouraged when I know your state.
²⁰ Because I have no one likeminded, who will naturally care for your state.
²¹ Because all seek their own, not the things which are Jesus Christ's.
²² But you know his proven character, that like a son with *his* father, he served with me in the gospel.
²³ Therefore I hope to send him at once, as soon as I see how it will go with me.
²⁴ But I trust in the Lord that I myself shall also come shortly.
²⁵ Yet I considered it necessary to send to you Epaphroditus, my brother, fellow worker, and fellow soldier, but your messenger and he who ministered to my need;
²⁶ since he was longing for you all, and was full of heaviness, because you had heard that he had been sick.
²⁷ Because, indeed he was sick almost to death; but God had mercy on him, and not only on him but on me also, lest I should have sorrow upon sorrow.
²⁸ Therefore I sent him the more eagerly, that when you see him again you may rejoice, and I may be less sorrowful.
²⁹ Receive him therefore in the Lord with all gladness, and hold such men in esteem;
³⁰ because for the work of Christ he came close to death, not regarding his life, to supply what was lacking in your service toward me.

CHAPTER 3

¹ Finally, my brethren, rejoice in the Lord. For me to write the same things to you *is* not tedious, but for you *it is* safe.
² Beware of dogs, beware of evil workers, beware of the mutilation!
³ Because, we are the circumcision, who worship God in the Spirit, rejoice in Christ Jesus, and have no confidence in the flesh,
⁴ though I also might have confidence in the flesh. If anyone else

thinks he may have confidence in the flesh, I more so:
⁵ circumcised the eighth day, of the stock of Israel, *of* the tribe of Benjamin, a Hebrew of the Hebrews; concerning the law, a Pharisee;
⁶ concerning zeal, persecuting the church; concerning the righteousness which is in the law, blameless.
⁷ But what things were gain to me, these I have counted loss for Christ.
⁸ Yet indeed I also count all things *as* loss for the excellence of the knowledge of Christ Jesus my Lord, for whom I have suffered the loss of all things, and count them *as* manure, that I may gain Christ
⁹ and be found in Him, not having my own righteousness, which is from the law, but that which is through the faith of Christ, the righteousness which is from God by faith;
¹⁰ that I may know Him and the power of His resurrection, and the fellowship of His sufferings, being conformed to His death,
¹¹ if, by any means, I may attain to the resurrection from the dead.
¹² Not that I have already attained, or am already perfected; but I press on, that I may apprehend that for which Christ Jesus has also laid hold of me.
¹³ Brethren, I do not count myself to have attained; but *this* one thing *I do*, forgetting those things which are behind and reaching forward to those things which are ahead,
¹⁴ I press toward the goal for the prize of the upward call of God in Christ Jesus.
¹⁵ Therefore let us, as many as are perfect, have this mind; and if in anything you think otherwise, God will reveal even this to you.
¹⁶ Nevertheless, to the degree that we have already attained, let us walk by the same rule, let us be of the same mind.
¹⁷ Brethren, join in following my example, and note those who so walk, as you have us for an example.
¹⁸ Because many walk, of whom I have told you often, and now tell you even weeping, *that they are* the enemies of the cross of Christ:
¹⁹ whose end *is* destruction, whose god *is their* belly, and *whose* glory *is* in their shame, who mind earthly things.
²⁰ Because, our citizenship is in heaven, from which we also eagerly wait for the Savior, the Lord Jesus Christ,
²¹ who will transform our vile body that it may be conformed to His glorious body, according to the working by which He is able even to subdue all things to Himself.

CHAPTER 4

¹ Therefore, my greatly beloved and longed for brethren, my joy and crown, so stand fast in the Lord, *my* greatly beloved.
² I implore Euodia and I implore Syntyche to be of the same mind in

the Lord.

³ And I urge you also, true companion, help those women who labored with me in the gospel, with Clement also, and the rest of my fellow workers, whose names *are* in the Book of Life.

⁴ Rejoice in the Lord always. *And* again I will say, rejoice!

⁵ Let your gentleness be known to all men. The Lord is at hand.

⁶ Be anxious for nothing, but in everything by prayer and supplication, with thanksgiving, let your requests be made known to God;

⁷ and the peace of God, which surpasses all understanding, will guard your hearts and minds through Christ Jesus.

⁸ Finally, brethren, whatever things are true, whatever things *are* honest, whatever things *are* just, whatever things *are* pure, whatever things *are* lovely, whatever things *are* of good report, if *there is* any virtue and if *there is* anything praiseworthy, meditate on these things.

⁹ Those things which you learned and received and heard and saw in me, these do also, and the God of peace will be with you.

¹⁰ But I rejoiced in the Lord greatly that now at last your care for me has flourished again; though you surely did care, but you lacked opportunity.

¹¹ Not that I speak in regard to need, because I have learned in whatever state I am, to be content *with it*:

¹² I know both how to be abased, and I know how to abound. Everywhere and in all things I am instructed both to be full and to be hungry, both to abound and to suffer need.

¹³ I can do all things through Christ who strengthens me.

¹⁴ Nevertheless you have done well that you shared in my affliction.

¹⁵ Now you Philippians know also that in the beginning of the gospel, when I departed from Macedonia, no church shared with me concerning giving and receiving but you alone.

¹⁶ Because even in Thessalonica you sent aid once and again for my necessities.

¹⁷ Not because I desire the gift, but I desire the fruit that abounds to your account.

¹⁸ But I have all and abound. I am full, having received from Epaphroditus the things *that were sent* from you, a sweet smelling aroma, an acceptable sacrifice, well pleasing to God.

¹⁹ And my God will supply all your need according to His riches in glory by Christ Jesus.

²⁰ Now to our God and Father *be* glory forever and ever. Amen.

²¹ Greet every saint in Christ Jesus. The brethren who are with me greet you.

²² All the saints greet you, but especially those who are of Caesar's household.

²³ The grace of our Lord Jesus Christ be with you all. Amen.

To the Philippians written from Rome, by Epaphroditus.

THE LETTER OF PAUL THE APOSTLE TO THE
COLOSSIANS

CHAPTER 1

¹ Paul, an apostle of Jesus Christ by the will of God, and Timothy *our* brother,

² To the saints and faithful brethren in Christ who are at Colosse: Grace *be* to you and peace from God our Father and the Lord Jesus Christ.

³ We give thanks to the God and Father of our Lord Jesus Christ, always praying for you,

⁴ since we heard of your faith in Christ Jesus, and of the love *that you have* for all the saints;

⁵ because of the hope which is laid up for you in heaven, of which you heard before in the word of the truth of the gospel,

⁶ which has come to you, *as it* has also in all the world, and is bearing fruit, as *it is* also among you since the day you heard *about it*, and knew the grace of God in truth;

⁷ as you also learned from Epaphras, our dear fellow servant, who is a faithful minister of Christ on your behalf,

⁸ who also declared unto us your love in the Spirit.

⁹ For this reason we also, since the day we heard *it*, do not cease to pray for you, and to desire that you may be filled with the knowledge of His will in all wisdom and spiritual understanding;

¹⁰ that you may walk worthy of the Lord, fully pleasing *Him*, being fruitful in every good work and increasing in the knowledge of God;

¹¹ strengthened with all might, according to His glorious power, for all patience and longsuffering with joy;

¹² giving thanks to the Father who has qualified us to be partakers in the inheritance of the saints in the light,

¹³ who has delivered us from the power of darkness and translated *us* into the kingdom of His beloved Son,

¹⁴ in whom we have redemption through His blood *even* the forgiveness of sins.

¹⁵ He is the image of the invisible God, the firstborn over all creation.

¹⁶ Because, all things were created by Him that are in heaven and that are on earth, visible and invisible, whether *they are* thrones or dominions or principalities or powers. All things were created by Him and for Him.

¹⁷ And He is before all things, and by Him all things consist.

¹⁸ And He is the head of the body, the church, who is the beginning, the firstborn from the dead, that in all *things* He may have the preeminence.

¹⁹ Because, it pleased *the Father* that

in Him all the fullness should dwell, ²⁰ and by Him, having made peace through the blood of His cross, to reconcile all things to Himself, by Him, whether things on earth or things in heaven.

²¹ And you, who once were alienated and enemies in *your* mind by wicked works, yet now He has reconciled ²² in the body of His flesh through death, to present you holy, and blameless, and above reproach in His sight, ²³ if you continue in the faith, grounded and steadfast, and *are* not moved away from the hope of the gospel which you heard, *and* which was preached to every creature under heaven, of which I, Paul, became a minister.

²⁴ I now rejoice in my sufferings for you, and fill up in my flesh what is lacking in the afflictions of Christ, for the sake of His body, which is the church, ²⁵ of which I became a minister according to the stewardship from God which was given to me for you, to fulfill the word of God, ²⁶ *even* the mystery which has been hidden from ages and from generations, but now has been revealed to His saints.

²⁷ To them God desired to make known what are the riches of the glory of this mystery among the Gentiles: which is Christ in you, the hope of glory.

²⁸ Him we preach, warning every man and teaching every man in all wisdom, that we may present every man perfect in Christ Jesus.

²⁹ To this *end* I also labor, striving according to His working which works in me mightily.

CHAPTER 2

¹ Because, I want you to know what a great conflict I have for you and *for* those in Laodicea, and *for* as many as have not seen my face in the flesh, ² that their hearts may be encouraged, being knit together in love, and *attaining* to all the riches of the full assurance of understanding, to the knowledge of the mystery of God, both of the Father and of Christ, ³ in whom are hidden all the treasures of wisdom and knowledge.

⁴ Now this I say lest anyone should deceive you with persuasive words. ⁵ Because, though I am absent in the flesh, yet I am with you the spirit, rejoicing to see your order and the firmness of your faith in Christ.

⁶ Therefore, as you have received Christ Jesus the Lord, *so* walk in Him, ⁷ rooted and built up in Him and established in the faith, just as you have been taught, abounding in it with thanksgiving.

⁸ Beware lest anyone rob you through philosophy and vain deceit, according to the tradition of men, according to the basic princi-

ples of the world, and not according to Christ.

⁹ Because, in Him dwells all the fullness of the Godhead bodily;

¹⁰ and you are complete in Him, who is the head of all principality and power.

¹¹ In Him you were also circumcised with the circumcision made without hands, by putting off the body of the sins of the flesh, by the circumcision of Christ,

¹² buried with Him in baptism, in which you also were raised with *Him* through the faith of the working of God, who has raised Him from the dead.

¹³ And you, being dead in your sins and the uncircumcision of your flesh, He has made alive together with Him, having forgiven you all trespasses,

¹⁴ having erased the written record of commands that were against us, which was contrary to us, and took it out of the way, nailing it to the cross.

¹⁵ Having disarmed principalities and powers, He made a spectacle of them, triumphing over them in it.

¹⁶ Therefore let no man judge you in food or in drink, or regarding a holyday, or of the new moon, or of the sabbath days,

¹⁷ which are a shadow of things to come, but the body *is* of Christ.

¹⁸ Let no one rob you of your reward, delighting in *false* humility and worship of angels, meddling into those things which he has not seen, vainly puffed up by his fleshly mind,

¹⁹ And not clinging to the Head, from whom all the body, nourished and knit together by joints and ligaments, increases with the increase from God.

²⁰ Therefore, if you are dead with Christ from the basic principles of the world, why, as *though* living in the world, are you subject to regulations,

²¹ ("Do not touch, do not taste, do not handle,"

²² which all concern things which perish with the using) according to the commandments and doctrines of men?

²³ These things certainly have an appearance of wisdom in self willed worship and humility, and neglecting of the body, but have no value against the indulgence of the flesh.

CHAPTER 3

¹ If then you are risen with Christ, seek those things which are above, where Christ is sitting at the right hand of God.

² Set your affections on things above, not on things on the earth.

³ Because, you are dead, and your life is hidden with Christ in God.

⁴ When Christ *who is* our life appears, then you also will appear with Him in glory.

⁵ Therefore put to death your members which are on the earth; fornication, uncleanness, inordinate passion, evil desire, and

covetousness, which is idolatry.

⁶ Because of these things the wrath of God is coming upon the children of disobedience,

⁷ in which you also once walked when you lived in them.

⁸ But now you also put off all these: anger, wrath, malice, blasphemy, filthy language out of your mouth.

⁹ Do not lie to one another, seeing you have put off the old man with his deeds,

¹⁰ and have put on the new *man*, who is renewed in knowledge according to the image of Him who created him,

¹¹ where there is neither Greek nor Jew, circumcised nor uncircumcised, Barbarian, Scythian, slave nor free: but Christ *is* all and in all.

¹² Therefore, as the elect of God, holy and beloved, put on heartfelt compassion, kindness, humility of mind, meekness, longsuffering;

¹³ bearing with one another, and forgiving one another, if anyone has a complaint against another; just as Christ forgave you, so you *do* likewise.

¹⁴ And above all these things *put on* love, which is the bond of perfection.

¹⁵ And let the peace of God rule in your hearts, to which you also were called in one body; and be thankful.

¹⁶ Let the word of Christ dwell in you richly in all wisdom, teaching and admonishing one another in psalms and hymns and spiritual songs, singing with grace in your hearts to the Lord.

¹⁷ And whatever you do in word or deed, *do* all in the name of the Lord Jesus, giving thanks to God and the Father by Him.

¹⁸ Wives, submit to your own husbands, as is acceptable in the Lord.

¹⁹ Husbands, love *your* wives, and do not be bitter against them.

²⁰ children, obey *your* parents in all things, because this is well pleasing to the Lord.

²¹ Fathers do not provoke your children *to anger*, lest they become discouraged.

²² Servants, obey your masters according to the flesh in all things, not with eye service, as men pleasers, but in singleness of heart, reverencing God.

²³ And whatever you do, do *it* with all your heart, as to the Lord and not to men,

²⁴ knowing that from the Lord you will receive the reward of the inheritance; because you serve the Lord Christ.

²⁵ But he who does wrong will be repaid for the wrong that he has done, and there is no personal favoritism.

CHAPTER 4

¹ Masters, give to *your* servants that which is just and balanced, knowing that you also have a Master in heaven.

² Continue in prayer, and watch in it with thanksgiving;

³ meanwhile praying also for us, that God would open to us a door for the word, to speak the mystery of Christ, for which I am also in chains,

⁴ that I may make it manifest, as I ought to speak.

⁵ Walk in wisdom toward those who are outside, redeeming the time.

⁶ Let your speech always *be* with grace, seasoned with salt, that you may know how you ought to answer each person.

⁷ Tychicus, *who is* a beloved brother, a faithful minister and fellow servant in the Lord, will tell you about my state of *affairs*

⁸ whom I have sent to you for the same purpose, that he might know your circumstances, and comfort your hearts,

⁹ with Onesimus, a faithful and beloved brother, who is *one* of you. They will make known to you all things that *are happening* here.

¹⁰ Aristarchus my fellow prisoner greets you, with Mark, the sister's son of Barnabas, (about whom you received instructions: if he comes to you, receive him),

¹¹ and Jesus, who is called Justus, who are of the circumcision. These *are my* only fellow workers for the kingdom of God who have proven to be a comfort to me.

¹² Epaphras, who is *one* of you, a servant of Christ, greets you, always laboring fervently for you in prayers, that you may stand perfect and complete in all the will of God.

¹³ Because, I bear him record, that he has a great zeal for you, and those *who are* in Laodicea, and those in Hierapolis.

¹⁴ Luke, the beloved physician and Demas greet you.

¹⁵ Greet the brethren who are in Laodicea, and Nymphas, and the church that is in his house.

¹⁶ Now when this letter is read among you, see that it is read in the church of the Laodiceans also, and that you likewise read the *letter* from Laodicea.

¹⁷ And say to Archippus, "Take heed to the ministry that you have received in the Lord, that you fulfill it."

¹⁸ The salutation of Paul, by my own hand. Remember my chains. Grace *be* with you. Amen.

Written from Rome to the Colossians, by Tychicus and Onesimus.

THE FIRST LETTER OF PAUL THE APOSTLE TO THE
THESSALONIANS

CHAPTER 1

¹ Paul, Silvanus, and Timothy, to the church of the Thessalonians *which is* in God the Father and *in* the Lord Jesus Christ: Grace *be* to you and peace from God our Father and the Lord Jesus Christ.

² We always give thanks to God for you all, making mention of you in our prayers,

³ remembering without ceasing your work of faith, labor of love, and patience of hope in our Lord Jesus Christ in the sight of God even our Father,

⁴ knowing, beloved brethren, your election by God.

⁵ Because, our gospel did not come to you in word only, but also in power, and in the Holy Spirit and in much assurance, as you know what sort of men we were among you for your sake.

⁶ And you became followers of us and of the Lord, having received the word in much affliction, with joy of the Holy Spirit,

⁷ so that you were examples to all who believe in Macedonia and Achaia.

⁸ Because, from you the word of the Lord sounded forth, not only in Macedonia and Achaia, but also in every place your faith towards God is proclaimed, so that we do not need to say anything.

⁹ Because, they themselves declare concerning us what sort of entry we had to you, and how you turned to God from idols to serve the living and true God,

¹⁰ and to wait for His Son from heaven, whom He raised from the dead, *even* Jesus, who delivered us from the wrath to come.

CHAPTER 2

¹ Because, you yourselves know brethren, that our coming to you was not in vain.

² But even after we had suffered beforehand and were disgraced at Philippi, as you know, we were bold in our God to speak to you the gospel of God in much conflict.

³ Because, our exhortation *did* not *come* from deception, nor of uncleanness, nor in trickery.

⁴ But as we have been approved by God to be entrusted with the gospel, even so we speak, not as pleasing men, but God, who tests our hearts.

⁵ Because, neither at any time did we use flattering words, as you know, nor a cloak of covetousness, God *is* witness.

⁶ Nor did we seek glory from men, either from you or from others, when we might have been burdensome, as the apostles of Christ.

⁷ But we were gentle among you,

even as a nursing mother cherishes her children.

⁸ So affectionately longing for you, we were willing to impart to you, not just the gospel of God, but also our own souls, because you were dear to us.

⁹ Because you remember, brethren, our labor and toil; because, laboring night and day, since we did not want to be a burden to any of you, we preached to you the gospel of God.

¹⁰ You *are* witnesses, and God *also*, how holy and justly and blamelessly we behaved ourselves among you who believe;

¹¹ as you know how we exhorted and comforted and commanded every one of you, as a father *does to* his children,

¹² that you would walk worthy of God, who has called you into His kingdom and glory.

¹³ For this reason also we thank God without ceasing, because when you received the word of God which you heard from us, you did not receive *it as* the word of men, but as it is in truth, the word of God, which also effectually works in you who believe.

¹⁴ Because you, brethren, became followers of the churches of God which in Judea are in Christ Jesus. Because, you also have suffered similar things from your own countrymen, just as they *have* from the Jews,

¹⁵ who killed both the Lord Jesus and their own prophets, and have persecuted us; and they do not please God, and are contrary to all men,

¹⁶ forbidding us to speak to the Gentiles that they may be saved, to always fill up their sins; because of which the wrath is coming upon them to the uttermost.

¹⁷ But we, brethren, being taken away from you for a short time in presence, not in heart, endeavored more eagerly to see your face with great longing.

¹⁸ Therefore we wanted to come to you, even I, Paul, time and again, but Satan hindered us.

¹⁹ Because what is our hope, or joy, or crown of rejoicing? *Is it* not even you in the presence of our Lord Jesus Christ at His coming?

²⁰ Because you are our glory and joy.

CHAPTER 3

¹ Therefore when we could no longer endure it, we thought it good to be left in Athens alone,

² and sent Timothy, our brother and minister of God, and our fellow laborer in the gospel of Christ, to establish you and to encourage you concerning your faith,

³ that no one should be shaken by these afflictions; because you yourselves know that we are appointed to this.

⁴ Because indeed, we told you before when we were with you that we would suffer tribulation, just as

it came to pass, and you know.

⁵ Because of this reason, when I could no longer endure it, I sent to know your faith, lest by some means the tempter had tempted you, and our labor might be in vain.

⁶ But now when Timothy came to us from you, and brought us good news of your faith and love, and that you always have good remembrance of us, earnestly desiring to see us, as we also to *see* you,

⁷ therefore, brethren, in all our affliction and distress we were comforted concerning you by your faith.

⁸ Because now we live, if you stand firmly in the Lord.

⁹ Because, what thanks can we offer back to God for you, for all the joy with which we rejoice for your sake before our God,

¹⁰ night and day praying exceedingly that we may see your face and would perfect that which is lacking in your faith?

¹¹ Now may God Himself even our Father, and our Lord Jesus Christ, direct our way to you.

¹² And the Lord make you to increase and abound in love towards one another, and towards all *men*, just as we *do* towards you,

¹³ so that He may establish your hearts blameless in holiness before God, even our Father, at the coming of our Lord Jesus Christ with all His saints.

CHAPTER 4

¹ Furthermore then brethren, we urge you and exhort *you* by the Lord Jesus, that just as you have received from us how you ought to walk and to please God, *that* you should abound more and more.

² Because, you know what commandments we gave you by the Lord Jesus.

³ Because, this is the will of God, your sanctification: that you should abstain from sexual immorality;

⁴ that every one of you should know how to possess his vessel in sanctification and honor,

⁵ not in the passion of lust, just as the Gentiles who do not know God;

⁶ that no *one* should take advantage of and defraud his brother in *any* matter, because the Lord *is* the avenger of all such, as we have also forewarned you and testified.

⁷ Because, God has not called us to uncleanness, but to holiness.

⁸ Therefore he who despises, does not despise man, but God, who has also given to us His Holy Spirit.

⁹ But concerning brotherly love you do not need that I should write to you, because you yourselves are taught by God to love one another;

¹⁰ and indeed you do so toward all the brethren who are in all Macedonia. But we urge you, brethren, that you increase more and more;

¹¹ that you also study to be quiet, and to do your own business, and to work with your own hands, as we commanded you,

¹² that you may walk appropriately toward those who are outside, and *that* you may lack nothing.

¹³ But I do not want you to be ignorant, brethren, concerning those who are asleep, that you do not mourn just like others who have no hope.

¹⁴ Because, if we believe that Jesus died and rose again, in the same way, God will bring with Him those who sleep in Jesus.

¹⁵ Because, we say this to you by the word of the Lord, that we who are alive *and* remain until the coming of the Lord will not go before those who are asleep.

¹⁶ Because, the Lord Himself will descend from heaven with a shout, with the voice of an archangel, and with the trumpet of God. Then the dead in Christ will rise first.

¹⁷ Then we who are alive *and* remain will be caught up together with them in the clouds to meet the Lord in the air. And then we will always be with the Lord.

¹⁸ Therefore comfort one another with these words.

CHAPTER 5

¹ But concerning the times and the seasons, brethren, you do not have any need that I write to you.

² Because, you yourselves know perfectly that the day of the Lord comes as a thief in the night.

³ Because, when they say, "Peace and safety!" then sudden destructtion comes upon them, like labor pains upon a pregnant woman. And they will not escape.

⁴ But you, brethren, are not in darkness, that this Day should overtake you like a thief.

⁵ You are all the children of light, and the children of the day, we are not of the night, nor of darkness.

⁶ Therefore let us not sleep, as others do, but let us watch and be sober.

⁷ Because, those who sleep, sleep at night, and those who are drunk are drunk at night.

⁸ But let us who are of the day be sober, putting on the breastplate of faith and love, and as a helmet, the hope of salvation.

⁹ Because, God has not appointed us to wrath, but to obtain salvation by our Lord Jesus Christ,

¹⁰ who died for us, that whether we wake or sleep, we should live together with Him.

¹¹ Therefore comfort each other and edify one another, just as you also are doing.

¹² And we urge you, brethren, to recognize those who labor among you, and are over you in the Lord and advise you,

¹³ and to esteem them very highly in love for their work's sake. *And* be at peace among yourselves.

¹⁴ Now we exhort you, brethren, warn those who are disorderly, comfort the feebleminded, support the weak, be patient towards everyone.

¹⁵ See that no one renders evil for

evil to *anyone*, but always pursue that which is good both for yourselves, and for everyone.

¹⁶ Rejoice always,

¹⁷ pray without ceasing,

¹⁸ in everything give thanks; because this is the will of God in Christ Jesus concerning you.

¹⁹ Do not quench the Spirit.

²⁰ Do not despise prophecies.

²¹ Test all things; hold firmly to that which is good.

²² Abstain from every appearance of evil.

²³ And may the God of peace sanctify you completely; and *I ask God* that your entire spirit, soul, and body be preserved blameless at the coming of our Lord Jesus Christ.

²⁴ He who calls you *is* faithful, who also will do *it*.

²⁵ Brethren, pray for us.

²⁶ Greet all the brethren with a holy kiss.

²⁷ I command you by the Lord that this letter be read to all the holy brethren.

²⁸ The grace of our Lord Jesus Christ *be* with you. Amen.

The first letter to the Thessalonians was written from Athens.

THE SECOND LETTER OF PAUL THE APOSTLE TO THE
THESSALONIANS

CHAPTER 1

¹ Paul, Silvanus, and Timothy, to the church of the Thessalonians in God our Father and the Lord Jesus Christ:

² Grace to you and peace from God our Father and the Lord Jesus Christ.

³ We are bound to thank God always for you, brethren, as it is fitting, because your faith grows exceptionally, and the love of every one of you all abounds toward each other,

⁴ so that we ourselves boast about you in the churches of God for your patience and faith in all your persecutions and afflictions that you endure,

⁵ *which is* clear evidence of the righteous judgment of God, that you may be counted worthy of the kingdom of God, for which you also suffer;

⁶ seeing *it is* a righteous thing with God to repay with tribulation those who trouble you,

⁷ and you who are troubled rest with us, when the Lord Jesus will be revealed from heaven with His mighty angels,

⁸ in flaming fire taking vengeance on those who do not know God, and who do not obey the gospel of our Lord Jesus Christ.

⁹ These will be punished with everlasting destruction from the presence of the Lord, and from the glory of His power,

¹⁰ when He comes in that Day to be glorified in His saints, and to be admired among all those who believe, because our testimony among you was believed.

¹¹ Therefore we also pray always for you, that our God would count you worthy of *this* calling, and fulfill all the good pleasure of *His* goodness, and the work of faith with power,

¹² that the name of our Lord Jesus Christ may be glorified in you, and you in Him, according to the grace of our God and the Lord Jesus Christ.

CHAPTER 2

¹ Now brethren, concerning the coming of our Lord Jesus Christ, and by our gathering together to Him, we urge you,

² not to be suddenly shaken in mind or to be troubled, either by a spirit or by a word, or by a letter as if from us, as though the Day of Christ is at hand.

³ Let no one deceive you by any means; because, *that Day will not come* unless a falling away comes first, and that man of sin is revealed, the son of perdition,

⁴ who opposes and exalts himself above all that is called God or that

is worshiped, so that he sits as God in the temple of God, declaring that he himself is God.

⁵ Do you not remember that when I was still with you, I told you these things?

⁶ And now you know what is restraining that he might be revealed in his time.

⁷ Because, the mystery of iniquity is at work already; only He who now restrains will restrain, until He is taken out of the way.

⁸ And then that wicked one will be revealed, whom the Lord will consume with the Spirit of His mouth and will destroy with the brightness of His coming.

⁹ *Even him*, whose coming is according to the working of Satan with all power, signs, and lying wonders,

¹⁰ and with all unrighteous deception amongst those who perish, because they did not receive the love of the truth, that they might be saved.

¹¹ And for this reason God will send them strong delusion, that they should believe a lie,

¹² that they all might be damned who did not believe the truth but had pleasure in unrighteousness.

¹³ But we are bound to give thanks to God always for you, brethren beloved by the Lord, because God has chosen you from the beginning for salvation through sanctification of the Spirit and belief of the truth,

¹⁴ to which He called you by our gospel, for the obtaining of the glory of our Lord Jesus Christ.

¹⁵ Therefore, brethren, stand firm, and hold the traditions which you were taught, whether by word or our letter.

¹⁶ Now may our Lord Jesus Christ Himself, and God, even our Father, who has loved us and has given *us* everlasting help and good hope through grace,

¹⁷ encourage your hearts and establish you in every good word and work.

CHAPTER 3

¹ Finally, brethren, pray for us, that the word of the Lord may have a *free* course, and be glorified, just as *it is* with you,

² and that we may be delivered from unreasonable and wicked men; because not everyone has faith.

³ But the Lord is faithful, who will establish you and keep *you* from evil.

⁴ And we have confidence in the Lord concerning you, both that you do and will do the things that we command you.

⁵ Now may the Lord direct your hearts into the love of God and into the perseverance for Christ.

⁶ Now we command you, brethren, in the name of our Lord Jesus Christ, that you withdraw yourselves from every brother who walks disorderly and not according to the tradition which he received

from us.

⁷ Because you yourselves know how you ought to follow us, because we were not disorderly among you;

⁸ Neither did we eat anyone's bread free of charge, but worked with labor and toil night and day, that we might not be a burden to any of you,

⁹ not because we do not have authority, but to make of ourselves an example of how you should follow us.

¹⁰ Because, even when we were with you, we commanded you this: That if anyone will not work, neither should he eat.

¹¹ Because, we hear that there are some who walk among you in a disorderly manner, not working at all, but are busybodies.

¹² Now those who are such we command and exhort by our Lord Jesus Christ that they work in quietness and eat their own bread.

¹³ But as for you, brethren, do not become weary in doing good.

¹⁴ And if anyone does not obey our word in this letter, note that person, and do not keep company with him, that he may be ashamed.

¹⁵ Yet count *him* not as an enemy, but instruct *him* as a brother.

¹⁶ Now may the Lord of peace Himself give you peace always in every way. The Lord *be* with you all.

¹⁷ The salutation of Paul with my own hand, which is confirmation in every letter; so I write.

¹⁸ The grace of our Lord Jesus Christ *be* with you all. Amen.

The second letter to the Thessalonians was written from Athens.

THE FIRST LETTER OF PAUL THE APOSTLE TO

TIMOTHY

CHAPTER 1

¹ Paul, an apostle of Jesus Christ, by the commandment of God our Savior and the Lord Jesus Christ, *who* is our hope,

² To Timothy, *my* own son in the faith: Grace, mercy, *and* peace from God our Father and Jesus Christ our Lord.

³ As I urged you when I went into Macedonia, remain in Ephesus that you may command some that they teach no other doctrine,

⁴ nor give heed to fables and endless genealogies, which minister questions rather than godly edification which is in faith, *so do*.

⁵ Now the purpose of the commandment is love from a pure heart, *from* a good conscience, and *from* sincere faith,

⁶ from which some, having strayed, have turned aside to idle talking,

⁷ desiring to be teachers of the law, understanding neither what they say nor the things which they affirm.

⁸ But we know that the law *is* good if one uses it lawfully,

⁹ knowing this: that the law is not made for a righteous person, but for the lawless and disobedient, for the ungodly and for sinners, for the unholy and profane, for murderers of fathers and murderers of mothers, for manslayers,

¹⁰ for fornicators, for those who defile themselves with mankind, for kidnappers, for liars, for perjurers, and if there is any other thing that is contrary to sound doctrine,

¹¹ according to the glorious gospel of the blessed God which was committed to my trust.

¹² And I thank Christ Jesus our Lord who has enabled me, because He counted me faithful, putting me into the ministry,

¹³ who was formerly a blasphemer, a persecutor, and an abusive man; but I obtained mercy because I did *it* ignorantly in unbelief.

¹⁴ And the grace of our Lord was exceedingly abundant, with faith and love which are in Christ Jesus.

¹⁵ This *is* a faithful saying and worthy of all acceptance, that Christ Jesus came into the world to save sinners, of whom I am chief.

¹⁶ However, for this reason I obtained mercy, that in me first Jesus Christ might show forth all longsuffering, as a pattern to those who are going to believe on Him for everlasting life.

¹⁷ Now to the King eternal, immortal, invisible, to God who alone is wise, *be* honor and glory forever and ever. Amen.

¹⁸ This command I commit to you, son Timothy, according to the

prophecies previously made concerning you, that by them you may wage the good warfare,

¹⁹ holding *to* faith and a good conscience, which some having rejected, concerning the faith have suffered shipwreck,

²⁰ of whom are Hymenaeus and Alexander, whom I delivered to Satan that they may learn not to blaspheme.

CHAPTER 2

¹ Therefore I exhort first of all that supplications, prayers, intercessions, *and* giving of thanks be made for all men,

² for kings and *for* all who are in authority, that we may lead a quiet and peaceable life in all godliness and honesty.

³ Because, this *is* good and acceptable in the sight of God our Savior,

⁴ who desires all men to be saved and to come to the knowledge of the truth.

⁵ Because *there is* one God and one Mediator between God and men, the Man Christ Jesus,

⁶ who gave Himself a ransom for all, to be testified in due time,

⁷ because of which I was ordained a preacher and an apostle, I am speaking the truth in Christ *and* not lying, a teacher of the Gentiles in faith and truth.

⁸ I desire therefore that the men pray everywhere, lifting up holy hands, without wrath and doubting;

⁹ in like manner also, that the women adorn themselves in modest apparel, with propriety and moderation, not with braided hair or gold or pearls or costly clothing,

¹⁰ but, which is proper for women professing godliness, with good works.

¹¹ Let the woman learn in silence with all submission.

¹² And I do not permit the woman to teach or to have authority over the man, but to be in silence.

¹³ Because Adam was formed first, then Eve.

¹⁴ And Adam was not deceived, but the woman being deceived, fell into transgression.

¹⁵ Nevertheless she will be saved in childbearing if they continue in faith, love, and holiness, with self control.

CHAPTER 3

¹ This *is* a faithful saying: If a man desires the position of a bishop, he desires a good work.

² A bishop then must be blameless, the husband of one wife, temperate, sober, of good behavior, given to hospitality, able to teach;

³ not prone to drink wine, not violent, not greedy for dishonest gain, but gentle, not hostile, not covetous;

⁴ one who rules his own house well, having his children in submission with all reverence

⁵ (because, if a man does not know how to rule his own house, how will

he take care of the church of God?);

⁶ not a novice, lest being puffed up with pride he fall into the same condemnation as the devil.

⁷ Moreover he must have a good testimony among those who are outside, lest he fall into reproach and the snare of the devil.

⁸ Likewise deacons must be reverent, not double tongued, not slaves to wine bingeing, not greedy for dishonest gain,

⁹ holding the mystery of the faith with a pure conscience.

¹⁰ But let these also first be tested; then let them serve as deacons, being *found* blameless.

¹¹ Likewise, *their wives* must *be* reverent, not slanderers, sober, faithful in all things.

¹² Let deacons be the husbands of one wife, ruling their children and their own houses well.

¹³ Because, those who have served well as deacons obtain for themselves a good standing and great boldness in the faith which is in Christ Jesus.

¹⁴ These things I write to you, though I hope to come to you shortly;

¹⁵ but if I am delayed, so that you may know how you ought to conduct yourself in the house of God, which is the church of the living God, the pillar and ground of the truth.

¹⁶ And without controversy great is the mystery of godliness: God was manifested in the flesh, justified in the Spirit, seen by angels, preached among the Gentiles, believed on in the world, received up into glory.

CHAPTER 4

¹ Now the Spirit expressly says that in latter times some will depart from the faith, giving heed to seducing spirits and doctrines of demons,

² speaking lies in hypocrisy, having their own conscience seared with a hot iron,

³ forbidding to marry, *and commanding* to abstain from foods which God has created to be received with thanksgiving by those who believe and know the truth.

⁴ Because, every creature of God *is* good, and nothing is to be refused if it is received with thanksgiving;

⁵ because it is sanctified by the word of God and prayer.

⁶ If you put the brethren in remembrance of these things, you will be a good minister of Jesus Christ, nourished in the words of faith and of the good doctrine which you have carefully pursued.

⁷ But reject profane and old wives' fables, and *instead* exercise yourself toward godliness.

⁸ Because, bodily exercise profits a little, but godliness is profitable for all things, having promise of the life that now is and of that which is to come.

⁹ This is a faithful saying and worthy of all acceptance.

¹⁰ Because, to this end we both labor and suffer reproach, because we trust in the living God, who is the Savior of all men, especially of those who believe.
¹¹ These things command and teach.
¹² Let no one despise your youth, but be an example to the believers in word, in conduct, in love, in spirit, in faith, in purity.
¹³ Until I come, give attention to reading, to exhortation, to doctrine.
¹⁴ Do not neglect the gift that is in you, which was given to you by prophecy with the laying on of the hands of the eldership.
¹⁵ Meditate on these things; give yourself entirely to them, that your progress may be evident to all.
¹⁶ Take heed to yourself and to the doctrine. Continue in them, because in doing this you will save both yourself and those who hear you.

CHAPTER 5

¹ Do not rebuke an older man, but exhort *him* as a father, younger men as brethren,
² older women as mothers, *and* younger women as sisters, with all purity.
³ Honor widows who are truly widows.
⁴ But if any widow has children or grandchildren, let them first learn to show piety at home and to repay their parents; because, this is good and acceptable before God.
⁵ Now she who is truly a widow, and desolate, trusts in God and continues in supplications and prayers night and day.
⁶ But she who lives in pleasure is dead while she lives.
⁷ And these things give in commands, that they may be blameless.
⁸ But if anyone does not provide for his own, and especially for those of his household, he has denied the faith and is worse than an unbeliever.
⁹ Do not let a widow under sixty years old be taken into the number, and not unless she has been the wife of one man,
¹⁰ well reported for good works: if she has brought up children, if she has lodged strangers, if she has washed the saints' feet, if she has relieved the afflicted, if she has diligently followed every good work.
¹¹ But refuse the younger widows; because, when they have, begun to grow immoral against Christ, they desire to marry,
¹² having damnation because they have cast off their first faith.
¹³ And besides they learn *to be* idle, wandering about from house to house, and not only idle but also gossips and busybodies, speaking things which they ought not.
¹⁴ Therefore I desire that the younger women marry, bear children, manage the house, give no opportunity to the adversary to

speak reproachfully.

¹⁵ Because, some have already turned aside after Satan.

¹⁶ If any believing man or woman has widows, let them relieve them, and do not let the church be burdened, that it may relieve those who are truly widows.

¹⁷ Let the older men who rule well be counted worthy of double honor, especially those who labor in the word and doctrine.

¹⁸ Because, the Scripture says, "You shall not muzzle an ox while it treads out the grain," and, "The laborer *is* worthy of his wages."

¹⁹ Do not receive an accusation against an older man except from two or three witnesses.

²⁰ Those who are sinning rebuke in the presence of all, that others also may have reverence.

²¹ I command *you* before God and the Lord Jesus Christ and the elect angels that you observe these things without prejudice, doing nothing with personal favoritism.

²² Do not lay hands on anyone hastily, nor be a partaker in other people's sins; keep yourself pure.

²³ No longer drink *only* water, but use a little grape juice for your stomach's sake and your frequent weaknesses.

²⁴ Some men's sins are clearly evident, preceding them to judgment, but those of some *men* follow afterwards.

²⁵ Likewise also, the good works *of some* are clearly manifest beforehand, and those that are otherwise cannot be hidden.

CHAPTER 6

¹ Let as many servants as are under the yoke count their own masters worthy of all honor, so that the name of God and *His* doctrine may not be blasphemed.

² And those who have believing masters, let them not despise *them* because they are brethren, but rather serve *them* because those who are benefited are faithful and beloved. Teach and exhort these things.

³ If anyone teaches otherwise and does not consent to wholesome words, *even* the words of our Lord Jesus Christ, and to the doctrine which is according to godliness,

⁴ he is proud, knowing nothing, but is obsessed with disputes and arguments over words, from which come envy, strife, reviling, evil suspicions,

⁵ useless disputations of men of corrupt minds and destitute of the truth, who suppose that gain is godliness. From such withdraw yourself.

⁶ Now godliness with contentment is great gain.

⁷ Because, we brought nothing into *this* world, *and it is* certain we can carry nothing out.

⁸ And having food and clothing, with these we should be content.

⁹ But those who desire to be rich fall into temptation and a snare,

and into many foolish and harmful lusts which drown men in destructtion and perdition.

¹⁰ Because, the love of money is the root of all evil, for which some have strayed from the faith in their covetousness, and pierced themselves through with many sorrows.

¹¹ But you, O man of God, flee these things and pursue righteousness, godliness, faith, love, patience, meekness.

¹² Fight the good fight of faith, lay hold on eternal life, to which you were also called and have confessed a good confession before of many witnesses.

¹³ I command you in the sight of God who gives life to all things, and *before* Christ Jesus who witnessed a good confession before Pontius Pilate,

¹⁴ that you keep *this* commandment without spot, blameless until the appearing of our Lord Jesus Christ,

¹⁵ which He will reveal in His own timeframe, *who is* the blessed and only Potentate, the King of kings and Lord of lords,

¹⁶ who alone has immortality, dwelling in unapproachable light, whom no man has seen or can see, to whom *be* honor and everlasting power. Amen.

¹⁷ Command those who are rich in this present age not to be arrogant, nor to trust in uncertain riches but in the living God, who gives us richly all things to enjoy.

¹⁸ That they do good, that they be rich in good works, ready to distribute, willing to share,

¹⁹ storing up for themselves a good foundation for the time to come, that they may lay hold on eternal life.

²⁰ O Timothy! Guard that which was committed to your trust, avoiding profane *and* idle babblings and contradictions of what is falsely called science,

²¹ by professing it some have strayed concerning the faith. Grace *be* with you. Amen.

The first letter to Timothy was written from Laodicea, which is the largest city of Phrygia Pacatiana.

THE SECOND LETTER OF PAUL THE APOSTLE TO
TIMOTHY

CHAPTER 1

¹ Paul, an apostle of Jesus Christ by the will of God, according to the promise of life which is in Christ Jesus,

² To Timothy, *my* dearly beloved son. Grace, mercy, and peace from God the Father and Christ Jesus our Lord.

³ I thank God, whom I serve with a pure conscience, *as my* forefathers did, that without ceasing I remember you in my prayers night and day,

⁴ greatly desiring to see you, being mindful of your tears, that I may be filled with joy,

⁵ when I call to remembrance the genuine faith that is in you, which dwelt first in your grandmother Lois and your mother Eunice, and I am persuaded is in you also.

⁶ Therefore I remind you to stir up the gift of God which is in you through the laying on of my hands.

⁷ Because, God has not given us the spirit of fear, but of power and of love and of a sound mind.

⁸ Therefore do not be ashamed of the testimony of our Lord, nor of me His prisoner, but share with me in the afflictions for the gospel according to the power of God,

⁹ who has saved us and called *us* with a holy calling, not according to our works, but according to His own purpose and grace which was given to us in Christ Jesus before the ages began,

¹⁰ but has now been revealed by the appearing of our Savior Jesus Christ, who has abolished death and brought life and immortality to light through the gospel,

¹¹ to which I was appointed a preacher, an apostle, and a teacher of the Gentiles.

¹² For this reason I also suffer these things; nevertheless I am not ashamed, because I know whom I have believed and am persuaded that He is able to keep what I have committed to Him until that Day.

¹³ Hold fast the pattern of sound words which you have heard from me, in faith and love which are in Christ Jesus.

¹⁴ That good thing which was committed to you, keep by the Holy Spirit who dwells in us.

¹⁵ This you know, that all those in Asia have turned away from me, among whom are Phygellus and Hermogenes.

¹⁶ The Lord grant mercy to the household of Onesiphorus, because he often refreshed me, and was not ashamed of my chain;

¹⁷ but when he was in Rome, he sought me out very diligently and found *me*.

¹⁸ The Lord grant to him that he

may find mercy from the Lord in that Day, and you know very well how many ways he ministered to me at Ephesus.

CHAPTER 2

[1] You therefore, my son, be strong in the grace that is in Christ Jesus.

[2] And the things that you have heard from me among many witnesses, commit the same to faithful men who will be able to teach others also.

[3] You therefore endure hardship as a good soldier of Jesus Christ.

[4] No one engaged in warfare entangles himself with the affairs of *this life*, that he may please him who enlisted him as a soldier.

[5] And likewise if anyone competes in athletics, he is not crowned unless he competes according to the rules.

[6] The hardworking farmer must be first to partake of the crops.

[7] Consider what I say, and may the Lord give you understanding in all things.

[8] Remember that Jesus Christ, of the seed of David, was raised from the dead according to my gospel,

[9] for which I suffer trouble as an evildoer, *even* to the point of chains; but the word of God is not bound.

[10] Therefore I endure all things for the sake of the elect, that they also may obtain the salvation which is in Christ Jesus with eternal glory.

[11] *This is* a faithful saying: because if we died with Him, we will also live with *Him*.

[12] If we suffer, we will also reign with *Him*. If we deny Him, He also will deny us.

[13] If we are faithless, He remains faithful; He cannot deny Himself.

[14] Remind *them* of these things, commanding *them* before the Lord not to strive about words to no profit, to the ruin of the hearers.

[15] Study to present yourself approved to God, a worker who does not need to be ashamed, rightly dividing the word of truth.

[16] But shun profane *and* vain babblings, because they will increase to more ungodliness.

[17] And their word will eat like gangrene. Hymenaeus and Philetus are of this sort,

[18] who have strayed concerning the truth, saying that the resurrection is already past; and they overthrow the faith of some.

[19] Nevertheless the foundation of God stands firm, having this seal: "The Lord knows those who are His," and, "Let everyone who names the name of Christ depart from iniquity."

[20] But in a great house there are not only vessels of gold and silver, but also of wood and clay, some for honor and some for dishonor.

[21] Therefore if anyone cleanses himself from the latter, he will be a vessel for honor, sanctified and useful for the Master, *and* prepared for every good work.

[22] Flee youthful lusts also; but pur-

sue righteousness, faith, love, peace with those who call on the Lord out of a pure heart.

²³ But avoid foolish and ignorant disputes, knowing that they generate strife.

²⁴ And a servant of the Lord must not be hostile but be gentle to all *people*, able to teach, patient,

²⁵ in humility correcting those who are in opposition, if God perhaps will grant them repentance, so that they may know the truth,

²⁶ and that they may come to their senses and *escape* the snare of the devil, having been taken captive by him to do his will.

CHAPTER 3

¹ Also know this, that in the last days perilous times will come:

² Because, men will be lovers of themselves, covetous, boasters, proud, blasphemers, disobedient to parents, unthankful, unholy,

³ without natural affection, covenant breakers, slanderers, without self control, brutal, despisers of those who are good,

⁴ traitors, headstrong, haughty, lovers of pleasure rather than lovers of God,

⁵ having a form of godliness but denying its power. And from such *people* turn away!

⁶ Because, of this sort are those who creep into households and make captives of gullible women loaded down with sins, led away by various lusts,

⁷ always learning and never able to come to the knowledge of the truth.

⁸ Now as Jannes and Jambres resisted Moses, so do these also resist the truth: men of corrupt minds, disapproved concerning the faith;

⁹ but they will progress no further, because their folly will be manifest to all *people*, as theirs also was.

¹⁰ But you have fully followed my doctrine, manner of life, purpose, faith, longsuffering, love, perseverance,

¹¹ persecutions, afflictions, which happened to me at Antioch, at Iconium, at Lystra, what persecutions I endured, but the Lord delivered me out of *them* all.

¹² Yes, and all who desire to live godly in Christ Jesus will suffer persecution.

¹³ But evil men and seducers will grow worse and worse, deceiving and being deceived.

¹⁴ But you must continue in the things which you have learned and been assured of, knowing from whom you have learned *them*,

¹⁵ and that from childhood you have known the Holy Scriptures, which are able to make you wise for salvation through faith which is in Christ Jesus.

¹⁶ All Scripture *is* given by inspiration of God, and *is* profitable for doctrine, for reproof, for correction, for instruction in righteousness,

¹⁷ that the man of God may be per-

fect, thoroughly equipped for every good work.

CHAPTER 4

¹ I command *you* therefore before God and the Lord Jesus Christ, who will judge the living and the dead at His appearing and His kingdom:

² Preach the word! Be ready in season and out of season. Convince, rebuke, exhort, with all longsuffering and doctrine.

³ Because, the time will come when they will not endure sound doctrine, but according to their own desires, they will heap up for themselves teachers, having itching ears,

⁴ and they will turn their ears away from the truth, and will be turned aside to fables.

⁵ But you be watchful in all things, endure afflictions, do the work of an evangelist, make your ministry complete.

⁶ Because, I am now ready to be offered, and the time of my departure is at hand.

⁷ I have fought the good fight, I have finished *my* race, I have kept the faith.

⁸ After this, there is laid up for me the crown of righteousness, which the Lord, the righteous Judge, will give me at that Day, and not to me only but also to all who love His appearing.

⁹ Be diligent to come to me quickly;

¹⁰ because Demas has forsaken me, having loved this present world, and has departed for Thessalonica, Crescens for Galatia, Titus for Dalmatia.

¹¹ Only Luke is with me. Get Mark and bring him with you, because he is profitable to me for the ministry.

¹² And Tychicus I have sent to Ephesus.

¹³ When you come, bring the cloak *with* you that I left with Carpus at Troas, and the books, *but* especially the parchments.

¹⁴ Alexander the coppersmith did me much evil. May the Lord repay him according to his works.

¹⁵ You also must beware of him, because he has greatly resisted our words.

¹⁶ At my first defense no one stood with me, but everyone forsook me. *I ask God* that it may not be charged against them.

¹⁷ But the Lord stood with me and strengthened me, so that through me the preaching might be fully known, and *that* all the Gentiles might hear. Also I was delivered out of the mouth of the lion.

¹⁸ And the Lord will deliver me from every evil work and will preserve *me* for His heavenly kingdom. To Him *be* glory forever and ever. Amen!

¹⁹ Greet Prisca and Aquila, and the household of Onesiphorus.

²⁰ Erastus stayed in Corinth, but Trophimus I have left in Miletus sick.

²¹ Do your utmost to come before winter. Eubulus greets you, as well

as Pudens, Linus, Claudia, and all the brethren.

²² The Lord Jesus Christ *be* with your spirit. Grace *be* with all of you. Amen.

The second *letter* to Timothy, ordained the first bishop of the church of the Ephesians, was written from Rome, when Paul was brought before Nero the second time.

THE LETTER OF PAUL TO

TITUS

CHAPTER 1

¹ Paul, a servant of God and an apostle of Jesus Christ, according to the faith of God's elect and the acknowledgment of the truth which is according to godliness,

² in hope of eternal life which God, who cannot lie, promised before the ages began,

³ but has in due time manifested His word through preaching, which is committed to me according to the commandment of God our Savior;

⁴ To Titus, *my* own son according to the common faith: Grace, mercy, *and* peace from God the Father and the Lord Jesus Christ our Savior.

⁵ I left you in Crete for this purpose, that you should set in order the things that are lacking, and ordain elders in every city as I had appointed you.

⁶ If any is blameless, the husband of one wife, having faithful children not accused of riotous behavior or insubordination.

⁷ Because, a bishop must be blameless, as a steward of God, not self willed, not hostile, not prone to drink wine, not violent, not greedy for dishonest gain,

⁸ but a lover of hospitality, a lover of good men, sober, just, holy, self controlled,

⁹ holding fast the faithful word as he has been taught, that he may be able, by sound doctrine, both to exhort and convict those who contradict.

¹⁰ Because, there are many insubordinate, idle talkers, and deceivers, especially those of the circumcision,

¹¹ whose mouths must be stopped, who subvert entire households, teaching things which they ought not *to*, for the sake of dishonest gain.

¹² One of them, *even* a prophet of their own, said, "The Cretans *are* always liars, evil beasts, lazy gluttons."

¹³ This testimony is true. Therefore rebuke them sharply, that they may be sound in the faith,

¹⁴ not giving heed to Jewish fables and commandments of men who turn from the truth.

¹⁵ To the pure all things *are* pure, but to those who are defiled and unbelieving nothing *is* pure; but even their mind and conscience are defiled.

¹⁶ They profess that they know God, but in works they deny *Him*, being abominable, disobedient, and disqualified for every good work.

CHAPTER 2

¹ But as for you, speak the things which are proper for sound doc-

trine:

² that the older men be sober, reverent, self controlled, sound in faith, in love, in patience;

³ the older women likewise, that they demonstrate holiness in behavior, not slanderers, not slaves to wine bingeing, teachers of good things;

⁴ that they may teach the young women to be sober, to love their husbands, to love their children,

⁵ *to be* discreet, chaste, homemakers, good, obedient to their own husbands, that the word of God may not be blasphemed.

⁶ Likewise, exhort the young men to be sober minded,

⁷ in all things showing yourself to be a pattern of good works; in doctrine *showing* incorruptibility reverence, integrity,

⁸ sound speech that cannot be condemned, that one who is an opponent may be ashamed, having no evil thing to say of you.

⁹ *Exhort* servants to be obedient to their own masters, *and* to be well pleasing in all *things*, not answering back,

¹⁰ not stealing, but showing all good fidelity, that they may adorn the doctrine of God our Savior in all things.

¹¹ Because, the grace of God that brings salvation has appeared to all men,

¹² teaching us that, denying ungodliness and worldly lusts, we should live soberly, righteously, and godly in the present age,

¹³ looking for that blessed hope and the glorious appearing of the great God even our Savior Jesus Christ,

¹⁴ who gave Himself for us, that He might redeem us from all iniquity and purify for Himself His own special people, zealous for good works.

¹⁵ Speak these things, exhort, and rebuke with all authority. Let no one despise you.

CHAPTER 3

¹ Remind them to be subject to rulers and authorities, to obey magistrates, to be ready for every good work,

² to speak evil of no one, not hostile *but* gentle, showing all meekness to all men.

³ Because, we ourselves were also once foolish, disobedient, deceived, serving various lusts and pleasures, living in malice and envy, hateful *and* hating one another.

⁴ But when the kindness and the love of God our Savior toward man appeared,

⁵ not by works of righteousness which we have done, but according to His mercy He saved us, through the washing of regeneration and renewing of the Holy Spirit,

⁶ whom He poured out on us abundantly through Jesus Christ our Savior,

⁷ that having been justified by His grace we should become heirs according to the hope of eternal

life.

⁸ *This is* a faithful saying, and these things I want you to affirm constantly, that those who have believed in God should be careful to maintain good works. These things are good and profitable to men.

⁹ But avoid foolish disputes, genealogies, contentions, and strivings about the law; because they are unprofitable and vain.

¹⁰ A person who is a heretic reject after the first and second admonition,

¹¹ knowing that such a person is warped and sinning, being self condemned.

¹² When I send Artemas to you, or Tychicus, be diligent to come to me at Nicopolis, as I have decided to spend the winter there.

¹³ Send Zenas the lawyer and Apollos on their journey with care, that they may lack nothing.

¹⁴ And let our *people* also learn to maintain good works for necessary uses, that they may not be unfruitful.

¹⁵ All who are with me greet you. Greet those who love us in the faith. Grace *be* with you all. Amen.

It was written to Titus, ordained the first bishop of the church of the Cretians, from Nicopolis of Macedonia.

THE LETTER OF PAUL TO

PHILEMON

CHAPTER 1

¹ Paul, a prisoner of Jesus Christ, and Timothy *our* brother, to Philemon our beloved friend, and fellow laborer,

² to *our* beloved Apphia, Archippus our fellow soldier, and to the church in your house:

³ Grace to you and peace from God our Father and the Lord Jesus Christ.

⁴ I thank my God, making mention of you always in my prayers,

⁵ hearing of your love and faith which you have toward the Lord Jesus and toward all *the* saints,

⁶ that the sharing of your faith may become effectual by acknowledging every good thing that is in you in Christ Jesus.

⁷ Because, we have great joy and consolation in your love, because, the hearts of the saints have been refreshed by you, brother.

⁸ Therefore, although I could be very bold in Christ to command you that which is appropriate,

⁹ yet for love's sake I rather make request of you, being such a one as Paul the aged, and now also a prisoner of Jesus Christ:

¹⁰ I make request of you for my son Onesimus, whom I have begotten *while* in my chains,

¹¹ who was formerly unprofitable to you, but is now profitable to you and to me.

¹² Whom I have sent again. Therefore you receive him, that is, my own heart,

¹³ whom I would have kept with me, that in your position, he might have ministered to me in the chains of the gospel.

¹⁴ But I did not want to do anything without your consent, that your goodness might not be of obligation, but voluntary.

¹⁵ Because, perhaps he departed for a season for this *reason*, that you might receive him forever,

¹⁶ not now as a servant, but more than a servant, a beloved brother, especially to me but how much more to you, both in the flesh and in the Lord?

¹⁷ If you count me as a partner, receive him as you would me.

¹⁸ If he has wronged you, or owes *you* anything, put that on my account.

¹⁹ I Paul have written *this* with my own hand, I will repay *it*, not to mention to you how you also owe to me even your own lives.

²⁰ Yes, brother, let me have joy from you in the Lord; refresh my heart in the Lord.

²¹ Having confidence in your obedience, I wrote to you, knowing that you will also do *even* more than I say.

²² But, meanwhile, prepare *for* me a guest room also, because I trust that through the prayers of you all I shall be given to you all.

²³ Epaphras, my fellow prisoner in Christ Jesus, greets you,

²⁴ *also* Mark, Aristarchus, Demas, Luke, my fellow laborers.

²⁵ The grace of our Lord Jesus Christ *be* with your spirit. Amen.

Written from Rome to Philemon, by Onesimus a servant.

THE LETTER OF PAUL THE APOSTLE TO THE
HEBREWS

CHAPTER 1

¹ God, who at various times and in diverse ways spoke in time past to the fathers through the prophets,

² has in these last days spoken to us by *His* Son, whom He has appointed heir of all things, by whom also He made the ages;

³ who being the brightness of *His* glory and the express image of His person, and upholding all things by the word of His power, when He had by Himself purged our sins, sat down at the right hand of the Majesty on high,

⁴ being made so much better than the angels, as He has by inheritance obtained a more excellent name than they.

⁵ Because, to which of the angels did He ever say: "You are My Son, today I have begotten You"? And again: "I will be to Him a Father, and He will be to Me a Son"?

⁶ And again when He brings in the firstborn into the world, He says: "Let all the angels of God worship Him."

⁷ And of the angels He says: "Who makes His angels spirits and His ministers a flame of fire."

⁸ But to the Son *He says*: "Your throne, O God, *is* forever and ever; a scepter of righteousness *is* the scepter of Your kingdom.

⁹ You have loved righteousness and hated iniquity; Therefore God, *even* Your God, has anointed You with the oil of gladness above Your companions."

¹⁰ And: "You, LORD, in the beginning laid the foundation of the earth, and the heavens are the work of Your hands.

¹¹ They will perish, but You remain; and they will all grow old like clothing;

¹² And like a cloak You will fold them up, and they will be changed. But You are the same, and Your years will not fail."

¹³ But to which of the angels has He ever said: "Sit at My right hand, until I make Your enemies Your footstool"?

¹⁴ Are they not all ministering spirits sent forth to minister for those who will inherit salvation?

CHAPTER 2

¹ Therefore we ought to earnestly pay attention to the things we have heard, lest at any time we should let *them* slip *away*.

² Because, if the word spoken through angels proved steadfast, and every transgression and disobedience received a just reward,

³ how shall we escape if we neglect so great a salvation, which at the first began to be spoken by the

Lord, and was confirmed to us by those who heard *Him*,

⁴ God also bearing *them* witness both with signs and wonders, with various miracles, and gifts of the Holy Spirit, according to His own will?

⁵ Because, He has not put the world to come, of which we speak, in subjection to angels.

⁶ But one testified in a certain place, saying: "What is man that You are mindful of him, or the son of man that You visit him?

⁷ You have made him a little lower than the angels; You have crowned him with glory and honor, and set him over the works of Your hands.

⁸ You have put all things in subject-tion under his feet." Because, in that He put all in subjection under him, He left nothing *that* is not put under him. But now we do not yet see all things put under him.

⁹ But we see Jesus, who was made a little lower than the angels, for the suffering of death crowned with glory and honor, that He, by the grace of God, might taste death for everyone.

¹⁰ Because, it was fitting for Him, for whom *are* all things and by whom *are* all things, in bringing many sons to glory, to make the captain of their salvation perfect through sufferings.

¹¹ Because, both He who sanctifies and those who are being sanctified *are* all of one, for which reason He is not ashamed to call them brethren,

¹² saying: "I will declare Your name to My brethren; in the midst of the church I will sing praise to You."

¹³ And again: "I will put My trust in Him." And again: "Here am I and the children whom God has given Me."

¹⁴ Inasmuch then as the children are partakers of flesh and blood, He Himself likewise shared in the same, that through death He might destroy him who had the power of death, that is, the devil,

¹⁵ and deliver those who through fear of death were all their lifetime subject to bondage.

¹⁶ Because indeed He did not take upon *Himself the nature* of angels, but He took on *himself* the seed of Abraham.

¹⁷ Therefore, in all things He had to be made like *His* brethren, that He might be a merciful and faithful High Priest in things *pertaining* to God, to make reconciliation for the sins of the people.

¹⁸ Because, in that He Himself has suffered, being tempted, He is able to help those who are tempted.

CHAPTER 3

¹ Therefore, holy brethren, par-takers of the heavenly calling, consider the Apostle and High Priest of our confession, Christ Jesus,

² who was faithful to Him who appointed Him, as Moses also *was faithful* in all His house.

³ Because, this *Man* was counted

worthy of more glory than Moses, inasmuch as He who built the house has more honor than the house.

⁴ Because every house is built by someone, but He who built all things *is* God.

⁵ And truly Moses *was* faithful in all His house as a servant, for a testimony of those things which would be spoken *afterward*,

⁶ but Christ as a Son over His own house, whose house we are if we hold firmly to the confidence and the rejoicing of the hope firmly to the end.

⁷ Therefore, as the Holy Spirit says: "Today, if you will hear His voice,

⁸ do not harden your hearts as in the provocation, in the day of trial in the wilderness,

⁹ where your fathers tested Me, tried Me, and saw My works forty years.

¹⁰ Therefore I was angry with that generation, and said, 'They always deceive in *their* heart, and they have not known My ways.'

¹¹ So I swore in My wrath, 'They will not enter into My rest.' "

¹² Beware, brethren, lest there be in any of you an evil heart of unbelief in departing from the living God;

¹³ but exhort one another daily, while it is called "Today," lest any of you be hardened through the deceitfulness of sin.

¹⁴ Because, we have become partakers of Christ if we hold the beginning of our confidence firmly to the end,

¹⁵ while it is said: "Today, if you will hear His voice, do not harden your hearts as in the provocation."

¹⁶ Because some, having heard, did provoke. However not all who came out of Egypt by Moses.

¹⁷ Now with whom was He angry forty years? *Was it* not with those who sinned, whose corpses fell in the wilderness?

¹⁸ And to whom did He swear that they would not enter His rest, but to those who did not believe?

¹⁹ So we see that they could not enter in because of unbelief.

CHAPTER 4

¹ Therefore, since a promise remains of entering His rest, let us have reverence lest any of you seem to have come short of it.

² Because, the gospel was preached to us as well as to them; but the word preached did not profit them, not being mixed with faith in those who heard *it*.

³ Because, we who have believed do enter into rest, as He has said: "So I swore in My wrath, 'If they will enter into My rest,'" although the works were finished from the foundation of the world.

⁴ Because, He spoke in a certain place of the seventh *day* in this way: "And God rested on the seventh day from all His works";

⁵ and again in this *place*: "If they will enter into My rest."

⁶ Since therefore it remains that some must enter it, and those to

whom it was first preached did not enter because of unbelief,

⁷ again He declares a certain day, saying in David, "Today," after such a long time, as it has been said: "Today, if you will hear His voice, do not harden your hearts."

⁸ Because, if Joshua had given them rest, then He would not have afterward spoken about another day.

⁹ There remains therefore a rest for the people of God.

¹⁰ Because, he who has entered His rest has himself also ceased from his own works as God *did* from His.

¹¹ Therefore let us labor to enter into that rest, lest anyone fall according to the same example of unbelief.

¹² Because, the word of God *is* living and powerful, and sharper than any two edged sword, piercing even to the division of soul and spirit, and of the joints and marrow, and is a discerner of the thoughts and intents of the heart.

¹³ Neither is there any creature that is not manifest in His sight, but all things *are* naked and open to the eyes of Him to whom we *must give* account.

¹⁴ Seeing then that we have a great High Priest who has passed into the heavens, Jesus the Son of God, let us hold fast *our* confession.

¹⁵ Because, we do not have a High Priest who cannot sympathize with our weaknesses, but was in all points tempted as *we are, yet* without sin.

¹⁶ Let us therefore come boldly to the throne of grace, that we may obtain mercy and find grace to help in time of need.

CHAPTER 5

¹ Because, every high priest taken from among men is ordained for men in things *pertaining* to God, that he may offer both gifts and sacrifices for sins.

² He can have compassion on those who are ignorant and on those who are going astray, since he himself is also subject to weakness.

³ And because of this he ought, just as for the people so also for himself, to offer for sins.

⁴ And no man takes this honor to himself, but he who is called by God, just as Aaron *was*.

⁵ So also Christ did not glorify Himself to become a High Priest, but *it was* He who said to Him: "You are My Son, today I have begotten You."

⁶ As He also says in another place: "You are a priest forever according to the order of Melchizedek";

⁷ who, in the days of His flesh, when He had offered up prayers and supplications, with strong cries and tears to Him who was able to save Him from death, and was heard because He had respect,

⁸ though He was a Son, *yet* He learned obedience by the things which He suffered.

⁹ And having been perfected, He became the author of eternal salva-

tion to all who obey Him,

¹⁰ called by God as High Priest "according to the order of Melchizedek,"

¹¹ of whom we have much to say, and hard to explain, since you have become dull of hearing.

¹² Because, though by this time you ought to be teachers, you require that someone teaches you again what *are* the first principles of the oracles of God; and you have become such as have need of milk and not solid food.

¹³ Because, everyone who partakes *only* of milk is unskilled in the word of righteousness, because he is a babe.

¹⁴ But solid food belongs to those who are of full age, *that is*, those who by reason of use have their senses exercised to discern both good and evil.

CHAPTER 6

¹ Therefore, leaving the *elementary* principles of the doctrine of Christ, let us go on to perfection, not laying again the foundation of repentance from dead works and of faith toward God,

² of the doctrine of baptisms, of laying on of hands, of resurrection of the dead, and of eternal judgment.

³ And this we will do if God permits.

⁴ Because, *it is* impossible for those who were once enlightened, and have tasted the heavenly gift, and have become partakers of the Holy Spirit,

⁵ and have tasted the good word of God and the powers of the age to come,

⁶ if they shall fall away, to renew them again to repentance, since they crucify again for themselves the Son of God, and put *Him* to an open shame.

⁷ Because, the earth which drinks in the rain that often comes upon it, and bears herbs useful for those by whom it is cultivated, receives blessing from God;

⁸ but that which bears thorns and briers *is* rejected and is near to being cursed, whose end *is* to be burned.

⁹ But, beloved, we are persuaded of better things concerning you, yes, things that accompany salvation, though we speak in this manner.

¹⁰ Because, God *is* not unrighteous to forget your work and labor of love which you have shown toward His name, in that you have ministered to the saints, and do minister.

¹¹ And we desire that each one of you show the same diligence to the full assurance of hope until the end,

¹² that you do not become slothful, but followers of those who through faith and patience inherit the promises.

¹³ Because, when God made a promise to Abraham, because He could swear by no one greater, He swore by Himself,

¹⁴ saying, "Surely blessing I will

bless you, and multiplying I will multiply you."

¹⁵ And so, after he had patiently endured, he obtained the promise.

¹⁶ Because, men indeed swear by the greater, and an oath for confirmation is for them an end of all dispute.

¹⁷ In this way, God, determining to show more abundantly to the heirs of promise the immutability of His counsel, confirmed *it* by an oath,

¹⁸ that by two immutable things, in which *it is* impossible for God to lie, we might have strong consolation, who have fled for refuge to lay hold of the hope set before *us*.

¹⁹ This *hope* we have as an anchor of the soul, both sure and steadfast, and which enters into that which is behind the veil,

²⁰ where the forerunner has entered for us, *even* Jesus, having become High Priest forever according to the order of Melchizedek.

CHAPTER 7

¹ Because, this Melchizedek, king of Salem, priest of the Most High God, who met Abraham returning from the slaughter of the kings and blessed him,

² to whom also Abraham gave a tenth part of all, first being translated as "king of righteousness," and then also king of Salem, that is "king of peace,"

³ without father, without mother, without genealogy, having neither beginning of days nor end of life, but made like the Son of God, remains a priest continually.

⁴ Now consider how great this man *was*, to whom even the patriarch Abraham gave a tenth of the spoils.

⁵ And indeed those who are of the sons of Levi, who receive the office of the priesthood, have a commandment to receive tithes from the people according to the law, that is, from their brethren, though they have come from the loins of Abraham;

⁶ but he whose genealogy is not derived from them received tithes from Abraham and blessed him who had the promises.

⁷ Now beyond all contradiction the lesser is blessed by the better.

⁸ And here mortal men receive tithes, but there he *receives them*, of whom it is witnessed that he lives.

⁹ And Levi also, who receives tithes, paid tithes through Abraham, so to speak,

¹⁰ because he was still in the loins of his father when Melchizedek met him.

¹¹ Therefore, if perfection were through the Levitical priesthood (because under it the people received the law), what further need *was there* that another priest should rise according to the order of Melchizedek, and not be called according to the order of Aaron?

¹² Because, the priesthood being changed, of necessity there is also a change of the law.

¹³ Because, He of whom these things are spoken belongs to another tribe, from which no man has served at the altar.

¹⁴ Because, *it is* evident that our Lord arose out of Judah, of which tribe Moses spoke nothing concerning priesthood.

¹⁵ And it is yet far more evident if, in the likeness of Melchizedek, there arises another priest

¹⁶ who is made, not according to the law of a fleshly commandment, but according to the power of an endless life.

¹⁷ Because He testifies: "You *are* a priest forever according to the order of Melchizedek."

¹⁸ Because, on the one hand there is truly an annulling of the former commandment because of its weakness and unprofitableness,

¹⁹ because, the law made nothing perfect; but the bringing in of a better hope *did*, by which we draw near to God.

²⁰ And inasmuch as *He was* not *made* priest without an oath

²¹ (because, they have become *priests* without an oath, but He with an oath by Him who said to Him: "The LORD has sworn and will not relent, 'You are a priest forever according to the order of Melchizedek' "),

²² by so much more Jesus has become a surety of a better testament.

²³ Also truly there were many priests, because they were prevented by death from continuing.

²⁴ But this *Man*, because He continues forever, has an unchangeable priesthood.

²⁵ Therefore He is also able to save to the uttermost those who come to God by Him, since He always lives to make intercession for them.

²⁶ Because, such a High Priest was fitting for us, *who is* holy, harmless, undefiled, separate from sinners, and has become higher than the heavens;

²⁷ who does not need daily, as those high priests, to offer up sacrifices, first for His own sins and then for the people's, because this He did once when He offered up Himself.

²⁸ Because, the law appoints men as high priests who have weakness, but the word of the oath, which came after the law, *appoints* the Son who is consecrated forever.

CHAPTER 8

¹ Now *this is* the summary of the things we are saying: We have such a High Priest, who is seated at the right hand of the throne of the Majesty in the heavens,

² a Minister of the sanctuary and of the true tabernacle which the Lord set up, and not man.

³ Because, every high priest is ordained to offer both gifts and sacrifices. Therefore *it is* necessary that this Man also have something to offer.

⁴ Because, if He were on earth, He would not be a priest, since there

are priests who offer the gifts according to the law;

⁵ who serve the copy and shadow of the heavenly things, as Moses was admonished by God, when he was about to make the tabernacle. Because, He said, "See *that* you make all things according to the pattern shown you on the mountain."

⁶ But now He has obtained a more excellent ministry, inasmuch as He is also Mediator of a better covenant, which was established on better promises.

⁷ Because, if that first *covenant* had been faultless, then no place would have been sought for a second.

⁸ Because, finding fault with them, He says: "Behold, the days are coming, says the LORD, when I will make a new covenant with the house of Israel and with the house of Judah,

⁹ not according to the covenant that I made with their fathers in the day when I took them by the hand to lead them out of the land of Egypt; because they did not continue in My covenant, and I disregarded them, says the LORD."

¹⁰ Because, this *is* the covenant that I will make with the house of Israel after those days, says the LORD: I will put My laws in their mind and write them on their hearts; and I will be to them a God, and they will be to Me a people.

¹¹ None of them will teach his neighbor, and none his brother, saying, 'Know the LORD,' because all will know Me, from the least of them to the greatest.

¹² Because, I will be merciful to their unrighteousness, and their sins and their iniquities I will remember no more."

¹³ In that He says, "A new *covenant*," He has made the first obsolete. Now that which has become obsolete and has become old *is* ready to vanish away.

CHAPTER 9

¹ Then indeed, even the first *covenant* had ordinances of divine service and the earthly sanctuary.

² Because, a tabernacle was prepared: the first part, in which was the lampstand, the table, and the showbread, which is called the sanctuary;

³ and behind the second veil, the part of the tabernacle which is called the Holiest of All,

⁴ which had the golden censer and the ark of the covenant overlaid on all sides with gold, in which *were* the golden pot that had the manna, Aaron's rod that budded, and the tablets of the covenant;

⁵ and above it were the cherubim of glory overshadowing the mercy seat. Of these things we cannot now speak in detail.

⁶ Now when these things had been prepared like this, the priests always went into the first part of the tabernacle, performing the services *of God*.

⁷ But into the second part the high priest *went* alone once a year, not without blood, which he offered for himself and *for* the errors of the people;

⁸ the Holy Spirit indicating this, that the way into the Holiest of All was not yet made manifest while the first tabernacle was still standing.

⁹ Which *was* symbolic for the present time in which both gifts and sacrifices are offered which could not make him who performed the service perfect in regard to the conscience;

¹⁰ *concerned* only with foods and drinks, various washings, and fleshly ordinances imposed *on them* until the time of reformation.

¹¹ But Christ came as High Priest of the good things to come, with the greater and more perfect tabernacle not made with hands, that is, not of this creation.

¹² Not with the blood of goats and calves, but with His own blood He entered in once into the Holy Place, having obtained eternal redemption *for* us.

¹³ Because, if the blood of bulls and goats and the ashes of a heifer, sprinkling the unclean, sanctifies for the purifying of the flesh,

¹⁴ how much more will the blood of Christ, who through the eternal Spirit offered Himself without spot to God, cleanse your conscience from dead works to serve the living God?

¹⁵ And for this reason He is the Mediator of the new testament, that by means of death, for the redemption of the transgressions *that were* under the first testament, that those who are called may receive the promise of the eternal inheritance.

¹⁶ Because, where there *is* a testament, there must also of necessity be the death of the testator.

¹⁷ Because, a testament *is* in force after men are dead, since it has no force at all while the testator lives.

¹⁸ Therefore not even the first *testament* was dedicated without blood.

¹⁹ Because, when Moses had spoken every precept to all the people according to the law, he took the blood of calves and goats, with water, scarlet wool, and hyssop, and sprinkled both the book itself and all the people,

²⁰ saying, "This *is* the blood of the testament which God has commanded you."

²¹ Then likewise he sprinkled with blood both the tabernacle and all the vessels of the ministry.

²² And according to the law almost all things are purified with blood, and without shedding of blood there is no remission.

²³ Therefore *it was* necessary that the pattern of the things in the heavens should be purified with these, but the heavenly things themselves with better sacrifices than these.

²⁴ Because, Christ has not entered the holy places made with hands, *which are* figures of the true, but into heaven itself, now to appear in the presence of God for us;

²⁵ not that He should offer Himself often, as the high priest enters the Most Holy Place every year with blood of another;

²⁶ He then would have had to suffer often since the foundation of the world; but now, once at the end of the ages, He has appeared to put away sin by the sacrifice of Himself.

²⁷ And as it is appointed for men to die once, but after this the judgment,

²⁸ so Christ was offered once to bear the sins of many. To those who eagerly wait for Him, He will appear a second time, apart from sin, for salvation.

CHAPTER 10

¹ Because the law, having a shadow of the good things to come, *and* not the very image of the things, can never with those same sacrifices, which they offered continually year by year, make those who approach perfect.

² Because then would they not have ceased to be offered? Because, the worshipers, once purified, would have had no more consciousness of sins.

³ But in those *sacrifices there is* again a reminder *made* for sins every year.

⁴ Because *it is* not possible that the blood of bulls and goats could take away sins.

⁵ Therefore, when He came into the world, He said: "Sacrifice and offering You did not desire, but a body You have prepared for Me.

⁶ In burnt offerings and *sacrifices* for sin You had no pleasure.

⁷ Then I said, 'Behold, I have come (in the volume of the book it is written of Me) to do Your will, O God.'"

⁸ Previously saying, "Sacrifice and offering, burnt offerings, and *offerings* for sin You did not desire, nor had pleasure *in them*" (which are offered according to the law),

⁹ then He said, "Behold, I have come to do Your will, O God." He takes away the first that He may establish the second.

¹⁰ By that will, we are sanctified through the offering of the body of Jesus Christ once *for all*.

¹¹ And every priest stands ministering daily and offering repeatedly the same sacrifices, which can never take away sins.

¹² But this Man, after He had offered one sacrifice for sins forever, sat down at the right hand of God,

¹³ from that time waiting until His enemies are made His footstool.

¹⁴ Because by one offering He has perfected forever those who are sanctified.

¹⁵ But the Holy Spirit also witnesses to us; because after that He had said beforehand,

¹⁶ "This *is* the covenant that I will make with them after those days, says the LORD: I will put My laws into their hearts, and in their minds I will write them,"

¹⁷ "Their sins and their iniquities I will remember no more."

¹⁸ Now where there *is* remission of these, *there is* no longer an offering for sin.

¹⁹ Therefore, brethren, having boldness to enter the Holiest by the blood of Jesus,

²⁰ by a new and living way which He consecrated for us, through the veil, that is to say, His flesh,

²¹ and *having* a High Priest over the house of God,

²² let us draw near with a true heart in full assurance of faith, having our hearts sprinkled from an evil conscience and our bodies washed with pure water.

²³ Let us hold fast the confession of *our* faith without wavering, because He who promised *is* faithful.

²⁴ And let us consider one another in order to provoke love and good works,

²⁵ not forsaking the assembling of ourselves together, as *is* the manner of some, but exhorting *one another*, and so much the more as you see the Day approaching.

²⁶ Because, if we sin willfully after we have received the knowledge of the truth, there no longer remains a sacrifice for sins,

²⁷ but a certain fearful expectation of judgment, and fiery indignation which will devour the adversaries.

²⁸ Anyone who has rejected Moses' law died without mercy on the testimony of two or three witnesses.

²⁹ Of how much worse punishment, do you suppose, will he be thought worthy who has trampled the Son of God underfoot, counted the blood of the covenant by which he was sanctified an unholy thing, and insulted the Spirit of grace?

³⁰ Because, we know Him who said, "Vengeance is Mine, I will repay," says the Lord. And again, "The LORD will judge His people."

³¹ *It is* a fearful thing to fall into the hands of the living God.

³² But recall the former days in which, after you were illuminated, you endured a great fight of afflicttions:

³³ partly while you were made a spectacle both by reproaches and afflictions, and partly while you became companions of those who were so treated;

³⁴ because you had compassion on me in my chains, and joyfully accepted the plundering of your goods, knowing in yourselves that you have a better and enduring substance in heaven.

³⁵ Therefore do not cast away your confidence, which has great reward.

³⁶ Because, you have need of endurance, so that after you have done the will of God, you may receive the promise:

³⁷ Because, "Yet a little while, and He who is coming will come and will not delay.
³⁸ Now the just will live by faith; but if *anyone* draws back, My soul will have no pleasure in him."
³⁹ But we are not of those who draw back to perdition, but of those who believe to the saving of the soul.

CHAPTER 11

¹ Now faith is the substance of things hoped for, the evidence of things not seen.
² Because by it the elders obtained a good testimony.
³ Through faith we understand that the ages were framed by the word of God, so that the things which are seen were not made of things which are visible.
⁴ By faith Abel offered to God a more excellent sacrifice than Cain, by which he obtained witness that he was righteous, God testifying of his gifts; and by it he being dead still speaks.
⁵ By faith Enoch was taken away so that he did not see death, "and was not found, because God had taken him"; because before he was taken he had this testimony, that he pleased God.
⁶ But without faith *it is* impossible to please *Him*, because, he who comes to God must believe that He is, and *that* He is a rewarder of those who diligently seek Him.
⁷ By faith Noah, being warned by God of things not yet seen, moved with reverence, prepared an ark for the saving of his household, by which he condemned the world and became heir of the righteousness which is by faith.
⁸ By faith Abraham obeyed when he was called to go out to the place which he would receive as an inheritance. And he went out, not knowing where he was going.
⁹ By faith he dwelt in the land of promise as *in* a foreign country, dwelling in tents with Isaac and Jacob, the heirs with him of the same promise;
¹⁰ because, he waited for the city which has foundations, whose builder and maker *is* God.
¹¹ By faith Sarah herself also received strength to conceive seed, and she bore a child when she was past the age, because she judged Him faithful who had promised.
¹² Therefore from one man, and him as good as dead, were born as *many* as the stars of the sky in multitude, innumerable as the sand which is by the seashore.
¹³ These all died in faith, not having received the promises, but having seen them afar off were persuaded of *them*, embraced *them* and confessed that they were strangers and pilgrims on the earth.
¹⁴ Because those who say such things declare plainly that they seek a homeland.
¹⁵ And truly if they had called to mind that *country* from which they had come out, they would have had

opportunity to return.

¹⁶ But now they desire a better, that is, a heavenly *country*. Therefore God is not ashamed to be called their God, because He has prepared a city for them.

¹⁷ By faith Abraham, when he was tested, offered up Isaac, and he who had received the promises offered up his only begotten *son*,

¹⁸ of whom it was said, "In Isaac your seed will be called,"

¹⁹ concluding that God *was* able to raise *him* up, even from the dead, from which he also received him in a figurative sense.

²⁰ By faith Isaac blessed Jacob and Esau concerning things to come.

²¹ By faith Jacob, when he was dying, blessed both of the sons of Joseph, and worshiped, *leaning* on the top of his staff.

²² By faith Joseph, when he was dying, made mention of the departure of the children of Israel, and gave instructions concerning his bones.

²³ By faith Moses, when he was born, was hidden three months by his parents, because they saw *he was a* beautiful child; and they were not afraid of the king's command.

²⁴ By faith Moses, when he became of age, refused to be called the son of Pharaoh's daughter,

²⁵ choosing rather to suffer affliction with the people of God than to enjoy the passing pleasures of sin,

²⁶ esteeming the reproach of Christ greater riches than the treasures in Egypt; because he looked to the reward.

²⁷ By faith he forsook Egypt, not fearing the wrath of the king; because he endured as seeing Him who is invisible.

²⁸ Through faith he kept the Passover and the sprinkling of blood, lest he who destroyed the firstborn should touch them.

²⁹ By faith they passed through the Red Sea as by dry *land*, whereas the Egyptians, attempting to do so, were drowned.

³⁰ By faith the walls of Jericho fell down after they were encircled for seven days.

³¹ By faith the harlot Rahab did not perish with those who did not believe, when she had received the spies with peace.

³² And what more shall I say? Because, the time would fail me to tell of Gideon and Barak and Samson and Jephthah, also *of* David and Samuel and the prophets:

³³ who through faith subdued kingdoms, worked righteousness, obtained promises, stopped the mouths of lions,

³⁴ quenched the violence of fire, escaped the edge of the sword, out of weakness were made strong, became valiant in battle, turned to flight the armies of the foreigners.

³⁵ women received their dead raised to life again. Others were tortured, not accepting deliverance, that they might obtain a better resurrection.

³⁶ And others had trial of *cruel* mockings and scourgings, yes, and of chains and imprisonment.

³⁷ They were stoned, they were sawn in two, were tempted, were slain with the sword. They wandered about in sheepskins and goatskins, being destitute, afflicted, tormented;

³⁸ of whom the world was not worthy. They wandered in deserts and *in* mountains, *in* dens and caves of the earth.

³⁹ And all these, having obtained a good testimony through faith, did not receive the promise,

⁴⁰ God having provided something better for us, that they should not be made perfect apart from us.

CHAPTER 12

¹ Therefore seeing we also are surrounded by so great a cloud of witnesses, let us lay aside every weight, and the sin which so easily ensnares *us*, and let us run with endurance the race that is set before us,

² looking to Jesus, the author and finisher of *our* faith, who for the joy that was set before Him endured the cross, despising the shame, and has sat down at the right hand of the throne of God.

³ Because, consider Him who endured such hostility from sinners against Himself, lest you become weary and faint in your minds.

⁴ You have not yet resisted to bloodshed, striving against sin.

⁵ And you have forgotten the exhortation which speaks to you as to children: "My son, do not despise the chastening of the LORD, nor be discouraged when you are rebuked by Him;

⁶ Because, whom the Lord loves He chastens, and scourges every son whom He receives."

⁷ If you endure chastening, God deals with you as with sons; because what son is there whom a father does not chasten?

⁸ But if you are without chastening, of which all have become partakers, then you are illegitimate and not sons.

⁹ Furthermore, we have had human fathers who corrected *us*, and we gave *them* respect. Should we not much more readily be in subjection to the Father of spirits and live?

¹⁰ Because, they indeed for a few days chastened *us* as seemed best to them, but He for *our* profit, that *we* may be partakers of His holiness.

¹¹ Now no chastening seems to be joyful for the present, but painful; nevertheless, afterward it yields the peaceable fruit of righteousness to those who have been trained by it.

¹² Therefore strengthen the hands which hang down, and the feeble knees,

¹³ and make straight paths for your feet, so that what is lame may not be turned out of the way, but rather let it be healed.

¹⁴ Pursue peace with all *people*, and

holiness, without which no one will see the Lord;

¹⁵ looking diligently lest anyone fall short of the grace of God; lest any root of bitterness springing up cause trouble, and by this many become defiled;

¹⁶ lest there *be* any fornicator or profane person like Esau, who for one morsel of food sold his birthright.

¹⁷ Because, you know that afterward, when he wanted to inherit the blessing, he was rejected, because he found no place for repentance, though he sought it diligently with tears.

¹⁸ Because, you have not come to the mountain that may be touched and that burned with fire, and to blackness and darkness and tempest,

¹⁹ and the sound of a trumpet and the voice of words, which *voice* those who heard *it* begged that the word should not be spoken to them anymore.

²⁰ (Because, they could not endure what was commanded: "And if so much as a beast touches the mountain, it shall be stoned or shot with an arrow."

²¹ And so terrifying was the sight *that* Moses said, "I am exceedingly afraid and trembling.")

²² But you have come to Mount Zion and to the city of the living God, the heavenly Jerusalem, to an innumerable company of angels,

²³ to the general assembly and church of the firstborn *who* are written in heaven, to God the Judge of all, to the spirits of just men made perfect,

²⁴ to Jesus the Mediator of the new covenant, and to the blood of sprinkling that speaks better things than *that of* Abel.

²⁵ See that you do not refuse Him who speaks. Because, if they did not escape who refused Him who spoke on earth, much more *will* we *not escape* if we turn away from Him who *speaks* from heaven,

²⁶ whose voice then shook the earth; but now He has promised, saying, "Yet once more I shake not only the earth, but also heaven."

²⁷ Now this *phrase*, "Yet once more," indicates the removal of those things that are being shaken, as of things that are made, that the things which cannot be shaken may remain.

²⁸ Therefore, since we are receiving a kingdom which cannot be shaken, let us have grace, by which we may serve God acceptably with respect and godly reverence.

²⁹ Because our God *is* a consuming fire.

CHAPTER 13

¹ Let brotherly love continue.

² Do not forget to entertain strangers, because by *doing so* some have unknowingly entertained angels.

³ Remember the prisoners as if chained with them, *and* those who suffer adversity, since you your-

selves are in the same body.

⁴ Marriage *is* honorable among all, and the bed undefiled; but fornicators and adulterers God will judge.

⁵ *Let your* conduct *be* without covetousness; *and be* content with such things as you have. Because He Himself has said, "I will never leave you nor forsake you."

⁶ So that we may boldly say: "The LORD is my helper, and I will not fear what man shall do to me!"

⁷ Remember your leaders, who have spoken the word of God to you, whose faith follow, considering the outcome of *their* conduct.

⁸ Jesus Christ, the same yesterday, today, and forever.

⁹ Do not be carried about with various and strange doctrines. Because, *it is* good that the heart be established with grace, not with foods which have not profited those who have been occupied with them.

¹⁰ We have an altar from which those who serve the tabernacle have no right to eat.

¹¹ Because, the bodies of those animals, whose blood is brought into the sanctuary by the high priest for sin, are burned outside the camp.

¹² Therefore Jesus also, that He might sanctify the people with His own blood, suffered outside the gate.

¹³ Therefore let us go forth to Him, outside the camp, bearing His reproach.

¹⁴ Because, here we have no continuing city, but we seek the one to come.

¹⁵ Therefore by Him let us continually offer the sacrifice of praise to God, that is, the fruit of *our* lips, giving thanks to His name.

¹⁶ But do not forget to do good and to share, because with such sacrifices God is well pleased.

¹⁷ Obey those who lead you, and be submissive, because they watch out for your souls, as those who must give account. Let them do so with joy and not with grief, because that *is* unprofitable for you.

¹⁸ Pray for us; because, we are confident that we have a good conscience in all things, desiring to live honorably.

¹⁹ But I especially urge *you* to do this, that I may be restored to you the sooner.

²⁰ Now may the God of peace who brought up our Lord Jesus from the dead, that great Shepherd of the sheep, through the blood of the everlasting covenant,

²¹ make you complete in every good work to do His will, working in you what is well pleasing in His sight, through Jesus Christ, to whom *be* glory forever and ever. Amen.

²² And I urge you, brethren, bear with the word of exhortation, because I have written to you in few words.

²³ Know that *our* brother Timothy

has been set free, with whom I shall see you if he comes shortly. ²⁴ Greet all those who rule over you, and all the saints. Those from Italy greet you.

²⁵ Grace *be* with you all. Amen.

Written to the Hebrews from Italy, by Timothy.

THE GENERAL LETTER OF
JAMES

CHAPTER 1

¹ James, a servant of God and of the Lord Jesus Christ, to the twelve tribes which are scattered abroad: Greetings.

² My brethren, count it all joy when you fall into various trials,

³ knowing *this*, that the testing of your faith produces perseverance.

⁴ But let perseverance have *her* perfect work, that you may be perfect and complete, lacking nothing.

⁵ If any of you lacks wisdom, let him ask of God, who gives to all *people* liberally and without reproach, and it will be given to him.

⁶ But let him ask in faith, nothing wavering, because, he who wavers is like a wave of the sea driven and tossed by the wind.

⁷ Because, do not let that man think that he will receive anything from the Lord;

⁸ a double minded man *is* unstable in all his ways.

⁹ Let the lowly brother rejoice in his exaltation,

¹⁰ but the rich in his humiliation, because as a flower of the field he will pass away.

¹¹ Because, no sooner has the sun risen with a burning heat than it withers the grass; its flower falls, and its beautiful appearance perishes. So the rich man likewise will fade away in his ways.

¹² Blessed *is* the man who endures temptation; because, when he has been approved, he will receive the crown of life which the Lord has promised to those who love Him.

¹³ Let no one say when he is tempted, "I am tempted by God"; because, God cannot be tempted by evil, nor does He tempt anyone.

¹⁴ But each one is tempted when he is drawn away by his own lust and enticed.

¹⁵ Then, when lust has conceived, it brings forth sin; and sin, when it is finished, brings forth death.

¹⁶ Do not be deceived, my beloved brethren.

¹⁷ Every good gift and every perfect gift is from above, and comes down from the Father of lights, with whom there is no variation or shadow of turning.

¹⁸ Of His own will He begot us by the word of truth, that we might be a type of firstfruits of His creatures.

¹⁹ So then, my beloved brethren, let every man be swift to hear, slow to speak, slow to wrath;

²⁰ because, the wrath of man does not produce the righteousness of God.

²¹ Therefore lay aside all filthiness and overflow of wickedness, and receive with meekness the implanted word, which is able to save your souls.

²² But be doers of the word, and not hearers only, deceiving yourselves.
²³ because, if anyone is a hearer of the word and not a doer, he is like a man observing his natural face in a mirror;
²⁴ because, he observes himself, goes away, and immediately forgets what kind of man he was.
²⁵ But he who looks into the perfect law of liberty and continues *in it*, and is not a forgetful hearer but a doer of the work, this one will be blessed in what he does.
²⁶ If anyone among you seems to be religious, and does not bridle his tongue but deceives his own heart, this one's religion *is* vain.
²⁷ Pure and undefiled religion before God and the Father is this: to visit orphans and widows in their affliction, *and* to keep oneself unspotted from the world.

CHAPTER 2

¹ My brethren, do not hold the faith of our Lord Jesus Christ, *the Lord* of glory, with personal favoritism.
² Because, if there should come into your assembly a man with a gold ring, in fine apparel, and there should also come in a poor man in filthy clothes,
³ and you have respect to the one wearing the fine clothes and say to him, "You sit here in a good place," and say to the poor *person*, "You stand there," or, "Sit here at my footstool,"
⁴ have you not shown personal favoritism among yourselves, and have become judges with evil thoughts?
⁵ Listen, my beloved brethren: Has not God *also* chosen the poor of this world to be rich in faith and heirs of the kingdom which He promised to those who love Him?
⁶ But you have despised the poor. Do not *also* the rich oppress you and drag you before the courts?
⁷ Do they not blaspheme that worthy name by which you are called?
⁸ If you fulfill the royal law according to the Scripture, "You shall love your neighbor as yourself," you do well;
⁹ but if you show personal favoritism, you commit sin, and are convicted by the law as transgressors.
¹⁰ Because, whoever shall keep the entire law, and yet stumble in one *point*, he is guilty of all.
¹¹ Because, He who said, "Do not commit adultery," also said, "Do not murder." Now if you do not commit adultery, but you do murder, you have become a transgresssor of the law.
¹² So speak and so do as those who will be judged by the law of liberty.
¹³ Because, judgment is without mercy to the one who has shown no mercy. And mercy triumphs over judgment.
¹⁴ What *does* it profit, my brethren, if someone says he has faith but does not have works? Can faith save

him?

¹⁵ If a brother or sister is naked and destitute of daily food,

¹⁶ and one of you says to them, "Depart in peace, be warmed and filled," but you do not give them the things which are needed for the body, what *does it* profit?

¹⁷ So likewise faith by itself, if it does not have works, is dead.

¹⁸ Yes, someone may say, "You have faith, and I have works." Show me your faith without your works, and I will show you my faith by my works.

¹⁹ You believe that there is one God. You do well. Even the demons believe, and tremble!

²⁰ But do you want to know, O vain man, that faith without works is dead?

²¹ Was not Abraham our father justified by works when he offered Isaac his son upon the altar?

²² Do you see that faith was working together with his works, and by works faith was made perfect?

²³ And the Scripture was fulfilled which says, "Abraham believed God, and it was imputed to him for righteousness." And he was called the Friend of God.

²⁴ You see then how that a man is justified by works, and not by faith only.

²⁵ Likewise, was not Rahab the harlot also justified by works when she received the messengers and sent *them* out another way?

²⁶ Because, as the body without the spirit is dead, so faith without works is dead also.

CHAPTER 3

¹ My brethren, do not let many of you be teachers, knowing that we will receive a stricter judgment.

² Because, we all offend in many things. If anyone does not offend in word, he *is* a perfect man, *and* able also to bridle the whole body.

³ Behold, we put bits in horses' mouths that they may obey us, and we turn their entire body.

⁴ Look also at ships: although *they are so* large and *are* driven by fierce winds, yet they are turned about by a very small rudder wherever the pilot desires.

⁵ Even so the tongue is a little member and boasts great things. See how large an object a little fire kindles!

⁶ And the tongue *is* a fire, a world of iniquity. The tongue is so set among our members that it defiles the entire body, and sets on fire the course of nature; and it is set on fire by hell.

⁷ Because, every kind of beast and bird, of reptile and things in the sea, is tamed and has been tamed by mankind.

⁸ But no man can tame the tongue. *It is* an unruly evil, full of deadly poison.

⁹ With it we bless our God and Father, and with it we curse men, who have been made in the simil-

itude of God.

¹⁰ Out of the same mouth proceed blessing and cursing. My brethren, these things ought not to be so.

¹¹ Does a spring send forth fresh *water* and bitter from the same opening?

¹² Can a fig tree, my brethren, bear olives, or a grapevine bear figs? Thus no spring yields both salt water and fresh.

¹³ Who *is* wise and knowledgeable among you? Let him show by good conduct that his works are done in the meekness of wisdom.

¹⁴ But if you have bitter envy and selfish ambition in your hearts, do not boast and lie against the truth.

¹⁵ This wisdom does not descend from above, but *is* earthly, sensual, demonic.

¹⁶ Because, where envy and selfish ambition *exist*, confusion and every evil thing *are* there.

¹⁷ But the wisdom that is from above is first pure, then peaceable, gentle, *and* willing to yield, full of mercy and good fruits, without personal favoritism and without hypocrisy.

¹⁸ And the fruit of righteousness is sown in peace by those who make peace.

CHAPTER 4

¹ Where do wars and fights *come* from among you? Do *they* not *come* from your lust for pleasure that war in your members?

² You lust and do not have. You murder and covet and cannot obtain. You fight and war. Yet you do not have because you do not ask.

³ You ask and do not receive, because you ask amiss, that you may spend *it* on your pleasures.

⁴ You adulterers and adulteresses! Do you not know that friendship with the world is enmity with God? Whoever therefore wants to be a friend of the world is the enemy of God.

⁵ Or do you think that the Scripture says in vain, *that* the spirit that dwells within us lusts enviously?

⁶ But He gives more grace. Therefore He says: "God resists the proud, but gives grace to the humble."

⁷ Therefore submit to God. Resist the devil and he will flee from you.

⁸ Draw near to God and He will draw near to you. Cleanse *your* hands, *you* sinners; and purify *your* hearts, *you* double minded.

⁹ Lament and mourn and weep! Let your laughter be turned to mourning and *your* joy to gloom.

¹⁰ Humble yourselves in the sight of the Lord, and He will lift you up.

¹¹ Do not speak evil of one another, brethren. He who speaks evil of *his* brother and judges his brother, speaks evil of the law and judges the law. But if you judge the law, you are not a doer of the law but a judge.

¹² There is one Lawgiver, who is able to save and to destroy. Who are you to judge another?

¹³ Come now, you who say, "Today

or tomorrow we will go to such and such a city, spend a year there, buy and sell, and make a profit";
¹⁴ whereas you do not know what *will happen* tomorrow. Because what *is* your life? It is even a vapor that appears for a little time and then vanishes away.
¹⁵ Instead you *ought* to say, "If the Lord wills, we shall live and do this or that."
¹⁶ But now you boast in your arrogance. All such boasting is evil.
¹⁷ Therefore, to him who knows to do good and does not do *it*, to him it is sin.

CHAPTER 5

¹ Come now, *you* rich men, weep and howl for your miseries that will come upon you!
² Your riches are corrupted, and your clothes are moth eaten.
³ Your gold and silver are corroded, and their corrosion will be a witness against you and will eat your flesh like it was fire. You have heaped up treasure in the last days.
⁴ Behold, the wages of the laborers who harvested your fields, which you kept back by fraud, cries out; and the outcry of the reapers have reached the ears of the Lord of Sabaoth.
⁵ You have lived on the earth in pleasure and luxury; you have fattened your hearts as in a day of slaughter.
⁶ You have condemned *and* murdered the just; *and* he does not resist you.
⁷ Therefore be patient, brethren, until the coming of the Lord. See how the farmer waits for the precious fruit of the earth, and waits patiently for it until he receives the early and latter rain.
⁸ You also be patient. Establish your hearts, for the coming of the Lord draws near.
⁹ Do not hold a grudge against one another, brethren, lest you be condemned. Behold, the Judge is standing at the door!
¹⁰ My brethren, take the prophets, who have spoken in the name of the Lord, as an example of suffering affliction and of patience.
¹¹ Behold, we count them blessed who endure. You have heard of the perseverance of Job and seen the end intended by the Lord, that the Lord merciful is very compasssionate and merciful.
¹² But above all, my brethren, do not swear, either by heaven or by earth or with any other oath. But let your "Yes" be "Yes," and *your* "No," "No," lest you fall into condemnation.
¹³ Is anyone among you afflicted? Let him pray. Is anyone cheerful? Let him sing psalms.
¹⁴ Is anyone among you sick? Let him call for the elders of the church, and let them pray over him, anointing him with oil in the name of the Lord.
¹⁵ And the prayer of faith will save the sick, and the Lord will raise him

up. And if he has committed sins, he will be forgiven.

¹⁶ Confess *your* faults to one another, and pray for one another, that you may be healed. The effective, fervent prayer of a righteous man avails much.

¹⁷ Elijah was a man subject to passions as we are, and he prayed earnestly that it would not rain; and it did not rain on the land for three years and six months.

¹⁸ And he prayed again, and the heaven gave rain, and the earth produced her fruit.

¹⁹ Brethren, if any of you wanders from the truth, and someone converts him

²⁰ let him know that he who converts a sinner from the error of his way will save a soul from death and cover a multitude of sins.

THE FIRST GENERAL LETTER OF

PETER

CHAPTER 1

¹ Peter, an apostle of Jesus Christ, to the pilgrims scattered throughout Pontus, Galatia, Cappadocia, Asia, and Bithynia,

² elect according to the foreknowledge of God the Father, through sanctification of the Spirit to obedience, and sprinkling of the blood of Jesus Christ: Grace to you and peace be multiplied.

³ Blessed *be* the God and Father of our Lord Jesus Christ, who according to His abundant mercy has begotten us again to a living hope by the resurrection of Jesus Christ from the dead,

⁴ to an inheritance incorruptible, undefiled, and that does not fade away, reserved in heaven for you,

⁵ who are kept by the power of God through faith for salvation ready to be revealed in the last time.

⁶ In this you greatly rejoice, though now for a season, if need be, you are in heaviness through various trials,

⁷ that the testing of your faith, being much more precious than gold that perishes, though it be tested by fire, may be found to praise, honor, and glory at the appearing of Jesus Christ,

⁸ whom having not seen, you love. In whom, though now you do not see *Him*, yet believing, you rejoice with unspeakable joy, and full of glory,

⁹ receiving the end of your faith, *even* the salvation of *your* souls.

¹⁰ Of this salvation, the prophets inquired and searched diligently, who prophesied of this grace *that would come* to you;

¹¹ searching for what, or which particular time, the Spirit of Christ who was in them signified when He testified beforehand of the sufferings of Christ and the glory that would follow.

¹² To them it was revealed that, not to themselves, but to us they ministered the things that are now reported to you by those who have preached the gospel to you by the Holy Spirit sent down from heaven, things which the angels desire to look into.

¹³ Therefore gird up the loins of your mind, be sober, and hope until the end for the grace that is to be brought to you at the revelation of Jesus Christ;

¹⁴ as obedient children, not conforming yourselves according to the former lusts, as in your ignorance,

¹⁵ but just as He who has called you is holy, you also be holy in all your conduct,

¹⁶ because it is written, "Be holy, because I am holy."

¹⁷ And if you call on the Father, who

without personal favoritism judges according to each one's work, pass the time of your pilgrimage here in reverence;

¹⁸ knowing that you were not redeemed with corruptible things, like silver or gold, from your vain conduct received by tradition from your fathers,

¹⁹ but with the precious blood of Christ, as of a lamb without blemish and without spot.

²⁰ He indeed was foreordained before the foundation of the world, but was manifest in these last times for you

²¹ who now by Him believe in God, who raised Him up from the dead and gave Him glory, so that your faith and hope might be in God.

²² Seeing you have purified your souls in obeying the truth through the Spirit in sincere love of the brethren, *see that you* love one another fervently with a pure heart,

²³ having been born again, not of corruptible seed, but of incorruptible, by the word of God which lives and abides forever.

²⁴ Because, "All flesh *is* like grass, and all the glory of man like the flower of the grass. The grass withers, and its flower falls away,

²⁵ but the word of the LORD endures forever." Now this is the word which by the gospel is preached to you.

CHAPTER 2

¹ Therefore laying aside all malice, all deceit, hypocrisy, envy, and evil speaking,

² as newborn babes, desire the pure milk of the word, that you may grow thereby,

³ if indeed you have tasted that the Lord *is* gracious.

⁴ Coming to Him *as to* a living stone, rejected indeed by men, but chosen by God *and* precious,

⁵ you also, as living stones, are built up as a spiritual house, a holy priesthood, to offer up spiritual sacrifices acceptable to God by Jesus Christ.

⁶ Therefore it is also contained in the scripture, "Behold, I lay in Zion a chief cornerstone, elect, precious, and he who believes on Him will not be put to shame."

⁷ Therefore, to you who believe, *He* is precious; but to those who are disobedient, "The stone which the builders rejected, has become the head cornerstone,"

⁸ and "A stone of stumbling and a rock of offense," *which is to those* who stumble at the word, being disobedient, to which they are also appointed.

⁹ But you *are* a chosen generation, a royal priesthood, a holy nation, a special people, that you may proclaim the praises of Him who has called you out of darkness into His marvelous light;

¹⁰ who once *were* not a people, but *are* now the people of God, who had not obtained mercy, but now have obtained mercy.

¹¹ Beloved, I urge *you* as foreigners and pilgrims, abstain from fleshly lusts, which war against the soul,

¹² having your conduct honorable among the Gentiles, that while they speak against you as evildoers, they may, by your good works which they observe, glorify God in the day of visitation.

¹³ Submit yourselves to every ordinance of man for the Lord's sake, whether it be to the king as supreme,

¹⁴ or to governors, as to those who are sent by him for the punishment of evildoers and for the praise of those who do good.

¹⁵ Because, this is the will of God, that by doing good you may put to silence the ignorance of foolish men,

¹⁶ as free, yet not using your liberty as a cover for maliciousness, but as the servants of God.

¹⁷ Honor all *people*. Love the brotherhood. Reverence God. Honor the king.

¹⁸ Servants, *be* submissive to *your* masters with all reverence, not only to the good and gentle, but also to the harsh.

¹⁹ Because, this *is* admirable, if because of conscience toward God a person endures grief, suffering wrongfully.

²⁰ Because, what glory *is it* if, when you are punished for your faults, you take it patiently? But when you do good and suffer *for it*, if you take it patiently, this *is* acceptable before God.

²¹ Because, to this were you called, because Christ also suffered for us, leaving us an example, that you should follow His steps:

²² "Who did no sin, nor was deceit found in His mouth";

²³ who, when He was reviled, did not revile in return; when He suffered, He did not threaten, but committed *Himself* to Him who judges righteously;

²⁴ who Himself bore our sins in His own body on the tree, that we, being dead to sins, should live for righteousness, by whose stripes you were healed.

²⁵ Because, you were like sheep going astray, but have now returned to the Shepherd and Overseer of your souls.

CHAPTER 3

¹ Likewise, wives, *be* in subjection to your own husbands, so that if any do not obey the word, they also without the word may be won by the conduct of their wives,

² when they observe your chaste conduct *accompanied* with reverence.

³ Do not let your adornment be only an outward appearance, *arranging* the hair, wearing gold, or putting on of clothes,

⁴ but *let it be* the hidden person of the heart, with that which is incorruptible, *even the adornment* of a meek and quiet spirit, which is of great value in the sight of God.

⁵ Because, in this manner, in old times, the holy women who trusted in God also adorned themselves, being in submission to their own husbands,

⁶ just as Sarah obeyed Abraham, calling him lord, whose daughters you are if you do good and are not afraid with any terror.

⁷ Husbands, likewise, dwell with *them* according to knowledge, giving honor to the wife, as to the weaker vessel, and as being heirs together of the grace of life, that your prayers may not be hindered.

⁸ Finally, all of *you be* of one mind, having compassion for one another; love as brethren, *be* tenderhearted, *be* courteous;

⁹ not returning evil for evil or reviling for reviling, but on the contrary blessing, knowing that you are called to this, that you should inherit a blessing.

¹⁰ Because, "He who would love life and see good days, let him refrain his tongue from evil, and his lips from speaking deceit.

¹¹ Let him turn away from evil, and do good; let him seek peace and pursue it.

¹² Because, the eyes of the LORD *are* on the righteous, and His ears *are* open to their prayers; but the face of the LORD *is* against those who do evil."

¹³ And who *is* he who will harm you if you be followers of that which is good?

¹⁴ But even if you suffer for righteousness' sake, *you are* blessed. "And do not be afraid of their threats, nor be troubled."

¹⁵ But sanctify the Lord God in your hearts, and always *be* ready to *give* an answer to everyone who asks you a reason for the hope that is in you, with meekness and reverence;

¹⁶ having a good conscience, that when they defame you as evildoers, those who falsely accuse your good conduct in Christ may be ashamed.

¹⁷ Because, *it is* better, if it is the will of God, that you suffer for doing good than for doing evil.

¹⁸ Because, Christ also suffered once for sins, the just for the unjust, that He might bring us to God, being put to death in the flesh but made alive by the Spirit,

¹⁹ by whom also He went and preached to the spirits in prison,

²⁰ who formerly were disobedient, when once the longsuffering of God waited in the days of Noah, while the ark was being prepared, in which a few, that is, eight souls, were saved by water.

²¹ This is also figurative of that which also now saves us, *even* baptism (not the removal of the filth of the flesh, but the answer of a good conscience toward God), by the resurrection of Jesus Christ,

²² who has gone into heaven and is on the right hand of God, angels and authorities and powers having been made subject to Him.

CHAPTER 4

¹ Therefore, since Christ suffered for us in the flesh, arm yourselves likewise with the same mind, because, he who has suffered in the flesh has ceased from sin,

² that he no longer should live the rest of *his* time in the flesh for the lusts of men, but for the will of God.

³ Because, we *spent* enough of *our* former life in doing the will of the Gentiles, when we walked in lustfulness, desires, drunkenness, partying, drinking parties, and abominable idolatries,

⁴ in concerning these things they think it is strange that you do not run with *them* in the same excessive rioting, speaking evil of *you*,

⁵ who will give an account to Him who is ready to judge the living and the dead.

⁶ Because, for this reason was the gospel also preached to those who are dead, that they might be judged according to men in the flesh, but live according to God in the spirit.

⁷ But the end of all things is at hand; therefore be sober and watchful in prayer.

⁸ And above all things have fervent love among yourselves, because "love will cover the multitude of sins."

⁹ Be hospitable to one another without grumbling.

¹⁰ As each one has received the gift, *even* so also minister the same to one another, as good stewards of the manifold grace of God.

¹¹ If anyone speaks, *let him speak* as the oracles of God. If anyone ministers, *let him do* it as with the ability which God gives, that in all things God may be glorified through Jesus Christ, to whom be the praise and dominion forever and ever. Amen.

¹² Beloved, do not think it strange concerning the fiery trial which is to test you, as though some strange thing happened to you;

¹³ but rejoice to the degree that you participate in Christ's sufferings, that when His glory will be revealed, you may also be glad with exceeding joy.

¹⁴ If you are reproached for the name of Christ, you *are* blessed, because the Spirit of glory and of God rests upon you. On their part He is blasphemed, but on your part He is glorified.

¹⁵ But let none of you suffer as a murderer, *as* a thief, *as* an evildoer, or as a busybody in other people's matters.

¹⁶ Yet if *anyone suffers* as a Christian, let him not be ashamed, but let him glorify God in this matter.

¹⁷ Because, the time *has come* that judgment must begin at the house of God; and if *it begins* with us first, what will *be* the end of those who do not obey the gospel of God?

¹⁸ Now "if the righteous are scarcely saved, where will the ungodly and the sinner appear?"

¹⁹ Therefore let those who suffer according to the will of God commit the preservation of their souls to

Him in doing good, as to a faithful Creator.

CHAPTER 5

¹ The elders who are among you I exhort, who am also an elder and a witness of the sufferings of Christ, and also a partaker of the glory that will be revealed:

² Feed the flock of God which is among you, serving as overseers, not by obligation but willingly, not for dishonest gain, but with an eager mind;

³ nor as being lords over *God's* heritage, but being examples to the flock;

⁴ and when the Chief Shepherd will appear, you will receive a crown of glory that does not fade away.

⁵ Likewise you younger ones, submit yourselves to the elders. Yes, all of *you* be submissive to one another, and be clothed with humility, because, "God resists the proud, but gives grace to the humble."

⁶ Therefore humble yourselves under the mighty hand of God, that He may exalt you in due time,

⁷ casting all your burdens upon Him, because He cares for you.

⁸ Be sober, be vigilant; because your adversary the devil walks about like a roaring lion, seeking whom he may devour.

⁹ Resist him steadfast in the faith, knowing that the same afflictions are experienced by your brethren who are in the world.

¹⁰ But may the God of all grace, who has called us to His eternal glory by Christ Jesus, after you have suffered a while, perfect, establish, strengthen, and settle *you*.

¹¹ To Him *be* glory and dominion forever and ever. Amen.

¹² By Silvanus, a faithful brother to you as I consider him, I have written to you briefly, exhorting and testifying that this is the true grace of God in which you stand.

¹³ The *church who is* in Babylon, elect together with *you*, greets you; and *so does* Mark my son.

¹⁴ Greet one another with a kiss of love. Peace *be* to you all who are in Christ Jesus. Amen.

THE SECOND GENERAL LETTER OF
PETER

CHAPTER 1

¹ Simon Peter, a servant and an apostle of Jesus Christ, to those who have obtained like precious faith with us through the righteousness of God even our Savior Jesus Christ:

² Grace and peace be multiplied to you through the knowledge of God and of Jesus our Lord,

³ in the same way as His divine power has given to us all things that *pertain* to life and godliness, through the knowledge of Him who has called us to glory and virtue,

⁴ by which are given to us exceedingly great and precious promises, that by these you might be partakers of the divine nature, having escaped the corruption that is in the world through lust.

⁵ And beside this, giving all diligence, add to your faith virtue, and to virtue knowledge,

⁶ and to knowledge self control, and to self control perseverance, and to perseverance godliness,

⁷ And to godliness brotherly kindness, and to brotherly kindness love.

⁸ Because, if these things are in you and abound, they make *you that you will be* neither barren nor unfruitful in the knowledge of our Lord Jesus Christ.

⁹ But he who lacks these things is short sighted and blind, and has forgotten that he was cleansed from his old sins.

¹⁰ Therefore instead brethren, be diligent to make your calling and election certain, because if you do these things you will never fall;

¹¹ because, then an entrance will be provided for you abundantly into the everlasting kingdom of our Lord and Savior Jesus Christ.

¹² Therefore I will not be negligent to constantly remind you of these things, though you know *them* and are established in the present truth.

¹³ Yes, I think it is right, as long as I am in this tent, to stir you up by reminding you,

¹⁴ knowing that shortly I must put off my tent, just as our Lord Jesus Christ has shown me.

¹⁵ Moreover I will endeavor that after my decease you may be able to have these things in remembrance.

¹⁶ Because, we did not follow cunningly devised fables when we made known to you the power and coming of our Lord Jesus Christ, but were eyewitnesses of His majesty.

¹⁷ Because, He received from God the Father honor and glory when a voice came to Him from the Excellent Glory: "This is My beloved Son, in whom I am well pleased."

¹⁸ And we heard this voice which came from heaven when we were with Him on the holy mountain.

¹⁹ We also have an additional confirmed word of prophecy, which you do well to observe as a light that shines in a dark place, until the day dawns and the day star rises in your hearts;

²⁰ knowing this first, that no prophecy of Scripture is of any private interpretation.

²¹ because, the prophecy in old times did not come by the will of man, but holy men of God spoke *as they were* moved by the Holy Spirit.

CHAPTER 2

¹ But there were false prophets also among the people, even as there will be false teachers among you, who will secretly bring in damnable heresies, even denying the Lord who bought them, and bring upon themselves swift destruction.

² And many will follow their destructive ways, because of whom the way of truth will be blasphemed.

³ And through covetousness they will exploit you with deceptive words for profit; for a long time their judgment has not been idle, and their damnation does not slumber.

⁴ Because, if God did not spare the angels who sinned, but cast *them* down to hell and delivered *them* into chains of darkness, to be reserved for judgment;

⁵ and did not spare the old world, but saved Noah *one of* eight *people*, a preacher of righteousness, bringing in the flood upon the world of the ungodly;

⁶ and turning the cities of Sodom and Gomorrah into ashes, condemned *them* with destruction, making *them* an example to those who afterward would live ungodly;

⁷ and delivered righteous Lot, who was oppressed with the filthy conduct of the wicked

⁸ (because, that righteous man, dwelling among them, tormented his righteous soul from day to day by seeing and hearing *their* lawless deeds).

⁹ The Lord knows how to deliver the godly out of temptations and to reserve the unjust for the day of judgment to be punished,

¹⁰ but especially those who walk according to the flesh in the lust of uncleanness and despise authority. *They are* presumptuous, self willed, they are not afraid to speak evil of dignitaries,

¹¹ whereas angels, who are greater in power and might, do not bring a reviling accusation against them before the Lord.

¹² But these, like natural brute beasts, made to be captured and destroyed, speak evil of the things that they do not understand, and will utterly perish in their own corruption,

¹³ and will receive the wages of unrighteousness, *as* those who count it pleasure to be riotous in the daytime. *They are* spots and blemishes, delighting themselves

with their own deceptions while they feast with you,

¹⁴ having eyes full of adultery, and that cannot cease from sin, enticing unstable souls. They have a heart trained with covetous practices, and are cursed children.

¹⁵ They have forsaken the right way and have gone astray, following the way of Balaam *the son* of Beor, who loved the wages of unrighteousness;

¹⁶ but was rebuked for his iniquity: the mute donkey speaking with a man's voice restrained the madness of the prophet.

¹⁷ These are wells without water, clouds that are carried by a tempest, for whom is reserved the blackness of darkness forever.

¹⁸ Because, when they speak great swelling *words* of emptiness, they allure through the lusts of the flesh, *through* unrestrained lusts, those who had completely escaped from those who live in error.

¹⁹ While they promise them liberty, they themselves are the servants of corruption; because by whom a person is overcome, by him also is he brought in bondage.

²⁰ Because if, after they have escaped the pollutions of the world through the knowledge of the Lord and Savior Jesus Christ, they are again entangled in them and overcome, the latter end is worse for them than the beginning.

²¹ because, it would have been better for them not to have known the way of righteousness, than after having known *it*, to turn from the holy commandment delivered to them.

²² But it has happened to them according to the true proverb: "The dog returned to his own vomit again," and, "a sow, having washed, to her wallowing in the mire."

CHAPTER 3

¹ Beloved, I now write to you this second letter, in *both* which I stir up your pure minds by the method of remembrance,

² that you may be mindful of the words which were spoken beforehand by the holy prophets, and of the commandment of us, the apostles of the Lord and Savior'

³ knowing this first, that scoffers will come in the last days, walking according to their own lusts,

⁴ and saying, "Where is the promise of His coming? Because, since the fathers fell asleep, all things continue *as they were* from the beginning of creation."

⁵ Because, they are willfully ignorant of this: that by the word of God the heavens were of old, and the earth standing out of water and in the water,

⁶ by which the world that then existed perished, being flooded with water.

⁷ But the heavens and the earth which are now preserved by the same word, are reserved for fire until the day of judgment and

perdition of ungodly men.

⁸ But, beloved, do not be ignorant of this one thing, that with the Lord one day *is* as a thousand years, and a thousand years as one day.

⁹ The Lord is not slack concerning His promise, as some count slackness, but is longsuffering toward us, not willing that any should perish but that all should come to repentance.

¹⁰ But the day of the Lord will come as a thief in the night, in which the heavens will pass away with a great noise, and the elements will melt with fervent heat; both the earth and the works that are in it will be burned up.

¹¹ *Seeing* then *that* all these things will be dissolved, what manner of *persons* ought you to be in *all* holy conduct and godliness,

¹² looking for, and moving rapidly toward, the coming of the day of God, in which the heavens will be dissolved, being on fire, and the elements will melt with fervent heat?

¹³ Nevertheless we, according to His promise, look for new heavens and a new earth in which righteousness dwells.

¹⁴ Therefore, beloved, seeing that you look for such things, be diligent to be found by Him in peace, without spot and blameless;

¹⁵ and consider *that* the longsuffering of our Lord is salvation, just as also our beloved brother Paul according to the wisdom given to him, has written to you,

¹⁶ as also in all *his* letters, speaking in them of these things, in which are some things which are hard to understand, which unlearned and unstable people twist, as *they do* also the other Scriptures, to their own destruction.

¹⁷ You therefore, beloved, since you know this beforehand, beware lest you also fall from your own steadfastness, being led away with the error of the wicked;

¹⁸ but grow in grace and *in* the knowledge of our Lord and Savior Jesus Christ. To Him *be* glory both now and forever. Amen.

THE FIRST GENERAL LETTER OF
JOHN

CHAPTER 1

¹ That which was from the beginning, which we have heard, which we have seen with our eyes, which we have looked upon, and our hands have handled, concerning the Word of life;

² (because, the life was manifested, and we have seen *it*, and bear witness, and show to you that eternal life, which was with the Father, and was manifested to us:)

³ that which we have seen and heard we declare to you, that you also may have fellowship with us; and truly our fellowship *is* with the Father and with His Son Jesus Christ.

⁴ And these things we write to you that your joy may be full.

⁵ This then is the message which we have heard from Him and declare to you, that God is light and in Him is no darkness at all.

⁶ If we say that we have fellowship with Him, and walk in darkness, we lie and do not practice the truth.

⁷ But if we walk in the light as He is in the light, we have fellowship one with another, and the blood of Jesus Christ His Son cleanses us from all sin.

⁸ If we say that we have no sin, we deceive ourselves, and the truth is not in us.

⁹ If we confess our sins, He is faithful and just to forgive us *our* sins and to cleanse us from all unrighteousness.

¹⁰ If we say that we have not sinned, we make Him a liar, and His word is not in us.

CHAPTER 2

¹ My little children, these things I write to you, so that you do not sin. And if anyone sins, we have an Advocate with the Father, Jesus Christ the righteous.

² And He is the propitiation for our sins, and not for ours only but also for *the sins* of the entire world.

³ Now by this we know that we know Him, if we keep His commandments.

⁴ He who says, "I know Him," and does not keep His commandments, is a liar, and the truth is not in him.

⁵ But whoever keeps His word, truly the love of God is perfected in him. By this we know that we are in Him.

⁶ He who says he abides in Him should also himself so walk just as He walked.

⁷ Brethren, I write no new commandment to you, but an old commandment which you have had from the beginning. The old commandment is the word which you heard from the beginning.

⁸ Again, a new commandment I

write to you, which thing is true in Him and in you, because the darkness has passed away, and the true light now shines.

⁹ He who says he is in the light, and hates his brother, is in darkness until now.

¹⁰ He who loves his brother abides in the light, and there is no cause for stumbling in him.

¹¹ But he who hates his brother is in darkness, and walks in darkness, and does not know where he is going, because that darkness has blinded his eyes.

¹² I write to you, little children, because your sins are forgiven you for His name's sake.

¹³ I write to you, fathers, because you have known Him *who is* from the beginning. I write to you, young men, because you have overcome the wicked one. I write to you, little children, because you have known the Father.

¹⁴ I have written to you, fathers, because you have known Him *who is* from the beginning. I have written to you, young men, because you are strong, and the word of God abides in you, and you have overcome the wicked one.

¹⁵ Do not love the world or the things *that are* in the world. If anyone loves the world, the love of the Father is not in him.

¹⁶ Because, everything that *is* in the world, the lust of the flesh, the lust of the eyes, and the pride of life, is not of the Father, but is of the world.

¹⁷ And the world is passing away, and the lust of it; but he who does the will of God abides forever.

¹⁸ Little children, it is the last time; and as you have heard the Antichrist is coming, even now there are many antichrists, by whom we know that it is the last time.

¹⁹ They went out from us, but they were not of us; because, if they had been of us, *no doubt* they would have continued with us ; but *they went out* that they might be made manifest, that they were not all of us.

²⁰ But you have an anointing from the Holy One, and you know all things.

²¹ I have not written to you because you do not know the truth, but because you know it, and that no lie is of the truth.

²² Who is a liar but he who denies that Jesus is the Christ? He is antichrist who denies the Father and the Son.

²³ Whoever denies the Son, the same does not have the Father: *but* he who acknowledges the Son has the Father also.

²⁴ Therefore let that abide in you which you have heard from the beginning. If what you heard from the beginning remains in you, you also will continue in the Son and in the Father.

²⁵ And this is the promise that He has promised us, *even* eternal life.

²⁶ These *things* I have written to you

concerning those who seduce you.

²⁷ But the anointing which you have received from Him abides in you, and you do not need that anyone teach you; but as the same anointing teaches you concerning all things, and is true, and is not a lie, and just as it has taught you, you shall abide in Him.

²⁸ And now, little children, abide in Him; that when He appears, we may have confidence and not be a-shamed before Him at His coming.

²⁹ If you know that He is righteous, you know that everyone who practices righteousness is born of Him.

CHAPTER 3

¹ Behold what manner of love the Father has given to us, that we should be called the sons of God! Therefore the world does not know us, because it did not know Him.

² Beloved, now we are the sons of God, and it has not yet been revealed what we will be, but we know that when He appears, we will be like Him, because we will see Him as He is.

³ And everyone who has this hope in Him purifies himself, just as He is pure.

⁴ Whoever commits sin also transgresses the law, because sin is the transgression of the law.

⁵ And you know that He was manifested to take away our sins, and in Him is no sin.

⁶ Whoever abides in Him does not sin. Whoever sins has neither seen Him nor known Him.

⁷ Little children, let no one deceive you. He who does righteousness is righteous, just as He is righteous.

⁸ He who commits sin is of the devil, because the devil has sinned from the beginning. For this purpose the Son of God was manifested, that He might destroy the works of the devil.

⁹ Whoever is born of God does not commit sin, because, His seed remains in him; and he cannot sin, because he is born of God.

¹⁰ In this the children of God and the children of the devil are revealed: whosoever does not practice righteousness is not of God, nor he who does not love his brother.

¹¹ Because, this is the message that you heard from the beginning, that we should love one another,

¹² not as Cain who was of that wicked one and murdered his brother. And why did he kill him? Because his own works were evil and his brother's righteous.

¹³ Do not marvel, my brethren, if the world hates you.

¹⁴ We know that we have passed from death to life, because we love the brethren. He who does not love *his* brother abides in death.

¹⁵ Whoever hates his brother is a murderer, and you know that no murderer has eternal life abiding in him.

¹⁶ By this we perceive the love of God, because He laid down His life for us. And we also should lay down

our lives for the brethren.

¹⁷ But whoever has this world's goods, and sees his brother in need, and shuts up his heart *of compassion* from him, how does the love of God abide in him?

¹⁸ My little children, let us not love in word or in tongue, but in deed and in truth.

¹⁹ And by this we know that we are of the truth, and will assure our hearts before Him.

²⁰ Because, if our heart condemns us, God is greater than our heart, and knows all things.

²¹ Beloved, if our heart does not condemn us, *then* have we confidence toward God.

²² And whatever we ask we receive from Him, because we keep His commandments and do those things that are pleasing in His sight.

²³ And this is His commandment: that we should believe on the name of His Son Jesus Christ and love one another, as He gave us commandment.

²⁴ Now he who keeps His commandments abides in Him, and He in him. And by this we know that He abides in us, by the Spirit whom He has given us.

CHAPTER 4

¹ Beloved, do not believe every spirit, but test the spirits whether they are of God; because many false prophets have gone out into the world.

² By this you know the Spirit of God: Every spirit that confesses that Jesus Christ came in the flesh is of God,

³ and every spirit that does not confess that Jesus Christ came in the flesh is not of God. And this is that *spirit* of antichrist, which you have heard was coming and even now it is already in the world.

⁴ You are of God, little children, and have overcome them, because greater is He who is in you than he who is in the world.

⁵ They are of the world. Therefore they speak from the world, and the world hears them.

⁶ We are of God. He who knows God hears us; he who is not of God does not hear us. By this we know the spirit of truth and the spirit of error.

⁷ Beloved, let us love one another, because love is of God; and everyone who loves is born of God and knows God.

⁸ He who does not love does not know God, because God is love.

⁹ In this the love of God was manifested toward us, in that God sent His only begotten Son into the world, that we might live through Him.

¹⁰ In this is love, not that we loved God, but that He loved us and sent His Son *to be* the propitiation for our sins.

¹¹ Beloved, if God loved us so much, we also should love one another.

¹² No one has seen God at any time. If we love one another, God abides

in us, and His love is perfected in us.

¹³ By this we know that we abide in Him, and He in us, because He has given us of His Spirit.

¹⁴ And we have seen and do testify that the Father has sent the Son *to be* the Savior of the world.

¹⁵ Whoever confesses that Jesus is the Son of God, God abides in him, and he in God.

¹⁶ And we have known and believed the love that God has toward us. God is love, and he who abides in love abides in God, and God in him.

¹⁷ By this is our love perfected, that we may have boldness in the day of judgment; because as He is, so are we in this world.

¹⁸ There is no fear in love; but perfect love casts out fear, because fear involves torment. He who fears has not been made perfect in love.

¹⁹ we love Him because He first loved us.

²⁰ If anyone says, "I love God," and yet hates his brother, he is a liar; because, he who does not love his brother whom he has seen, how can he love God whom he has not seen?

²¹ And this commandment we have from Him: that he who loves God should love his brother also.

CHAPTER 5

¹ Whoever believes that Jesus is the Christ is born of God, and everyone who loves Him who begot also loves him who is begotten of Him.

² By this we know that we love the children of God, when we love God and keep His commandments.

³ Because, this is the love of God, that we keep His commandments. And His commandments are not burdensome.

⁴ Because, whatever is born of God overcomes the world. And this is the victory that overcomes the world, *even* our faith.

⁵ Who is he who overcomes the world, but he who believes that Jesus is the Son of God?

⁶ This is He who came by water and blood, *even* Jesus Christ; not only by water, but by water and blood. And it is the Spirit who bears witness, because the Spirit is truth.

⁷ Because there are three that bear record in heaven, the Father, the Word, and the Holy Spirit; and these three are one.

⁸ And there are three that bear witness on earth, the spirit, the water, and the blood; and these three agree in one.

⁹ If we receive the witness of men, the witness of God is greater; because this is the witness of God which He has testified of His Son.

¹⁰ He who believes on the Son of God has the witness in himself; he who does not believe God has made Him a liar, because he does believe the record that God gave of His Son.

¹¹ And this is the record: that God has given to us eternal life, and this life is in His Son.

¹² He who has the Son has life; *and* he who does not have the Son of God does not have life.

[13] These things I have written to you who believe on the name of the Son of God, that you may know that you have eternal life, and that you may believe on the name of the Son of God.

[14] Now this is the confidence that we have in Him, that if we ask anything according to His will, He hears us.

[15] And if we know that He hears us, whatever we ask, we know that we have the petitions that we desired from Him.

[16] If anyone sees his brother sin a sin *which* is not *leading* to death, he shall ask, and He will give him life for those who commit sin not *leading* to death. There is a sin *leading* to death. I do not say that he should pray for that.

[17] All unrighteousness is sin, and there is a sin not *leading* to death.

[18] We know that whoever is born of God does not sin; but he who has been begotten of God keeps himself, and that wicked one does not touch him.

[19] *And* we know that we are of God, and the entire world lies in wickedness.

[20] And we know that the Son of God came, and has given us an understanding, that we may know Him who is true; and we are in Him who is true, even in His Son Jesus Christ. This is the true God and eternal life.

[21] Little children, keep yourselves from idols. Amen.

THE SECOND GENERAL LETTER OF
JOHN

CHAPTER 1

¹ The elder to the elect lady and her children, whom I love in the truth, and not I only, but also all those who have known the truth'

² for the truth's sake which dwells in us, and will be with us forever:

³ Grace be with you, mercy, *and* peace, from God the Father and from the Lord Jesus Christ, the Son of the Father in truth and love.

⁴ I rejoiced greatly that I found *some* of your children walking in truth, as we have received a commandment from the Father.

⁵ And now I urge you, lady, not as though I wrote a new commandment to you, but that which we had from the beginning: that we love one another.

⁶ And this is love, that we walk according to His commandments. This is the commandment, that as you have heard from the beginning, you should walk in it.

⁷ Because many deceivers have entered into the world, who do not confess that Jesus Christ came in the flesh. This is a deceiver and an antichrist.

⁸ Look to yourselves, that we do not lose those things which we have worked for, but that we receive a full reward.

⁹ Whoever transgresses and does not abide in the doctrine of Christ does not have God. He who abides in the doctrine of Christ, he has both the Father and the Son.

¹⁰ If anyone comes to you, and does not bring this doctrine, do not receive him into *your* house, neither greet him with a blessing:

¹¹ Because he who greets him with a blessing shares in his evil deeds.

¹² Having many things to write to you, I did not wish to *write* with paper and ink; but I hope to come to you and speak face to face, that our joy may be full.

¹³ The children of your elect sister greet you. Amen.

THE THIRD GENERAL LETTER OF
JOHN

CHAPTER 1

¹ The elder to the well beloved Gaius, whom I love in the truth:

² Beloved, I wish above all things that you may prosper and be in health, just as your soul prospers.

³ Because I rejoiced greatly, when the brethren came and testified of the truth that is in you, just as you walk in the truth.

⁴ I have no greater joy than to hear that my children walk in truth.

⁵ Beloved, you do faithfully whatever you do for the brethren, and for strangers,

⁶ who have borne witness of your love before the church; whom if you send them forward on their journey in a manner worthy of God, you will do well,

⁷ because they went forth for His name's sake, taking nothing from the Gentiles.

⁸ We therefore ought to receive such, that we may become fellow workers for the truth.

⁹ I wrote to the church, but Diotrephes, who loves to have the preeminence among them, does not receive us.

¹⁰ Therefore, if I come, I will remember his deeds which he does, prating against us with malicious words. And not satisfied with that, he himself does not receive the brethren, and forbids those who want to, throwing *them* out of the church.

¹¹ Beloved, do not follow that which is evil, but that which is good. He who does good is of God, but he who does evil has not seen God.

¹² Demetrius has a good report from all *men*, and from the truth itself. Yes, and we *also* bear record, and you all know that our record is true.

¹³ I had many things to write, but I will not write to you with ink and pen;

¹⁴ but I hope I shall see you shortly, and we will speak face to face. Peace be to you. Our friends greet you. Greet the friends by name.

THE GENERAL LETTER OF
JUDE

CHAPTER 1

¹ Jude, a servant of Jesus Christ, and brother of James, to those who are sanctified by God the Father, and preserved in Jesus Christ: *and* called
² Mercy to you, and peace, and love, be multiplied.
³ Beloved, while I was very diligent to write to you about the common salvation, it was necessary for me to write to *you*, and urge you that you should earnestly contend for the faith which was once delivered to the saints.
⁴ Because, there are certain men who crept in unnoticed, who long ago were ordained to this condemnation, ungodly men, turning the grace of our God into lustfulness and denying the only Lord God and our Lord Jesus Christ.
⁵ Therefore I want to remind you, although you once knew this, that the Lord, having saved the people out of the land of Egypt, afterward destroyed those who did not believe.
⁶ And the angels who did not keep their first domain, but left their own habitat, He has reserved in everlasting chains under darkness for the judgment of the great day.
⁷ Likewise, Sodom and Gomorrah, and the cities about them in the same manner, giving themselves over to sexual immorality and going after other flesh, are set forth as an example, suffering the vengeance of eternal fire.
⁸ Likewise also these *filthy* dreamers defile the flesh, despise authority, and speak evil of those highly esteemed.
⁹ Yet Michael the archangel, while contending with the devil, when he disputed about the body of Moses, dared not bring against him a railing accusation, but said, "The Lord rebuke you!"
¹⁰ But these speak evil of those things they know nothing of; but what they know naturally, like brute beasts, in these things they corrupt themselves.
¹¹ Woe to them! Because, they have gone in the way of Cain, have run greedily in the error of Balaam for profit, and perished in the rebellion of Korah.
¹² These are spots in your love feasts, while they feast with you, feeding themselves without reverence. *They are* clouds without water, carried about by winds; trees whose fruit withers, without fruit, twice dead, pulled up by the roots;
¹³ raging waves of the sea, foaming out their own shame; wandering stars for whom is reserved the blackness of darkness forever.
¹⁴ Now Enoch, the seventh from Adam, also prophesied about these

men, saying, "Behold, the Lord comes with ten thousands of His saints,

¹⁵ to execute judgment upon all, to convict all who are ungodly among them of all their ungodly deeds which they have committed in an ungodly manner, and of all their harsh *words* which ungodly sinners have spoken against Him."

¹⁶ These are grumblers, complainers, walking according to their own lusts; and their mouth speaks great swelling *words*, flattering people to gain advantage.

¹⁷ But you, beloved, remember the words which were spoken beforehand by the apostles of our Lord Jesus Christ:

¹⁸ how that they told you there would be mockers in the last time who would walk according to their own ungodly lusts.

¹⁹ These are those who separate sensual, not having the Spirit.

²⁰ But you, beloved, building yourselves up on your most holy faith, praying in the Holy Spirit,

²¹ keep yourselves in the love of God, looking for the mercy of our Lord Jesus Christ to eternal life.

²² And on some have compassion, making a distinction;

²³ but others save with fear, pulling *them* out of the fire, hating even the clothing defiled by the flesh.

²⁴ Now to Him who is able to keep you from falling, and to present *you* faultless before the presence of His glory with exceeding joy,

²⁵ To the only wise God our Savior, *be* glory and majesty, dominion and power, both now and forever. Amen.

THE REVELATION

OF JOHN THE DIVINE

CHAPTER 1

¹ The Revelation of Jesus Christ, which God gave to Him to show to His servants, things that will come to pass suddenly. And He sent and signified *it* by His angel to His servant John,

² who bore record to the word of God, and of the testimony of Jesus Christ, and of everything that he saw.

³ Blessed *is* he who reads and those who hear the words of this prophecy, and keep those things which are written in it; because the time is at hand.

⁴ John, to the seven churches which are in Asia: Grace *be* to you and peace from Him who is and who was and who is to come, and from the seven Spirits who are before His throne,

⁵ and from Jesus Christ, *who is* the faithful witness, the firstborn from the dead, and the ruler of the kings of the earth. To Him who loved us and washed us from our sins in His own blood,

⁶ and has made us kings and priests to God and His Father, to Him be glory and dominion forever and ever. Amen.

⁷ Behold, He is coming with clouds, and every eye will see Him, and *also* those who pierced Him. And all tribes of the earth will mourn because of Him. Even so, Amen.

⁸ "I am Alpha and Omega, the Beginning and the End," says the Lord, "who is and who was and who is to come, the Almighty."

⁹ I John, who am also your brother and companion in tribulation and in the kingdom and patience of Jesus Christ, was on the island that is called Patmos for the word of God and for the testimony of Jesus Christ.

¹⁰ I was in the Spirit on the Lord's day, and heard behind me a loud voice, as of a trumpet,

¹¹ saying, "I am Alpha and Omega, the First and the Last," and, "What you see, write in a book and send *it* to the seven churches which are in Asia: to Ephesus, to Smyrna, to Pergamos, to Thyatira, to Sardis, to Philadelphia, and to Laodicea."

¹² Then I turned to see the voice that spoke with me. And having turned I saw seven golden lampstands,

¹³ and in the midst of the seven lampstands *One* like the Son of Man, clothed with a garment down to the feet and wrapped about the chest with a golden band.

¹⁴ His head and *his* hair *were* white like wool, as white as snow, and His eyes *were* like a flame of fire;

¹⁵ His feet were like fine brass, as if being refined in a furnace, and His

voice as the sound of many waters; ¹⁶ and He had in His right hand seven stars, out of His mouth went a sharp two edged sword, and His countenance *was* like the sun shining in its strength.

¹⁷ And when I saw Him, I fell at His feet as dead. But He laid His right hand on me, saying to me, "Do not fear; I am the First and the Last.

¹⁸ I am He who lives, and was dead, and behold, I am alive forevermore. Amen. And I have the keys of Hell and of Death.

¹⁹ Write the things which you have seen, and the things which are, and the things which will be after this.

²⁰ The mystery of the seven stars which you saw in My right hand, and the seven golden lampstands: The seven stars are the angels of the seven churches, and the seven lampstands which you saw are the seven churches.

CHAPTER 2

¹ To the angel of the church of Ephesus write, 'These things says He who holds the seven stars in His right hand, who walks among the seven golden lampstands:

² "I know your works, your labor, your endurance, and how you cannot bear those who are evil. And you have tested those who say they are apostles and are not, and have found them liars;

³ and you have persevered and have endurance, and have labored for My name's sake and have not become weary.

⁴ But I have *some things* against you, that you have left your first love.

⁵ Remember therefore from where you have fallen; and repent and do the first works, or else I will come to you suddenly and remove your lampstand from its place, unless you repent.

⁶ But you have this, that you hate the works of the Nicolaitans, which I also hate.

⁷ "He who has an ear, let him hear what the Spirit says to the churches. To him who overcomes I will give to eat from the Tree of Life, which is in the midst of the Paradise of God." '

⁸ "And to the angel of the church in Smyrna write, 'These things says the First and the Last, who was dead, and is alive:

⁹ "I know your works, tribulation, and poverty (but you are rich); and *I know* the blasphemy of those who say they are Jews and are not, but *are* the synagogue of Satan.

¹⁰ Do not fear any of those things which you are about to suffer. Behold, the devil is about to throw *some* of you into prison, that you may be tested, and you will all have tribulation ten days. Be faithful until death, and I will give you the crown of life.

¹¹ "He who has an ear, let him hear what the Spirit says to the churches. He who overcomes will not be hurt by the second death." '

¹² "And to the angel of the church

in Pergamos write, 'These things says He who has the sharp two edged sword:

¹³ "I know your works, and where you dwell, *even* where Satan's throne is. And you hold fast to My name, and did not deny My faith even in those days in which Antipas *was* My faithful martyr, who was killed among you, where Satan dwells.

¹⁴ But I have a few things against you, because you have those there who hold the doctrine of Balaam, who taught Balak to cast a stumbling block before the children of Israel, to eat things sacrificed to idols, and to commit sexual immorality.

¹⁵ And also you have those who hold the doctrine of the Nicolaitans, which thing I hate.

¹⁶ Repent, or else I will come to you suddenly and will fight against them with the sword of My mouth.

¹⁷ "He who has an ear, let him hear what the Spirit says to the churches. To him who overcomes I will give to eat from the hidden manna. And I will give him a white stone, and on the stone a new name written which no one knows except he who receives it."'

¹⁸ "And to the angel of the church in Thyatira write, 'These things says the Son of God, who has eyes like a flame of fire, and His feet *are* like fine brass:

¹⁹ "I know your works, love, service, faith, endurance and your works; and the last *to be* more than the first.

²⁰ But I have a few things against you, because you permit that woman Jezebel, who calls herself a prophetess, to teach and seduce My servants to commit sexual immorality and eat things sacrificed to idols.

²¹ And I gave her time to repent of her sexual immorality, and she did not repent.

²² Behold, I will throw her into a bed, and those who commit adultery with her into great tribulation, unless they repent of their deeds.

²³ I will kill her children with death, and all the churches will know that I am He who searches the minds and hearts. And I will give to each one of you according to your works.

²⁴ "Now to you I say, and to the rest in Thyatira, as many as do not have this doctrine, and who have not known, as they say, the depths of Satan, I will put on you no other burden.

²⁵ But what you *already* have, hold firmly until I come.

²⁶ And he who overcomes, and keeps My works until the end, to him I will give authority over the nations:

²⁷ 'He will rule them with a rod of iron; they will be broken to pieces like the potter's vessels' just as I have received from My Father;

²⁸ and I will give him the morning star.

²⁹ "He who has an ear, let him hear

what the Spirit says to the churches." '

CHAPTER 3

¹ "And to the angel of the church in Sardis write, 'These things says He who has the seven Spirits of God and the seven stars: "I know your works, that you have a name that you are alive, but you are dead.
² Be watchful, and strengthen the things which remain, that are about to die, because I have not found your works perfect before God.
³ Remember therefore how you have received and heard; and hold firmly and repent. Therefore if you will not watch, I will come upon you as a thief, and you will not know what hour I will come upon you.
⁴ You have a few names even in Sardis who have not defiled their garments; and they will walk with Me in white, because they are worthy.
⁵ He who overcomes, these will be clothed in white garments, and I will not blot out his name from the Book of Life; but I will confess his name before My Father and before His angels.
⁶ "He who has an ear, let him hear what the Spirit says to the churches." '
⁷ "And to the angel of the church in Philadelphia write, 'These things says He who is holy, He who is true, "He who has the key of David, He who opens and no one shuts, and shuts and no one opens":
⁸ "I know your works. Behold, I have set before you an open door, and no one can shut it; because, you have a little strength, have kept My word, and have not denied My name.
⁹ Behold, I will make those of the synagogue of Satan, who say they are Jews and are not, but do lie, behold, I will make them come and worship before your feet, and to know that I have loved you.
¹⁰ Because you have kept My word to persevere, I also will keep you from the hour of trial that will come upon the entire world, to test those who dwell on the earth.
¹¹ Behold, I am coming suddenly! Hold firmly to what you have, that no one may take your crown.
¹² He who overcomes, I will make a pillar in the temple of My God, and he will go out no more. And I will write on him the name of My God and the name of the city of My God, *which is* New Jerusalem, which comes down out of heaven from My God. And I *will write on him* My new name.
¹³ "He who has an ear, let him hear what the Spirit says to the churches." '
¹⁴ "And to the angel of the church of the Laodiceans write, 'These things says the Amen, the Faithful and True Witness, the beginning of the creation of God:
¹⁵ "I know your works, that you are neither cold nor hot. I wish that you were cold or hot.

¹⁶ So then, because you are lukewarm, and neither cold nor hot, I will vomit you out of My mouth.

¹⁷ Because you say, 'I am rich, am increased with possessions, and have need of nothing,' but do not know that you are wretched, miserable, poor, blind, and naked;

¹⁸ I counsel you to buy from Me gold refined in the fire, that you may be rich; and white clothing, that you may be clothed, so *that* the shame of your nakedness does not appear; and anoint your eyes with eye salve, that you may see.

¹⁹ As many as I love, I rebuke and chasten. Therefore be zealous and repent.

²⁰ Behold, I stand at the door and knock. If anyone hears My voice and opens the door, I will come in to him and will dine with Him, and he with Me.

²¹ To him that overcomes will I allow to sit with Me on My throne, just as I also overcame and have sat down with My Father on His throne.

²² He who has an ear, let him hear what the Spirit says to the churches." ' "

CHAPTER 4

¹ After these things I looked, and behold, a door was opened in heaven. And the first voice which I heard *was* like it was of a trumpet speaking with me, which said, "Come up here, and I will show you things that must be after this."

² And immediately I was in the spirit; and behold, a throne was set in heaven, and *One* sat on the throne.

³ And He who sat there looked like a jasper and a sardine stone; and *there was* a rainbow around about the throne, which looked like an emerald.

⁴ And around the throne *were* twenty four thrones, and on the thrones I saw twenty four elders sitting, clothed in white clothing; and they had golden crowns on their heads.

⁵ And lightnings, thunderings, and voices proceeded from the throne. And *there were* seven lamps of fire burning before the throne, which are the seven Spirits of God.

⁶ And before the throne *there* was a sea of glass, like crystal. And in the midst of the throne, and around the throne, *were* four creatures full of eyes in the front and the back.

⁷ And the first creature was like a lion, and the second creature like a calf, and the third creature had a face like a man, and the fourth creature *was* like a flying eagle.

⁸ And the four creatures, each of them having six wings around *him*, also *were* full of eyes inside. And they do not rest day or night, saying: "Holy, holy, holy, Lord God Almighty, Who was, and is and is to come!"

⁹ And whenever the creatures give glory and honor and thanks to Him who sits on the throne, who lives

forever and ever,

¹⁰ the twenty four elders fall down before Him who sits on the throne and worship Him who lives forever and ever, and throw their crowns before the throne, saying:

¹¹ "You are worthy, O Lord, to receive glory and honor and power; because, You have created all things, and for Your pleasure they are and were created."

CHAPTER 5

¹ And I saw in the right hand of Him who sat on the throne a scroll written inside and on the back, sealed with seven seals.

² Then I saw a strong angel proclaiming with a loud voice, "Who is worthy to open the scroll and to loose its seals?"

³ And no one in heaven or on earth or under the earth was able to open the scroll, or to look at it.

⁴ So I wept greatly, because no one was found worthy to open and to read the scroll, or to look at it.

⁵ But one of the elders said to me, "Do not weep. Behold, the Lion of the tribe of Judah, the Root of David, has prevailed to open the scroll and to loose its seven seals."

⁶ And I looked, and behold, in the midst of the throne and of the four creatures, and amongst the elders, stood a Lamb as though it had been slain, having seven horns and seven eyes, which are the seven Spirits of God sent out into all the earth.

⁷ Then He came and took the scroll out of the right hand of Him who sat on the throne.

⁸ Now when He had taken the scroll, the four creatures and twenty four elders fell down before the Lamb, each having harps and golden bowls full of incense, which are the prayers of saints.

⁹ And they sang a new song, saying: "You are worthy to take the scroll, and to open its seals; because, You were slain, and have redeemed us to God by Your blood out of every tribe and language and people and nation,

¹⁰ and have made us kings and priests to our God; and we will reign on the earth."

¹¹ Then I looked, and I heard the voice of many angels surrounding the throne, and the creatures and the elders; and the number of them was ten thousand times ten thousand, and thousands of thousands,

¹² saying with a loud voice: "Worthy is the Lamb who was slain to receive power and riches and wisdom, and strength and honor and glory and blessing!"

¹³ And I heard every creature which is in heaven and on the earth and under the earth and such as are in the sea, and all that are in them, saying: "Blessing and honor and glory and power, *be* to Him who sits on the throne, and to the Lamb forever and ever!"

¹⁴ And the four creatures said, "Amen!" And the twenty four elders fell down and worshiped

Him who lives forever and ever.

CHAPTER 6

¹ Now I saw when the Lamb opened one of the seals; and I heard one of the four creatures saying with a voice like thunder, "Come and see."

² And I looked, and behold, a white horse. And he who sat on him had a bow; and a crown was given to him, and he went out conquering and to conquer.

³ And when He opened the second seal, I heard the second creature say, "Come and see."

⁴ And another horse *that was* red went out. And *authority* was given to the one who sat on it to take peace from the earth, and that they should kill one another; and there was given to him a large sword.

⁵ Then when He had opened the third seal, I heard the third creature say, "Come and see." So I looked, and behold, a black horse, and he who sat on it had a pair of scales in his hand.

⁶ And I heard a voice in the midst of the four creatures saying, "A measure of wheat for a denarius, and three measures of barley for a denarius; and *see* you do not harm the oil and the grape juice."

⁷ And when He opened the fourth seal, I heard the voice of the fourth creature say, "Come and see."

⁸ So I looked, and behold, a pale horse. And the name of him who sat on it was Death, and Hell followed with him. And authority was given to them over a quarter of the earth, to kill with sword, with hunger, with death, and by the beasts of the earth.

⁹ And when He opened the fifth seal, I saw under the altar the souls of those who had been slain for the word of God and for the testimony which they held.

¹⁰ And they shouted out with a loud voice, saying, "How long, O Lord, holy and true, until You judge and avenge our blood on those who inhabit the earth?"

¹¹ Then white robes were given to each of them; and it was said to them that they should rest a little while longer, until their fellow servants and also their brethren, who should be killed just as they *were*, should be fulfilled.

¹² And I looked when He opened the sixth seal, and behold, there was a large earthquake; and the sun became black as sackcloth of hair, and the moon became like blood.

¹³ And the stars of heaven fell to the earth, just as a fig tree drops her untimely figs when she is shaken by a strong wind.

¹⁴ Then the heaven receded like a scroll when it is rolled up, and every mountain and island was moved out of its place.

¹⁵ And the kings of the earth, and the great men, and the rich men, and the commanders, and the mighty men, and every slave and every free man, hid themselves in the caves and in the rocks of the

mountains,

¹⁶ and said to the mountains and rocks, "Fall on us and hide us from the face of Him who sits on the throne and from the wrath of the Lamb!

¹⁷ Because, the great day of His wrath has come, and who shall be able to stand?"

CHAPTER 7

¹ Now after these things I saw four angels standing on the four corners of the earth, holding the four winds of the earth, that the wind should not blow on the earth, nor on the sea, nor on any tree.

² Then I saw another angel ascending from the east, having the seal of the living God. And he shouted out with a loud voice to the four angels to whom it was granted to harm the earth and the sea,

³ saying, "Do not harm the earth, neither the sea, nor the trees, until we have sealed the servants of our God in their foreheads."

⁴ And I heard the number of them who were sealed. *And* one hundred *and* forty four thousand of all the tribes of the children of Israel *were* sealed:

⁵ of the tribe of Judah twelve thousand *were* sealed; of the tribe of Reuben twelve thousand *were* sealed; of the tribe of Gad twelve thousand *were* sealed;

⁶ of the tribe of Asher twelve thousand *were* sealed; of the tribe of Naphtali twelve thousand *were* sealed; of the tribe of Manasseh twelve thousand *were* sealed;

⁷ of the tribe of Simeon twelve thousand *were* sealed; of the tribe of Levi twelve thousand *were* sealed; of the tribe of Issachar twelve thousand *were* sealed.

⁸ of the tribe of Zebulun twelve thousand *were* sealed; of the tribe of Joseph twelve thousand *were* sealed; of the tribe of Benjamin twelve thousand *were* sealed.

⁹ After this I looked, and behold, a large multitude which no one could number, of all nations, tribes, peoples, and languages, standing before the throne, and before the Lamb, clothed with white robes, with palm branches in their hands,

¹⁰ and shouting out with a loud voice, saying, "Salvation *belongs* to our God who sits upon the throne, and to the Lamb!"

¹¹ And all the angels stood surrounding the throne and *among* the elders and the four creatures, and fell on their faces before the throne and worshiped God,

¹² saying: "Amen! Blessing and glory and wisdom, thanksgiving and honor and power and might, *be* to our God forever and ever. Amen."

¹³ Then one of the elders responded, saying to me, "Who are these that are clothed in white robes and where did they come from?"

¹⁴ And I said to him, "Sir, you know." So he said to me, "These are

those who have come out of great tribulation, and have washed their robes, and made them white in the blood of the Lamb.

¹⁵ Therefore are they before the throne of God, and serve Him day and night in His temple. And He who sits on the throne will live among them.

¹⁶ They will not hunger anymore nor thirst anymore; neither will the sun strike them, nor any heat;

¹⁷ Because, the Lamb who is in the midst of the throne will feed them and will lead them to living fountains of waters. And God will wipe away every tear from their eyes."

CHAPTER 8

¹ Then when He had opened the seventh seal, there was silence in heaven for about the period of half an hour.

² And I saw the seven angels who stand before God, and to them were given seven trumpets.

³ Then another angel having a golden censer came and stood at the altar. And a large amount of incense was given to him, that he should offer *it* with the prayers of all saints upon the golden altar which was before the throne.

⁴ And the smoke of the incense, *which came* up with the prayers of the saints, ascended up before God from the angel's hand.

⁵ Then the angel took the censer, filled it with fire from the altar, and threw *it* to the earth. Then there were noises, thunderings, lightnings, and an earthquake.

⁶ So the seven angels who had the seven trumpets prepared themselves to sound.

⁷ The first angel sounded: And hail and fire mingled with blood followed, and they were thrown to the earth. Then a third of all the trees were burnt up, and all green grass was burnt up.

⁸ Then the second angel sounded: And a thing like a huge mountain burning with fire was thrown into the sea, then a third of all the sea became blood.

⁹ And a third of all the creatures in the sea that had life died, and a third of all the ships were destroyed.

¹⁰ Then the third angel sounded: And a large star fell from heaven, burning like a torch, and it fell on a third of all the rivers and on the springs of waters.

¹¹ And the name of the star is Wormwood. Then a third of all the waters became wormwood, and many people died from the water, because it was made bitter.

¹² Then the fourth angel sounded: And a third of the sun was struck, a third of the moon, and a third of the stars, so that a third of them were darkened. And a third of the day did not shine, and likewise the night.

¹³ And I looked, and heard an angel flying through the midst of heaven, saying with a loud voice, "Woe,

woe, woe, to the inhabitants of the earth, because of the remaining blasts of the trumpet of the three angels who are about to sound!"

CHAPTER 9

¹ Then the fifth angel sounded: And I saw a star fall from heaven to the earth. And to him was given the key to the bottomless pit.

² And he opened the bottomless pit, and smoke arose out of the pit, like the smoke of a large furnace. So the sun and the air were darkened because of the smoke of the pit.

³ Then out of the smoke came locusts upon the earth. And to them was given authority, as the scorpions of the earth have authority.

⁴ And they were commanded not to harm the grass of the earth, or any green thing, or any tree, but only those men who do not have the seal of God in their foreheads.

⁵ And they were not given permission to kill them, but that they should be tormented *for* five months. And their torment *was like* the torment of a scorpion when it strikes a man.

⁶ And in those days men will seek death and will not find it; and will desire to die, and death will flee from them.

⁷ And the shape of the locusts *were* like horses prepared for battle. And on their heads *were* like crowns of gold, and their faces *were* like the faces of men.

⁸ And they had hair like women's hair, and their teeth were like lions' *teeth.*

⁹ And they had breastplates like breastplates of iron, and the sound of their wings *was* like the sound of chariots with many horses running to battle.

¹⁰ And they had tails like scorpions, and there were stings in their tails. And their power *was* to hurt men five months.

¹¹ And they had a king over them, *who is* the angel of the bottomless pit, whose name in the Hebrew language *is* Abaddon, but in the Greek language *his* name *is* Apollyon.

¹² One woe is past, *and* behold, still two more woes are coming after this.

¹³ Then the sixth angel sounded: And I heard a voice from the four horns of the golden altar which is before God,

¹⁴ saying to the sixth angel who had the trumpet, "Release the four angels who are bound at the great river Euphrates."

¹⁵ So the four angels, who had been prepared for the hour and day and month and year, were released to kill the third of mankind.

¹⁶ Now the number of the army of the horsemen *was* two hundred million; and I heard the number of them.

¹⁷ And thus I saw the horses in the vision: So those who sat on them had breastplates of fire, and sapphire, and sulfur; and the heads of

the horses were like the heads of lions; and out of their mouths came fire, smoke, and brimstone.

¹⁸ By these three a third part of mankind was killed, by the fire and the smoke and the brimstone which came out of their mouths.

¹⁹ Because, their power is in their mouth and in their tails; because their tails were like serpents, having heads; and with them they do harm.

²⁰ But the rest of mankind who were not killed by these plagues, yet did not repent of the works of their hands, that they should not worship demons, and idols of gold, and silver, brass, stone, and wood, which can neither see nor hear nor walk;

²¹ neither did they repent of their murders or of their sorceries or of their sexual immorality or of their thefts.

CHAPTER 10

¹ And I saw another mighty angel come down from heaven, clothed with a cloud. And a rainbow was on his head, his face was like the sun, and his feet like pillars of fire.

² And he had a little book open in his hand. And he set his right foot on the sea and his left foot on the land,

³ and shouted out with a loud voice, like when a lion roars. And when he had shouted out, seven thunders uttered their voices.

⁴ Now when the seven thunders had spoken their voices, I was about to write; but I heard a voice from heaven saying to me, "Seal up those things which the seven thunders spoke, and do not write them."

⁵ And the angel whom I saw standing on the sea and on the land lifted up his hand to heaven

⁶ and swore by Him who lives forever and ever, who created heaven and the things that are in it, the earth, and the things that are in it, and the sea, and the things that are in it, that there should no longer be a delay,

⁷ but in the days of the voice of the seventh angel, when he will begin to sound, the mystery of God would be finished, as He has declared to His servants the prophets.

⁸ Then the voice which I heard from heaven spoke to me again and said, "Go and take the little book which is open in the hand of the angel who stands on the sea and on the land."

⁹ So I went to the angel and said to him, "Give me the little book." And he said to me, "Take it and eat it; and it will make your stomach bitter, but it will be as sweet as honey in your mouth."

¹⁰ Then I took the little book out of the angel's hand and ate it up, and it was sweet as honey in my mouth. But as soon as I had eaten it, my stomach became bitter.

¹¹ And he said to me, "You must prophesy again before many peoples, and nations, and languages, and kings."

CHAPTER 11

¹ Then I was given a reed like a measuring rod. And the angel stood, saying, "Rise and measure the temple of God, the altar, and those who worship in it.

² But leave out the court which is outside the temple, and do not measure it, because it has been given to the Gentiles. And they will tread the holy city under foot *for* forty two months.

³ And I will give *power* to my two witnesses, and they will prophesy one thousand two hundred *and* sixty days, clothed in sackcloth."

⁴ These are the two olive trees and the two lampstands standing before the God of the earth.

⁵ And if anyone wants to hurt them, fire proceeds from their mouth and devours their enemies. And if anyone wants to hurt them, he must be killed in this manner.

⁶ These have power to shut heaven, so that no rain falls in the days of their prophecy; and have power over waters to turn them to blood, and to strike the earth with all plagues, as often as they desire.

⁷ And when they will have finished their testimony, the beast that ascends out of the bottomless pit will make war against them, will overcome them, and kill them.

⁸ And their dead bodies *will lie* in the street of the great city which spiritually is called Sodom and Egypt, where also our Lord was crucified.

⁹ And those from the peoples, tribes, languages, and nations will see their dead bodies three and a half days, and will not allow their dead bodies to be put in graves.

¹⁰ And those who dwell on the earth will rejoice over them, and will be glad, and will send gifts to one another, because these two prophets tormented those who dwell on the earth.

¹¹ Now after three and a half days the Spirit of life from God entered into them, and they stood on their feet, and great fear fell on those who saw them.

¹² And they heard a loud voice from heaven saying to them, "Come up here." And they ascended up to heaven in a cloud, and their enemies saw them.

¹³ And in the same hour there was a large earthquake, and a tenth of the city fell. And in the earthquake seven thousand people were killed, and the rest were afraid and gave glory to the God of heaven.

¹⁴ The second woe is past. *And* behold, the third woe is coming suddenly.

¹⁵ Then the seventh angel sounded: And there were loud voices in heaven, saying, "The kingdoms of this world have become *the kingdoms* of our Lord and of His Christ, and He will reign forever and ever!"

¹⁶ And the twenty four elders who sat before God on their thrones fell on their faces and worshiped God,

¹⁷ saying: "We give You thanks, O

Lord God Almighty, who is and was and is to come, because You have taken to Yourself Your great power and reigned.

¹⁸ And the nations were angry, and Your wrath has come, and the time of the dead, that they should be judged, and that You should give rewards to Your servants the prophets and the saints, and those who reverence Your name, small and great, and should destroy those who destroy the earth."

¹⁹ Then the temple of God was opened in heaven, and the ark of His testament was seen in His temple. And there were lightnings, voices, thunderings, an earthquake, and large hail.

CHAPTER 12

¹ Now there appeared a great sign in heaven: a woman clothed with the sun, with the moon under her feet, and on her head a crown of twelve stars.

² And being with child cried out in labor and in pain to give birth.

³ Then another sign appeared in heaven: and behold a great red dragon having seven heads and ten horns, and seven crowns on his heads.

⁴ And his tail drew a third of the stars of heaven and threw them to the earth. And the dragon stood before the woman who was ready to give birth, to devour her Child as soon as it was born.

⁵ And she bore a male Child who was to rule all nations with a rod of iron. And her Child was caught up to God and to His throne.

⁶ Then the woman fled into the wilderness, where she has a place prepared by God, that they should feed her there one thousand two hundred *and* sixty days.

⁷ And there was war in heaven: Michael and his angels fought against the dragon; and the dragon and his angels fought,

⁸ but did not prevail; nor was a place found for them in heaven any longer.

⁹ So the great dragon was cast out, that serpent of old, called the Devil and Satan, who deceives the entire world; he was cast out into the earth, and his angels were cast out with him.

¹⁰ Then I heard a loud voice saying in heaven, "Now salvation, and strength, and the kingdom of our God, and the authority of His Christ have come, because the accuser of our brethren, who accused them before our God day and night, has been cast down.

¹¹ And they overcame him by the blood of the Lamb and by the word of their testimony, and they did not love their lives to the death.

¹² Therefore rejoice, *you* heavens, and you who dwell in them! Woe to the inhabitants of the earth and of the sea! Because the devil has come down to you, having fierce wrath, because he knows that he only has a short time."

¹³ Now when the dragon saw that he had been cast to the earth, he persecuted the woman who gave birth to the male *Child.*

¹⁴ But the woman was given two wings of a great eagle, that she might fly into the wilderness into her place, where she is nourished for a time and times and half a time, from the face of the serpent.

¹⁵ So the serpent spewed out water from his mouth like a flood after the woman, that he might cause her to be carried away by the flood.

¹⁶ But the earth helped the woman, and the earth opened its mouth and swallowed up the flood which the dragon spewed out of his mouth.

¹⁷ And the dragon was enraged with the woman, and went to make war with the remainder of her seed, who keep the commandments of God and have the testimony of Jesus Christ.

CHAPTER 13

¹ Then I stood on the sand of the sea. And saw a beast rise up out of the sea, having seven heads and ten horns, and on his horns ten crowns, and on his heads a blasphemous name.

² Now the beast which I saw was like a leopard, and his feet were like the *feet* of a bear, and his mouth like the mouth of a lion, and the dragon gave him his power, throne, and great authority.

³ And I saw one of his heads as it had been mortally wounded, and his deadly wound was healed, and the entire world followed after the beast.

⁴ And they worshiped the dragon who gave authority to the beast; and they worshiped the beast, saying, "Who is like the beast? Who *is* able to make war with him?"

⁵ And he was given a mouth speaking grand things and blasphemies, and he was given authority to continue for forty two months.

⁶ And he opened his mouth in blasphemy against God, to blaspheme His name, and His tabernacle, and those who dwell in heaven.

⁷ And it was granted to him to make war with the saints and to overcome them. And authority was given to him over every tribe, and language, and nation.

⁸ And all who live on the earth will worship him, whose names are not written in the Book of Life of the Lamb slain from the foundation of the world.

⁹ If anyone has an ear, let him hear.

¹⁰ He who leads into captivity will go into captivity; he who kills with the sword must be killed with the sword. Here is the perseverance and the faith of the saints.

¹¹ Then I saw another beast coming up out of the earth, and he had two horns like a lamb and he spoke like a dragon.

¹² And he exercises all the authority of the first beast in his presence, and causes the earth and those who dwell in it to worship the first beast,

whose deadly wound was healed.

¹³ And performs great wonders, so that he makes fire come down from heaven on the earth in the sight of men.

¹⁴ And deceives those who dwell on the earth *because* of those miracles which he had authority to do in the sight of the beast, saying to those who live on the earth, that they should make an image to the beast who had the wound by a sword, and lived.

¹⁵ And he had authority to give life to the image of the beast, that the image of the beast should both speak and cause as many as would not worship the image of the beast to be killed.

¹⁶ And he causes all, both small and great, rich and poor, free and slave, to receive a mark in their right hand or in their foreheads,

¹⁷ and that no one may buy or sell except one who had the mark or the name of the beast, or the number of his name.

¹⁸ Here is wisdom. Let him who has understanding calculate the number of the beast, because it is the number of a man: and his number *is* six hundred and sixty six.

CHAPTER 14

¹ Then I looked, and saw a Lamb standing on mount Zion, and with Him one hundred *and* forty four thousand, having His Father's name written in their foreheads.

² And I heard a voice from heaven, like the voice of many waters, and like the voice of loud thunder. And I heard the sound of harpists playing with their harps.

³ And they sang as it were a new song before the throne, before the four creatures, and the elders; and no one could learn that song except the one hundred *and* forty four thousand who were redeemed from the earth.

⁴ These are those who were not defiled with women, because they are virgins. These are those who follow the Lamb wherever He goes. These were redeemed from among men, *being* the firstfruits to God and to the Lamb.

⁵ And no deception was found in their mouths, because they are without fault before the throne of God.

⁶ Then I saw another angel flying in the midst of heaven, having the everlasting gospel to preach to those who live on the earth, and to every nation, tribe, language, and people,

⁷ saying with a loud voice, "Reverence God and give glory to Him, because, the hour of His judgment has come; and worship Him who made heaven and earth, the sea and springs of water."

⁸ And another angel there followed, saying, "Babylon is fallen, is fallen, that great city, because she made all nations drink of the wine of the wrath of her fornication."

⁹ Then the third angel followed

them, saying with a loud voice, "If anyone worships the beast and his image, and receives his mark *in* his forehead or in his hand,

¹⁰ they will drink of the wine of the wrath of God, which is poured out without mixture into the cup of His indignation. Then he will be tormented with fire and brimstone in the presence of the holy angels and in the presence of the Lamb.

¹¹ And the smoke of their torment ascends up forever and ever; and they have no rest day or night, who worship the beast and his image, and whoever receives the mark of his name."

¹² Here is the patience of the saints; here *are* those who keep the commandments of God and the faith of Jesus.

¹³ Then I heard a voice from heaven saying to me,

"Write: 'Blessed are the dead who die in the Lord from now on.'" "Yes," says the Spirit, "that they may rest from their labors; and their works follow them."

¹⁴ Then I looked, and behold a white cloud, and on the cloud sat *One* like the Son of Man, having on His head a golden crown, and in His hand a sharp sickle.

¹⁵ And another angel came out of the temple, shouting out with a loud voice to Him who sat on the cloud, "Thrust in Your sickle and reap, because, the time has come for You to reap, because the harvest of the earth is ripe."

¹⁶ So He who sat on the cloud thrust in His sickle on the earth, and the earth was reaped.

¹⁷ Then another angel came out of the temple which is in heaven, he also having a sharp sickle.

¹⁸ And another angel came out from the altar, who had authority over fire, and he shouted out with a loud shout to him who had the sharp sickle, saying, "Thrust in your sharp sickle and gather the clusters of the vine of the earth, because her grapes are fully ripe."

¹⁹ So the angel thrust in his sickle into the earth and gathered the vine of the earth, and threw *it* into the large grape juice press of the wrath of God.

²⁰ And the grape juice press was trodden outside the city, and blood came out of the grape juice press, up to the horse bridles, for the distance of one thousand and six hundred stadiums.

CHAPTER 15

¹ Then I saw another sign in heaven, great and marvelous: seven angels having the seven last plagues, because in them the wrath of God is complete.

² And I saw something like a sea of glass mingled with fire, and those who have attained the victory over the beast, over his image over his mark *and* over the number of his name, standing on the sea of glass, having the harps of God.

³ And they sing the song of Moses, the servant of God, and the song of the Lamb, saying: "Great and marvelous *are* Your works, Lord God Almighty! Just and true *are* Your ways, You King of saints!

⁴ Who will not reverence You, O Lord, and glorify Your name? Because *You* alone *are* holy. Because, all nations will come and worship before You, because Your judgments are being manifested."

⁵ And after these things I looked, and saw, the temple of the tabernacle of the testimony in heaven was opened.

⁶ And the seven angels came out of the temple having the seven plagues, clothed in pure and white linen, and having their chests wrapped with golden belts

⁷ Then one of the four creatures gave to the seven angels seven golden bowls full of the wrath of God who lives forever and ever.

⁸ And the temple was filled with smoke from the glory of God and from His power, and no one was able to enter into the temple until the seven plagues of the seven angels were completed.

CHAPTER 16

¹ Then I heard a loud voice from the temple saying to the seven angels, "Go your way and pour out the bowls of the wrath of God upon the earth."

² So the first went and poured out his bowl upon the earth, and a dreadful and harmful sore came *upon* the men who had the mark of the beast and upon those who worshiped his image.

³ Then the second angel poured out his bowl upon the sea, and it became like the blood of a dead *man*; and every living creature in the sea died.

⁴ Then the third angel poured out his bowl upon the rivers and springs of water, and they became blood.

⁵ And I heard the angel of the waters saying: "You are righteous, O Lord, who is and who was and who will be, because You have judged these things.

⁶ Because, they have shed the blood of saints and prophets, and You have given them blood to drink, because they deserve it."

⁷ And I heard another from the altar saying, "Even so, Lord God Almighty, true and righteous *are* Your judgments."

⁸ Then the fourth angel poured out his bowl upon the sun, and authority was given to him to scorch men with fire.

⁹ And men were scorched with intense heat, and blasphemed the name of God who has authority over these calamities; and they did not repent to give Him glory.

¹⁰ Then the fifth angel poured out his bowl upon the throne of the beast, and his kingdom became full of darkness; and they gnawed their tongues because of the pain.

¹¹ They blasphemed the God of heaven because of their pains and their sores, and yet did not repent of their deeds.

¹² Then the sixth angel poured out his bowl upon the great river Euphrates, and its water dried up, *so* that the way of the kings of the east might be prepared.

¹³ And I saw three unclean like frogs come out of the mouth of the dragon, and out of the mouth of the beast, and out of the mouth of the false prophet.

¹⁴ Because, they are the spirits of demons, doing miracles, *which* go out to the kings of the earth and of the entire world, to gather them to the battle of that great day of God Almighty.

¹⁵ "Behold, I come as a thief. Blessed *is* he who watches, and keeps his garments, lest he walk naked and they see his shame."

¹⁶ And he gathered them together into a place called in the Hebrew language, Armageddon.

¹⁷ Then the seventh angel poured out his bowl into the atmosphere, and a loud voice came from the temple of heaven, from the throne, saying, "It is done!"

¹⁸ And there were noises and thunders and lightnings; and there was a large earthquake, such a mighty *and* very large earthquake as had not occurred since men were on the earth.

¹⁹ Now the large city was divided into three parts, and the cities of the nations fell. And great Babylon was remembered before God, to give her the cup of the wine of the ferocity of His wrath.

²⁰ Then every island fled away, and the mountains were not found.

²¹ And large hail fell from heaven upon men, *every hailstone* about the weight of a talent. And men blasphemed God because of the calamity of the hail, because its calamity was exceptionally brutal.

CHAPTER 17

¹ Then one of the seven angels who had the seven bowls came and talked with me, saying to me, "Come here, I will show you the judgment of the great harlot who sits on many waters,

² with whom the kings of the earth have committed fornication, and the inhabitants of the earth have been made drunk with the wine of her fornication."

³ So he carried me away in the Spirit into the wilderness. And I saw a woman sitting on a scarlet colored beast, full of names of blasphemy, having seven heads and ten horns.

⁴ And the woman was arrayed in purple and scarlet colors, and adorned with gold and precious stones and pearls, having a golden cup in her hand full of abominations and the filthiness of her fornication.

⁵ And on her forehead a name *was* written: MYSTERY, BABYLON THE

GREAT, THE MOTHER OF HARLOTS AND ABOMINATIONS OF THE EARTH.

⁶ And I saw the woman drunk with the blood of the saints and with the blood of the martyrs of Jesus. And when I saw her, I marveled with great amazement.

⁷ But the angel said to me, "Why did you marvel? I will tell you the mystery of the woman and of the beast that carries her, which has the seven heads and ten horns.

⁸ The beast that you saw was, and is not, and will ascend out of the bottomless pit and go to perdition. And those who dwell on the earth will marvel, whose names are not written in the Book of Life from the foundation of the world, when they see the beast that was, and is not, and yet is.

⁹ "And here *is* the mind that has wisdom: The seven heads are seven mountains on which the woman sits.

¹⁰ And there are seven kings. Five have fallen, one is, and the other has not yet come. And when he comes, he must continue a short time.

¹¹ And the beast that was, and is not, he is also the eighth, and is of the seven, and goes to perdition.

¹² "And the ten horns which you saw are ten kings who have received no kingdom as yet, but receive authority as kings for one hour with the beast.

¹³ These are all of one mind, and will give their power and authority to the beast.

¹⁴ These will make war with the Lamb, and the Lamb will overcome them, because He is Lord of lords and King of kings; and those who are with Him *are* called, chosen, and faithful."

¹⁵ Then he said to me, "The waters that you saw, where the harlot sits, are peoples, multitudes, nations, and languages.

¹⁶ And the ten horns which you saw upon the beast, these will hate the harlot, and will make her desolate and naked, will eat her flesh and burn her with fire.

¹⁷ Because, God has put into their hearts to fulfill His will, to be in agreement, and give their kingdom to the beast, until the words of God will be fulfilled.

¹⁸ And the woman whom you saw is that great city which reigns over the kings of the earth."

CHAPTER 18

¹ Now after these things I saw another angel coming down from heaven, having great authority, and the earth was illuminated with his glory.

² And he shouted out mightily with a loud voice, saying, "Babylon the great is fallen, is fallen, and has become the dwelling place for demons, and the prison for every foul spirit, and a cage for every unclean and hateful bird!

³ Because all the nations have

drunk of the grape juice of the wrath of her fornication, and the kings of the earth have committed fornication with her, and the merchants of the earth have become rich through the abundance of her luxury."

⁴ And I heard another voice from heaven saying, "Come out of her, my people, that you do not be partakers of her sins, and that you do not receive of her plagues.

⁵ Because her sins have reached to heaven and God has remembered her iniquities.

⁶ Repay her just as she paid you, and pay back to her double according to her works; in the cup which she has mixed, mix to her double.

⁷ In the measure that she glorified herself and lived lavishly, in the same measure give her torment and sorrow; because she says in her heart, 'I sit as queen, and am no widow, and will see no sorrow.'

⁸ Therefore her plagues will come in one day, death and mourning and famine. And she will be utterly burned with fire, because mighty *is* the Lord God who judges her.

⁹ "And the kings of the earth who have committed fornication and lived lavishly with her will weep for her, and lament for her, when they see the smoke of her burning,

¹⁰ standing at a distance for fear of her torment, saying, 'Alas, alas, that great city Babylon, that mighty city! Because in one hour your judgment has come.'

¹¹ And the merchants of the earth will weep and mourn over her, because no one buys their merchandise anymore:

¹² the merchandise of gold and silver, precious stones and pearls, fine linen and purple, silk and scarlet, and every kind of citron wood, and every kind of object of ivory, and every kind of object of most precious wood, bronze, iron, and marble;

¹³ and cinnamon and incense, and fragrant oil and frankincense, grape juice and oil, fine flour and wheat, cattle and sheep, horses and chariots, slaves and souls of men.

¹⁴ And the fruits that your soul lusted after have departed from you, and all things which were dainty and splendid have departed from you, and you will not find them anymore.

¹⁵ The merchants of these things who became rich by her, will stand at a distance because of the fear of her torment, weeping and wailing,

¹⁶ and saying, 'Alas, alas, that great city that was clothed in fine linen, purple, and scarlet, and adorned with gold and precious stones and pearls!

¹⁷ Because in one hour such great riches came to nothing.' And every shipmaster, all who travel by ship, sailors, and as many as trade on the sea, stood at a distance

¹⁸ and cried out when they saw the smoke of her burning, saying,

'What city *is* like this great city!'

¹⁹ And threw dust on their heads and shouted out, weeping and wailing, saying, 'Alas, alas, that great city, in which all who had ships on the sea became rich by her wealth! Because in one hour she is made desolate.

²⁰ Rejoice over her, *you* heaven, and you holy apostles and prophets, because God has avenged you on her!"

²¹ Then a mighty angel took up a stone like a large millstone and threw it into the sea, saying, "Thus with violence will that great city Babylon be thrown down, and will not be found anymore.

²² And the sound of harpists, musicians, flutists, and trumpeters will not be heard in you anymore. And no craftsman of any craft *he is*, will be found in you anymore, and the sound of a millstone will not be heard in you anymore.

²³ And the light of a lamp will not shine in you anymore, and the voice of the bridegroom and bride will not be heard in you anymore. Because, your merchants were the great men of the earth, because by your sorceries all the nations were deceived.

²⁴ And in her was found the blood of prophets and of saints, and all who were slain on the earth."

CHAPTER 19

¹ And after these things I heard a loud voice of many people in heaven, saying, "Alleluia! Salvation and glory and honor and power belong to the Lord our God!

² Because, His judgments *are* true and righteous, because He has judged the great harlot who corrupted the earth with her fornication; and has avenged the blood of His servants by her hand."

³ And again they said, "Alleluia! And her smoke rose up forever and ever!"

⁴ And the twenty four elders and the four creatures fell down and worshiped God who sat on the throne, saying, "Amen! Alleluia!"

⁵ Then a voice came from the throne, saying, "Praise our God, all you His servants, and those who reverence Him, both small and great!"

⁶ And I heard, as it were, the voice of a large multitude, as the voice of many waters and as the voice of mighty thunderings, saying, "Alleluia! Because the Lord God Omnipotent reigns!

⁷ Let us be glad and rejoice and give honor to Him, because the marriage of the Lamb has come, and His wife has made herself ready."

⁸ And to her was granted that she should be arrayed in fine linen, clean and white, because the fine linen is the righteousness of the saints.

⁹ Then he said to me, "Write 'Blessed *are* those who are called to the marriage supper of the Lamb!' "

And he said to me, "These are the true sayings of God."

¹⁰ And I fell at his feet to worship him. But he said to me, "See that *you* do not *do that*! I am your fellow servant, and of your brethren who have the testimony of Jesus. Worship God! Because the testimony of Jesus is the spirit of prophecy."

¹¹ Now I saw heaven opened, and behold a white horse. And He who sat on him was called Faithful and True, and in righteousness He judges and makes war.

¹² His eyes *were* like a flame of fire, and on His head *were* many crowns. And He had a name written that no one knew except Himself.

¹³ And He *was* clothed with a robe dipped in blood, and His name is called The Word of God.

¹⁴ And the armies *which were* in heaven, clothed in fine linen, white and clean, followed Him on white horses.

¹⁵ Now out of His mouth goes a sharp sword, that with it He should smite the nations. And He will rule them with a rod of iron. And He treads the grape juice press of the fierceness and wrath of Almighty God.

¹⁶ And He has on *His* robe and on His thigh a name written, KING OF KINGS AND LORD OF LORDS.

¹⁷ Then I saw an angel standing in the sun; and he shouted out with a loud voice, saying to all the birds that fly in the midst of heaven, "Come and gather yourselves together to the supper of the great God,

¹⁸ that you may eat the flesh of kings, the flesh of captains, the flesh of mighty men, the flesh of horses, and of those who sit on them, and the flesh of all *people*, *both* free and slave, both small and great."

¹⁹ And I saw the beast, and the kings of the earth, and their armies, gathered together to make war against Him who sat on the horse and against His army.

²⁰ Then the beast was captured, and with him the false prophet who worked miracles before him, by which he deceived those who had received the mark of the beast and those who worshiped his image. These two were cast alive into the lake of fire burning with brimstone.

²¹ And the rest were killed with the sword which proceeded from the mouth of Him who sat on the horse. And all the birds were filled with their flesh.

CHAPTER 20

¹ Then I saw an angel coming down from heaven, having the key to the bottomless pit and a large chain in his hand.

² And he laid hold of the dragon, that serpent of old, which is the Devil and Satan, and bound him for a thousand years;

³ and cast him into the bottomless pit, and shut him up, and set a seal

on him, so that he should deceive the nations no more, until the thousand years were finished. But after that he must be released for a little season.

⁴ And I saw thrones, and they sat upon them, and judgment was committed to them. Then *I saw* the souls of those who had been beheaded for the witness of Jesus and for the word of God, those who had not worshiped the beast, or his image, neither had received *his* mark on their foreheads or in their hands. And they lived and reigned with Christ a thousand years.

⁵ But the rest of the dead did not live again until the thousand years were finished. This is the first resurrection.

⁶ Blessed and holy *is* he who has part in the first resurrection. Upon such the second death has no power, but they will be priests of God and of Christ, and will reign with Him a thousand years.

⁷ Now when the thousand years have expired, Satan will be released from his prison

⁸ and will go out to deceive the nations which are in the four quarters of the earth, Gog and Magog, to gather them together to battle, whose number *is* as the sand of the sea.

⁹ And they went up on the breadth of the earth and surrounded the camp of the saints and the beloved city. And fire came down from God out of heaven and devoured them.

¹⁰ And the devil who deceived them was cast into the lake of fire and brimstone, where the beast and the false prophet *are*. And they will be tormented day and night forever and ever.

¹¹ Then I saw a large white throne and Him who sat on it, from whose face the earth and the heaven fled away. And there was found no place for them.

¹² And I saw the dead, small and great, standing before God, and the books were opened. And another book was opened, which is *the Book of Life*. And the dead were judged according to their works by those things that were written in the books.

¹³ And the sea gave up the dead who were in it, and death and hell delivered up the dead who were in them. And they were judged, every one according to their works.

¹⁴ Then death and hell were cast into the lake of fire. This is the second death.

¹⁵ And whoever was not found written in the Book of Life was thrown into the lake of fire.

CHAPTER 21

¹ Now I saw a new heaven and a new earth, because the first heaven and the first earth had passed away, and there was no more sea.

² And I, John, saw the holy city, New Jerusalem, coming down from God out of heaven, prepared as a bride adorned for her husband.

³ And I heard a loud voice from heaven saying, "Behold, the tabernacle of God *is* with men, and He will dwell with them, and they will be His people. God Himself will be with them *and be* their God.

⁴ And God will wipe away every tear from their eyes; there will be no more death, nor sorrow, nor crying, neither will there be any more pain, because the former things have passed away."

⁵ Then He who sat on the throne said, "Behold, I make all things new." And He said to me, "Write, because these words are true and faithful."

⁶ And He said to me, "It is done! I am Alpha and Omega, the Beginning and the End. I will give to him who thirsts of the fountain of the water of life freely.

⁷ He who overcomes will inherit all things, and I will be his God and he will be My son.

⁸ But the fearful, unbelieving, abominable, murderers, fornicators, sorcerers, idolaters, and all liars will have their part in the lake which burns with fire and brimstone, which is the second death."

⁹ Then one of the seven angels who had the seven bowls filled with the seven last plagues came to me and talked with me, saying, "Come here, I will show you the bride, the Lamb's wife."

¹⁰ And he carried me away in the Spirit to a great and high mountain, and showed me the great city, the holy Jerusalem, descending out of heaven from God,

¹¹ having the glory of God. And her light *was* like a most precious stone, like a jasper stone, clear as crystal.

¹² And having a large and high wall with twelve gates, and twelve angels at the gates, and names written on them, which are *the names* of the twelve tribes of the children of Israel:

¹³ three gates on the east, three gates on the north, three gates on the south, and three gates on the west.

¹⁴ And the wall of the city had twelve foundations, and in them were the names of the twelve apostles of the Lamb.

¹⁵ And he who talked with me had a gold reed to measure the city, its gates, and its wall.

¹⁶ And the city layout is square; and its length is as large as its breadth. And he measured the city with the reed: twelve thousand stadiums. Its length, breadth, and height are equal.

¹⁷ And he measured its wall: one hundred *and* forty four cubits, *according to* the measure of a man, that is, of the angel.

¹⁸ And the material of the wall was *of* jasper; and the city *was* pure gold, like clear glass.

¹⁹ And the foundations of the wall of the city *were* adorned with every kind of precious stone. The first foundation was jasper, the second sapphire, the third chalcedony, the

fourth emerald,

²⁰ the fifth sardonyx, the sixth sardius, the seventh chrysolite, the eighth beryl, the ninth topaz, the tenth chrysoprase, the eleventh jacinth, and the twelfth amethyst.

²¹ And the twelve gates *were* twelve pearls: each separate gate was of one pearl. And the street of the city *was* pure gold, just like transparent glass.

²² And I saw no temple in it, because the Lord God Almighty and the Lamb are its temple.

²³ The city had no need of the sun or of the moon to shine in it, because the glory of God lit it up. The Lamb *is* its light.

²⁴ And the nations of those who are saved will walk in its light, and the kings of the earth bring their glory and honor into it.

²⁵ And its gates will not be shut at all by day, because there will be no night there.

²⁶ And they will bring the glory and honor of the nations into it.

²⁷ But there will by no means enter into it anything that defiles, nor *anything that* causes an abomination or *makes* a lie, except those who are written in the Lamb's Book of Life.

CHAPTER 22

¹ And he showed me a pure river of water of life, clear as crystal, proceeding from the throne of God and of the Lamb.

² In the middle of its street, and on either side of the river, *was* the tree of life, which bore twelve *types of* fruit, *and* yielded her fruit every month. And the leaves of the tree *were* for the healing of the nations.

³ And there will be no more curse, but the throne of God and of the Lamb will be in it, and His servants will serve Him.

⁴ And they will see His face, and His name *will be* in their foreheads.

⁵ And there will be no night there: And they need no lamp nor the light of the sun, because the Lord God gives them light. And they will reign forever and ever.

⁶ And he said to me, "These sayings *are* faithful and true." And the Lord God of the holy prophets sent His angel to show to His servants the things which must suddenly take place.

⁷ "Behold, I come suddenly! Blessed *is* he who keeps the sayings of the prophecy of this book."

⁸ And I, John saw these things and heard *them*. And when I had heard and saw, I fell down to worship before the feet of the angel who showed me these things.

⁹ Then he said to me, "See *that you do* not *do that*, because, I am your fellow servant, and of your brethren the prophets, and of those who keep the sayings of this book. Worship God."

¹⁰ And he said to me, "Do not seal the sayings of the prophecy of this book, as the time is at hand.

¹¹ He who is unjust, let him be unjust still; he who is filthy, let him be

filthy still; he who is righteous, let him be righteous still; and he who is holy, let him be holy still."

¹² "And behold, I am coming suddenly; and My reward *is* with Me, to give *to* every one according as his work shall be.

¹³ I am Alpha and Omega, the beginning and the end, the first and the last."

¹⁴ Blessed *are* those who do His commandments, that they may have right to the tree of life, and may enter in through the gates into the city.

¹⁵ Because outside *are* dogs and sorcerers and fornicators and murderers and idolaters, and whoever loves and practices a lie.

¹⁶ "I Jesus, have sent My angel to testify to you these things in the churches. I am the Root and the Offspring of David, *and* the Bright and Morning Star."

¹⁷ And the Spirit and the bride say, "Come!" And let him who hears say, "Come!" And let him who thirsts come. And whoever wills, let him take the water of life freely.

¹⁸ Because, I testify to everyone who hears the words of the prophecy of this book: If anyone will add to these things, God will add to him the plagues that are written in this book;

¹⁹ and if anyone will take away from the words of the book of this prophecy, God will take away his part out of the Book of Life, out of the holy city, and *from* the things which are written in this book.

²⁰ He who testifies these things says, "Surely I am coming suddenly." Amen. Even so, come, Lord Jesus!

²¹ The grace of our Lord Jesus Christ *be* with you all. Amen.